Through a Canadian Periscope

HMCS/M *Ojibwa* at sea.

Through a Canadian Periscope

THE STORY OF THE CANADIAN SUBMARINE SERVICE

JULIE H. FERGUSON

DUNDURN PRESS

Toronto • Oxford

Canadian Dolphins on title page drawn by Janet Bell
Edited by Doris Cowan
Printed and bound in Canada by Webcom

The publisher wishes to acknowledge the generous assistance and ongoing support of the **Canada Council**, the **Book Publishing Industry Development Program** of the **Department of Canadian Heritage**, the **Ontario Arts Council**, the **Ontario Publishing Centre** of the **Ministry of Citizenship, Culture and Recreation**, and the **Ontario Heritage Foundation**.

Care has been taken to trace the ownership of copyright material used in the text (including the illustrations). The author and publisher welcome any information enabling them to rectify any reference or credit in subsequent editions.

J. Kirk Howard, Publisher

Canadian Cataloguing in Publication Data

Ferguson, Julie, 1945–
    Through a Canadian periscope : the story of the Canadian Submarine Service

Includes bibliographical references and index.
ISBN 1-55002-217-2

1. Canada.   Canadian Armed Forces.   Canadian
Submarine Service - History.   I. Title.

V859.C3F4 1995   359.9'33'0971   C95-931360-5

Dundurn Press Limited	Dundurn Distribution	Dundurn Press Limited
2181 Queen Street East	73 Lime Walk	1823 Maryland Avenue
Suite 301	Headington, Oxford	P.O. Box 1000
Toronto, Canada	England	Niagara Falls, N.Y.
M4E 1E5	0X3 7AD	U.S.A. 14302-1000

CONTENTS

PART THREE 1946 TO THE PRESENT

LIST OF MAPS

LIST OF TABLES

FOREWORD

Julie Ferguson has done a great service for those who are interested in naval history. She has produced a detailed account of an almost unknown branch of Canada's least understood service. Canada's submarine service has had a checkered history. Through eighty years of "ups and downs" this small force continues today to fight and struggle for survival. From *CC1* to *Grilse* and *Okanagan* it is a fascinating tale.

Maitland-Dougall, Johnson, Sherwood, Forbes, Bonnell, Ruse, and others are not well-known names even within the naval community and I am hopeful that this book will in some small measure recognize them for the true professionals that they really were. The adventures of the RCNVR officers who served with the Royal Navy in WWII in chariots and X-craft should have long been enshrined in our naval history but, for most of us, we will learn of their feats for the first time in this book.

My own naval career has been inextricably involved with submarines since 1965, through training with the Royal Navy, the commissioning of *Onondaga* and *Rainbow*, my Perisher and the commands that followed it, and various staff appointments. I experienced the era when submarines truly became Canadian – when we took the best from both the American and British systems and applied it in our own way. During these thirty years we recognized that we could independently operate submarines and that we were damn good at it.

At the same time the navy also had several flirtations with nuclear power. While these were exciting times in themselves, in my view the energy they expended was probably detrimental to the acceptance of submarines as an essential arm of Canada's small balanced navy.

Julie Ferguson does not believe our small submarine force will survive in today's climate of weak government resolve. I hope she is in error. The advantages that accrue to a small navy that operates submarines are slowly being realized by Canada's decision-makers. Their stealth, ability to sustain independent operations, extraordinary surveillance capability with modern sensors, capability to operate in areas where we do not have air superiority, their fire power and range are seen as essential requirements in a modern navy. The potential of a modern diesel/electric submarine with air-independent propulsion opens new horizons. Submarines have traditionally only been considered as war fighting or training vehicles. Today their utility in operations short of hostilities such as sovereignty surveillance, fishery patrols and counter drug operations is well accepted.

In this period of reduced budgets, Canada needs ships that can work effectively in all her maritime areas of interest. These ships need to have small crews to reduce personnel costs and have low operating and mainte-nance costs. The modern conventional submarine meets these criteria. The equivalent of one frigate crew can man four modern submarines. It is estimated that these submarines would consume as little as one percent of the dollar amount on operations and maintenance in the three elements of the Canadian Forces. The "operational imperative" and the bottom-line "business case" cry out for maintaining a submarine capability in Canada's navy.

The young Canadians who wear the "Dolphin" are a different breed. They live and work in an environment that is incomprehensible to the non-submariner. Their history is one of dedication and professionalism in adversity. Their story needed to be told. I thank Julie Ferguson for telling it.

February 1995   Vice-Admiral Peter W. Cairns, CMM, CD. (Ret.),
Commander, Maritime Command, 1992–1994

PREFACE

Through a Canadian Periscope has taken ten fascinating years to complete during which I met lofty admirals and enthusiastic leading seamen, patient archivists and irritated politicians, hundreds of submariners, and a few "surface pukes." They were years when I fired make-believe torpedoes in HMS *Dolphin*'s Attack Teacher, crawled around in the bowels of submarines, and studied thousands of naval documents. If I had a nickel for every beer I drank while interviewing submariners, I'd be rich.

The result of these experiences is this book. It presents the story of the Canadian Submarine Service from an *outsider's* viewpoint. I make no apologies to naval historians or even to the submariners themselves about the book's levity or lack of technical detail. I never intended *Through a Canadian Periscope* to be solely for them – it has been written to promote an interest in and an understanding of the Canadian Submarine Service in a much wider audience. As a history intended for a general as well as a naval readership, the book has been edited to conform with "civilian" style, particularly in the matter of capitalization. In addition, some terms that will be well known to readers familiar with naval traditions are explained in the text to help newcomers to the subject.

Through a Canadian Periscope tells the tale of the service from its unexpected inauguration in British Columbia on the first day of the Great War to its uncertain future today, with an emphasis on the submariners themselves. While there was plenty of official documentary evidence available to assist me in reconstructing the story from 1914 to 1968, none has been released for the period of 1969 to the present. Relying on interviews and media accounts is always worrying, but I have chosen to take the risk in the interests of bringing the story up to date. I hope the key players in the current long-playing submarine acquisition will be inspired to write insider accounts and complete the tale.

This book is not an official history of the Canadian Submarine Service. It was not commissioned by, nor does it represent the opinions or policies of, Maritime Command, the Department of National Defence, any other public or private organization, or any individual. It is solely my work, my interpretation of events, and my opinion. Any mistakes are also mine.

In my attempt to do this subject justice, my first draft produced enough to fill two books. Thus many of you will find your memories, photos, and explanations missing from this single volume and still others, insiders all, will wonder why I did not include some "essential" facts. Although every cut was arduous and I, no doubt, made a few poor choices, the result is what I wanted – the whole story in one volume at a reasonable price.

Securing financial support for the preparation of this book proved almost to be its undoing. As I am not affiliated with any university, not a published historian, and not independently wealthy, the usual sources of research money were closed to me. A two-year search located a little-known federal agency which would consider a proposal from an "independent scholar." In the end the costly research for *Through a Canadian Periscope* was made possible by the Canadian Studies Directorate of the Department of the Secretary of State and International Submarine Engineering Ltd. of Port Coquitlam, B.C., who jointly provided the funds with their matching private sector grant. Their confidence in me has, at last, been rewarded.

When I began to work on this book in 1984 I never guessed that I might be writing the obituary of the Canadian Submarine Service. The submariners have swung from euphoria to melancholia and back again several times during the last few years and have braced themselves for the possibility that government might axe their proud service. If the Canadian Submarine Service is disbanded, this book will be their eulogy. If not, it will be a celebration of their commitment.

Port Moody, B.C.   J.H.F.
May 1995

ACKNOWLEDGEMENTS

While non-fiction authors get public recognition, there is always a team behind the writer, which gets little, save a mention in the acknowledgements. They deserve better and my team was the best.

Two people always had faith in my ability to complete this book and get it published, even when I did not. Dr. Jim McFarlane, OC, CD, P.Eng., president of International Submarine Engineering Ltd., has been there for me since the idea tentatively emerged. He and his company actually provided more money for the project than the grant specified, as well as the use of a photocopier, office supplies, and a telephone credit card. However, it has been Jim's willingness to act as a sounding-board, to ask penetrating questions, to explain engineering mysteries, and to provide contacts in the submarine community that I will always remember. (Nor can I forget ISE's secretaries, Janene, Renée, and Chris.) My project officer with the Canadian Studies Directorate, Michelle Bonin-Stewart, gave me much appreciated support, encouragement, and hospitality. Now that the work is over, I miss her.

Hundreds of other individuals also served on my team. Without exception, their infinite patience and courtesy to an unpublished author and non-submariner was noteworthy. Each pushed my learning curve toward the vertical and many increased my capacity for beer.

My "board of advisers" kept me out of many difficulties. They were: Dr. James Boutilier, Royal Roads Military College; Dr. Michael Hadley, University of Victoria and author of *U-boats Against Canada*; Isaac Brower-Berkhoven (technical); James Ferguson (operations); and, of course, Dr. Jim McFarlane.

The First Canadian Submarine Squadron and its commander in 1990, Capt. (N) Allan Dunlop, CD, were far and away the most welcoming, helpful, and hospitable group I encountered. They were the only organization who did not question my credentials, my qualifications (or rather lack of), or my gender. Bravo zulu!

The commanders, Maritime Command, who served during the book's preparation were always available and all talked to me more frankly than I expected. The personnel in National Defence Headquarters and the now defunct CASAP Project Office were equally accommodating. I overstayed my welcome on many occasions and no one complained. They are listed among the "Interviews" at the back.

Other organizations opened their doors to me and their staff provided invaluable assistance with the research materials that were made available to me. They were British Columbia House in Ottawa, which provided me with a private office for interviews on several occasions; the Department of National Defence's Directorate of History (Dr. Carl Christie and Dr. Marc Milner, now at the University of New Brunswick); the CF Photo Unit; the Imperial War Museum, London; the Maritime Museum of the Atlantic; the Maritime Museum of British Columbia; the Maritime Museum of Vancouver; the Ministry of Defence Navy Records Centre, London; the National Archives of Canada (especially Glenn Wright); the National Personnel Record Centre; the Naval Historical Branch of the Ministry of Defence, London; the Port Moody Public Library who found many rare (to them) books for me; the Port Moody Writers' Workshop, whose leader, Eileen Kernahan, and members kept me on track; the Provincial Archives of British Columbia; the Public Record Office, London; the Royal Navy Submarine School at HMS *Dolphin*; the Royal Navy Submarine Museum (Gus Britton and Margaret Bidmead); the Submarine Procurement Executive of the Ministry of Defence, Bath (especially Peter Davies); the Submariners Old Comrades Association, Canadian Pacific Branch; and, the Vancouver City Archives.

There are even more people to thank in the "individual" category. This includes all the retired submariners, their families, other naval personnel in Canada and abroad, and many non-affiliated people who were involved in my quest for information. To list them would take another volume, so I refer the reader to the endnotes for their names. I enjoyed working with them all and appreciated every interview, every tape, every letter, and every picture that they so generously offered for my use.

I am greatly indebted to my good friend, Elspeth Naismith, for her listening ear and her couch in Ottawa; Ken Ducommun for his interest and his flat in London; Dave Perkins for his generosity in sharing information; Bill Herman and David Rolfe whose references helped me secure funding; Gary Wiseman, Carl Sorrell, and several others for their assistance in piecing together the events during the recent nuclear-powered submarine acquisition program; the late Pat MacDonald who was encouragement itself; my boss at Eagle Ridge Hospital, Rosemary Groves, who has never complained in eight years about my "other job;" my late mother, Deborah Holbard, who read all the drafts except the final one; my sister-in-law, Janet Bell, for her empathy and the exquisite art work in this book; and my husband, James, for putting up with my reduced earning capacity for ten years.

Lastly, a word about Canadian publishers. Not once did I experience the horror stories that unpublished authors dread when they submit a manuscript. All the companies I dealt with treated me with respect and the utmost courtesy. However it was Kirk Howard of Dundurn Press in Toronto who made the quickest decision and the best offer. Throughout the production phase, Dundurn's staff has displayed remarkable tolerance with my inexperience and have provided me with outstanding assistance – particularly Judith Turnbull, Dirk Lehman, and my editor, Doris Cowan.

*To all Canadian submariners – past,
present, and future*

PART ONE
1914–1922

CHAPTER ONE

THE BIRTH OF THE CANADIAN SUBMARINE SERVICE, 1914

"My God, what do we do now?"

Two small vessels crept slowly into Canadian waters in the pre-dawn of a summer's morning. It was 0445* on 5 August 1914 – warm, calm and hazy. The vessels were submarines, arriving secretly after an escape under cover of darkness from their American shipyard.

At that moment the Canadian Submarine Service was born.

Its conception had not been planned by the Royal Canadian Navy, and its delivery turned out to be precipitate and furtive, unheralded by the usual naval ceremonies. Like all unexpected events, the acquisition of the submarines was surrounded by urgency and confusion.

The Canadian Submarine Service began not in Halifax as one might assume, but in the middle of the Strait of Juan de Fuca, the seaway that separates Canada from the United States on the Pacific coast. Astonishingly, it was the Province of British Columbia, not the Canadian government, that had taken the initiative and acquired the twin submarines at the outbreak of the Great War.

The two vessels appeared insignificant as they made their way into Esquimalt Harbour on that warm, hazy morning, around breakfast time. Many people saw them; few paid any attention. But those on board the examination vessel, MV *Malaspina*, took one look at the unusual craft,

---

*Throughout the book, the time is given military style, which is based on the twenty-four-hour system. Thus, 9:30 a.m. is written as "0930," and 8 p.m. as "2000."

failed to challenge them, turned tail, and ran at full speed for the harbour entrance. They "went round the corner off Fisgard Light, [and] bloody near skidded," signalling, "Two German torpedo boats approaching the harbour."[1]

The situation also alarmed the militia who were manning the shore-based guns on the first day of World War I. "My God, what are we going to do now?"[2] groaned one officer when he heard the news. But at the Black Rock gun battery the gunners had no doubts about what to do – they rammed home their shells and trained the twelve-pounders' barrels on the submarines. As soon as the boats* were within range, they would fire.

Fortunately, the infant Canadian Submarine Service got a reprieve. The officer in charge of the Black Rock guns looked again through his telescope and stopped to think. The submarines were on the surface in plain sight, not submerged as an enemy would be, and they looked like British C-class boats. His pause saved the submarines. At that moment they hoisted a flag: some say it was the Red Ensign, but rumour has it that it was a pillow case. The gunners held their fire and wondered why the dockyard had not notified them to expect the submarines. Later they discovered that they had nearly blown Canada's first submarines to kingdom come.

Meanwhile, the *Malaspina* had alerted the entire dockyard – she came into port "wailing like a banshee"[3] with the lanyard of her siren tied to the rail. One confident civilian went to investigate. He was B.L. "Barney" Johnson, a master mariner and B.C. pilot, who had volunteered to assist the navy for one month with their navigation in the difficult coastal waters of B.C. Speaking later of the submarines' arrival he recalled, "My naval career had commenced without my realizing it."[4] The boats changed his life irrevocably.

No naval band played "Heart of Oak" to mark the historic birth of the Canadian Submarine Service, no flags or coloured streamers fluttered in the breeze, and no crowd cheered. Only two men stood on the jetty in the sunshine to greet the new arrivals. They were Sir Richard McBride, the premier of British Columbia, and Lt. Henry Pilcher, RN (Royal Navy), temporarily in charge of the naval base.

Although tired, Sir Richard took much pride in his accomplishment: he had secured the submarines for the Pacific coast in the nick of time, and he was relieved that his bold and hurried plan had succeeded. He was also anxious about the cost; he later took a man aside who had come with

---

*Submariners always refer to submarines as *boats*, never *subs*.

the submarines and asked him if he thought the price was fair. James V. Paterson was probably not the right person to ask; he was the president of the shipyard that had built the boats. He assured the premier that it was.

Lieutenant Pilcher, on the other hand, suffered only anxiety at the scale of the events that had overtaken him while he was burdened with responsibilities for which he was too junior in rank – the senior naval officer having gone to sea and left him alone. He reacted to the event by issuing a stream of ill-conceived orders, which no one obeyed.

Half an hour later McBride and Pilcher returned to their respective offices for another long and taxing day preparing for war, which they both believed would soon be unleashed upon their city. When he was settled at his desk the first task that McBride undertook, and one that gave him great pleasure, was the composition of a press release for the Canadian and British newspapers. The Victoria *Daily Colonist* published it at noon in an extra and it caused a sensation. It read:

> ... Sir Richard McBride, representing the Province of British Columbia, some days ago completed the purchase of two submarines, which are now lying at anchor in British waters ready for action ... The submarines are newly built and said to be of the most destructive class.[5]

Another version of events paints a more dramatic picture, but is probably less reliable as history. According to this account, two other men were scrutinizing the boats with intense interest. They had just been released from the naval prison, but were in fact there to join the submarines. Lt. Adrian St.V. Keyes, RN, had been appointed to command the flotilla and Midshipman John G. (Jock) Edwards, RCN, was shortly to become the third officer of the second boat.[6]

The two had met in early July 1914, at a weekend house party at Georgian Bay, north of Toronto. In conversation over drinks, they discovered that they had much in common: both were former naval officers, and both wished to return to England if war broke out. The younger man, Edwards, aged twenty, had been invalided out of the Royal Naval College at Dartmouth before completing his training. Keyes at thirty-one was a pioneer submariner who had retired from the Royal Navy two years previously. When they parted, they promised to keep in touch.

Edwards returned to Toronto. Then, the story goes, he impulsively decided to join the army. He continued to work at his clerical job, but was issued a rifle and uniform.

At the end of July, when war looked certain, the two men met again. Keyes asked Edwards to assist him with the enrollment of naval volunteers in Toronto, and the younger man did so, without bothering to arrange for time off work. His employer promptly fired him. Next, with a fine disregard for the fact that he had already enlisted in the army, Edwards volunteered for the Royal Canadian Navy. Several days later he and Keyes were on their way to the west coast and the submarines. Edwards felt guilty about the fact that technically, he was a deserter from the army, and preparing to leave for B.C. was a nerve-racking experience for him. He hid his rifle under his bed at home and concealed his army uniform by wrapping it in a parcel, which he planned to throw off the train into a river. He passed up the farewell party in case he was arrested as a deserter and crept furtively onto the train, avoiding Keyes's boisterous friends who were saying goodbye.

Toward the end of their journey, the two friends persuaded the train conductor to part with his gold braid. They applied it to the sleeves of Keyes's civilian suit so that he could make a suitable entrance to the Esquimalt dockyard. From here the story becomes more dramatic and is certainly apocryphal. The two men were arrested at the gate by guards armed with revolvers, then thrown into the brig – hardly a fitting end to their bold enterprise – and subsequently released in time to watch the submarines' arrival on 5 August 1914.

The historical record throws cold water on this exciting tale. The evidence shows that these first Canadian submariners were never arrested and that they were not in Esquimalt to witness the submarines' arrival. Keyes and Edwards were still in Toronto on 5 August 1914, not yet having been appointed to the submarine service. That would happen on the 6th. McBride and the director of the Naval Service (DNS), who posted the pair, did not know of the availability of the boats until 3 August 1914, and without jet planes Keyes and Edwards could never have been at the dockyard on the evening of the 4th. Nor were they expected: no signal was sent. The origins of the story may lie in the fact that the naval prison had been hastily converted into officers' quarters, to accommodate the influx of personnel when war began. It is easy to see how the story became exaggerated over time. Edwards had embellished the story into a wonderful after-dinner yarn – it is recorded here in full because it was the very first of the Canadian Submarine Service.

The Canadian Submarine Service was born of crisis and opportunity, and of sheer daring by the premier of British Columbia. The birth was a complicated one – the boats departed covertly from Seattle in the dead of night and narrowly avoided being shelled by their own side. Although the local press had alerted the population of Victoria, and they knew how vulnerable the Pacific coast would be in case of war, the citizens did not react to the information until after the boats arrived. On reading their newspapers the next morning, the Victorians, barely used to the idea of being at war, did not know whether to feel alarmed or reassured.

If the citizenry had known what McBride and Pilcher knew, they would have felt extreme anxiety. Those privy to the facts were very concerned, because Ottawa had warned them that an attack from German cruisers prowling in the western Pacific was imminent. It was this intelligence that had provoked the premier into risking the unilateral submarine purchase. The population learned this later, though postwar accounts would have readers believe otherwise.

The background to the story of the submarine acquisition was this: on 29 July 1914, only six days before war was declared,[7] a group of politicians and prominent local citizens gathered for lunch at the Union Club in Victoria. They knew the government was preparing for war, and they discussed how it might affect British Columbia, in view of the dismal defences of the Pacific coast. One of those present was James Paterson, the president of the Seattle Dry Dock and Construction Company, who listened intently, perhaps sniffing a deal in the wind. He mentioned to his companions that two brand new submarines were available at his yard. He did not tell them that Chile, the country for which they had been built, had just refused to accept the boats, because of their failure to meet performance specifications.

Paterson had sown his seed. Another guest at the Union Club was Captain William H. Logan, a man of sound judgement and responsible opinions, who was not only a master mariner but also the local representative of Lloyd's of London. Through Logan's position as an insurer, he knew about the finished submarines and probably knew the reason Chile had refused them. However, he was not aware that they were for sale until the luncheon at the Union Club.

A few days later, on 2 August, a citizen called on Logan, asking him to join a local committee planning to buy a battleship. Logan casually suggested that perhaps they should consider two new submarines instead. Later that day another acquaintance urged him to inform the premier of British Columbia of the unusual opportunity. Because McBride had frequently demonstrated his concern about the defence of B.C., and was sympathetic to all naval matters, Logan thought it was a good idea.

Early on 3 August Logan telephoned the premier and his suggestion was received with enthusiasm. Sir Richard McBride was only too keen to do something, because another telegram had arrived at the dockyard: "Relations very strained with Germany. Guard against surprise attack." Ottawa knew through Admiralty intelligence that two German light cruisers, the *Leipzig* and *Nürnberg*, of Vice-Admiral Count Von Spee's Far Eastern Squadron were steaming north up the Pacific coast of North America. The Canadian Naval Service did not provide these details to the naval base at Esquimalt until after the declaration of war.

Logan's timing was perfect. The dynamic and energetic McBride made a quick decision and gave Logan a mandate to pursue the matter with all dispatch. Logan immediately telephoned Paterson at the shipyard in Seattle to confirm the availability of the submarines. After mentioning that it was the Electric Boat Company (EBCo) in the eastern United States which held the Chilean navy contract for the boats, Paterson assured Logan that the submarines were still for sale because Chile had defaulted on their payments. They did not discuss the price, but it appears that Paterson had already worked one out with EBCo. Logan then advised McBride of their conversations and praised the submarines, probably reiterating Paterson's sales pitch. He said nothing about the submarines' deficiencies, which Chile had discovered, and which had been widely reported in American newspapers.

The submarines, named *Iquique* and *Antofagasta*, had been ordered by the Chilean government in 1911 from EBCo of Connecticut, which had subcontracted the work to the Seattle Dry Dock and Construction Company. EBCo had designed and built the boats in knock-down form and shipped the parts to Seattle for assembly. Chile's purchase price at $409,000 each was a bargain according to Paterson. When Chile allowed their progress payments to fall into arrears during 1914, both Paterson and EBCo became seriously concerned that, after Chile's rejection of the boats, they would be left with two white elephants. McBride's sudden interest in them was a heaven-sent opportunity to the American.

The boats were very small diesel-electric submarines designed for coastal defence operations – about 150 feet (45 m) in overall length, with a fifteen-foot beam and a displacement of 421 tons (408.2 tonnes) submerged. To a casual observer the submarines looked smaller than their dimensions suggested, because they floated low in the water with much of their hulls hidden. They were probably painted grey and the conning towers were little taller than a man. The deck or casing was narrow, barely wide enough for three men to stand side by side at its widest point. The boats were slightly different – one had three 18-inch torpedo tubes, and the other five, all in the bow. They had no deck guns. Surfaced, the submarines could do 13 knots, and submerged a maximum of 10 knots.

McBride, wanting to test the Canadian government's reaction, asked Logan to discuss the acquisition with a Cabinet minister from Ottawa and the local member of Parliament, both of whom were in Victoria. Later, these men gathered in McBride's office, with the attorney general of British Columbia and Logan, to decide what should be done. There was consensus on the necessity of acquiring the boats, but McBride's private diary shows that there was no agreement over how that might be achieved. When Logan was asked the price of the submarines, he made a guess at $375,000 each, having forgotten to establish the cost with Paterson.

The group's next objective was to gain the navy's agreement and they went off to the dockyard, leaving McBride in his office. Lieutenant Pilcher, still temporarily in charge, needed little persuasion but also wanted to know the asking price. Logan telephoned Paterson. He was stunned when he heard Paterson demand $575,000 for each, adding that the price was not negotiable. Logan passed the phone to Burrell, the federal minister of agriculture, to get confirmation (and presumably a witness) of the amount. This was $332,000 more than Chile had contracted for, but Paterson recognized when a client was in a tight spot and pushed his advantage.

The four men then sat down and composed a telegram for Pilcher to send later to Vice-Admiral Kingsmill, the director of the Naval Service in Ottawa:

> Two submarines actually completed for Chilian [sic] Government Seattle, estimated cost [$575,000] each. Could probably purchase. Ready for action torpedoes on board [This was incorrect]. Chilian Government cannot take possession. I consider it most important to acquire immediately. Burrell concurs. Provincial Government will advance money pending remittance.

This cable, dated 3 August 1914, was the first communication about submarines between the west coast and Ottawa, and proves Keyes could not have already been on his way to Esquimalt with Edwards.

Paterson was so sure of his sale that he began to prepare the submarines to sail for Canada that night. Logan had to forestall him with a telegram saying "Don't move." The key players in B.C. settled down to wait for a response from Ottawa. A speedy answer was expected, but did not materialize.

It is difficult to establish when the decision was made for B.C. to go it alone in the event that permission was not given, or not given soon enough, by Ottawa. However, it appears to have occurred in the early hours of 4 August, when Pilcher, alarmed by another signal to prepare for war, summoned the federal politicians and Logan to the dockyard. It is quite astonishing today to realize that the decision to buy Canada's first submarines was made without regard for price or authority by a very junior naval officer who was about to have a nervous breakdown. His sole advice stemmed from the federal minister of agriculture, a backbench MP, the Lloyd's agent for Victoria, and a provincial premier – none of whom had even seen the vessels. Pilcher had received no counsel from the RCN at this point. Although McBride organized the acquisition, and found the money for the boats when Ottawa dragged its feet, he maintained all along that he had merely facilitated the purchase.

After the historic decision had been taken, two major hurdles had to be overcome. The money had to be raised, and the submarines had to be removed from the United States quickly, before the president signed the Neutrality Act, which would prohibit the sale of war materials to belligerent nations.

Sir Richard McBride ordered Logan to depart for Seattle immediately and to take someone to assist him in getting the boats to Canada. Pilcher found a reserve volunteer, Able Seaman (AB) Thomas A. Brown, and instructed him to dress in plain clothes to avoid recognition as a Canadian sailor. It has often been reported that Able Seaman Brown disguised himself as a "hobo" to spy on the shipyard workers and establish if there were any German sympathizers among them who might scuttle the plan to spirit the submarines out of the country. However, according to Brown's son, there was no such plan. His father was simply taken along so that there would be a Canadian on board the second boat. Logan and Brown left hurriedly to catch the Seattle ferry.

The premier then concentrated on getting the money. He confessed all to the lieutenant-governor who lent a sympathetic ear, and then hurried to get the British Columbian Cabinet's approval to spend $1,200,000 for the boats, a very tidy sum in those days. The minutes of the executive council meeting shows only that a cheque for $1.2 million was approved and made out to McBride. There is no record that the submarines were discussed or the purchase was approved by a Cabinet vote.

The cheque was issued after the lieutenant-governor signed an order-in-council. Later on 4 August, McBride composed a cable to the prime minister, Sir Robert Borden, which he did not send until after the submarines had arrived safely. It said, in part, "... have advanced tonight one million and fifty thousand dollars ... for purchase of two modern submarines ... Congratulate Canada if this operation successful." The amount was decoded incorrectly, and should have read $1,200,000.

The Naval Service in Ottawa had also been busy – cabling the Royal Navy for advice on whether or not to buy the boats. The director of the Naval Service showed no independence of action as he waited for the British Admiralty's go-ahead. Pilcher, in an agony of indecision, kept nagging him by wire and finally cabled: "[I] shall not act without authority." However, he did.

Then the bell tolled – the British Empire declared war on Germany at 1500 Pacific time on 4 August 1914, taking Canada with it. The sudden reality put a different complexion on the submarine acquisition, and markedly increased McBride's anxiety. There was now more chance that he might lose the submarines because of America's impending declaration of neutrality, but the need for them was even greater. The scheme had to proceed now, even if it meant acting alone.

On his way home, McBride took the cheque to the dockyard and gave it to Pilcher. He then ordered his messenger, Richard Ryan, to witness the hand-over of the cheque at sea following the inspection of the submarines. The premier's daughter recalls that her father informed his family of the submarine acquisition after dinner, and appeared to be very concerned and preoccupied throughout the evening. He did not go to bed, but paced the floor downstairs all night, and left the house before dawn to attend to an urgent cable received by the dockyard.

The message brought the disturbing intelligence that the two light cruisers of Vice-Admiral Count Von Spee's squadron were indeed steaming north from Mexico up the Pacific coast of North America. McBride and Pilcher drew but one conclusion – as the enemy was not about to attack the neutral United States, the ships were heading straight for Victoria.

In the afternoon of 4 August, Logan and Brown had been met at the ferry by James Paterson. He took them to his Seattle shipyard to finalize the plans for the submarines' departure that night, following the acceptance of his offer. To cover his actions Paterson demanded that McBride personally guarantee payment before sailing, but he was persuaded to let payment be made at the time of delivery in Canadian waters. During this telephone conversation, confirmed by telegram at 2000, Logan asked McBride to have the tug *Salvor* sent out to meet the boats at dawn in the international waters of the Strait of Juan de Fuca, for the inspection and payment to be made. The premier concluded the call by urging Logan to avoid all unnecessary risks.

Then, with the Chilean naval inspectors still in the shipyard and unaware of what was to happen, preparations began in earnest to "steal" the boats from under their noses. AB Brown, looking rather disreputable, did at this point mingle with the yard crews to establish if they were still willing to go to sea that night for special trials. By 2100 the hatches were secured and the submarines were ready for their maiden voyage. With all the lights doused in the yard at 2200, the yard crews silently boarded the boats. Logan, Paterson, a retired U.S. naval officer, and the Pacific construction manager for EBCo, were in the *Antofagasta*, with Brown in the *Iquique*. Brown was told to stay close astern and within hail (he had never been on board a submarine before).

The stealthy departure was aided by a slight fog – no authorities were informed, no clearances arranged. The submarines sailed without navigation lights, using their quiet electric motors; later, when it was deemed they would not be caught, they switched over to the diesel engines. Working up to full power, the boats raced for Canadian waters.

After making a successful getaway, Logan sighted the tug on station at 0445 on the morning of 5 August 1914. Paterson, who had been most anxious throughout the night, fearing that British Columbia would not keep their end of the bargain, was profoundly relieved. Then the submarines moved alongside *Salvor* and into Canadian territory, and not a moment too soon – the president of the United States signed the Neutrality Act at 0530 Pacific time and Paterson narrowly avoided violating the laws of his land and losing his sale. Two hours before, while the submarines were still en route, the Admiralty had finally recommended the purchase to the Royal Canadian Navy. The Naval Service cabled inquiring of Esquimalt if the submarines could still be bought. Pilcher replied, "Have purchased submarines."

Those on the tug lined the rails to get their first glimpse of the new Canadian submarines, which looked rather sinister in the half light. Lt. Bertram Jones, RN, a retired submariner who had just reported for duty in Esquimalt, carried the cheque in his pocket. He was under strict instructions not to hand it over to Paterson until he was satisfied that the boats were suitable and well-found.

Jones transferred to the first boat, the *Antofagasta*, to start his inspection and was joined by the U.S. trials captain, who had piloted the *Iquique*. With irritation born of worry, Paterson demanded the cheque immediately, but Logan told him he had to wait until Jones had finished. Paterson was as yet unaware that the U.S.A. had declared its neutrality after they had entered Canadian waters – thus the sale was legal – and that the Admiralty had finally approved the purchase. When Jones moved on to inspect the other submarine, Paterson complained impatiently, but Jones calmly proceeded. When he was finished, the boats headed for Esquimalt and at 0700 Jones handed over the cheque and asked Paterson for a receipt. Paterson retorted that he felt the boats were receipt enough, but grudgingly obliged by writing it on the back of an envelope which he held against the side of the conning tower. At that moment, McBride's messenger, Ryan, remembers that someone hoisted a White Ensign and the crew gave three cheers. Their timing was excellent – it prevented the shore-based guns opening up on the unannounced flotilla. But Logan told a reporter soon afterwards that they remembered just in time to make their intentions clear to the naval authorities, and because they could not find an ensign they employed a pillow case instead.

The first Canadian submarines arrived alongside about 0830. Paterson, feeling a bit happier by now, and sure that the deal would stick, met McBride who had acted so promptly in his favour and told him expansively that the boats were the finest possible and the price was extraordinarily fair. He then rushed off to the bank.

Pilcher's increasingly excited behaviour peaked with the arrival of the new submarines. He sent a cable to Ottawa announcing that he had named the boats *McBride* and *Paterson* and then he announced several promotions, most of which were not confirmed by Ottawa. However, one was: the young naval volunteer, Tom Brown, who went down to Seattle an able seaman, returned with the submarines as a sub-lieutenant.

That evening McBride got into his stride and began to take command of the dockyard. Realizing something was seriously wrong with Pilcher, he sent him home for twenty-four hours. The fleet surgeon who later examined Pilcher found him suffering from nervous exhaustion and made his sick leave indefinite. Without authority, McBride placed the submariner Lieutenant Jones in charge, assisting him late into the night. The war situation was worsening rapidly. A radio station in San Diego had intercepted a message from the *Leipzig* that day. It confirmed that she was steaming north up the Pacific coast of the United States.

The reactions to the submarine acquisition came rapidly. They varied between fear, reassurance, shock, anxiety, and fury. The citizens of Victoria had no information, and they reacted emotionally. The better-informed politicians and naval personnel felt both relief, because they had achieved a means of defence, and fear, because of the real threat of shelling by German cruisers. The Americans and Chileans responded with anger because they had lost face over the secret deal.

"Victoria [was] in an awful state," recalled a member of the militia.[8] The First World War was a frightening surprise for the majority of B.C.'s population, because they were so isolated from the events in Europe. Many had no idea of the world situation; right up to the last moment, few believed war was possible. When the inadequacy of the Pacific defences came home to them after the submarines materialized, many Victorians evacuated to the mainland. The banks removed their cash and securities to inland towns and young men enlisted in huge numbers. Others stayed, reassured by the submarine presence. They saw the boats as "modern submarines of high speed and wide radius of activity ... [which] could cope with a hostile fleet."[9] The fact that they were without torpedoes was suppressed.

The fact that their new submarines were unarmed was a severe blow to the prime movers of the purchase, and quite unexpected. The boats did not have any spare parts either – another major oversight – to say nothing of experienced crews. Keeping his business hush-hush because of U.S. neutrality laws, Logan returned to Seattle to negotiate with Paterson for the weapons and parts. His efforts were exposed when Paterson received a cable from a Canadian bureaucrat asking in plain language for torpedoes. The U.S. Navy quickly learned of the plot and tightened security around the shipyard to prevent its success. Logan was willing to continue the undercover operation, but when suitable torpedoes were found in Halifax McBride terminated the scheme.

The United States viewed the disappearance of the submarines with anger. On 5 August, they dispatched their cruiser, USS *Milwaukee*, to intercept the boats, but of course, they were too late. In a diplomatic note to the U.S. government, Chile strongly objected to losing their boats. However, their protest carried little weight as they had failed to make payments and had recommended non-acceptance. Some of the senior management at EBCo were shocked at the precipitate action that had been taken by Paterson's company, but they carefully avoided comment.

The appalling state of the seaward defences in British Columbia had been a major thorn in McBride's side for many years, and had clearly been a factor in his hasty decision to buy the first Canadian submarines. The reason that the protection of the Pacific coast, and indeed all the coastline of Canada, had fallen so low in priority is to be found in earlier history, and is inextricably entwined with the naval policy of the British Empire, of which Canada was a part.

McBride's bold and decisive action displayed an unusual confidence in naval matters, which a provincial premier of today could not hope to emulate. Was his confidence merely the bravado of a strong personality, or was it based on a thorough knowledge of the subject? Was it political opportunism, or was it patriotism in its purest form? Did he overstep his authority in taking the leadership role of the dockyard while the senior officer was at sea?

While McBride knew that the sensational purchase of the boats would garner his political party some points, his confidence was rooted in a surprisingly deep knowledge of Imperial defence, the naval history of the British Empire and Canada, and the current naval requirements for the Pacific coast. The premier had continually rubbed shoulders with the leading men of the day at home and abroad during his time in power and had attended three imperial conferences on defence. He numbered among his friends Winston Churchill, who became First Lord of the Admiralty; Sir Robert Borden, the Canadian prime minister from 1911 to 1920; and, Adm. "Jacky" Fisher, the famous British First Sea Lord who was the father of the modern submarine, as well as the dreadnoughts. These men trusted and respected McBride and strongly influenced his emerging opinions. Later they listened to his views on defence, and allowed him access to classified material.

When Paterson offered *Iquique* and *Antofagasta*, McBride knew that Canada's navy was in a mess and the west coast was defenceless. There was no Canadian naval policy in place and the RCN was lacking both ships and men. He also knew that this state of affairs stemmed from the withdrawal of the British navy from the Dominion earlier in the century and the ideological clash of the Conservatives and Liberals over Canadian naval defence. The parties could not agree on the question of whether they should contribute ships, money and men to the mother country to combat Germany's growing aggression, or take an independent position and keep the RCN separate from Britain's navy. In the meantime the young RCN declined, both under the Liberals of Sir Wilfrid Laurier who had established it, and later under Borden's Conservatives who saw little point in having a Canadian navy. McBride saw no hope of an early resolution of the problem, which might have improved the naval protection for his province.

When Laurier's Liberals established the RCN in 1910 they acknowledged the country's duty to assume some of its own defence. Their policy called for four cruisers and six destroyers to be built, but McBride was aware that this did not meet the Admiralty's recommendation of one armoured and three unarmoured cruisers, six destroyers, and "three submarines."[10]

At its birth the RCN was a navy in name only, having administrative control over the dockyards on the Atlantic and Pacific coasts, but no operational control of the ships. This remained in the British Admiralty's hands. Britain sent two aging RN cruisers to each coast for training, which were recommissioned as His Majesty's Canadian Ships (HMCS) *Niobe* and *Rainbow*; and later still they sent two small sloops, HMS *Shearwater* and *Algerine*, to Esquimalt. All were manned by British naval personnel. These expatriates often left the navy as soon as they could, and often when they should not. In all, the crews were reduced by 271 desertions by 1914 and the Canadian government did nothing to replace the men, so the ships quickly became operational liabilities. Though the ship procurement was under way when Laurier lost power, the Liberals had not awarded any contracts for the ten ships they had wanted.

Just over a year after the RCN began, Robert Borden, a moderate imperialist, became the new Conservative prime minister in September 1911. Coming to the post with little interest in or knowledge of naval matters, Borden was faced with an immature and inadequate navy, an increasing threat from the German Kaiser, woeful coastal defence plans, and an obligation to maintain the Liberals' policy of independence from the Empire, with which he fundamentally disagreed. Despite the prime minister's desire to stimulate the Canadian shipbuilding industry, he cancelled the entire Liberal warship program, while endeavouring to learn more about the threat in Europe and the requirements needed to meet it. He consulted the Admiralty, his own Naval Service, and McBride to assist in the development of a new naval policy.

The triangle of leaders in London, Ottawa, and Victoria began to work up to full speed in early 1912. Churchill, knowing Borden was friendlier than the anti-imperialist Laurier, endeavoured to influence Borden directly, and indirectly through McBride, by offering all the help he could to make Canada's flagging naval policy a brilliant success. The First Lord had little trouble convincing Borden that the German threat was serious, and that Canada had a moral obligation to assist her mother country. He forcefully encouraged Borden to make a Canadian cash contribution to the Admiralty for three new dreadnoughts a part of his new policy. Churchill's strategy was not entirely altruistic: if successful it would give the RN three more ships at no expense. During a sojourn in Britain, Borden endeavoured to gain more of a voice for Canada in the Imperial defence decision process, as well as a promise that the Admiralty would consider placing contracts for small warships in Canadian yards, in exchange for the Canadian dollars. The British Prime Minister agreed in principle with Borden's conditions, but nothing was ever formalized.

Once back in Ottawa Borden went to work on a temporary naval policy of contribution to the Empire and postponed the development of a permanent one that would deal with the RCN. This decision ensured that the RCN and coastal defence continued their decline. McBride supported his friend's position on contributing funds to the imperial navy, but deplored the Tory PM's neglect of the young Canadian navy.

Foreseeing the difficulties the controversial policy would bring his government, Borden asked Churchill to prepare two memoranda to assist him in selling it at home. One of the memoranda was secret, the other was designed for public consumption: McBride was privy to both. The one for general release described in broad terms the "emergency" facing Britain and the urgent need for Canada's financial contribution to build three battleships to strengthen the Empire's defence. The secret memorandum contained a more specific threat appreciation, which stated that raids on undefended or poorly defended Canadian ports could be expected from enemy cruisers seeking coal and supplies. It recommended that the naval bases of Halifax and Esquimalt develop "small local defence flotillas, consisting of torpedo boats and submarines"[11] to respond to an attack. For McBride's province, the report specifically suggested an examination service, four torpedo boats, and three submarines to be based in Esquimalt. These recommendations were not lost on the B.C. premier.

Borden used the secret memo in Cabinet to assist the ministers' understanding of his proposed answer to naval defence – the Naval Aid Bill. The bill was short, only containing Borden's temporary contribution policy, the requirements recommended for the RCN being ignored. The Naval Aid Bill stated that $35 million should be given to Britain for the "purpose of immediately increasing the effective naval forces of the Empire."[12]

Churchill's delight knew no bounds when he heard of Borden's bill, which assisted Britain but did little for Canada. He wrote to McBride, "Canada has surpassed herself."[13] McBride, although pleased with the praise over the bill he helped develop, remained unhappy with the PM's neglect of the RCN, especially in Esquimalt.

Borden introduced the Naval Aid Bill to Parliament on 5 December 1912. The prime minister said, in his remarks about the bill, that he did not believe Canada should undertake the hazardous and costly experiment of building up a naval organization restricted to the Dominion. When he heard that, McBride was a very unhappy and worried man; he foresaw trouble on all fronts – for the success of the bill, for the navy in Canada, and in Europe.

One of the longest, most vociferous, and most famous debates since Confederation followed. The Liberals disagreed with the idea of a dollar contribution to Britain for two major reasons. First, they thought that the threat to Canada was grossly exaggerated, and secondly, that the payment would increase Canada's dependence on Britain. Laurier did all in his power to prevent passage of the bill, but it eventually passed third reading on 15 May 1913 by thirty-three votes.

Before being given royal assent, the Naval Aid Bill had to get through the Liberal Senate. The debate in the upper house was as loud and vitriolic as it had been in the lower, and McBride watched in frustration as the Bill was thrown out two weeks later. Despite Borden's earlier prediction of the coming conflict, the Tories made no attempt to amend the bill and try again. Borden chose instead to wait for a Tory majority to evolve in the Senate to get its approval.

Churchill complained to McBride, "my difficulties here will increase considerably"[14] and offered the services of the Second Sea Lord, Admiral Sir John Jellicoe, RN, to the Canadian government to help them develop another naval policy. But Borden did nothing as the world situation deteriorated; he did not accept the offer until twelve days before war was declared. The hostilities meant that Jellicoe never came and McBride, with seething frustration, decided to take some steps to protect his province.

So when McBride, a man of remarkable knowledge and leadership, was faced with the German cruisers heading his way, he felt fully justified in buying the available submarines to protect his province. He knew from Churchill that the Admiralty had recommended submarines for the west coast in 1912; he knew from Fisher that submarines were going to be a force to be reckoned with; and he knew from Borden that the Dominion was going to do nothing. Unfortunately he did not know how to judge the quality of the Seattle boats' construction, or how they compared with other classes of submarines, in price and capability.

The premier of British Columbia was motivated by patriotism, but he also knew full well that the decision to buy the submarines would not hurt him politically. He certainly made judgements in matters that were beyond his area of knowledge, both when he bought the boats and when he judged Pilcher to be too sick to be in charge of the dockyard, but was anyone else available who was better informed? If McBride had not assumed a leadership role, the submarines would have stayed in Seattle and the dockyard would have been in chaos.

McBride received many congratulatory messages from around the Empire for his decisive action. He had achieved a means of defence for the Pacific coast, contributed two warships to the Admiralty with Canadian dollars, and created the Canadian Submarine Service. Borden, who had been unable to achieve any of this, was nevertheless lavish in his praise of his friend both publicly and privately.

The government of British Columbia offered the submarines to the Dominion government, which gratefully accepted them and placed them at the disposal of His Majesty for general service in the Royal Navy on 7 August. The Admiralty ordered the boats to remain in B.C. for crew training and told the RCN to advertise their presence but to conceal their whereabouts, presumably to scare away the two German cruisers.

Ten days after the submarines were acquired, McBride learned of a plan to coal the German cruisers in Seattle. As they were steaming north, he cabled Churchill asking for help, instead of turning to the ineffective RCN. The First Lord reassured his friend with the promise that two powerful cruisers would arrive shortly to do battle with the foe. McBride had at last realized that, without torpedoes and a trained crew, the new submarine flotilla could do little to halt the enemy.

CHAPTER TWO

HMCS *CC1* AND *CC2* GO INTO SERVICE, 1914

"To a man they all stood fast!"[1]

When the Admiralty gave their belated approval for the RCN to buy the two submarines, it was only given provided that crews could be secured. In fact, crews were not available – they did not exist, even on paper. But by the time the cable had arrived, the purchase was a *fait accompli* and the boats were in Canadian waters.

As experienced submarine officers and men were a very rare breed in those days, and nonexistent in the RCN, the new Canadian Submarine Service had a difficult time manning the boats. William Logan, again under McBride's orders, made a desperate attempt to procure trained men from the United States Navy Yard in Bremerton, Washington. It failed, even though large financial inducements were offered to the sailors. When the flotilla's new commanding officer, Lt. Adrian Keyes, RN (Ret.), arrived on the scene on about the 9th or 10th of August, he tackled the manning problem without delay.

The RCN were very fortunate in finding Keyes, who had retired from the RN only two years before. Perhaps McBride knew he was in Toronto through his friendship with his elder brother, Roger Keyes, who was in charge of the British submarine service. Whatever the method used, the younger Keyes was located, and fast.

The energetic and raffishly good-looking Keyes, known as "Tubby," was a pioneer submariner. He had served in submarines since before their acceptance into the British Navy in 1904 and within two years commanded an A-class boat. Keyes had an excellent technical mind and became an RN submarine instructor of note. After several commands he had voluntarily retired in 1912, and emigrated to Toronto. When Keyes left the Royal Navy he held the rank of lieutenant-commander, but the RCN granted him only a lieutenancy in August 1914. The reason is not clear from his now-available Admiralty records[2] because, as far as the RN was concerned, Keyes remained a "two and a half" (lieutenant-commander) while in Canada.

Keyes not only had to train the crews for the new submarines, he also had to find them. He needed thirty-six men for the two boats, as well as some spare ratings for replacement purposes. Ideally he was looking for men with submarine experience, but it was too much to hope for in Canada and he had to opt for men who had potential. He wanted intelligent, brave men with initiative, who were willing to suffer hardship and stress and who could form a reliable team quickly. Time was short and the threat acute, so he did not follow the stringent selection process of the RN. The enrolment medical and a brief parade had to suffice.

From eager but inexperienced volunteer reservists, Keyes mustered fifty men into rough ranks. The men heard Keyes speak of the volunteer nature of the new Canadian Submarine Service and assure them that if anyone declined to volunteer for submarines, they would suffer no loss of respect. He then ordered, "All those not wishing to serve in submarines, fall out!"[3] Not one man moved. So Keyes continued his address outlining his expectations and stressing the importance of responsibility in each member of the crew: "If anyone fails to do his job properly and quickly, it could jeopardize the safety of the boat and all hands." Keyes finally selected the crews by ordering, "Seamen, one step forward. Stokers, one step to the rear. Electricians, fall out to the right. Steam fitters, to the left." Those remaining were thanked and dismissed.

In the end Keyes chose about twenty-eight RNCVRs to become submariners. They were farm boys, bankers, grocery clerks, electrical workers, and mechanics. Some had never seen the sea, and one or two had lied about their age and had yet to shave. "A pretty motley bunch," said an able seaman in retrospect.[4] Keyes was able to supplement the new ratings with a few experienced engine room artificers from HMCS *Rainbow* after she returned from sea, and with others who had deserted and had been granted the King's pardon. (The authorities had turned a blind eye to their desertion.) These individuals provided "one strand of disciplined [experienced] men, but not a thread with submarine experience."[5]

The new crews urgently needed formal submarine training, but the Esquimalt dockyard could provide neither the facilities nor the personnel. Keyes had to do it himself – almost single-handed. The retired U.S. naval officer who had sailed with the boats from Seattle remained with them at McBride's request to provide basic instruction.[6] Although no receipt survives to support it, the price paid for the boats was also intended to pay this American instructor, but he never received his fee from either James Paterson or the Electric Boat Company, and later, when he attempted to get it from McBride and the RCN, he was again unsuccessful.

Keyes, in charge of the flotilla, chose to command submarine *No. 1*, as she was now referred to. He appointed Lt. Bertram Jones, RN, who had inspected the boats for acceptance, as captain of *No. 2*. Jones had retired to B.C. in 1913, but before that he had been trained by Keyes and had served in British submarines for five years, commanding several. Although Jones did not have Keyes's instinctive gift for teaching, he provided a valuable leadership example for the Canadian Submarine Service over the next four years. He had wanted to return to Britain but accepted his temporary commission in the RCN with good grace. Keyes reported that he was competent and courageous, and that he conducted good attacks. There were no other submarine officers available, so Keyes made do with surface types. One of them was Jock Edwards, whom he had chosen personally in Toronto.

Keyes's manning plan called for a complement of three officers and eighteen ratings for each submarine. The officers consisted of the captain (at the rank of lieutenant), a first lieutenant (the term first lieutenant refers to the second in command of a submarine, not a rank) who was also the navigator, and a third hand (a midshipman under training). The crews included a coxswain (the most senior rating on board), a chief engine room artificer (CERA), two ERAs and about six stokers, one or two torpedomen, a wireless operator, two or three leading hands, and four able seamen, one of whom was the cook. On commissioning, Keyes used only thirteen volunteer reservists in *No. 1*'s crew and ten in *No. 2*'s. Thirteen British regulars, two with submarine experience, topped up the companies.

The recently recruited Canadian volunteer reservists had not received even basic naval training, and those who had joined the RNCVR company previously had little more. However, the need to get the boats operational was so urgent that the crews went straight to Keyes's crash submarine course.

Both the officers and the men began their informal basic submarine training in the bowels of the new boats, crawling about and learning the location and function of every valve and pipe, every switch and trim tank. It was a new and confusing world, complete with diesel engines, electric motors, high- and low-pressure air systems, torpedoes, and a huge number of electric storage batteries. Bankers learned about Kingston valves, grocery clerks learned about hydroplanes, and the officers, who were more used to navigating in two dimensions had to learn to contend with three, as well as mastering the art of watchkeeping through the periscope.

Able Seaman Frederick W. Crickard, aged twenty-three, was a typical submarine volunteer. Fired with the patriotism of the time, he enrolled in the Royal Naval Canadian Volunteer Reserve in Victoria in June 1914. Crickard was a wholesale grocery clerk who knew nothing of submarines, their machinery or equipment, but grew to love them. Another young recruit came from a farm and had never seen the sea in his life. This ordinary seaman had a difficult time adjusting to the navy and never felt that he belonged in submarines, though he did make a few good friends in his mess. Another, a fifteen-year-old from Vancouver, desperate not to miss the war, lied about his age and was believed despite his fair hair and smooth skin; he volunteered for submarines but grew to dislike them intensely as he became more familiar with them.

Canada's new submarine officers brought with them confidence, leadership, and the ability to inspire respect. The rest they learned as they went along. Several Canadians who served that apprenticeship developed the skills in full measure – most notably, the midshipman, William Maitland-Dougall from *No. 1*, and the first lieutenant, Barney Johnson, from *No. 2*.

While he was at a preparatory school on Vancouver Island, William Maitland-Dougall[7] had decided on a career in the Navy. Continuing a family tradition of distinguished naval service, he entered the Royal Naval College of Canada (RNCC) in Halifax when it opened in January 1911 and graduated with honours two years later, at the age of seventeen. Willie (as he was known) was an energetic high achiever even then, which boded well for his career in the newest branch of the navy. His year of sea time in a cruiser was interrupted for more schooling at RNCC, and it was there that he heard war declared. Maitland-Dougall was appointed to submarines and, on arrival in Esquimalt, he immediately began his practical training under Keyes in *No. 1*. He was put in charge of the torpedo compartment with one or two ratings reporting to him. Time was short: he had to learn all he could, gain experience in handling men who knew more than he did, and also practise ship handling and watchkeeping. Early reports indicated that Maitland-Dougall showed great promise as a submariner.

Barney Johnson, who had watched the submarines arrive, came from a very different background. He was a young master mariner of considerable repute in marine circles on the west coast of Canada. Johnson had been "lent" by the British Columbia Pilotage Authority for one month to the RCN to assist with the navigation of warships in the hazardous Inside Passage of B.C. He was an admirable choice – his twenty years of experience at sea, coupled with an instinct for brilliant seamanship gave him "an incomparable knowledge of every nook and cranny from Vancouver to Alaska."[8]

In the turmoil at the naval base in August 1914, Johnson found himself appointed to HMC Submarine *No. 2* as her first lieutenant because the surface ships he was meant to navigate were still at sea chasing the Germans. In fact, in the early days, he acted as navigator for whichever boat went to sea. Johnson was not yet officially in the Navy, wore no uniform and was addressed as "Mister." He diligently attended all Keyes's training classes, and he learned quickly.

During this period Johnson and Keyes developed a warm and abiding friendship (which would last until Keyes died in 1926), and in late September 1914, when Johnson should have returned to the B.C. Pilotage Authority, Keyes persuaded the pilots to let Johnson remain in the Navy for the duration of the war. Johnson donned his uniform as an acting lieutenant, RNCVR – a year over-age and never having had a medical. No wavy stripes (worn by reservists) were available, so he initially shipped the straight ones of the regulars. He protested his commission in the volunteer reserve because, being a foreign-going master, he was entitled to one of higher standing in the reserves. Johnson did not pursue the matter further at that stage as there was no time and his submarine career was on its way. His one-month loan from the Pilotage Authority would ultimately extend to nearly five years – all but a couple of weeks of it spent in submarines.

Other officers and men played a vital role in the early days of the infant service. Some were well suited and some were not; some were Canadian - born and some were not. But without them the Canadian Submarine Service would have perished in its cradle, and never reached the maturity that was later to provide experienced submariners to the Royal Navy.

Lt. Wilfred T. Walker, RN (Ret.), who had settled in Canada after being invalided out of the Royal Navy in 1908, became the first lieutenant of *No. 1* under Keyes. With no submarine experience at all, he offered his services to the dockyard on 4 August. Walker applied himself to his new task with energy and the best intentions, but according to Keyes he made too many mistakes – he never adjusted to three dimensions. This type of erratic behaviour sometimes occurs quite unexpectedly when an individual transfers to submarines from surface ships and has to deal with diving. By Christmas Keyes had replaced Walker, who returned to general service where he acquitted himself well throughout both world wars.

After inheriting a cash-strapped family estate, Jock Edwards emigrated to Canada in 1913 to take a job in a shipping firm (the job he left in Toronto to assist Keyes in B.C.). It was to be the only job he ever held, apart from naval service in the two wars. "Boy" was twenty and single when he became a Canadian midshipman on *No. 2*, and the nickname stemmed from his young and fresh-faced appearance. He was well-built, gregarious, fun, hard-working, and was rarely seen without a cigarette in one hand and a drink in the other. Early on, Edwards confessed to seasickness but never let it slow him down. After two and a half years with the submarines, working his way up to first lieutenant, Edwards transferred to the RN to supplement their crews in Europe, where he made it to command.

Among the "strand of disciplined men"[9] from the Royal Navy there were only two with previous submarine experience. Chief Petty Officer James Addison had spent four years in British boats and was on the *Rainbow* at the outbreak of hostilities when he became the cox'n of *No. 1*. He imparted his knowledge and discipline to the greenhorns for four and a half years, and undoubtedly served as a tower of strength to his successive captains.

Another experienced RN rating was tracked down in an electrical manufacturing plant in Ontario. By 8 August Gunner(T [torpedoman]) George Brisco was on his way to Esquimalt to report to Keyes. He was short, stocky, and tough, with a tendency to be pushy and harsh. He had no submarine time, but his experience with all things electrical, including torpedoes, proved indispensable. He was given responsibility for the training of torpedomen and the maintenance of the electrical equipment on both boats. Brisco was to remain with the submarines until just before the Armistice when, as a consequence of a misjudgement on his part, he was transferred to the surface.

The last key rating came from *Shearwater* and also stayed with the submarines until the end of the war. Chief Engine Room Artificer (CERA) Arthur J.S. Hunting joined *No. 2*. He was responsible for the unreliable diesels and the training of the ERAs and stokers. He became thoroughly respected for his work in one of the most difficult and trying positions in the boats.

These officers and men, and others like them, created the first close-knit teams in Canada's submarine service. Most were committed, hard-working and selfless individuals who always did their best in appalling conditions.

Canada's new submarines, intended for coastal defence, were tiny and primitive by today's standards. Habitability was not a concern. In design the two boats were not exactly alike, for reasons that are now unclear. *No. 2* had a much finer bow and was slightly longer than *No. 1*; it also carried only two bow torpedoes to *No. 1*'s four. They each had one stern tube.

When the teen-aged daughter of Sir Richard McBride went on board, her first impression was of a big bullet with partitions.[10] It is an apt description, because the essential structure of a submarine, even today, is a long metal cylinder called a pressure hull which contains the working and living space for the crew. Most of the equipment and machinery is housed inside it. The pressure hulls of the first Canadian submarines were designed to dive only to 200 feet (60 m) and had the main ballast and trim tanks inside; in submarines today, the main tanks and some of the trim tanks are external.

Both boats had casings of light steel on top of the pressure hulls, which provided a flat deck for the crews to work on when on the surface, and space for stowing anchors, lines, and other equipment. Also incorporated in the casings' structure were the conning towers with their periscope standards, battery ventilation shafts, and the bridge platforms for surface navigation. The casings allowed water to flood in and drain out at will when the boats were diving or surfacing.

The steel casings were only six feet across at their widest point amidships, and the tiny bridge platforms were only a few feet above the surface of the sea. They provided little protection from the weather for those on watch. Ventilation pipes behind the periscopes served as air intake pipes for the main engines. These were equipped with flap valves so that in rough seas the diesels could be run with the upper conning tower hatches closed. The magnetic compasses, electric steering controls, engine telegraphs, and vent-and-blow panels on the bridges could be sealed for diving. The upper conning tower hatches led down into the submarines through the conning towers. These had five round glass ports, which provided 360-degree visibility, and small periscopes for navigation. Each tower also had a compass, engine telegraphs, and a steering controller to enable the submarine to be conned (directed) from this position.

The submarines were entered by climbing vertically down through the upper and lower conning-tower hatches. Inside the pressure hulls the space was divided into four major watertight compartments, each filled with a bewildering array of pipes, wiring, engines, pumps, and all kinds of machinery. Below the wood-planked decks was space for the batteries, ballast, trim and fuel tanks, and the compressed air supplies.

A visitor climbing down the tower amidships entered the submarine's control room – the operating heart of any boat. It was only seven feet (2.1 m) long and contained the planesman's wheels with their depth gauges; the helm and the engine telegraphs; all the controls for venting and blowing the main ballast and trim tanks; the torpedo firing controls; and the main periscope. This periscope was used for attacks, and provided both natural-distance and high-power vision with a magnification of about two. It had no sky-search capability because it was designed before aircraft were perceived as a threat. With no hydraulics in the early submarines, periscopes were raised and lowered (only as far as the deck) with an electrically driven chain hoist.

The boats were conned and fought from the control room, and it was there that the white mice lived. The mice were kept as a barometer of the air quality. If the submarine was underwater for long periods, and the mice lost consciousness, it was time to surface – quickly! In the gasoline-fuelled C boats of the British navy, the mice were on the payroll. If the gas fumes built up, the mice would squeak and earn their shilling a day.

Stepping through a watertight door toward the bow, you would next enter another compartment called the "forward battery." Half the 120 cells of the storage batteries were housed below the deck; above it was the crew's accommodation. In a space smaller than the average living-room, most of the crew ate, slept, relaxed, and stored their belongings. Along the sides were wooden lockers for the men's personal kit, and lashed to the deckhead were two canvas bunks that could be swung down for two lucky sailors. The rest slept in hammocks or on the deck, either here or further forward. Two small heads (toilets) were provided, but no sinks or showers.

Further forward was the torpedo and stowage compartment, known as the "fore-ends." The remainder of the crew slept here, among the reload torpedoes, which lay on wooden cradles on the deck. The torpedo tube doors, with their controls, faced aft. On either side of the watertight door were two bunks for officers and, to port, the wireless cabinet. It was not an office, but more like an old-fashioned writing desk. Below the deck were some fuel tanks and compressed air bottles. In the deckhead were two hatches – an escape hatch and a torpedo loading scuttle.

Right in the bow of *No. 1*, forward of the torpedo tubes, lay the bow-cap operating mechanism and the valves for working the tubes. The single large bowcap covered all four outer torpedo doors and was rotated by gears to allow two torpedoes to be fired simultaneously. In the *No. 2*, instead of a bowcap, the two torpedo tubes had individual outer doors worked by handwheels. The compressed air tanks used to fire the torpedoes were on each side and were operated from the control room.

Going back aft through the control room, one next would reach the "after battery," which was part of the water-tight middle compartment. This area contained, below the deck, the other half of the storage batteries in their lead-lined, ventilated tank; and above the deck the electrical panels that controlled the main motors and auxiliary power distribution, and also regulated the battery charges. This "after battery" also served as the mess. There was a small galley on the port side, close to the control room, which boasted an electric range, oven, water boiler, and sink. Food was stored to starboard, and under the long refectory-style table. Six men slept here – four on the table and two in hammocks.

The aftermost and largest compartment in the submarines was the engine room. Its thirty-six-foot (10.8 m) length housed the diesel engines, the main motors, and the machinery space. The area was cramped and smelly and could be unbearably hot and noisy – orders had to be passed by sign language. Just like conventional submarines today, both boats had two means of propulsion. The direct-drive main engines, which needed air as well as diesel fuel to operate, drove the boats on the surface to a maximum of 15 knots. They also acted as generators to charge the huge battery. The 5,356 U.S. gallons (20,272 l) of diesel fuel for the main engines were stored below the deck in tanks throughout the length of the submarine.

Directly aft of the engines and connected to the propeller shafts were the two electric motors used for underwater propulsion. Using the stored electricity, the motors could drive the submarines at 10 knots underwater for about one hour, longer at slower speeds. The batteries and motors were also used to run the ballast pumps and air compressors located further aft in the machinery space. Above the power plant was another escape hatch. The propellers had three blades and were nearly five feet in diameter.

The stern torpedo tube lay in the centre of the aftermost bulkhead, with the two propeller shafts on either side of it. Underneath, the controls for the rudder and after hydroplanes passed through the bulkhead to the outside.

Early submarines had no air purification, heating, or cooling systems, and when they were submerged the air quickly became fetid and damp. The crews were rarely comfortable and the dress of the day was usually what best suited the wearer and his task.

The German cruisers continued their menacing prowls about the Pacific, alarming citizens and politicians alike, and the sailors were required to work hard, long hours to get the boats ready for sea. The inexperienced crews familiarized themselves with the new submarines by taking them apart and putting them back together again (a process made more difficult by the fact that all the tally plates were in Spanish).

Soon the crews and boats were ready for practice dives alongside the jetty, with the berthing lines slackened. This allowed the officers and men to experience their diving stations and the intricate routines in slow time and comparative safety. At first it took them forty-five minutes to dive instead of less than one. Soon afterwards, as the crews' confidence increased, the submarines were dived outside the harbour with positive buoyancy.

One volunteer reservist remembered that it was "very, very quiet and very tense"[11] in the control room during those first dives. As the air hissed out of the main tanks and water gurgled in to replace it, taking them down to periscope depth, the motors started, filling the boat with the sound of buzzing bees.

Keyes initially had some difficulties with the longitudinal stability of the boats and there was at least one awkward moment when the U.S. instructor was still on board. They were keeping a steady trim at periscope depth when suddenly the bow dropped and they headed for the bottom at about 45 degrees. The U.S. instructor ordered "Full ahead and blow forward tanks!" Keyes countered his order with "Full astern and blow everything!" The commanding officer, Keyes, was obeyed instantly and the boat surfaced safely.

The crews were made to rehearse their routines over and over again, with and without lights. As the officers and men learned more about their submarines, they were also developing trust in their captain – a vital necessity for their survival in the hazardous world of primitive boats. As Johnson, *No. 2*'s first lieutenant, later said, "We were endowed with the valour of ignorance."

As early as 13 August 1914 one of the submarines could be seen at sea: a development that reassured the population of Victoria. Although the boats were not "in all respects ready," the German cruiser scare was about to peak and the submarines were ordered out to respond to the threat. Still exercising and without torpedoes, *No. 2* bravely sailed into the Strait of Juan de Fuca to face down the *Leipzig*, which had been seen 130 miles (208 km) north of San Francisco on 14 August. A few days later the *Nürnberg* was reported off Prince Rupert, a town on the north coast of B.C., but this time the submarines were unable to respond.

By 20 August both boats were provisioned and the torpedoes arrived from Halifax, having been hurriedly adapted to fire from submarines instead of surface ships. At the end of the month the west coast fleet was augmented by two warships which Churchill had promised a worried McBride. The population began to feel a little more secure.

On the last day of August *No. 2* reported she was ready for sea; *No. 1* made a similar announcement three weeks later. The Pacific coast was at last prepared to defend herself from attack by sea, but now the threat was easing, as the Germans withdrew to the South Pacific.

During the lull, *No. 2* was docked in an attempt to correct her unpredictable diving and the crews began to learn how to maintain and fire the torpedoes. Halifax dockyard had sent Whitehead 18-inch, Mark IV, "cold" torpedoes, with a range of 1,000 yards (910 m) and a speed of 25 knots. The sailors exercised (practised) loading and unloading the torpedo tubes, flooding them prior to firing, firing the torpedoes when ordered, and then retrieving the torpedoes after their run. The experienced officers were able to hone their attack skills, using the sloop *Shearwater* as the target, and the new submarine officers started learning the difficult art. No leave was given to the ships' companies as patrols and exercises continued relentlessly.

In September 1914 the RCN decided to use the HMS *Shearwater* as the submarines' tender and she was refitted with workshops, a wireless, and crew accommodation. Shortly afterwards she was commissioned into the RCN. The *Shearwater* was a small sail- and steam-powered sloop of war built in 1899 for the Royal Navy. Her pre-war role had been the protection of British interests and citizens in the north Pacific, fishing and sealing patrols, and the training of volunteers. With the purchase of the submarines, the Naval Service instructed her to ensure that submarine training carried on without ceasing. She accompanied *No. 1* and *No. 2* everywhere for most of the war and, throughout it, was known to be a very happy ship.

On 26 September came another alarm – Ottawa believed that Von

Spee's cruisers were again approaching B.C. to attack Victoria and Vancouver simultaneously. The new submarines were made the first line of defence in the Strait of Juan de Fuca and they proceeded to sea alternately every twenty-four hours. During one patrol, Jones in *No. 2* thought he had made contact and prepared to receive the enemy. He altered course to meet the "stranger" on the surface, trimmed well down. However, he soon lost all trace of the vessel because someone put the engines astern (reversed) by mistake. It turned out that the error was of no account because the contact was HMCS *Rainbow* proceeding to sea to meet the threat too. The submariners were keen but clearly still lacked experience. By 2 October, the threat diminished when the German warships turned south once again.

The Naval Service was slow to name the new submarines after their rapid disapproval of Pilcher's misconceived suggestions. In October 1914 the flotilla learned that they were to be called *CC1* and *CC2*. The RCN chose to follow Australia's lead – designating the first letter to stand for the country and the second to show the class of boat. Though Canada's submarines were not British C-class boats, they looked quite similar.

With the desperate rush of the early weeks behind them, there was time in the fall to conduct some overdue submarine maintenance and to resume the crews' training. Keyes decided to get both boats docked in October 1914 to further investigate the problems of poor stability, and to repair defects. The crews tackled other essential tasks during this period as well – they changed the Spanish tally plates to English, they learned escape drill, and they began the vital cross-training, so that in the event of an emergency there would be another man capable of doing the job.

Keyes carried the heaviest burden of training the crews and enjoyed it. He was a natural and practised tutor, equally at home in the control room, the engine room, and the classroom, conveying the complexities of each system both by blackboard illustrations and by clear explanations. Keyes's lectures stimulated his students' interest and were conducted nightly in his cabin on HMCS *Shearwater*, recently designated the flotilla's depot ship. One of their favourite pastimes during that fall was a game called "Tubbing" whose name probably derived from Keyes's nickname, "Tubby." Keyes himself started the game to improve the new submariners' understanding of their boats: the object of the game was for one crew to confound the other with technical questions. By hard effort, much concentration, and no leave, Keyes quickly produced theoretical submariners from his novice crews. Later, the two COs encouraged practical rivalry between the boats and a good-humoured competition developed. They endeavoured to outdo each other by being the fastest to dive or to retrieve a torpedo, for example.

Escape drill was a requirement for all the new submariners. It is practised today in specially built diving towers, but Esquimalt then had neither towers nor instructors, so Keyes took the crews to Victoria's swimming pool. The officers and men donned heavy rubber jackets equipped with helmets and breathing apparatus and then they walked from the shallow end to the deep end on the bottom. Once there, they released some lead weights to surface and inflated the built-in lifebelts and opened the front of their helmets. (It helped if the survivors were conscious!) The students then floated until rescued. It was not uncommon for some participants to forget to inflate the life belt, but to open their helmets and be swamped – they had to be fished out quickly. The crews were considered qualified after two successful "escapes" in the pool.

Those first, mostly amateur crews were regarded by outsiders as efficient, confident, and most capable of attacking the enemy. The premier who created the Canadian Submarine Service was delighted with his "B.C. boys" and viewed them with proprietary interest. McBride commented, "They were handling their ships splendidly [in] only a few days."[12] A slight exaggeration, but caused by understandable pride. Keyes said later his sailors were bright and efficient seamen, and a snotty (midshipman) remembered forty years later that they were magnificent. They were certainly well motivated at the beginning.

Back in September Keyes and his officers had discussed the problems plaguing the submarines' performance. They identified three major problems that were potentially dangerous and needed to be solved, preferably during their first maintenance period in October. In *CC2*'s case, the difficulties were so severe she had to be docked earlier.

By far the worst fault was the boats' instability when diving. When all the main ballast tanks were vented, the submarines developed uncontrollable negative buoyancy, and if the tanks were left partly full dangerous nose or tail dives resulted. The only solution was to decrease weight: *CC1* and *CC2* were lightened by removing all unnecessary stores, fuel, and spare parts. This meant that patrols of more than a few days would never be possible.

The submarines also suffered temperamental emptying and flooding of their tanks. This was the urgent problem that led to *CC2*'s docking in September. Planks, rags, and a pair of coveralls were found in her tanks and pipelines, and the dockyard also discovered faulty valves that had to be reground and refitted. The performance of *CC2* improved substantially after this work was completed, and Keyes was able to report that she was finally controllable.

The last fault, and one which was to bedevil these boats during their whole commission, was the tendency of the cylinders of the diesel engines to overheat and crack after only six hours of running at full speed. Not much could be done about it as it was caused by the limitations of the early engine design and metallurgical inadequacies.

Following the October docking, both submarines conducted speed trials (*CC1* managed 15.1 knots on the surface), wireless telegraphy tests, and torpedo attacks. They also sailed to various ports to show the flag to British Columbians.

With the long hours of work and training under the threat of attack, and no leave, the submarine crews were getting desperate for some relief by November. When it was not forthcoming, the ratings dreamed up an escapade to give themselves a night on the town.[13] As the navy traditionally gives leave to members of a wedding party, the crew of *CC1* invented a wedding and one of her artificers requested leave to get married. Keyes granted it for the wedding party and guests (the rest of the crew). The groom picked his "bride" from among Victoria's willing sidewalk princesses and, minutes before the reception, the bridesmaids were gathered up the same way. That night the submariners held a "wedding" feast at Victoria's Westholme Grill. A couple of the submarines' officers witnessed the dinner and left satisfied that it was a real wedding. However, their commanding officer was not so convinced and decided to "give the beggars a wedding breakfast!" At 0400, after only three hours of rest, the crews of both submarines were ordered to sea in wild and windy weather to meet HMS *Newcastle* as she returned from sea. The sailors declared that the prank was worth the punishment.

A few weeks later the threat to British Columbia from the German cruisers dissolved forever. After Von Spee's Far Eastern Squadron decimated the British battle group of Rear Admiral "Kit" Cradock at the Battle of Coronel off Chile, the Germans themselves were vanquished on 8 December 1914 by Admiral Sturdee's South Atlantic squadron in the Battle of the Falkland Islands. With this news the RCN put both submarines into a care-and-maintenance routine for the winter, which meant that the crews got a well-deserved Christmas leave and did not go to sea again till the spring of 1915.

The news also signalled the departure of the popular Adrian Keyes, whom the Admiralty wanted back. McBride protested to the RN against his transfer, but to no avail. The first commanding officer of a Canadian submarine was sent on his way with a farewell party, the traditional gold watch, and an outpouring of affection and respect – Keyes had done them proud and went on to earn four rings and a DSO (Distinguished Service Order) for his part in the Gallipoli landings. Johnson missed his friend acutely and, though he had a wonderful capacity for friendship, it appears that no one really filled the gap that Keyes had left.

Repressing his desire to follow Keyes, Lieutenant Jones took over command of the flotilla, and retained *CC2*. Lt. Francis B. Hanson, RN, who had volunteered for submarines while serving in the Esquimalt shore establishment, was given command of *CC1*. He had no previous submarine experience and was not allowed to dive the submarine without Jones on board.

Johnson wrote in his memoirs that the winter of 1914–15 was "mouldy" and that morale "slumped noticeably" in the submarine flotilla. He had not been given command of *CC1* following Keyes's departure because his superiors felt that he did not have enough technical knowledge of submarines. Johnson did not record any disappointment at being passed over, but it is reasonable to assume he felt it keenly, especially as Hanson had far less experience. In the spring of 1915, following an exercise that, because of an inactive winter, was poorly executed, Johnson decided to "get away from this absurdly false position."

The Canadian submarines were not "blooded" in the Great War. They experienced only a few alarms in the early months, which failed to develop into engagements. They did not fire a single torpedo at the enemy and, indeed, never even saw a hostile warship. In spite of this *CC1* and *CC2* achieved the purpose for which they were purchased – they kept the German raiders at bay. Or did they?

The threat from Von Spee's squadron had been false. Once all the evidence was in after the war, it became clear that the German admiral's orders were to interrupt British trade and shipping in the Pacific; he had never been ordered to loot and pillage Canadian towns. Von Spee learned of the presence of the new submarines late on 6 August from a San Diego radio station, and he assumed that they had torpedoes. His squadron had only steamed to San Francisco to coal, and though the cruisers did continue to roam in that vicinity until 9 September, they came no further than Cape Mendocino (about 300 miles [480 km] north of San Francisco). The enemy cruisers did not return later in the month, as the

Naval Service had thought. The German records show nothing which would indicate that the presence of the Canadian boats influenced Von Spee's movements in any way.

However, the threat was alarmingly real to McBride, Pilcher, and the others coping with the intelligence reports at the outbreak of war and, even after the German squadron had been sunk in the Battle of the Falkland Islands, 8 December 1914, their worries persisted. Although the Dominion government considered that the chance of another attack on the west coast of Canada was exceedingly remote, the RCN kept the submarine flotilla in Esquimalt, training and exercising in a peacetime routine of two weeks at sea and two weeks alongside for two more years.

Were the boats suitable for their role in 1914?

Both boats were coastal submarines designed to make short defensive patrols in restricted waters and be back alongside in a couple of days. Their short-range capabilities were quite adequate for the defence of the two major coastal cities of British Columbia, because of the geography of the western seaboard. The narrow straits leading to Victoria and Vancouver could easily be patrolled, and even controlled, by such small submarines. Their mere presence would be enough to make a captain of a cruiser think twice before proceeding because, thousands of miles from his base, the risk of one torpedo damaging his ship was almost as catastrophic as being sunk .

Therefore both *CC1* and *CC2* were a suitable class of submarine to defend the Pacific coast of Canada. However, it is unlikely that McBride realized this when he decided to purchase both boats. The Admiralty, on the other hand, did appreciate the theatre of operations when they recommended the purchase of *Iquique* and *Antofagasta* after seeking advice from Sir Philip Watts. Watts had been the adviser to the Chilean government regarding these particular submarines, as well as the former director of naval construction for the Royal Navy.

Were the submarines well found?[14]

Although the CCs' design had been superseded by both British and American boats after their construction had begun in 1911, the submarines were brand new when McBride bought them. Their later engine failures and the inability of their batteries to survive prolonged use were common to most submarines of the period.

However, they did not appear well found to Keyes and his officers. Keyes had serious reservations about the performance and safety of the boats for the first two months after delivery. He attempted to rectify the faults in *CC2* very early on, and later in *CC1*. The efforts to correct the defects revealed some design faults and shoddy workmanship.

However, further evidence suggests that the Electric Boat Company and Watts had recognized the dangerous performance characteristics before the submarines were acquired by Canada. At some point after 11 August 1914, the Canadian high commissioner was informed that both submarines were "a menace to anyone using them." The credibility of the source of this information is unknown, but there is no doubt that a flurry of communication between London and Ottawa ensued, and the high commissioner, Sir George Perley, found it sufficiently disturbing to arrange a meeting in London with Sir Phillip Watts on 25 August to investigate the allegations.

The discussion was cordial, most thorough, and touched on all the defects that Keyes was contending with in Esquimalt. Watts agreed with the Chileans' assessment that the boats had been built too heavy and said that the Electric Boat Company had admitted to him that the submarines displayed some dangerous characteristics when diving. Watts made it clear that that EBCo had intended to provide him with suggested remedies, but had never delivered them because Canada had acquired the submarines before they could be developed. Watts told Perley that the Seattle builders had a definite responsibility to rectify the defects and he asked what arrangements had been made to have the work done. Of course, the submarines could not return to the neutral U.S.A., and the contractors knew it.

On 12 September 1914, a month after they first heard about it, the Prime Minister's Office (PMO) informed the Naval Service of the questionable safety of both boats. The deputy minister (DM) lost no time in soliciting Keyes's opinion, but his request arrived after Keyes had *CC2* docked. The deputy minister optimistically paraphrased Keyes's reply for the PMO – he reported that the behaviour of the submarines was "quite satisfactory ... they seem to handle well, and, while they may not have been built in exact accordance with their specifications, they seem to be seaworthy, and [are] useful for ... coastal defence." In fact, the DM relayed only part of the story. "*No. 2* submarine was not satisfactory," Kingsmill reminded him a week later,[15] and was still displaying a dangerous loss of buoyancy when diving. Keyes was unable to report *CC2* safe until 13 October 1914, after her second docking.

While no submarine in those pioneer days could be truly considered safe and reliable, neither submarine was built with as much attention to detail or quality control as they should have been. Once the faulty workmanship had been corrected, however, the boats were probably as safe and efficient as other coastal boats of that era.

Were *CC1* and *CC2* reasonably priced?

The purchase price of the Canadian submarines was definitely inflated – the newer, better designs were selling for under $500,000 each. However, as B.C. was not able to bargain from a position of strength and McBride probably did not know the current market prices, the province could do little but pay the piper.

The acquisition of the submarines caused a few heartaches for the politicians later; their need for maintenance and repairs kept the dry dock busy; the boats gained a little fame in 1917; and some of the Canadian officers went on to deeds of great distinction in British submarines.

CHAPTER THREE

QUESTIONING THE PURCHASE AND PERFORMANCE OF *CC1* AND *CC2*, 1915

"Kickbacks"

The warm glow of public acclaim surrounding Sir Richard McBride after the submarines arrived soon faded. In early 1915 the premier faced strident public censure for his actions, which resulted in two investigations.

Canada acquired *CC1* and *CC2* when submarines were poorly understood even by the navies that had adopted them, and later, when the potential of submarines was recognized they were judged to be inadequate. This rapidly changing climate of opinion affected McBride and also had its consequences on the Canadian submariners and their young service.

Before WWI, few naval officers disputed the value of coastal defence boats, but they were deeply divided over the offensive potential of long-range submarines. The majority seriously underestimated their capabilities.

Submarines had only been tested in fleet manoeuvres, never in war, either defensively or offensively, and in such manoeuvres unrealistic rules were imposed on them. Most senior officers believed that offensive submarines had to operate with the battle groups to be effective. As submarines were unable to keep up with the battleships and were thought to be "blind," the admirals concluded that they were unlikely to be much use. They never envisioned submarines as lone marauders able to threaten entire surface fleets and seaborne commerce and, in fact, many senior submariners believed that no civilized power would allow merchantmen to be torpedoed. The British Admiral of the Fleet in 1910 wrote, "... we cannot stop invention in this direction, but we can avoid doing anything to encourage it."[1]

The opposite view, and a most unpopular one, was held by a very few senior officers and the young submarine captains. These men, who accurately predicted the offensive value of submarines, were regarded as cranks; Admiral Lord Fisher being one of them. They knew with deep conviction that submarines were powerful and effective weapons – but their words went unheeded and their successes unnoticed, mostly because of the COs' junior rank and the boats' lack of appeal.

The RN fleet exercises in 1912–13 provided an inkling to the skeptics that enemy submarines could be a menace to the movements of the Grand Fleet in home waters. Their own boats had demonstrated that they could have destroyed 40 percent of the surface ships had they been permitted to fire their dummy torpedoes. However, even this revelation was not enough to convince the Admiralty: no plans were made to increase construction of offensive submarines or to employ them differently. They did form a committee to study anti-submarine measures, but it did not succeed in finding any until later in WWI.

We do not know what view the Canadian director of the Naval Service held, but it is likely to have been that of the majority, because he deferred to the wisdom of the Admiralty when the question of acquiring *CC1* and *CC2* emerged, even though they were coastal defence boats. Unfortunately, records that might have shed some light on his opinion have been lost or destroyed.

It only took the first month of the war to prove the skeptics wrong. In September 1914 the German *U9* sank three British cruisers in a single engagement and an RN boat (*E9*) dispatched the German *Hela* to the bottom with two torpedoes. Suddenly, there was a change of tactics and a rush to build offensive patrol boats. This change in attitude at the Admiralty caused several Canadian submariners to request transfers to the Royal Navy.

During the fall of 1914 and in early 1915 McBride sought to augment the new submarine flotilla, spurred on by Paterson, the builder of the CCs. Borden rejected the premier's suggestions after the Admiralty reminded Canada that the threat in the Pacific was slim and that the Dominion needed to concentrate on land forces.

After all his efforts to improve Pacific defence, McBride was shocked and saddened when an opposition MP attacked his actions during the submarine acquisition.[2] The MP alleged that financial wrongdoing had occurred and that McBride and his political party had benefited. Furthermore he claimed that *CC1* and *CC2* were overpriced, inadequate, and inefficient.

On 11 February 1915, the Hon. Mr. William Pugsley, Liberal member for Saint John, New Brunswick, rose in the House of Commons and initiated a series of events that brought Canada's first submarines into new prominence, caused much debate and speculation in the press, and created heartache for McBride. In fact, the incident consumed the premier's energies and almost certainly shortened his life.

Pugsley's speech contained some facts, some guesswork, and some imagination about the submarines, but, coming as it did on the heels of other scandals involving procurement of war supplies, it was considered by many as plausible. He impugned McBride's integrity and called the ability of the submarines to protect the west coast into serious question. The minister of the Naval Service, the Hon. Mr. J.D. Hazen, denied all Pugsley's accusations and announced that the relevant papers would be tabled in the House to prove that everyone's actions had been honourable, that the submarines were suitable, and that McBride had acted correctly and with the government's support. The prime minister, Sir Robert Borden, then came to the defence of his friend and accused Pugsley of wasting the House's time. However, Pugsley had the last word that day and an investigation into the manner of the submarine acquisition and the boats' seaworthiness was passed. It appears that the Liberal member had received some accurate intelligence regarding the poor diving characteristics of the boats, because his speech included the problems indicated by Sir Phillip Watts to the high commissioner in London and also those reported by Keyes, the flotilla commander.

The newspapers across the country reacted strongly to Pugsley's allegations. The eastern Liberal press gave the impression that B.C. and her politicians had behaved scandalously, and most of the western papers upheld the actions of the key players and praised the submarines.

McBride, the experienced and usually impervious premier, took the attack personally and made an impassioned rebuttal in the British Columbia Legislature on 24 February 1915, justifying his actions and denying that "kick-backs" had been given to any person or organization. That his motives had been misunderstood rankled for a very long time. In his speech, McBride asked for a "most searching investigation" to clear his name as he had "nothing to conceal,"[3] and followed this up with a written plea to the Canadian PM. Borden cabled a response asking McBride to let him deal with the whole matter and the B.C. premier agreed.

The deputy minister of the Naval Service began to prepare his next response for the House of Commons by asking Vice-Admiral Kingsmill for the care and maintenance reports on *CC1* and *CC2*. Kingsmill refused to provide them, citing security reasons, and instead prepared an unclassified summary, the gist of which was that the submarines, because of their hazardous operations, needed to be docked frequently. He made no mention of the shoddy workmanship that had rendered them unstable when newly arrived, or their constant engine problems. He also quoted Keyes saying that the boats were controllable and seaworthy, though these words were taken from a letter written after the early dockings had alleviated the defects.

Shortly after this, the purchase of *CC1* and *CC2* was included in an investigation by the Public Accounts Committee into expenditures under the War Appropriation Act. The auditor general of Canada presented his concerns to the committee about the way the transaction had been conducted. He thought there was something fishy about it and indeed, he had found evidence of improper commissions being paid in other, less costly war expenditures. The way in which the purchase and payment for the submarines had been accomplished, and the tardy response of the B.C. government to the auditor's questions did not help clear the air. Neither did the fact that McBride did not testify, although he was close by in New York at the time. The press censured the premier severely for not coming forward, and the investigation ended with nothing proved. The proud father of Canada's submarine service had quickly become the object of abuse rather than admiration and he resorted to writing letters to the editors of Canadian newspapers to clear his name.

The upshot of the inconclusive public accounts investigation was the establishment of a royal commission to inquire into the purchase of the submarines, among many other war appropriations. Ironically, the two men on either side of the dispute, Pugsley and McBride, got their wish.

In early 1915 changes were being made to both submarines' companies to fill the gaps left by postings to Europe and to provide more experienced ratings.

Lt. Francis B. Hanson, RN, who took command of *CC1*, was an average officer – steady but unimaginative. As he had had only two months' exposure to submarines when Keyes left, he was not allowed to take charge of *CC1* or to dive her alone for six months. Hanson knew less about submarines than Johnson, his experienced first lieutenant, and this made it difficult for both of them. He remained *CC1*'s captain, at the rank of lieutenant, throughout the war.

When Walker proved unsuitable for submarines, Geoffrey Lake, a retired merchant navy and RNR officer who was a watchkeeper on HMCS *Rainbow*, switched places with him. Lake became the first lieutenant of *CC1* under Hanson in February 1915, displacing Johnson, who transferred to *CC2*. Like Hanson, Lake was to stay with the boats for the duration and was not promoted. He was reliable and trustworthy, but lacked the aggressiveness required of a submarine CO. For the next year, under Jones's guidance, Lake learned about submarines and periscope attacks.

Midshipman William Maitland-Dougall of *CC1* was posted too at the beginning of 1915 and, though he had requested more "big-ship" time, he was sent to the naval headquarters in Ottawa for a few months. In May Maitland-Dougall decided to officially volunteer for submarines. It was a decision that was to have tragic consequences.

As Maitland-Dougall departed, a classmate of his from RNCC took his place. Midshipman Robert F. Lawson, RCN, served in *CC1* for nine months, undertaking the same responsibilities and training duties as his predecessor. Lawson became a first lieutenant while he was still too inexperienced to handle men well, and the RCN offered him to the RN for their submarines, and he was accepted.

By April 1915 *CC1* was commanded by Hanson, with Lake as his first lieutenant and navigator, and Lawson the midshipman. Jones was the flotilla commander and captain of *CC2*, with Johnson as his first lieutenant for a short while longer, and "Boy" Edwards as her snotty.

At the beginning of 1915, the ratio of experienced to inexperienced ratings changed in the submarines. The Naval Service added more RN-lent ratings to the crews and posted the original volunteers to the surface. Although not familiar with submarines, the new sailors brought valuable knowledge to the flotilla. This alteration in manning caused difficulties later, because the Canadian volunteers, and those in the RCN with previous RN service, earned more money than the RN men.

The accountants at headquarters, not noticing the make-up of the boats' crews in the confusion of the outbreak of war, had authorized all men in the submarines to be paid the higher Canadian rate. In 1916 the error was discovered and the British sailors were faced with a substantial pay cut and the possible requirement to return two years of overpayment. This was most unpalatable to the career sailors who saw those that had previously left the RN and the amateur sailors outdoing them in income. The submarine officers worried that a severe morale problem was developing.

The director of the Naval Service did not want to change the status quo and made a strong representation to the minister of the Naval Service. He explained that the sailors would suffer hardship and that discipline might be impaired if the pay scales were regularized, but his arguments did not influence the minister's decision to cut the sailors' wages. To the credit of those men affected, nothing detrimental ensued. The pay differential was not minor either – it meant a volunteer able seamen was earning more than a long-serving RN chief petty officer. The Canadian navy did not, in fact, pay vastly high rates – it was the British navy that persisted in underpaying its ratings. They earned far below the British average wage of the time.

Meanwhile, the two submarines, *CC1* and *CC2*, and their crews continued their boring but safe service on the Pacific coast. The logs of both boats show port visits and many practice attacks on their tender, HMCS *Shearwater*.[4] The submarines, shepherded by their mother ship, were generally at sea for three to six days at a time, with the crews using the *Shearwater* for meals and accommodation whenever feasible. There was a flurry of excitement in March 1915, when *CC1* and *CC2* patrolled the Straits of Juan de Fuca looking for a German steamer, the *Saxonia*, which was in Eagle Harbour near Seattle. Nothing came of the alert.

As an example of the submarines' employment during 1915, *CC2* spent eighty-four days at sea and made twenty-eight dives and torpedo runs. *CC1* did less. For vessels defending a nation at war, the submarines were underemployed. *CC2* spent thirty-seven days in the dockyard for regular maintenance and repairs, which generally involved the diesel engines. Crankshafts and pistons cracked or broke regularly, cylinders were damaged, and main shafts bent or fractured on a regular basis. *CC1* was in dock twice as often as *CC2*.

It is interesting to note that the maintenance reports from 1915 were scathing in their references to the construction of both boats. Echoing Sir Phillip Watts's concerns, the officer in charge of engineering in the Naval Service in Ottawa reviewed the reports and wrote, "the defects [were] likely to have grave results and ... vitally interfere with the efficiency of the operation of the boat[s]."[5] He concluded that the builders were culpably negligent, but decided that the RCN had no recourse because of the manner in which the submarines had been acquired. None of his damning opinions leaked out of headquarters or entered the testimony given at the Royal Commission, which was soon to get under way.

Costly repairs were made and borne by the RCN. Crews replaced leaky rivets in the fuel tanks and torpedo tubes, reseated Kingston valves, and cleaned out more debris found in the valve casings and trim tanks, to name some of the remedies. The rivets continued to be a problem and eventually the majority were replaced.

Efforts were made throughout 1915 to 1917 to improve the communications between the submarines, their tender, and the shore. Only Morse code was used, which was possible only over short distances and was frequently garbled. The small size, low profile, and high noise and vibration levels of *CC1* and *CC2* made reception almost impossible, even when the boats were within sight of each other. Eventually, taller and better insulated aerials were fitted, which dramatically improved the reception of both boats to over fifteen miles (24 km). This problem was not confined to the Canadian submarines – the British boats used carrier pigeons to convey urgent messages to their flotilla commanders. Birds were far more dependable than radios in those days.

Keyes disliked the periscopes with which *CC1* and *CC2* had been equipped, because their size invited detection. Before he left, he initiated a plan to replace them and keep the old ones as spares. In the log-strewn B.C. waters this was essential. *CC1* was fitted with her new periscope two years later, in March 1917, and *CC2* received hers not long after.

Jones, the flotilla commander, was keen to try the new periscopes, and when he met the captain of an auxiliary cruiser, HMS *Avoca*, at a party, an opportunity presented itself. Captain Hardy challenged Jones to "sink" his ship with the submarine, and the two laid a wager. At 1000 the next morning, *CC1* fired one exercise torpedo, at a range of 400 yards (364 m), and hit the *Avoca* amidships on the starboard side. Hardy graciously acknowledged Jones's success in a report, stating that *CC1*'s periscope had been sighted too late to take effective avoiding action. Hardy was happy to honour the wager – "Most men on board have never … seen the periscope of a submarine," he explained.[6] It was good training for both sides.

The second inquiry into the purchase and the efficiency of *CC1* and *CC2* began in the fall of 1915 and was closely watched by all British Columbians.

An order-in-council in June 1915 set up a Royal Commission to investigate questionable war appropriations, and named Sir Charles P. Davidson, the former chief justice of the Supreme Court of Quebec, as commissioner. Sir Richard McBride asked Sir Charles to have the circumstances of the acquisition of *CC1* and *CC2* included in the inquiry, and Davidson willingly agreed.

On 1 October 1915 people overflowed the legislative dining room in Victoria where the hearings took place. Many had just come to listen, hoping for a sensation. However, though it proved to be a sometimes entertaining investigation, they were to be disappointed.

The commission lawyer called numerous witnesses to testify about the purchase of the first Canadian submarines and they included the major players and minor onlookers; the well-informed and the ignorant; naval personnel and civilian janitors. The detailed evidence was recorded verbatim and gives, even today, a feel for the individuals' personalities and the emotions of the time. The testimony of the witnesses is remarkably consistent. All the key people were asked the same question: "Were you, or did you know of anyone who was, offered, given or asked for a commission?"[7] They all said no, including Sir Richard McBride. It was obvious to those who observed the proceedings that no one in Canada had benefited financially by the transaction, or had tried to do so. But Paterson, the president of the shipyard where the submarines had been built, collected $40,000 in "brokerage" fees which the Electric Boat Company, the prime contractors, eventually allowed him to keep. Paterson claimed the money was for expenses incurred by his yard during the sale, but as the delivery only cost $5,000, he personally profited by $35,000, a very large sum in 1914.

The evidence that was given publicly regarding the efficiency of the submarines was all positive, and all superficial; it gave little hint of the boats' poor construction and the builders' negligible quality control. Most of the naval testimony was given behind closed doors and, regrettably, has not survived. These sessions were held *in camera* to protect national security and Pilcher's reputation; they examined the defences of the Pacific coast, the organization of the dockyard, the August/September 1914 intelligence reports, and the submarines' condition on delivery.

The commission sat for five days in Victoria, then moved on to Vancouver to question two bankers; in November, the auditor of the Electric Boat Company gave his testimony in Montreal. This witness explained that the Chilean government was at least twelve months behind in its payments for the submarines and that in August 1914 the account was $150,000 in arrears. EBCo cleverly implied, and most believed, that the Chileans' complaint about the submarines' poor performance was fabricated to get out of their contract. Only a very few, including EBCo, knew that the Chileans' objections were justified, as Watts's letters and the RCN docking reports prove. Neither of these pieces of evidence appear to have been considered by the commission. Interestingly enough, it also came out that EBCo had asked only $555,000 for each boat. It was Paterson who had upped the asking figure to $575,000, thus securing a large commission for himself unbeknownst to the Canadians.

The major daily newspapers in British Columbia featured the reports of the hearings every day. These accounts were surprisingly accurate, detailed, and without sensationalism. However, their editors could not resist prejudging the transaction, two years before the official report was published. They all agreed, with varying grace, that neither the premier nor his political party had gained financially. A Tory-leaning paper praised McBride: "… he kept his head, [and] worked with great decision and dispatch."[8] An opposition paper, by contrast, remarked that the premier had acted high-handedly once again and that Paterson had extorted money from Canada in her hour of need.[9]

Although Sir Richard McBride had publicly demonstrated his innocence and integrity, he never regained his vitality and confidence, according to his family and intimate friends. Nine weeks after the commissioner left Victoria, Sir Richard resigned as premier of British Columbia at the age of forty-five. He accepted the post of agent-general for B.C. in London, England, effective January 1916. Family members maintain to this day that the bitter attacks on the premier in early 1915, which left him devastated, contributed to his precipitate departure from politics. The conclusions of the learned commissioner were long in coming and the report was not published for another two years.

CHAPTER FOUR

THE "CANADIAN" H BOATS, 1915–1916

"The Ford submersibles"

When Lt. "Barney" Johnson left *CC1* and *CC2* in May 1915, he had earned his shipmates' respect for his competence, and the farewell party they gave him bore witness to their affection for him. The day after the festivities, an excited Johnson set out for Montreal, where the Vickers shipyard was completing several American H-class submarines for the British Admiralty. One of the new boats was for him.

The H boat construction in Quebec took Prime Minister Borden completely by surprise.[1] He had not been consulted about it or informed of the contract award, despite a gentlemen's agreement between the Canadian government and the Admiralty which promised warship contracts for Canada. Borden learned of the submarine project only when it was well under way, within his borders but without his knowledge or consent. Although he was happy to have the depressed Canadian shipbuilding industry stimulated, he could not stomach what he saw as the deliberate exclusion of Canada from the negotiations. However, there was a war on, and Borden, seeing a possible way to augment the infant Canadian Submarine Service, swallowed his pride and said little to Britain.

The Admiralty had not intended to build the H-class submarines in Canada, but when the United States government refused to allow the construction to proceed at American yards, the Canadian Vickers yard was given the contract, without even having to ask for it.

The sudden realization, in the fall of 1914, of the potential of offensive submarines enabled Churchill, the First Lord of the Admiralty, to gain rapid Cabinet approval for twelve new long-range boats. Admiral Lord Fisher was named First Sea Lord shortly afterwards and undertook the procurement with his usual vigour. At that point, fate stepped in and took a helping hand; through happenstance, a colleague introduced Fisher to an American industrialist, Charles Schwab, the president of Bethlehem Steel Corporation. Schwab promised Fisher his firm could build submarines faster than anyone had ever done before. Fisher immediately ordered twenty, not twelve, submarines without thought to the American neutrality laws. "[I] made a wonderful coup with someone abroad for very rapid delivery of submarines ... it's a gigantic deal done in five minutes. That's what I call war!"[2] wrote the ebullient British admiral.

The boats were to be built at yards on both coasts of the U.S.A. in batches – the first four in five months, the next six in eight months, and the final ten, in ten – and shipped to Britain for assembly. All were to be fitted out by the Electric Boat Company (which had designed *CC1* and *CC2*). Schwab and Fisher negotiated a price of $500,000 each, which included a premium for fast delivery. The design and specifications of the submarines were similar to the boats being built for the American Navy, and the Admiralty designated the letter H to the class.

Even before Schwab returned home, work had begun on the twenty boats in two American shipyards. The U.S. State Department provisionally approved the contract on the basis of a legal precedent that allowed the submarines to be shipped in parts to a warring nation without violating the neutrality laws. However, President Wilson took a different view; the builders, he felt, were breaking the spirit of the law. He refused to allow Bethlehem Steel to proceed. Schwab announced that he would comply with the presidential order, but found excuses to delay, and his subcontractors continued the work.

Borden was aware of the difficulties the submarine project was in, and he saw Wilson's edict as his golden opportunity to gain shipbuilding contracts to ease unemployment in Quebec. He wrote to the Admiralty, offering Canadian companies to take over the contract. Fisher never replied.

Meanwhile, Schwab had been secretly setting up a scheme to rescue his floundering contract. Canadian Vickers in Montreal had had only two small contracts since Borden had cancelled Laurier's naval procurement program, and without consulting the Canadians, Schwab proposed to the Admiralty that the Canadian yard should build ten boats, using steel and components from the U.S.A., under American supervision. Fisher leaped at the chance; he accepted the contract and new conditions on 15 December 1914. The remaining ten submarines in the contract were to be constructed in the U.S. while Schwab sought ways to legally implement delivery to Britain.

The revised contract called for completed submarines, ready to sail, rather than for components for assembly, and yet despite this the delivery dates were brought forward. The Admiralty also agreed to pay $100,000 more for each boat and the expenses of the move to Vickers. Fisher never discussed the proposal with Borden, and did not notify him after the contract had been signed. When Schwab announced that he had cancelled the submarine contract, Borden believed that the H-class construction was history.

Without fanfare, Americans started to arrive in Montreal to prepare the Vickers facility. Bethlehem Steel took over the plant on 1 January 1915 and tightened security. Prime Minister Borden first heard about the project through newspaper speculation, and when he was able to verify the reports, he reacted with anger. The prime minister was further embarrassed when, not having received official word from Britain, he found he could not respond to questions from the press.

Two days after the first keel was laid, some details about the construction reached Borden through the Canadian governor general, who had withheld the information from the PM for a week. The rest came directly from Vickers, whose officials seemed embarrassed about their complicity in the affair. Borden, now armed with some hard data, seethed.

Borden asked his high commissioner in London for confirmation. Sir George Perley, his faithful diplomat, went immediately to the Admiralty to question them. Discovering the truth, Perley became as incensed as Borden. However, it was not till 16 January 1915 that the British Colonial Office officially notified Canada of the construction. The Royal Canadian Navy, which later supplied several officers for the H-class submarines, learned of their existence ten days after their government, and were as shocked as Borden had been by the deliberate subterfuge engaged in by the parties involved.

Canadian Vickers had submitted a proposal to Borden's government immediately after war broke out, to build two or three H-class submarines in eight months for the RCN at $6,000 less than the CC boats had cost. The government turned the idea down, because the Admiralty advised Borden against the construction, citing objections to the design and the impossibility of the early delivery date. Vickers and the RCN, who had been hoping to increase the Canadian Submarine Service for the defence of Halifax, were acutely disappointed – and consequently the RCN was doubly surprised to hear of the new contract.

When Borden replied to the official announcement from Britain regarding the H boat build, he wrote meekly that Canada was glad to have the work but would have appreciated earlier intimation of the plans. The contract for the ten H boats employed between 800 and 2,800 Canadians in a depressed Montreal. Borden concluded that Canada should not seem ungracious. He did, however, vent his anger at being treated so shabbily in a private letter sent to Perley later.

Even though Borden was justifiably annoyed when Canada was kept in the dark about the construction, he was incorrect in believing that Vickers could have undertaken the work without American expertise. Fearing the possibility of an international incident arising from the Americans' involvement in the construction of the H-class submarines, Borden asked his minister of the Naval Service to order an inquiry.

The investigation did not get under way until the end of April and then it found that the boats were not (as Borden had feared) being assembled exclusively by Americans from parts manufactured in the U.S.A. They were actually being built at Vickers: though the uncut steel and some components came from the States, most were fabricated from local sources, and only 150 of the 2800 men employed on the project at its height were Americans. Borden's concerns evaporated.

Vickers laid the first keel on 11 January 1915, and by the end of the summer, the ten H boats were delivered to the Royal Navy. Johnson was given command of *H8*. They were the first submarines to be built in Canada and were the fastest to reach completion in history. In the words of historian Gaddis Smith, "The speed … was breathtaking."[3] The first boat went down the ways at the end of April – nineteen weeks after she was begun and four months in advance of the earliest estimates. By mid-June the first four sailed to the Mediterranean via St. John's, Newfoundland, and Gibraltar, and the second six were on their way by the end of July. They were the first submarines to cross the Atlantic under their own power and their passage took thirteen days.

Vickers had done so well that by July the company was without work, or any prospect of it, because the second batch of ten in the Admiralty contract was being built in the U.S.A. Knowing Vickers was short of work, and because Borden and the RCN were still hoping to enlarge the Canadian Submarine Service, Canada asked the Admiralty for the last two H boats of the order, on the understanding that Canada would pay for the construction of two more at the end. The Admiralty refused, stating that the submarines were urgently needed by the RN and that the Canadian east coast was unlikely to be threatened. The Canadian navy disagreed with this appreciation, and when Vickers offered to build two more H boats after *H10* for $600,000 each, the RCN rejoiced. Borden, however, who had initiated the previous suggestion to augment the fleet, now inexplicably refused the RCN their two submarines (The reasons for his volte-face remain unclear to this day.) In the end, Vickers won contracts to build eight H-class submarines for Italy and six for Russia, which kept her work force employed, but the young Canadian Submarine Service did not expand.

The first four H-class submarines (*H1* to *H4*), manned by RN crews, left together for the Mediterranean in June 1915. The last six were finished with such unprecedented speed that the Admiralty did not have men available to deliver them to Britain. Admiral Kingsmill, DNS, offered the under-employed crews of *CC1* and *CC2* to man the boats and make the delivery. The Admiralty accepted with the proviso that the crews would then stay in Britain to man British submarines. Borden immediately withdrew the offer. He was still hoping to acquire two Canadian-built H boats and the RCN needed the CC crews' expertise. Furthermore, the prime minister was in no mood to help the Admiralty after what they had done to him.

As the H boats were now very short of manpower, the senior officer, Submarines, in Montreal asked for "Boy" Edwards of *CC2* by name. Edwards agreed to go, but the RCN decided to send Willie Maitland-Dougall, the midshipman from *CC1*, in his stead, because his navigational skills were better. Maitland-Dougall had scarlet fever, and missed delivering the first batch of H boats, but as soon as he recovered he joined *H10*, with sextant in hand, on 24 June. The delivery crews for the transatlantic passage were smaller than those manning operational boats – two officers (the commanding officer [CO] and a navigator) and about fifteen ratings in each submarine.

Even if Maitland-Dougall had sailed with the first batch of submarines, Barney Johnson would still have been the first Canadian submariner on the scene in Montreal.[4] His request for overseas service was granted on 7 May 1915 and the RN appointed him to HM Submarine *H8* as her CO. Johnson arrived in Montreal in time to see *H8* launched on 19 May and his sense of pride and anticipation was heightened by knowing that he was the first Canadian to command a submarine, and he was a reservist at that!

Johnson had two months to familiarize himself with his new command before sailing for England. He did so with his usual thoroughness: he observed the handling characteristics of *H8* during her acceptance trials on the St. Lawrence River, with the builders' crew in charge, and made plans for developing a cohesive team to man the submarine. However, the scramble for men was competitive, and *H8*'s delivery crew was not available until after her second set of trials with Johnson in command. He did the five weeks of fitting out and trials with a mostly borrowed crew. The deep dives were done at Murray Bay, more than three hundred miles (480 km) east of Montreal, and once *H8* was pronounced leakproof she returned to Quebec. The permanent crew finally arrived for *H8* on 15 June and the next day at 1000 Johnson watched proudly as his submarine was commissioned. He commenced the training of the new crew immediately, using Keyes's example of lectures and on-the-job training.

Despite the crew difficulties, Johnson was very pleased with *H8*; he found the two diesel engines and the boat's diving characteristics more reliable than those of *CC1* and *CC2*, of which he had long been critical. The acceptance trials of *H8* were conducted by the same retired USN officer who had been responsible for the trials of the CC boats and the instruction of their first crews. As an aside, this EBCo employee remarked to Johnson that he was amazed that the RCN had managed to solve the buoyancy problems of Canada's first submarines.

Johnson had trouble establishing his credibility with the regular RN officers of the other H boats while they worked together in Montreal – the Brits were reluctant to accept a colonial – a reservist to boot – in their midst. Relations did not improve until they were billeted together later and the RN officers had a chance to see Johnson in action.

Following a busy few days painting and provisioning, *H8* sailed for Halifax on 3 July 1915, in company with the five other H boats (*5, 6, 7, 9,* and *10*), and escorted by HMCS *Canada*. Commander Quicke, who had supervised the construction program for the Royal Navy, rode *H10* as the flotilla commander. They arrived four days later at midnight after a straightforward voyage. During two weeks in Halifax, as the submarines completed more trials, the frosty relationship between Johnson and the RN types began to thaw. The Brits began to see that Canadians were competent shiphandlers, and the RN officers also grudgingly acknowledged that the American submarine design, which they had earlier disparaged, was a good one.

The boats took on fuel and two torpedoes each for the transatlantic voyage, and early on 22 July 1915 the flotilla sailed with HMS *Carnavon* and two colliers as escorts. They arrived in Devonport on 4 August 1915, following an uneventful passage of thirteen days, more than a year ahead of a German U-boat that made the crossing west to New York and claimed to be the first ever to have done so. The submarines and their crews were welcomed in Britain by Commander Charles Little, RN, a submariner and future admiral, who was an assistant to the Commodore(S).*

The British submariners had prepared Lieutenant Johnson to expect bad news on arrival. They told him that he would have to relinquish his first submarine command – the Admiralty had only appointed him as commanding officer for the delivery. The RN planned to palm Johnson off with an ancient A boat used for training, and to insist that he take the basic training course. Johnson realized it was going to be difficult to retain *H8*. He was a reservist and a colonial – in 1915 British operational submarines were only commanded by their own career officers. The Canadian considered his response during the transatlantic crossing and decided to seek what he felt was his due. Johnson dug in his heels and took a risk – he respectfully but forthrightly told Commander Little that if he could not command *H8*, he would immediately request a transfer to General Service (surface fleet) because after twelve years of merchant command, he was unprepared to serve yet another apprenticeship.

It is to Johnson's and the Admiralty's immense credit that his appointment as *H8*'s commanding officer was confirmed a few days after they arrived in Portsmouth. The Admiralty sought to regularize what they saw as Johnson's peculiar position as a reserve submarine CO by offering him a commission in the Royal Navy, but Johnson refused, choosing instead to accept one in the Royal Navy Reserve, to which he was entitled by virtue of his merchant navy background. He remained a reservist, true to his principles, throughout the hostilities – the first reservist ever to command a submarine.

Johnson did not retain his command just because of his refusal to be pushed around – he earned it. His expert ship handling, well-trained crew, and well-kept submarine had been recognized and were undoubtedly the major reason a precedent was set. All the British H boat officers, with whom relations had been cool, dined Johnson out that night and he treasured their tribute all his life.[5] "I was taken into the family," he

---

*Commodore(S) refers to a specific command appointment in a submarine service. (S) is an abbreviation of submarine and is used to differentiate a sub-surface command from a surface command.

remembered. The same officers also assisted Johnson over the rough spots of command with consideration and tact. He was forever grateful for their support and enduring friendships.

On arrival in England, Midshipman Maitland-Dougall left *H10* to attend the Submarine Officers' Training Course (SOTC) at HMS *Dolphin* (the RN submarine service's headquarters at Gosport). He was the first Canadian naval officer to do so. This basic course for junior officers after their acceptance into the submarine service was generally taken before they were posted to their first boat. During the six-week course, Maitland-Dougall learned the details of the complicated operating systems common to all classes of submarines and how to make them work. In those days the officers had to create their own textbooks with very detailed drawings and notes, a practice that continued until 1960 when handbooks were introduced. Maitland-Dougall had a head start on the course with Keyes's lectures and his exposure to *CC1* and *H10*, and he did very well. On the successful completion of his SOTC, the young Canadian rejoined *H10* at Portsmouth, as her third and most junior officer.

The crews of *H8* and *H10* then settled down to a period of training and work-ups in Portsmouth to prepare for operational duties. A gyroscope, a wireless, and other additional equipment were installed in the submarines, and some battery cells, already showing signs of wear, were replaced. Two new officers reported to *H8*, one of whom was Sub-Lieutenant John Mansfield, RN, who later became flag officer, Submarines. Johnson welcomed his new first lieutenant, thankful that his predecessor, who had not believed reservists should command submarines, had left. The Canadian captain liked Mansfield's style which made *H8* into a happy and efficient ship. Lt. William Thompson, RNVR, who had made the Atlantic crossing in *H5*, became Johnson's third hand for a short time.

At the end of September 1915 *H8* joined other H boats of the Eighth Flotilla at Great Yarmouth on the east coast of England to begin operations in the North Sea. Commander Quicke was in overall command based in the depot ship, HMS *Alecto*. The D- and E-class submarines of the same flotilla were based further south at Harwich with HMS *Maidstone*.

When the H-class submarines came into service with the Royal Navy, they were rated as "overseas" boats, capable of long offensive patrols, and sent to work with the E-class, the best British submarines of the day. This classification pleased all who served in them, including Johnson, because it meant they were more likely to see action than if they were assigned to coastal defence. Their crews nicknamed the H-class the "Ford Submersibles" because of their assembly-line method of construction.

The early H-class submarines, of which *H8* was one, were almost the same size and displacement as the Canadian CC boats, having been designed for coastal defence, and their range was 2800 nautical miles. They were of similar riveted single-hull construction, with all the ballast and trim tanks placed internally. Outwardly *H8* looked slightly different – she had a higher, rounder bow and a long, tapered stern.

The H boats were able to run trimmed down on the surface in heavy seas without water entering the submarine through the conning tower hatches. They had a six-inch diameter air-induction pipe between the two periscopes, which had a flap valve on top to prevent waves entering. This pipe allowed the diesel engines to draw air into the boat when the conning tower hatches were shut and also served as the voice pipe from the bridge through which orders were relayed below. The value of this equipment was not fully recognized at the time, nor was it developed further until the middle of World War II when the Germans introduced it in their U-boats and called it a *schnorkel.* Today Canadians call it a *snorkel,* the Brits, a *snort. H8* had no deck gun or stern torpedo tube, but could fire four 18-inch torpedoes in a salvo from their bow tubes. The boats carried four reload torpedoes.

The control room was a separate watertight compartment in the H boats and the crews welcomed this change in configuration because it reduced the chances of sea water contaminating the batteries if it slopped into the boat during a dive. One other design difference was to save *H8* from disaster – there was a watertight bulkhead in the middle of the torpedo tubes.

The H boats were designed for a maximum diving depth of about 200 feet (60 m), though this was rarely resorted to in those days, and they could run at 12 knots on the surface and 9 knots submerged. Early on Johnson referred to the main engines as "sweet running diesels" and time certainly proved him to be right. The attention paid to habitability was limited and accommodation was much the same as *CC1* and *CC2.* The H-class turned out to be a most successful, reliable, and seaworthy design and some of the later ones served well into WWII.

By the beginning of November, Johnson and his submarine began to patrol in the North Sea, very close to Holland and Germany, in the

Heligoland Bight.[6] Their objectives included a blockade of German ports and surveillance of the High Seas Fleet movements – freelance hunting was forbidden.

The coastlines were treacherous, consisting of many low islands, shifting sandbars visible only at low tide, and in wartime the ever-present threat of mines and aircraft. The weather was very unpredictable – howling gales, rough seas or fog. Conditions for the crew of *H8* were more often than not very cold and wet, and were worsened by the unrelenting tension and fatigue. On station, *H8* would keep periscope watch by day and be on the surface at night, charging their batteries. It was in the darkness that the crew had to be constantly and almost superhumanly alert for both enemy and Allied patrols rushing at them from the blackness. It was not uncommon to be attacked with vigour by their own side.

After a patrol, *H8* would get a few days in port to remedy defects and sail again. Johnson and his crew lived a tough, uncomfortable existence – full of stress and spiced with real danger. In spite of the hardships, Johnson was growing to love submarines: "... it was a sight for the Gods to watch a sea roll over the conning tower and to see the little ship emerge like a porpoise and almost smile." By now Johnson was a submariner through and through, even though he had never taken a formal training course.

H10, with Maitland-Dougall as her third officer, was participating in the same kind of work in the same area, with the same orders as *H8*. Only occasionally were the submarines permitted to attack homeward-bound German ships. The Admiralty adopted this tactic to allow the German fleet to reach the open sea, where the surface ships could destroy them in a major sea battle. It led to boring, frustrating patrols for the submariners: on two outings in December 1915, *H10* saw nothing of the enemy.

In January 1916 Maitland-Dougall was promoted to sub-lieutenant and *H8* and *H10* were two of six submarines chosen to take part in Operation ARH. This was the first time they were allowed to act offensively. The Admiralty hoped to entice the German fleet to sea by bombing some Zeppelin sheds and they spread out the submarines to intercept them ahead of the surface fleet. Later they were to act as rescue boats for the Allied bomber pilots who ditched. *H8* and *H10* reached their assigned stations without incident and surfaced at dawn to watch for the Germans, but nothing hove in sight. A persistent fog and a stiffening breeze had prevented flying operations and the Admiralty cancelled ARH.

After the fruitless watch and no recall, *H8* sank to the seabed for the rest of the daylight hours to avoid the enemy. When Johnson resurfaced the boat at 1615, a force-9 gale was blowing from the southwest, which made the bridge untenable. Because *H8* had lost a large number of cells in her battery and could not make a long submerged passage to avoid the seas, Johnson had no choice but to return to the seabed until the weather moderated. A day later he was able to lay a course for home even though the seas were still frightful. In a very small submarine, which could not travel submerged, it meant an exhausting trip. The submarine lost her bridge screen and aerial at noon, but she behaved well, and was not attacked. Johnson remarked that the crew did well too, despite severe seasickness, in a storm that was considered to be one of the worst of the war. *H8* finally arrived in Great Yarmouth thirty-six hours overdue and a little battered. She was greeted with much rejoicing: the flotilla staff had not received the message giving the boat's revised arrival time, and had given *H8* up for lost. *H10* had managed the passage home on schedule because her batteries still allowed her to dive.

After this patrol, the officers and men of *H8* and *H10* enjoyed the pleasures of fresh air, hot baths, clean beds and clothes and, most especially, hot cooked meals with fresh bread and vegetables aboard their depot ship. The crew got two evenings ashore for each night on watch alongside, which gave them the chance to relax and go drinking with their shipmates. During the days in harbour the crew readied the submarine for her next patrol – topping up the batteries, loading torpedoes and stores, and repairing the defects caused by the weather.

After the cancellation of Operation ARH, both *H8* and *H10* received new batteries in Portsmouth. The old ones had lost too many cells to sustain the submarines underwater. *H8* was the fourth of her class to require a battery refit and the job was backbreaking for her crew, who did most of the removal and replacement of cells. These were about six feet (1.8 m) high, weighed over a thousand pounds (450 kg) each, and were difficult to manoeuvre in and out of the boat. When the task was finished, *H8* took part in several training exercises in the Solent and Johnson was pleased with their performance.

H8 returned from her refit to Harwich, instead of Great Yarmouth, joining the E boats of the Eighth Flotilla, and continued to patrol in the North Sea. The pressure on boat and crew was still relentless. Several submarines had been lost or damaged in action. All the crews were beginning to feel the losses personally.

Johnson was developing into a seasoned commanding officer of steely determination, courage, and decisiveness, which he tempered with kindness towards his crew. He believed in the capabilities of his submarine and men alike. The crew, whose training had begun so well during the transatlantic crossing, were now approaching their peak, having learned that they could put their trust in Johnson and that they were ready for anything.

It was not an easy billet serving under the Canadian. Johnson ran a very tight ship, tighter than most. He demanded nothing but the best from everyone, including himself. Every inch of his boat and every sailor came under his fierce scrutiny regularly. Johnson always rewarded outstanding skills and special effort immediately, but he would not tolerate even the smallest degree of sloppy seamanship. The erring sailor or officer would receive a thorough dressing down, with a few well-chosen words accompanied by disapproving looks from Johnson's piercing blue eyes. The captain knew that laziness and mistakes, if ignored, could seriously jeopardize the safety of everyone at critical moments. *H8* became a confident and well-run submarine through the strict but fair discipline practised by Johnson and Mansfield.

In 1916 the greatest enemy of the Allied submarines was the mine, whether friendly or hostile, and there were minefields throughout *H8* and *H10*'s operating areas. Surface ships were a lesser hazard as their only means of attack was by gunfire or ramming when the boat was surfaced; submerged submarines had little to fear from them as few vessels had any means of detecting them underwater. Aircraft and airships were more of a menace as they could bomb submarines on the surface and at periscope depth and force them deep to prevent them from attacking. Identification of friendly submarines was difficult and often incorrect; this regularly caused serious mistakes by nervous naval and merchant ships. Aircraft-dropped depth-charges as an anti-submarine device did not get into service until 1917.

After a delay caused by a vicious gale, *H8* proceeded to sea on 16 March 1916, in top form. In company with *E26* they went to patrol between Terschelling and Ameland islands off the coast of neutral Holland. The orders required *H8* to report on outbound enemy troopships and their escorts, but not to attack them. The patrol was uneventful for five days and was conducted in dense fog. When the fog suddenly thinned on 21 March, *H8* sighted a German destroyer and three large trawlers 3,000 yards (2,730 m) away. Johnson attacked the destroyer but was foiled on his second attempt by the fog thickening again and hiding the target. *H8* touched a submerged object at fifty feet (15 m) shortly after this attack, which Johnson thought was debris of some sort. He then took his submarine to the bottom for the night.

In the early morning of their sixth day on station, 22 March 1916, the weather cleared. At 1050 *H8* was keeping a constant periscope watch, when many on board heard a scraping noise near the starboard bow. Almost instantly a tremendous explosion battered the submarine and the sea started to pour into the boat. The crew leapt to their stations in total darkness and, with no need for reminders, slammed the watertight doors shut as the boat descended uncontrollably to the bottom. *H8* settled bow-down in ninety feet (27 m) of water at an angle of 30 degrees. Johnson thought they were lost.

In the glimmer of emergency lighting, the damage looked fairly minor to those in the control room – the forward planes and periscope were inoperable and a depth gauge was broken. The two after compartments were undamaged, but in the fore-ends the picture was grim. The sea was gushing in freely around the torpedo tube doors, and there was one huge dent in the pressure hull, which threatened to cave in at any moment. The ratings started the pumps within two minutes of the explosion and quickly began to shore up the buckled hull. Taking stock five minutes later, Johnson found his crew uninjured but the submarine firmly stuck on the sea bed.

Though the pumps kept pace with the leaks, *H8* had lost considerable buoyancy, and Johnson concluded that the forward main ballast tank had been destroyed. He dared not blow a fuel tank to regain the necessary forward buoyancy to surface, because this manoeuvre might disclose their position to the enemy seaplane that he believed had bombed them. *H8*'s captain attempted instead to blow the remaining two main ballast tanks and drive the boat full speed astern on her main motors to get her to surface – a choice reminiscent of Keyes's swift action with a plummeting CC boat. The first attempt failed. With a crackle and a spit, the fuses of the main motors blew and the remaining lights went out. While the problem was remedied, more damage reports came in to Johnson – the gyro compass had stopped, the wireless had been damaged, and a few other essential gauges were broken. This first pause in the race to survive gave most on board time to consider their fate – all knew they were facing death. "It didn't look like much of a chance," said one sailor. "It was a bad minute."[7]

Finally on the second attempt, everything held and *H8* shook herself free and surfaced stern first to wallow in the rough seas. Johnson was first through the hatch to check for the enemy and found, to his surprise, an empty sky. Johnson ordered the diesels started and, when the submarine began to proceed safely at slow ahead, he examined the damage from the bridge. "Things didn't look particularly promising,"[8] Johnson wrote later. Much of the bow was missing, No. 1 main ballast tank had been laid wide open, as he thought, as well as a trim tank, and the forward planes were gone. While on the bridge Johnson noticed four mines floating by which looked suspiciously British. Knowing *H8* should not be in an Allied minefield, he logged their position.

Johnson had to make a closer inspection of the twisted bow, as the damage below indicated that it was more serious than the buckled casing suggested. The intrepid CO slid hand over hand down the still-intact jumping wire, which ran forward from the conning tower. When he reached what was left of the bow he hung on grimly as the icy seas threatened to wash him away. From his precarious vantage point, he quickly realized the bow cap had been blown off, exposing the torpedoes' arming (firing) pistols. This meant that *H8*'s torpedoes could detonate at any time. Almost as troubling was his discovery that both forward watertight bulkheads in the bow were gone. The one left at the torpedo tube doors was holding, but only just.

Johnson knew he could do nothing to disarm the torpedoes, so he shinnied back up the wire to the bridge, very worried by what he had seen. "Carry on cooking!" ordered Johnson. He could think of no better order to encourage his crew because, like "Carry on smoking!" it meant that all was well. He deliberately withheld the bad news of the missing bow cap and told his officers that, although the submarine could not attack, she was seaworthy enough to get home on the surface in darkness if they were not attacked. They could not avoid or fight off enemy patrols as diving was next to impossible and *H8* had no deck gun. Johnson then blew a fuel tank in the bow to increase *H8*'s forward buoyancy, knowing now that there were no aircraft around to spot their oil slick.

With the navigational aids either broken or of questionable value and no landmarks to go by, Johnson set about pointing his boat towards Harwich. He put all his navigational skills to work and calculated the compass's new deviation by using the waves, which he knew were running from the northeast. Then Johnson turned *H8* towards the Dutch coast to find a village that would give him a reference point for departure. He also knew that if *H8* started to sink, the village could provide a landfall to save his crew.

Vibrating considerably and leaking like a sieve, the submarine held together as she approached the coast. The tight knots of fear in the sailors' stomachs slowly loosened as urgent repairs occupied them and they began to believe that their Canadian captain would get them back to England. They crossed their fingers tightly and offered up many impromptu prayers for invisibility.

Johnson slowly increased *H8*'s speed to 11 knots, but the crippled submarine soon protested. The bent propeller shafts caused the bearings to overheat and forced the captain to drop the diesels' revs. The implication of the slow-down was not lost upon the crew – the submarine would take twice as long to get home, greatly increasing their chances of detection. Stomachs churned again.

Just before dusk, and six hours after the explosion, the bridge lookout spotted the sails of a windmill off the starboard bow. The sighting signalled the location of the village Johnson had been seeking. He was now faced with the most difficult decision of his career. Would the torpedoes detonate if they continued? Should he risk the lives of the entire crew by turning for England? Should he take *H8* into a Dutch port and commit his officers and men to an internment camp for the duration? Johnson, slightly more certain now that the boat would stay afloat, swallowed hard and opted for home. He altered course as night thickened around the submarine and wondered briefly if he had chosen wisely. Johnson then ordered a hot meal for everyone, which gave his crew added comfort for the daunting overnight passage.

None of the sailors knew the full extent of the crippling blow their boat had suffered; they would not see the damage until they came alongside. They relied on their captain to "see" for them. In a lull in the activity, Johnson carefully told his men what he had told his officers, again withholding the information about the torpedoes. The crew expressed their relief that *H8* was seaworthy by cheering their captain lustily and set to with a will to "baby" their boat to safety. This was not to say that the crew were not badly shaken. Everyone was, but their belief in their captain and their own abilities was strongly rooted. However, one can only sympathize with the navigator of *H8* whose first submarine patrol it had been. He stayed on the bridge for the 300-mile (480 km) voyage and nothing could make him go below. Johnson understood and left him there.

While the hot supper was cooking, the CO, his first lieutenant, and CERA met hurriedly, and with some desperation, to work out a way to dive *H8* in case they encountered the enemy. The three men knew diving would be highly dangerous and the chances of surfacing afterwards almost nil. Nonetheless, they developed a plan which they thought might work, deciding to use it only if their lives were under direct threat from the enemy. They altered the submarine's buoyancy or "trim" in preparation.

During the long night, Johnson did not sleep. In his quieter moments he replayed the catastrophic event over in his mind. He became increasingly certain they had been blown up by one of their own mines. As soon as the radio transmitter was repaired, he sent a message to his Captain(S) giving his damage report and estimated position, and told him that a British mine was responsible. The message was repeated at 2240. Johnson wondered briefly what his reaction would be, and then dismissed his concern as unwarranted.

As dawn lightened the sky, *H8* was still afloat and the enemy, miraculously, had stayed away. The crew worked on steadily. They ensured that the pumps kept pace with the leaks; that the bearings stayed cool; that the cracks in the pressure hull did not grow; and that everyone got a little rest, however short.

When *H8* came alongside HMS *Maidstone* in Harwich twenty-six hours after the explosion at noon on 23 March 1916, she was greeted with utter astonishment. The flotilla staff, having received neither radio message, assumed the submarine had sunk with all hands.

After securing his boat and seeing his crew comfortable ashore, Johnson settled down to compose his patrol report which was succinct and understated. He described all that happened and concluded that a British minefield had been laid in his billet. He closed with the words, "I should like to place on record my appreciation of the coolness and promptitude with which Sub.Lt. Mansfield RN and Sub.Lt. Meadows RNR and the entire crew carried out my orders under exceptionally trying circumstances."[9]

In the morning, Johnson's opinion that his boat was in an unknown British minefield was not believed by his superior officer or the Admiralty. They both maintained that *H8* must have been badly off course at the time of the explosion and thus the Canadian had hazarded his command.

Johnson, not about to be branded as an incompetent and knowing a board of inquiry would soon be held, set about proving to the authorities that he had acted correctly throughout the patrol and the minefield was where he said it was. He immediately asked the flotilla navigator to check the amended compass deviations he had made after the accident and they proved to be accurate. This information demonstrated that *H8* was not off course at the time of the disaster and encouraged Captain(S) to support Johnson's theory to the Admiralty. He wrote that Johnson's and the crew's behaviour in the face of certain death was "an example of courage of which the whole Service may be proud."[10] The final piece of evidence proving that Johnson's theory was correct was the analysis of the fragments of mine casing found embedded in *H8*'s superstructure. The mine that blew off her bow indeed turned out to be British and the Admiralty acknowledged that a recently laid minefield must have dragged far to the westwards during the gale that delayed the boats' departure for the patrol, and had ended up in *H8*'s billet.

After that, the conclusion of the board of inquiry into the accident was inevitable. It absolved Johnson of any responsibility in the event and recognized his brilliant seamanship in bringing his damaged submarine back safely with its crew unharmed. Johnson knew that there were other reasons why *H8* had survived the harrowing experience. First, the explosives experts believed that the mine could not have detonated with full force; if it had, there would have been no hope. That theory turned out to be incorrect, though it was not discovered for several decades. The mine *had* detonated with full force, but at some distance away from *H8*'s hull. Studies showed that if the mine's slack mooring wire hooked around the fore plane and was jerked by the forward motion of the submarine, the movement was enough to set off its inertia-activated detonator. Secondly, the crew's training and Johnson's discipline had paid off magnificently, and, thirdly, the H-class submarines' watertight bulkhead forward of the torpedo tube doors had held. Without it, *H8* would not have stood a chance. No other RN class of submarine in WWI was blessed with this design feature.

On 30 March 1916, the Admiralty forwarded their appreciation to Barney Johnson, praising his highly meritorious conduct, gallantry and promptness of action on the occasion of the disaster. Even the Germans commented on the excellence of *H8* and her crew after the war saying "she was very lucky [and] her captain ... is to be congratulated."[11]

H8 was sent to Chatham for repairs, but the damage was so extensive that she was paid off and a new bow was fitted, which took several months. The Admiralty permitted a journalist access to the submarine and crew for propaganda purposes and Johnson was surprised to discover that the reporter was female. He showed her around *H8* and answered her questions. Jane Anderson's resulting article was suitably inspiring and appeared in May 1916.[12]

Just before the officers and men of *H8* dispersed, much against Johnson's better judgement, they gathered together in front of the other crews of their flotilla on the quarter deck of HMS *Maidstone* to be read a letter from the Admiralty. It was the commendation they so richly deserved, praising their "… steadiness and splendid behaviour under trying circumstances."[13]

Johnson had not only recovered his reputation, but had added to it substantially. The unfortunate mining of *H8* had provided the Canadian submariner with an opportunity to demonstrate his consummate skills to a Royal Navy unsure of colonials and reservists.

CHAPTER FIVE

CANADIAN SUBMARINERS IN EUROPE, 1915–1917

"Over half the crew was poisoned"

After the mining of *H8*, Barney Johnson was granted indefinite sick-leave to recover from the ordeal. By his own account, he was depressed, had nowhere to go and no friends to visit, and was probably suffering a reaction to the disaster. The Padre "took [him] in hand and taught [him] to golf."[1] Three weeks later Johnson applied for another command, hoping to be able to take his old crew to a new submarine.

The Admiralty quickly granted Johnson a new command and with it came his promotion to lieutenant-commander. He took over *D3* in mid-April 1916, a boat with a good reputation and an experienced crew, which was attached to the Eighth Flotilla at Harwich. Johnson soon realized that he could not replace the men of *D3* with his old crew, however much he might have liked to. The boat was a different class and he needed men who were familiar with it. The best he could do was to promise *H8*'s crew that he would fill any vacancy in *D3* from them. The first to occur was for a chief ERA and Johnson was delighted to offer it to his trusted CERA from *H8*, who accepted at once.

Less than a month after Johnson was appointed, another Canadian joined *D3*. Willie Maitland-Dougall, now a sub-lieutenant, became her first lieutenant and assisted in readying the boat for patrols. Johnson and Maitland-Dougall were in marked contrast – one who had been thought too old for submarines, the other very young; one a reservist, the other a career officer; one trained by experience, the other in the classroom. We know nothing about the relationship between the two men but, given the difference in age and rank, we can guess that it was fairly formal.

Still, Maitland-Dougall probably told his CO about the events of his last patrol in *H10*. In the early hours of 25 April 1916, six submarines of the Eighth Flotilla had been sent out to meet the German High Seas Fleet, which was threatening the east coast. When *H10* reached her billet, her lookouts could see the flashes of big guns lighting up the horizon to the south and the surfaced submarine altered course. The crew's excitement mounted as their first chance at the enemy became a possibility. Suddenly *H10* was shaken by the explosion of four bombs, dropped close to her by two aircraft that the lookouts had failed to spot. *H10* dived hurriedly and, after shaking off her adversaries, resumed her pursuit of the enemy. As they got close enough to attack, the Germans changed course at the last minute, costing *H10* her chance to score. She never regained it. Following *H10*'s narrow escape from the aircraft, which turned out to be British, all submarines had large white bull's-eyes painted on their casings for recognition purposes.

The British D boats had come into service in late 1909 and, being one of the few offensive classes available, were overworked during the first two years of the war. Although older and bigger than the H boats, they carried only two torpedoes in bow tubes and one in the stern. Johnson's boat had a deck gun fitted earlier in the war. The Ds were the first class to have saddle tanks – main ballast tanks outside the pressure hull – and their primitive periscopes made submerged attacks difficult. Officers shared one bunk and most of the hands slept on the deck. *D3*, commissioned in 1910, was overdue for a major refit when Johnson took over.

In mid-May 1916, *D3* recommenced patrols in the Heligoland Bight. Her orders were to patrol on the surface during the short nights and report the movements of enemy destroyers, remaining submerged in daylight to avoid detection. This meant spending up to twenty hours during the midsummer days on the bottom, and the air down below quickly became thick and foul. There was not enough oxygen to light a match and the crew panted with little or no exertion. Their reaction time and judgement suffered.

Johnson and his submarine missed the Battle of Jutland due to a defect and, though the rest of the Eighth Flotilla was involved, none of *D3*'s sisters saw the last great surface engagement either.

In the middle of June, *D3* was back on patrol again when the entire crew gradually became sick. Everyone began to complain of headaches, thirst, abdominal pain with nausea, and numbness in the fingers and toes, symptoms which later developed into jaundice. After one day, only four crew members managed to be on duty. When *D3* finished her patrol, nineteen sailors were very ill indeed. The cox'n and five others were admitted to hospital and thirteen more were sent to the sick bay on the depot ship. Johnson was chided for sticking out the patrol, but was unaware of the implications of doing so.

Johnson did not escape the symptoms either, though he was not as severely affected. Maitland-Dougall was, however, because those who remained below most of the time were the worst afflicted. Two weeks before, *D4* had been forced to return from patrol early with a similar problem.

Johnson's crew recovered quickly and *D3* was back on patrol three weeks later, after sealing the battery tanks better and after the symptoms had not recurred during several short cruises. Unfortunately, after a few days the mystery illness again spread rapidly through the crew, and Johnson abandoned the patrol. Two days later medical officers and scientists arrived to examine the sailors and their boats in the hope of determining the nature of the disease and its cause. Johnson slept through the first meeting with these specialists and had to be shaken to answer their questions. This was not surprising as Johnson turned out to be suffering from severe anaemia; his haemoglobin remained low for six months. Others were much worse.

The detailed investigation showed that the crews had been poisoned by arsennuiretted hydrogen gas, which the submarines' ancient battery plates had been emitting during charges. These lead plates contained small amounts of arsenic impurities, which combined with the hydrogen formed during a charge and seeped as a gas throughout the boat. If ventilation was adequate the gas would dissipate but, in the short summer nights, the submarine often dived before this could be completed. Fortunately *D3*'s crew recovered sufficiently to return to duty in ten days. (Johnson's account, written many years later, states that the level of toxicity was high enough for half the crew of *D3* to be invalided out of the submarine service altogether. Johnson's memory was inaccurate in this case.)

The Royal Navy took corrective action immediately. They instituted strict monitoring of the submarines' air quality, along with frequent medical checks for the crews. Five days later, *D3* sailed to Plymouth for a battery refit, and as many personnel as could be spared went on sick leave. Johnson took August off and said, "The antidote was sunshine, good food and plenty of port wine." His enjoyment of this holiday was in marked contrast to the depression that had marred his previous leave. Maitland-Dougall got away for a couple of weeks and spent a pleasant leave reunited with his younger brother, Hamish, who was now in the army.

When the work on *D3*'s new batteries was finished and trials were completed in September 1916, the submarine returned to operational status with the Third Flotilla at Immingham, near Hull on the river Humber. There was no more arsenic poisoning. Johnson and *D3* participated in short, uneventful patrols on the east coast of England, occasionally into the Bight, and spent time practising attacks and exercising with destroyers until being ordered to Ireland.

During the time on the Humber *D3* had no third officer, and Johnson and Maitland-Dougall ran the boat by themselves. Even with the added work both Canadians found time to golf and shoot duck in the Humber estuary. Johnson was delighted to be able to resume his friendship with Adrian Keyes, who, now married and a commander, was living close to Immingham following his distinguished service at Gallipoli.

By now Barney Johnson was recognized as having exceptional abilities and the hard-working Maitland-Dougall was promoted to acting lieutenant on 1 January 1917. He had already been earmarked for early command, partly because his time in *D3*, working closely with Johnson, had provided Maitland-Dougall with many fine examples of leadership to follow.

On 1 February 1917, Germany declared unrestricted submarine warfare, as Fisher had predicted, and their U-boat successes escalated. This forced the Admiralty to employ their flotillas in anti-submarine patrols and to reduce their defensive operations. This tactical change required more long-range submarines and one admiral suggested that twelve more H boats should be built in Canada. If Borden had heard of the proposal, he would have jumped at it, but the Admiralty kept quiet and built them at home.

In response to the Admiralty's decision, the Third Flotilla relocated to Ireland to defend the still-unconvoyed Allied shipping in the Western Approaches. The objective of the flotilla was to hunt for and destroy the enemy submarines that were prowling around the shipping lanes leading to British ports.

The Canadian team, now healthy and full of energy, worked harder than ever in this new type of warfare in the North Atlantic, from their base in Queenstown (now Cobh) in Cork harbour on the south coast of Ireland. Johnson's own written recollections of this period have a different tone from those he penned about patrols in the North Sea. The sentences convey spirit and interest to the reader as Johnson began to enjoy his role.

On arrival in Queenstown there was little familiarization for the crews, and within a few days *D3* was off to sea. They sailed with their sister submarines, accompanied by *Q13* which had operational control of the flotilla. Q ships were merchant vessels fitted with cleverly concealed guns whose purpose was to act as tempting targets for U-boats and, when they approached, shoot them out of the sea. In her cooperative role, *Q13* let the submarines attack the U-boats.

Submarine-versus-submarine was a new game. It had not been exercised before the war, and the Third Flotilla learned as they went along. The boats worked together, strung out across the shipping lanes, carrying out diving patrols in daylight, occasionally surfacing for a better look for the enemy, and shadowing friendly ships underwater to have a better chance of tangling with a U-boat. At night they patrolled on the surface while recharging their batteries. The practice of resting on the bottom for a good night's sleep was over for good. The boats remained on patrol for longer periods than before – *D3* set the flotilla record of twenty-three days.

D3's first two patrols were uneventful, but March 1916 saw Johnson get his eye in and have some exciting moments. *D3* rescued forty-eight survivors from *Q27*, which had been torpedoed by *U-61* near Galway Bay, before moving in April to Buncrana on Lough Swilley in the north of Ireland. There *D3* joined other Ds of the Second Flotilla based on HMS *Platypus*.

On 23 April 1917, Johnson was patrolling in calm weather off the northwest coast of Ireland and sighted a three-masted barque sailing southeastwards at 1040. Johnson dived his submarine at 1100 and kept station on the vessel at a distance of three miles hoping that she might lure a U-boat to her. At 1340 gunfire was heard on the hydrophones and Johnson saw through the periscope that the vessel had stopped and lowered her topsails. He brought *D3*'s crew to action stations at 1355. Johnson crept towards the stricken vessel underwater, using the periscope as little as possible. As he came round the barque's stern, he had a brief look and, sure enough, there was a U-boat on the surface tucked alongside the ship. Johnson waited until the U-boat disengaged and manoeuvred *D3* into position for a shot. He fired both bow torpedoes 1,300 yards (1,183 m) at 1528 – a long shot in those days. The captain quickly ordered eighteen feet so he could watch the results of his attack, but regrettably the planesman heard eighty feet. Less than a minute later a muffled explosion was heard on *D3*, which was taken to be a hit on the U-boat, but, because of the mistaken order, *D3* was well on her way down and Johnson saw nothing. "Periscope depth!" he ordered. At 1545, up went the periscope and to Johnson's surprise he saw what he thought was another submarine steering north away from the scene and no sign of the barque. He attempted to get into position to attack this one with his stern tube, but the U-boat dived. "Prepare to surface" sounded throughout *D3* and, when she did so at 1700, Johnson saw yet another submarine. At 1740 *D3* passed through wreckage and a small quantity of oil. Johnson was elated with the action, so long awaited.

The attack had been a good one and Johnson and his Captain(S) believed that he had scored. It was not until after the war that careful checking of German records proved that both torpedoes missed the target and the U-boat lived to fight another day. Johnson's adversary had been *UC66*, a U-boat which operated around Belfast and the Clyde laying mines and attacking shipping. The explosion Johnson had heard was not a torpedo hitting the U-boat, but the scuttling charges exploding in the sailing ship, S.V. *Arethusa*.

A typical attack in a First World War submarine usually began when the boat was trimmed well down on the surface and the officer of the watch (OOW) and the lookout were on the bridge platform.

"Contact bearing three-four-zero, Sir!" yelled the sharp-eyed lookout.

As he raced to get below, the lookout's feet slid non-stop down the outside of the ladder. The OOW, now alone, took a last quick look at the target, pressed the diving alarm and tumbled down the ladder too, closing the upper hatch behind him. The boat slid under the waves as the officer's sea boots hit the deck in the control room.

The *Ooh gaa! Ooh gaa!* of the klaxon had sent the crew who were not on watch scrambling to their diving stations.

"Half ahead, group up! Open main vents!"

The boat pitched down, accompanied by the roar of water rushing into the ballast tanks, followed by sudden silence as the diesels were stopped and unclutched.

"Slow ahead together!"

The CERA made some minor adjustments to the trim, and the crew, in their places now, were quiet and ready.

"Close main vents!"

"Half ahead together! Blow Q!"

"Thirty feet!"

"Up periscope!"

"Down periscope!"

The captain took an all-round look. These were necessary for safety reasons as well as for the location of targets. No submarine wanted to be run down by a ship they had not seen. Periscopes have a limited arc of visibility so they need to be walked around in a circle to provide a complete 360-degree picture of what is happening on the surface. An all-round look takes about ten seconds – a short time to absorb all that is happening.

Another look through the periscope – never too long. The enemy might catch a glimpse of the tell-tale feather of spray or a flash of light reflected from the periscope window which would give the submarine away. The crouching CO memorized the location of the target, its range, and its speed in relation to his submarine and then determined its angle on the submarine's bow. Then as the periscope came down, he chose the best tactic for success, did his mental arithmetic, and repositioned his boat to sink the target. Early torpedoes had no guidance systems; the boat itself had to be the captain's instrument of aim.

"Make number 1 and number 2 tubes ready!"

The first lieutenant, or the third hand, was now in the fore-ends supervising the flooding of the torpedo tubes which hissed and spluttered.

"Number 1 and 2 tubes ready!" came back the report.

The captain was now fully focused on the surface situation, knowing that the officers and men would ready the boat for attack. His brain methodically calculated the best approach and the possibilities of detection. He took another quick look, saw that the target had changed course, and altered his own to bring the submarine to bear again. Pause … Another look. A small change in course. A longer pause, harder to bear without signs of impatience. An all-round look.

"Damn! He's turned away!"

A change in speed and course to get the submarine around to lead the target. Another look. Wait again … a picture in his mind of the surface; a question to himself as to what the target might do next. Would he anticipate its moves correctly?

A fast look to check the angle on the bow. All is unchanged, and if it stays that way the bow tubes will be brought to bear in about two minutes. More patience. No one speaks, they almost hold their breath – the submarine is within 400 yards (364 m) of the target and, for a few minutes, very vulnerable.

"Up periscope!"

The crew watch the CO's face to see if they can tell what is happening by his expression. Another look to check his judgement and a small course change.

"Stand by number 1 and number 2 tubes!

"Fire one! ... Fire two!

"Down periscope!"

Those in the fore-ends hear a thud and a rattle as the torpedoes leave the tubes. The torpedo vents are immediately opened and the tubes flooded to compensate for the loss of weight. Now complete silence as everyone waits for the result of the captain's attack. It feels like an hour but, if he judged it well, two clanging reports will be heard. There is a collective sigh as they all release their breath and then a cheer from the crew, who *knew* their CO would succeed, and a broad, sweaty grin from the captain. A couple of seconds maybe, to take a look at the effect of the torpedoes, and then a sharp order to avoid the enemy's reprisal.

"One hundred feet! Course two-four-zero!"

"Watch diving! Reload number 1 and number 2 tubes!"

This is a description of an uncomplicated attack, without escorts or multiple targets, which might attack the submarine. The tension, excitement and activity are much greater when the boat has to contend with the extras. The pioneer submarine captains did not have mechanical or electronic devices to assist them in computing the data for an attack – they had to do it by "eye" and guesswork.

Two weeks after the first attack on the U-boat, *D3* found another in the same area. This time Johnson got in close, about 400 yards, and fired the two bow tubes in a textbook attack. Johnson watched the torpedoes' progress to the target through the periscope, which was camouflaged by a choppy sea. The first one kept breaking the surface during the entire run, due to a defect in the depth-keeping mechanism. It missed. Johnson thought the second hit the enemy's bow and *D3* quickly dived to sixty feet to avoid any retaliation. When *D3* returned to periscope depth, the submarine had vanished.

There is no record in the log of Johnson positively identifying the target – he thought it was a large type of U-boat with a high conning tower and a deck gun. But Johnson was wrong. It was *E48*, sent in error to a billet which overlapped *D3*'s by HMS *Vulcan*. Communication was immediately improved between the two commands to prevent such an incident occurring again and the patrol areas were redistributed. It had been a very close call – Johnson's torpedo had missed by no more than twenty yards.

Maitland-Dougall and Johnson acted upon many sightings during the rest of their Atlantic patrols together, though none of them matched those of the spring. The Canadians saw the Allied merchant losses drop dramatically when convoys were finally instituted by a hesitant Admiralty, forcing the U-boats, at their most plentiful then, to expose themselves more often to attack. More effective anti-submarine tactics and heavier depth charges were enabling the British navy to sink U-boats faster than they were being produced.

William Maitland-Dougall left *D3* in July 1917, with both regrets and anticipation. It had been a most satisfying time, with Barney Johnson as his commanding officer, learning and practising the art of attacking; but he was ambitious and knew that the next step up the ladder towards his own command meant separating from *D3*. With a last look around, he heaved his lanky form out of the submarine, gathered up his kit and left for Portsmouth and HMS *Dolphin* once more. Captain(S) wrote, "[He] is likely to make a determined and capable CO."[2] Maitland-Dougall had just turned twenty-two years old.

The Royal Navy was the first armed service to benefit from the entry of the United States into the war in 1917. U.S. naval officers were attached to various operations as observers before their ships and submarines arrived. The *Platypus* flotilla was one command which hosted the Americans.

Captain(S) asked *D3* to "entertain" Commander Boyd, USN, for four days at the start of an operational patrol. (Johnson was told to "bring him back in one piece, or else!") *D3* headed off into the Atlantic in heavy weather to show the Yank their business. On their second day they sighted a submarine and were fired on by a friendly sloop – before breakfast. Later, when the visibility suddenly cleared, *D3* found themselves too close to a large Allied convoy. Johnson hit the diving alarm button and Boyd ran the signalman a close second down the conning tower. The American got a shower of seawater down his neck though, as Johnson was later than usual in closing the lid. Boyd did not enjoy the experience and neither did Johnson, because "three men on the bridge is one too many for quick work." He did not allow his guest on the bridge again after that. *D3*'s American visitor was disembarked on schedule and none the worse for wear – just a little chastened and minus his brass hat which had vanished in the scramble below. *D3* returned to patrol immediately but the remainder of it was uneventful.

Johnson had no more excitement in *D3* – just two quiet patrols and a refit – before he turned over his command to Willie Maitland-Dougall on 22 November 1917.

On 2 November, Barney Johnson learned that he had been awarded the Distinguished Service Order for his gallant conduct in recovering *H8* after she was mined in 1916. But such were the exigencies of war that he had to wait until 1919 to receive his decoration from King George V. The citation also included mention of Johnson's long and arduous service in command and the sinking of *UC66* which was not disproved until after the war. Johnson was the only Canadian submariner decorated in the First World War.

CHAPTER SIX

HMCS *CC1* AND *CC2*, 1917

"An absurd undertaking"[1]

Back at home in October 1917, the first Canadian submarines had arrived in Halifax after a very tough seven-thousand-mile (11,200 km) voyage from Esquimalt. They had earned some fame for their having been the first warships flying the White Ensign to pass through the newly opened Panama Canal, and some notoriety for their continual engine breakdowns.

The Admiralty had been considering the transfer of *CC1* and *CC2* to the east coast for more than two years. The idea was first mooted immediately after the Battle of the Falkland Islands, which removed the threat of German cruisers from Victoria and Vancouver. However, nothing came of it until early 1917, when the U-boats were sinking too many merchantmen in the Western Approaches, and the RN, in need of reinforcements for their flotillas, resurrected the plan. They ordered the under-utilized *CC1* and *CC2* to Europe. The RCN responded favourably, saying the boats were "useless where they are [and] are rapidly deteriorating,"[2] but they regretted losing the depot ship, *Shearwater*, which was to accompany the submarines from Esquimalt.

Preparations[3] began in earnest after the RCN chose 20 June as the sailing date. The flurry of naval signals exchanged with the RN demonstrate the RCN's uncertainty about the boats' ability to undertake such a voyage and, as a consequence, their plans changed constantly. Initially the submarines were to travel mostly alone, with HMCS *Shearwater* accompanying them only as far as San Francisco. After many revisions, the RCN ordered *Shearwater* to escort the boats all the way to Halifax, carrying spare crew, fuel, and other gear. Both *CC1* and *Shearwater* went into refit to prepare. Ottawa also had to remind the Admiralty to pay for the passage to Halifax. The final itinerary estimated that they would arrive in Halifax about 14 August – a voyage of two months.

The RCN promulgated the final orders for the expedition at the end of May. They appointed Bertram Jones, now a lieutenant-commander, in overall command of the venture in *Shearwater* and the long-time lieutenants, Hanson and Lake, in command of the submarines. Both boats carried new officers from British Columbia – Lt. Arthur C.S. Pitts, RNCVR, in *CC1*, and Lt. George H.S. Edwardes, RNCVR, in *CC2*. Neither boat had a third officer. The cox'ns were Chief Petty Officers Addison (*CC1*) and Purvis (*CC2*), and the flotilla CERA, who was to bear the brunt of the voyage, was Arthur Hunting.

"Panther" Pitts, whose nickname referred to his outstanding hunting skills, was a confirmed bachelor with a quiet, modest disposition, who remained single until he reached the age of seventy-six. He joined Victoria's Volunteer Reserve Company at its inception and *CC1* in July 1915. Pitts became a keen and trustworthy submariner.

Edwardes joined *CC2* in May 1917, just in time for the epic voyage to Halifax. He had volunteered for the navy at the outbreak of war and soon commanded the small harbour patrol in Esquimalt and the local RNCVR company. He was experienced with engines of all types, and this, coupled with his energetic approach, proved invaluable during the submarine flotilla's journey.

Under a cloak of secrecy, HMS *Shearwater* and the two Canadian submarines sailed out of Esquimalt on 21 June 1917, never to return. Jones's orders included strict instructions to make no statements about their route or destination, and to allow no shore leave until they had passed through the Panama Canal. He was to approach ports in daylight only, and he was authorized to make unscheduled stops if necessary.

Soon *CC1* and *CC2* were out in the Pacific, with many of the crews were unprepared for the rigours of the open sea. *Shearwater* was towing *CC1* when a nasty gale blew up off Cape Blanco, Oregon, and *CC2* lost her station in the murk. She remained on the surface, rolling to 60 degrees, and seawater seriously contaminated her batteries. Her crew, laid low with seasickness, which they had rarely experienced, were exposed to chlorine gas and half were incapacitated.

The high seas caused another problem, which was to have a more enduring effect. Every time the propellers were flung out of the sea, the diesels over-revved. To avoid this, the COs ordered a running charge put into the batteries; the shafts were direct drives, and this stratagem loaded the screws and prevented their speeding up. As this could only be done safely on a depleted battery, *CC1* and *CC2* ran on their electric motors until the batteries were low, then started the diesels and put on the running charge at the same time. Soon they established a routine of twenty minutes on the batteries and ten minutes on engines, which continued until they reached Halifax.

However, this solution caused almost as many problems as it solved – the continual charging and discharging caused the battery cells to start to break down and then to short-circuit, causing electrical fires. This alarming occurrence could only be prevented by disconnecting the affected cells and thus reducing the battery capacity. The unreliable diesel engines broke down frequently under the repeated abuse and both submarines adopted the continuous routine of repairing one engine while proceeding on the other.

CC2 was separated from the other two vessels for a day before *Shearwater* located her; her engines cooperated as far as San Francisco. *CC1* was towed all the way, after an abortive attempt to run independently when her tow parted. The flotilla spent one day in San Francisco provisioning, making repairs, and ordering new parts for delivery at the next port. The submarines sailed for San Diego with *CC1* still in tow, though running on one engine to improve the speed of advance. The weather was kind to them and they arrived safely on 29 June 1917 – though *CC1* had broken down again. This time both her engines were unserviceable.

San Diego was a welcome respite for the boats' crews when they arrived in time for the famous Fourth of July celebrations. The city made a great fuss of the Canadian crews because the United States had recently entered the war and the Americans were now comrades-in-arms. The sailors of *CC1* and *CC2* led the Independence Day parade through the city streets to a tumultuous reception, but got no shore leave. They returned to their submarines immediately afterwards.

Unexpected engineering work had to be done on both submarines and the parts, ordered in San Francisco, were late arriving. The stokers and ERAs worked night and day while alongside, supervised by Lieutenant Edwardes and CERA Hunting. It was in San Diego that Jones realized that the original itinerary, which allowed only one day in port to prepare for the next leg, was over-optimistic. He wrote to the director of the Naval Service detailing his concerns and predicted that the submarines' engines would overheat in the tropics and create more problems. He appended a revised schedule to his report and warned that the flotilla probably could not keep to it.

Nine days late, with *CC1* under tow, *CC2* and *Shearwater* headed out of San Diego into a hotter climate than they had ever known. They port-hopped down the coast of Mexico in fine weather, experiencing difficulty obtaining fresh food. To alleviate the unvarying diet of canned pork and beans, "Panther" Pitts persuaded a coastal farmer to sell him a cow, which he drove onto the beach, slaughtered, butchered, and had loaded into the boats.

As they sailed south the temperature in the engine rooms rose as high as 140 degrees Fahrenheit and caused the stokers great discomfort. Heat prostration was not uncommon. One ERA could not continue and had to be given duties in *Shearwater*, and several stokers requested transfers, which could not be granted. The increasing humidity with its resultant condensation added to the misery by causing frequent defaults in the electrical systems.

After a brief stop in Acapulco and Salina Cruz the flotilla pushed on to the Canal Zone, with *Shearwater* towing both submarines in deteriorating weather. *CC1* could not run either engine or charge her batteries, and *CC2*'s battery was again contaminated with seawater, causing chlorine gas to fill the boat.

Life for the seamen was unpleasant enough in the submarines, but it was aggravated for the younger sailors in *CC2* by a much-disliked chief petty officer, Gunner(T) Brisco. He made a habit of picking on one or two, and making their lives a misery. The junior men drew closer together for protection from the NCO's unjustified persecutions and frequent charges.

Crippled and barely moving, the little flotilla eventually made it to Balboa, at the western entrance of the Panama Canal, on 31 July 1917. There were thirty-two items on the submarines' defect list and their stay extended to twelve days, with the ERAs working around the clock.

On 12 August, when most of the work was done, *CC1* and *CC2* undertook the fifty-mile transit of the canal. The boats took nine hours to pass through and, judging by the number of photographs taken by the crew that still survive, it was the highlight of the voyage. The immense locks dwarfed the little submarines and the crews watched with awe as the tow locomotives (know as "electric mules") moved the vessels through the canal with precision. It was to be fifty years before another Canadian submarine, HMCS *Grilse*, followed in their wake.

The flotilla sailed from Colón on 15 August, once again in heavy weather. One account written thirty-six years later indicates that the Canadian submarines participated in exercises with American submarines at this time, but the Reports of Proceedings make no mention of it. The high seas immediately took their toll – *CC1*'s engine died again and *CC2* suffered the same dangerous consequences of shipping salt water as she had off Oregon and Mexico. Jones was most perturbed by the implications of this continuing defect in *CC2*, and decided to stop in Kingston, Jamaica, to fix it. The flotilla was half-way to Halifax by now and, according to the original schedule, they should have arrived.

Jamaica proved to be a good choice for repairs – diesel fuel was available there and the islanders welcomed the sailors. Most got leave, when not repairing the engines, and one young able seaman found himself adopted by a local family, taken sightseeing, and fed decent meals. Another sailor, emboldened with booze, deserted rather than put up with another two months of the intolerable conditions. Needless to say, he was quickly caught and escorted off to jail with another rating who had gone AWOL. Both were left in Jamaica when the flotilla sailed, late as usual.

The submarines were now pointing towards Halifax, which encouraged all on board. Had they known what else they had to face, they would have been less cheerful. *CC2*, whose engines had run fairly well up till then, began to falter and needed regular towing. The tows parted continually in rougher seas than they had previously encountered. Very slowly the flotilla made their way to the big U.S. Navy base at Charleston, South Carolina, for more repairs. The submarines' chaperone commented, yet again, that both boats' engines were extremely unreliable.

The submarines sailed on 10 September 1917 after five days' hard work and with a depleted engine-room crew. Jones had put two sick sailors ashore and fired one of the two CERAs, with the over-burdened Hunting assuming the discharged man's duties in addition to his own.

The flotilla steamed north from Charleston into head seas with *Shearwater* towing *CC2*, and very soon *CC1* as well. After twenty hours of battling the swell and making minimal progress, they returned to port. The submarines' diesel engines, badly strained before, were now almost finished. Feverishly the crews worked to produce some reliable power, and four days later, on 15 September, the weather moderated enough for the boats to try again.

Twenty-four hours later a storm blew up, which turned out to be the worst of the voyage. *CC1*'s towing gear was carried away completely and the line fouled *Shearwater*'s propeller. The submarines, running on one engine each, were unable to dive to avoid the weather, and the crews again suffered from severe seasickness. Many were so badly affected that they could not carry on with their duties. On 18 September, the flotilla staggered into Norfolk, Virginia, broken and bleeding. Two weeks of repairs followed at the USN dockyard, in an attempt to resuscitate the dying submarines. Three more sailors deserted.

Despite their efforts, *Shearwater* had to tow *CC1* almost all the way to Newport, Rhode Island, with work continuing night and day on her engines. It took another six days to repair the submarine before they left on the last long-awaited leg to Halifax. The men, frustrated and exhausted, could almost smell their new home port. American warships escorted the flotilla for the final stage with *Shearwater, CC1,* and *CC2* coming thankfully alongside in Halifax on 14 October 1917.

The voyage had taken twice as long as planned – the flotilla had covered 7,252 nautical miles in four difficult months and *CC1* had been towed for most of it. The effort had been accomplished by dogged perseverance from every officer and man in the face of insurmountable problems. These problems were mainly caused by an engine cooling system that was inadequate for the tropics, condensation inside the hull affecting the electrical system, a flimsy pump shaft, and overstressed batteries. Jones felt that the safe arrival of the boats was largely due to the energy and devotion to duty of CERA Hunting.

The Admiralty immediately ordered *CC1* and *CC2* to refuel and proceed to the Mediterranean. This was clearly impossible – the submarines had "not [been] designed for such ... an absurd undertaking,"[4] wrote a commentator of the period.

In the end, the RCN commended Jones for his fine seamanship, resourcefulness, and endurance, and promoted him to acting commander on 1 November 1917. Jones had done his duty shepherding two terminally ill submarines, and had been rewarded, but he still longed to be in action in Europe. He was soon to be disappointed yet again.

Soon after the arrival of *CC1* and *CC2* in Halifax, the report of the royal commission into their purchase was published.[5] Sir Charles Davidson, the commissioner, applauded the faithful work of military officers and the honest performance of public officials in wartime procurement. He said that the popular view of malpractice in war appropriations was incorrect.

Davidson's report summarized the acquisition of the first Canadian submarines and then itemized the questionable points in the transaction, which hinged on the financial and legal arrangements, the price of the boats, the necessity of the purchase, and the efficacy of the submarines. The commissioner briefly described the facts around each point and concluded, "It is cause for congratulations to all Canadians that this ... enterprise was ... of blameless character. The ... submarines probably saved ... Victoria and Vancouver from attack."

Specifically, Sir Charles Davidson found that the suspicions aroused by the financing of the deal were caused by a decoding error and the lack of time available to properly execute the legal and accounting documents. He also proved that no Canadians or political parties had received or sought commissions during the acquisition of the submarines.

The commissioner decided that the purchase price of $1.2 million was not too high – in light of the cost of comparable boats and the desperate need to obtain a means of defence for the Pacific coast.

The evidence, which was considered by Sir Charles regarding the efficacy of *CC1* and *CC2*, led him to conclude that the boats were "effective fighting machines" of high quality. But he had not heard the whole story – the director of the Naval Service withheld the submarines' early buoyancy problems and continual engine breakdowns.

There is no doubt that, at the beginning of their commission, the buoyancy problems were severe and that they were caused by shoddy construction practices. Before the commission sat, EBCo knew it; Sir Phillip Watts, the adviser to the Chilean navy, knew it; through the high commissioner in London, the prime minister knew it; and, the Canadian submarine officers experienced it. Later the engineering commander at Naval Headquarters confirmed it. But most importantly, the director of the Naval Service knew it too when he gave evidence. He probably decided that, as the problem had been remedied the year before, there was little point in bringing it up and, as Canada was still at war, he certainly did not want to publicize the submarines' shortcomings. Similarly he did not mention their unreliable diesel engines.

The commissioner also had specific words for Sir Richard McBride, the provincial premier, whose actions had been misinterpreted and whose character had been so maligned: "what [he] accomplished deserves commendation ... for his motives were those of patriotism and his conduct that of an honourable man." However, these official words came too late for McBride – he had died in August 1917 of kidney failure. Indeed, the report received little attention and the memory of this energetic patriot, father of Canada's Submarine Service, has remained unnecessarily tarnished.

CC1 and *CC2* never went to Europe. "[Their] present condition absolutely forbids their undertaking an ocean passage," wrote the dockyard engineer officer. Jones had suggested that the submarines should have an extensive refit and be utilized to defend Halifax. At the end of October 1917, the Admiralty reluctantly agreed and ordered *CC1* and *CC2* to remain "where they might be useful if enemy submarines cross the Atlantic." Jones said a prayer of thanksgiving – he was, at last, going to be rid of his troublesome charges and the RCN would get two boats on the east coast, which they had wanted for three years.

The submarine crews began work in November on the major refit, and the construction of a shore-based submarine depot to service the needs of the flotilla. The facility included workshops, stores, and spartan accommodation to replace those previously available to the crews in their mother ship. *Shearwater* had sailed earlier for Bermuda in a training capacity, with Jones in command and Lake on board as well. Lake never returned to the submarines again – he died of pneumonia in the influenza epidemic of 1918, aged only thirty-eight.

"Twenty pushups, then twice round the shed! Look lively, there! Up-down! Up-down!" ordered Lieutenant Pitts.

Some sailors from *CC1* and *CC2* were out in the cold, damp air of a Halifax winter morning, doing their physical jerks at the submarine depot. Others were working on the submarines and the remaining officers were around and about supervising their men.

With no warning, the boats and the submariners heard and felt a monstrous explosion at 0906. The merchant ship *Mont Blanc*, carrying a highly explosive cargo, had caught fire in a collision with another ship and then had blown up, less than a mile away from the submarine depot. The Halifax Explosion was the most powerful man-made explosion to date, not surpassed in destructive force until the atomic bomb exploded over Hiroshima.

One petty officer, poking his head out of a hatch, was knocked upside down and hurled below. Pitts was blown over but not hurt and Edwardes was badly cut on his face after hitting a wall. Everyone on the jetty had to tumble for cover as pieces of metal rained down on them. Some pieces of shrapnel were small, but one rating saw the entire funnel of a ship sailing over his head. The immediate reaction of the submariners was the same as the Haligonians. They believed the Germans had attacked. "They've got us this time, and got us good!" said *CC2*'s cox'n.[6] A quick head count revealed that none of the submariners had been killed or badly injured. They had been incredibly lucky considering how close they were to the explosion that had atomized the *Mont Blanc*.

Later in the day, when the crews learned of the scale of the disaster, they were amazed. The sound of the explosion was heard more than two hundred miles (320 km) away and the North End of Halifax and the naval dockyard were flattened. One large gun was carried three and a half miles (5.6 km) from its original position and 1,600 souls perished in a second. The effect on the vessels in the harbour was no less devastating. The superstructures of ships were knocked off; hulls were punctured by the flying metal; sailors on deck were killed and stripped naked by the air blast; and the tidal wave that followed ripped ships from their moorings and sent them careering all over the harbour to collide with others or run aground. One tug ended up on a jetty.

The submarines broke adrift with the resulting tidal wave but were quickly secured again and Edwardes left for the hospital. Pitts then reported the damage sustained by the boats and the submarine depot to Hanson. *CC1* and *CC2* were unscathed but the blast had demolished the interior of the bunkhouse. Hanson ordered repairs begun at once and put Pitts in charge.

As Pitts's work party was leaving to get wood, they heard the cry: "Run for your lives!" The nearby ammunition dump was on fire and about to blow up. Hanson ordered the men to take cover and many of the submariners, including Pitts, jumped behind a wall into the water to shelter. Hanson stayed with the submarines and, when no explosion occurred, he decided to move the boats to safety. As Pitts and his work party could not scale the wall from the water side, they began to run back to the depot through the south gate of the dockyard. Hanson, unable to locate Pitts, asked Brisco to find him and tell him to take command of *CC1* and follow *CC2*. The gunner, failing to find Pitts, took command of *CC1* himself. Hanson, along with Edwardes, who had returned from the hospital, rapidly manoeuvred *CC2* out into the harbour, shortly pursued by *CC1*. When Pitts saw the boats leaving as he came running through the dockyard gate, he organized a motor boat to take the remaining crew over to *CC1* and *CC2*. The submarines returned to their jetty when it was obvious that the danger was over. The crews began to repair the depot and later helped to move the injured to makeshift hospitals and to fight fires in the dockyard.

CC1 and *CC2* were undamaged by the explosion, protected as they were by their pressure hulls of thick steel. A few dents in the casing were the only evidence that they had been close.

That night a ferocious winter storm hit Halifax. The gale caused many ships and smaller vessels to drag their anchors or come adrift for the second time in twenty-four hours. The submarines rode it out alongside and came to no harm.

CHAPTER SEVEN

CANADIAN SUBMARINERS IN EUROPE, 1917–1918

"A very promising submarine captain"

Lt. Willie Maitland-Dougall was the first and youngest career officer to command a submarine in the RCN. He took over *D1* on 28 August 1917, when she was transferred to HMS *Thames*, the home of the newly established Periscope School at Portsmouth. During "Perisher," as the course for commanding officers quickly became known, the prospective submarine captains learned the skills of submerged attack using the periscope. It is unclear whether Maitland-Dougall actually attended the first Commanding Officers' Qualifying Course (COQC), as his name does not appear on the class list, but he was certainly based there.[1] Perhaps *D1* was the boat being used for the course and Maitland-Dougall was not a participant.

After three months in *D1* Maitland-Dougall assumed command of his old submarine, *D3*, in Ireland, relieving Johnson. The young captain inherited a happy and efficient boat filled with familiar faces. They completed one uneventful patrol in the Western Approaches before returning to Portsmouth to begin A/S (anti-submarine) operations in the English Channel. *D3* worked from HMS *Dolphin* with the Sixth Flotilla, which was led by Commander Quicke, RN, Maitland-Dougall's old mentor from *H10*.

D3's patrols off the south coast were very different from those in the Atlantic: they were shorter, but in the restricted waters and heavy traffic of the Channel, they demanded all Maitland-Dougall's skill and nerve. The young Canadian experienced the combativeness of Allied vessels on many occasions – the surface ships attacked any submarine that showed itself, whether friend or foe. On a couple of occasions Maitland-Dougall was reprimanded for diving before identifying his submarine, but he preferred to risk a reprimand rather than stay exposed on the surface and invite disaster.

Maitland-Dougall wrote home regularly, but only one letter has survived from this period. In it he told his mother that he had made his will, and was leaving everything to her except his gold watch and chain. These were to go back to his father who had given them to him.

Meanwhile, Barney Johnson, who was still in Ireland, had taken over his third submarine, *E54*, while she was completing a refit. Together they remained on Atlantic patrol based on Ireland's southwest coast at Berehaven which had become the Western Approaches' anti-U-boat headquarters. Here Johnson rubbed shoulders with ten other distinguished submarine captains, six of whom were decorated; friendships were established, some of which would be lifelong.

Johnson, like many other COs, appreciated the characteristics of the offensive E-class submarines, especially their long range. They were the most modern boats in service: half as large again as the Ds and Hs, they combined many of their best features. The increase in size allowed for some improvement in accommodation but little in comfort. The Es operated in every theatre, from the Baltic to the Sea of Marmora, and were the most successful class built in the Great War.

The winter of 1917–18 brought Johnson many sightings of merchant ships, alone and in convoy, but he had no further engagements with U-boats. The only change in his dull routine was the arrival in January 1918 of an American flotilla of S boats, that had to be integrated with the British boats. The RN Captain(S) sent the American COs to sea in the Es to facilitate their introduction to anti-submarine warfare. In Johnson's opinion, his U.S. counterpart was a good shipmate, but lacked experience in wartime operations.

However, it was not all work for Johnson. He managed to get short periods of leave during his time in Ireland and generally spent it touring the countryside on a motorcycle. His private logbook identifies picnics, canoe trips, golf, and sleeping as his favourite pastimes. On 30 March 1918, *E54* returned to Portsmouth with the rest of the flotilla. Johnson was shocked by the news that awaited him.

Just before lunch on 12 March 1918, a French airship lumbered into the sky from Fécamp, a base in France that lay almost due south of Brighton.

It was a mild spring day. The young commanding officer, Ensign St.-Rémy, was looking for likely targets when his navigator sighted one through the haze to the northeast. The French CO altered course and increased speed to intercept the vessel. As they approached he could see it was a surfaced submarine, heading west, but he could not identify it. Suddenly the submarine fired on the airship with what the French officer described as "red rockets." St.-Rémy, believing his command to be under attack, ordered his gunner to fire back, using the machine gun. The shots missed initially but soon ricocheted off the casing causing the boat to dive.

As the boat slid beneath the waves, the airship dropped two bombs on her, but they missed astern by twenty metres. The French airman brought his craft round for another go and, by the time he was in position, the submarine was gone, leaving only its wake. St.-Rémy dropped four more bombs. Tall columns of water shot into the sky and within four minutes a French lookout reported a streak of bubbles and part of the conning tower showing above the waves. The submarine was desperately trying to surface.

The French crew believed the submarine was seriously damaged as she soon disappeared from their sight. By the time airship had stopped climbing after her bombs were dropped, her crew could see four men swimming in the sea. They approached to twenty metres, turned off their engines, and St.-Rémy tried to talk to the submariners. He heard, "You got us!" The airship CO quickly realized the dreadful mistake he had made and dropped lifebelts to the men who were struggling in the water. The airship made a useless attempt at saving them, fixed their position, sent off a message to their headquarters, and then flew off to find some rescue vessels. Together with a French torpedo boat, they returned to the scene where they had last seen the survivors and searched in vain till dusk. At 1810 the airship returned to her base and left the surface vessel to continue. St.-Rémy then reported his successful attack to his superiors, along with his serious concerns over the nationality of the submarine.

The French authorities conveyed the airship commander's report to HMS *Dolphin*, which received the news on 13 March. Commander Alexander Quicke, in charge of the Sixth Flotilla, waited until the 15th before posting one of his submarines missing. It was Maitland-Dougall's *D3*.

Quicke then had to inform the family. It was always a difficult duty, and this one was particularly so. Quicke knew that Maitland-Dougall's younger brother had been killed the previous year at Vimy and that Hamish and Willie were James and Winifred Maitland-Dougall's only children. He told them nothing of the circumstances of *D3*'s loss, saying simply that she was lost in action. Quicke mourned the Canadian's loss as well, having "fathered" Maitland-Dougall through three years of war.

The Admiralty informed Canada of the tragedy on 16 March, also without details.

Quicke searched for Maitland-Dougall's will, which he knew he had written, but failed to find it. He packed up Willie's few belongings and sent them to Mary, his relative in Scotland, whom the young captain had nominated as his next of kin, hoping to ease the pain for his mother if he died. The gold watch for Willie's father was not in the package – it had gone down with the submarine too.

Commander Quicke then investigated the disaster to determine what had happened, in the hope of preventing a recurrence. In his report, he made it very clear that *D3* was equipped with the correct British recognition signals for the period and also had her fore hatch cover painted with a white bull's-eye to aid identification from the air. Quicke noted that Maitland-Dougall had been fully briefed on British air and ship movements in his operational area. The conclusion stated that, when the airship approached unexpectedly from the sun, *D3* probably stayed on the surface to get a better look (as the haze precluded one through the periscope) and her captain, mindful of his previous reprimands, remained there to exchange recognition signals. These were red smoke grenades which the French reported as "rockets." As soon as Maitland-Dougall realized he was being relentlessly attacked, he did the only thing to save his command – he submerged.

Quicke also explained that the French and British commands had not established standard recognition signals or informed each other of their differing methods. Thus, neither *D3* nor the French airship could have established their identities for each other. For some reason the French crew did not see, or did not recognize, the white bull's-eye on *D3*'s casing, which would have saved the day. Despite Perkins's assertion in his book, *Canada's Submariners: 1914–1923*,[2] that the British did not inform the French forces of ship dispositions, evidence shows that the French were "fully acquainted with the fact that *D3* was operating in their area."[3]

Quicke determined that Maitland-Dougall had followed correct procedures throughout and could not have averted the tragedy. The saddened commander wrote in his closing paragraph that the Canadian was "in the very front rank of the younger Submarine captains, a most thorough, conscientious and resourceful officer."[4]

An Admiralty official remarked after the inquiries had been concluded on both sides of the Channel that "This most regrettable incident appears to have been due to a lack of discretion, combined with an excess of zeal, on the part of the commander of the French airship."[5] The French inquiry absolved St.-Rémy of all responsibility, saying that although he knew a British submarine was in his patrol area, he did not receive the correct recognition signals from *D3*. Hardly fair, when they did not know them.

Lt. William McKinstry Maitland-Dougall, RCN, achieved many submarine firsts in his short career. He was Canada's first submarine commanding officer to be lost at sea, and to date remains the only one. He was the first regular RCN officer to become a submarine CO, achieving command at an exceptionally early age; he was the first Canadian to take the Royal Navy's Submarine Officers' Training Course; he was the first RCN officer to cross the Atlantic in a submarine; and he was the first RCN officer to volunteer for the submarine service. Maitland-Dougall's accomplishments have never received official recognition from the RCN – his memory remains unknown and unsung, except by a few submariners.

It was not until after the war that Maitland-Dougall's family discovered how *D3* was sunk. Willie's mother was devastated by the details and never fully recovered from the shock. In 1921 she put up a handsome bronze memorial to her sons in the parish church where both Willie and Hamish had been christened and confirmed. It can still be seen above the Maitland-Dougall family pew in St. Peter's in Quamichan. It reads:

In loving memory of
Corp. Hamish Kinnear Maitland-Dougall
103rd and 102nd Bn.C.E.F.
Born April 4th 1898
Fell at Vimy Ridge April 9th 1917
Also
Lieut. William McKinstry Maitland-Dougall, RCN.
Born March 14th 1895
Killed on active service with his officers
and crew while in command of H.M.Sub *D3*, off Le Havre
March 12th 1918
"When thou passest through the waters, I will be with
thee ... When thou walkest through the fire,
thou shalt not be burned." Isa. 43.2.
"He went through fire and through waters ..." Ps. 66.2.

The plaque was dedicated on Sunday, 4 December 1921, at a small cere-mony. No one from the RCN attended, though the naval cadets from Esquimalt were invited.

Although Barney Johnson recorded nothing in his memoirs or his private notebooks about the tragic loss of *D3* and his shipmate, William Maitland-Dougall, he undoubtedly regretted the passing of his young friend. The scraps of personal notes that survive and the recollections of his WWII colleagues show Johnson to have been a sensitive man, who would have mourned deeply, but would not have allowed his grief to affect his duties.

In the closing months of the war Johnson and *E54* transferred to Portsmouth to join the RN's force that was waiting to intercept the German High Seas Fleet if they made a final sortie. However, the Germans stayed in port – immobilized by the near-mutiny of their crews – and *E54*'s patrols eased to vanishing point.

On 18 May, Johnson received an Admiralty letter announcing his appointment as senior officer in charge of *H14* and *H15*, two new boats that were being completed near Boston, U.S.A. These submarines were two of the twenty that Fisher ordered from Bethlehem Steel, and which President Wilson's stop-order had affected in 1915. When the States joined the war, work on the boats resumed and they were finished and released to Britain.

However, Johnson was ill and had to recover before picking up *H14* and *H15*. He was suffering from a stomach ulcer and partially collapsed lungs resulting from four years of appalling working conditions. Before taking sick leave in Canada, Johnson returned to Belfast, Ireland, for five days to say goodbye to his many firm friends. He played some golf and was wined and dined every evening. Johnson wrote that it was "a very sad parting."

On 1 June 1918 Johnson caught a ship in Liverpool bound for New York and luxuriated in the fine food served at every meal and the unbro-ken sleep he got every night. They sailed in a convoy with four other ships and an escort of six destroyers. Apart from one encounter with a U-boat, which the escorts depth-charged, Johnson had a quiet transatlantic crossing. Years later, in his unpublished memoirs, Johnson embellished this attack into a major engagement which the master of the passenger ship won. Records of the time prove otherwise.

Eleven days later they docked in New York. Johnson disembarked much refreshed, and was soon in touch with the American shipyard by telephone, to find out when the H boats would be ready for him. They told him to check back in about six weeks, so Johnson went straight home to Buccaneer Bay in the Gulf Islands of southern British Columbia to enjoy a long-overdue reunion with his wife and son, whom he had not seen in more than three years.

Five other Canadian submariners who had cut their teeth on *CC1* and *CC2* fought the war on the other side of the Atlantic too. Four served in home waters and one went to the Mediterranean. All survived the influenza epidemic of 1918 and some became commanding officers, but not before the Armistice.

Jock "Boy" Edwards, who had been the first midshipman on *CC2*, arrived at HMCS *Dolphin* in May 1917 to take his basic Submarine Officers' Training Course (three years late). Soon he was promoted to acting lieutenant and, after the obligatory time as a third hand, became first lieutenant of *E55* in the Eighth Flotilla based at Harwich. Edwards renewed his ties with his family, as well as with other Canadians who were with the Eighth. His sister vividly remembers her weekend visits to the submarine, where Jock greeted her, affecting a live white rat on his shoulder.

Edwards remained with *E55* for a year, operating briefly in the English Channel, but mostly in the North Sea on anti-submarine and surveillance patrols. He participated in several determined but unsuccessful attacks on U-boats, and when his boat went into refit in October 1918 he was selected for Perisher, the CO's course. Edwards did not take it immediately, but joined the R-class course designed to familiarize potential COs with the characteristics of the new hunter/killer submarines. Afterwards he took over an old gasoline-powered boat until his Perisher began.

Sub-Lieutenant Robert F. Lawson, RCN, followed in Maitland-Dougall's footsteps. The RCN transferred him to England after he showed interest in continuing in submarines while in *CC1* and he took his SOTC in April 1916. Lawson then became first lieutenant of *H10*, Maitland-Dougall's old boat, and patrolled in the North Sea. He saw submarines, Zeppelins, and enemy destroyers, but *H10* seldom attacked. By July 1917, the RN realized that Lawson, now an acting lieutenant, was not made of the right stuff to be a submariner and he was sent to the surface as unsuitable. His chronic seasickness, a series of below-average evaluations, and an illness all contributed to his departure. Lawson remained in the RCN as a career officer of no particular distinction. He died during World War II while serving in Montreal.

The third in the trio of submariners from the first graduating class of RNCC left for England in June 1916. Unlike Lawson, Sub-Lieutenant Ronald C. Watson, RCN, from Edmonton, thrived on responsibility. A clever, dedicated man, Watson easily passed his SOTC after nine months in the Canadian submarines and was quickly assigned to Brindisi in Italy as a spare officer attached to HMS *Adamant*. The three H boats and four older Bs of the Allied flotilla provided short anti-submarine patrols to control the Austro-Hungarian fleet in the Mediterranean. At first Watson performed administrative duties for the flotilla, staying mostly on land. But soon they moved to Venice, and at the beginning of November 1916 Watson became first lieutenant of *H2*, which was commissioned as the depot ship for *H1* and *H4*. Watson did well in this appointment, learning Italian to make his job easier. In March 1917 he joined *E11*, an operational submarine, and quickly rose to first lieutenant.

E11 was initially based in Malta and patrolled in the Ionian Sea. Later they worked in the Aegean off the Dardanelles in the hope of cutting off a German breakout. The numerous and effective enemy A/S patrols pursued Allied submarines relentlessly and the danger of mines was ever-present. It was a time of worry, frustration, and happiness for Watson. The sense that they were serving in a forgotten campaign, as well as the squabbles between the Allies, caused the frustration; the vigorous A/S patrols caused the worry; and an unusually attractive young woman was the reason for his happiness.

Aimée Fleury was Irish and appears to have been driving an ambulance in the Women's Auxiliary Corps in Italy, although this cannot be substantiated. She met Watson in Malta, where she was visiting her brother, a British naval officer. Watson was enchanted with Aimée, nicknaming her "Micky," and their friendship prospered under the warm Maltese sun. However, it was not all plain sailing for the young Canadian because Aimée had another sweetheart, with whom she had an understanding.

When *E11* went into refit in September 1917, Watson was lent to *E2* as her number one (first lieutenant) for three months, then did a brief spell of administrative work at Malta. In April 1918 Watson returned to England to take his Perisher, despite his lack of experience, but when it was delayed he went back as number one of *E11* for two months. *E11* went to Mudros in the Aegean but her patrols were short and uneventful. Watson finally got back to Britain and took his Perisher in August 1918, earning the right to call himself a submarine captain.

The RCN continued to produce young Canadian officers keen to go into submarines. Rupert Wood and Roy Beech, who had graduated from RNCC a year after Maitland-Dougall, Lawson, and Watson, also volunteered after serving in *CC1* and *CC2*.

Midshipman Rupert Wood, RCN, from Cowichan, British Columbia, did his SOTC in November 1916 and became the third hand of *D4* of the Third Flotilla at Immingham, when Johnson and Maitland-Dougall were there. *D4* sailed for Ireland with *D3* but saw few targets in the Western Approaches during the next year. Wood contracted syphilis at the end of 1917, but because of his good conduct and potential for command was allowed to stay in the submarine service. He was lucky; syphilis usually meant instant removal. It was not until Wood joined *E38* as her first lieutenant that he saw any action off Ireland. He participated in many spirited engagements with U-boats and experienced fire from the trigger-happy Allied ships. Wood stayed in *E38* till late 1919, accompanying her to the Clyde and to the Ninth Submarine Flotilla at Harwich. Then, after briefly serving in a big steam-driven K-class boat, he returned to Canada – without taking Perisher.

Wood's friend from the Canadian boats, W.J. "Roy" Beech, went with him to England and completed his SOTC in January 1917. He became the first lieutenant of *H9* in Great Yarmouth, and spent a quiet year operating in the North Sea. However, in January 1918 Great Yarmouth was bombarded by German ships, and the noise roused the crew of *H9*. They manned their boat and got her to sea in fifteen minutes, hoping to sink a few of the enemy. Sadly, they could not find them despite the good visibility, and *H9* was recalled at 0700. Later the officers and crew were commended for the smart manner in which *H9* got to sea. After joining the recently commissioned *L8* in 1918 as first lieutenant, Beech experienced his second enemy engagement with a U-boat in the English Channel, but they failed to sink her.

Beech remained with *L8* for six more months, during which time the Armistice was signed, and then spent a long leave in Canada to prepare for his next appointment. He was going to the China Station (the RN's base in the Far East), the only Canadian submariner to do so, and was about to get command of a boat without having taken Perisher.

CHAPTER EIGHT

HMCS *CC1* AND *CC2*, 1918

The first "clockwork mice"

By mid-1918, German U-boats were prowling around the coasts of Newfoundland and Nova Scotia and had even penetrated the Gulf of St. Lawrence, mining harbours and sinking ships. When the RCN realized that they had to respond to this unexpected threat, their first ASW effort was to deploy small patrol vessels armed with rifles. Later their eyes fell upon *CC1* and *CC2*.

At that time, the Canadian submarines were completing their lengthy refit in Halifax; by August, they were ready for service again. The submarines were not entirely restored to operational readiness standards – without new engines, that could not be done – but they were sufficiently rehabilitated to be used for training. Commander Bertram Jones, RN, now back from Bermuda with HMCS *Shearwater*, took overall command of the revived flotilla once more, with Hanson in command of *CC1* and Pitts in command of *CC2*. The Canadian Submarine Service was ready to help the RCN's first attempt at anti-submarine warfare.

Rifles quickly proved inadequate against the U-boats. The RCN issued five or six depth charges to each patrol vessel, and in early 1918 began to fit hydrophones to aid them in the location and prosecution of underwater targets. In its simplest form, a hydrophone was a microphone dropped over the side of a ship into the sea to listen for the sound of a submarine's propeller; it could indicate that a boat was present (detection), but was no help in ascertaining its position, range, course or speed (location). To locate the submarine, two or more vessels had to stop and listen together several times, taking cross bearings. This was difficult to coordinate, and both the tacticians and the listeners needed practice with a real submarine before they could hope to locate a U-boat with any accuracy, let alone sink one.

This was where the Canadian submarines came in – they became the targets for the patrol boats' ASW training. When the U-boat activity in Canadian waters intensified in August 1918, anti-submarine training became the RCN's first priority.[1] In a "MOST SECRET" memo, DNS ordered the flotilla to the Bras d'Or Lakes in Cape Breton, accompanied by HMCS *Shearwater,* to prepare for the hydrophone operators' training course. These salt-water lakes were ideal for classified activities, being well away from any naval base and safe from prying eyes.

Thus the first Canadian submarines became "clockwork mice" – beginning a tradition that still exists today.

CC1 and *CC2*'s involvement had two objectives. In addition to training the hydrophone operators as quickly as possible, the flotilla had to work up their submarine-versus-submarine tactics. After the courses the RCN planned to send the submarines out to the fishing grounds – to sink U-boats.

Following the refit, the Canadian Submarine Service was very short of experienced submariners; twenty-seven sailors had left the boats after the Panama passage. The RCN found that they could not replace them all. Those they did recruit had little naval training and no time in submarines. *CC2*, always the better boat, sailed to Cape Breton on 31 August, leaving the short-handed *CC1* behind in Halifax to follow when fully manned. Hanson, CO of *CC1,* rode *CC2* to give Pitts extra guidance for command. The faithful depot ship, *Shearwater,* went too. On 2 September 1918 they proceeded through the lock and canal into the Bras d'Or Lakes and on to Baddeck to commence their new operations.

Little is known about the submarines' time in the Bras d'Or Lakes from the naval point of view because the RCN files have been destroyed. However, tantalizing snippets from them were preserved in notes made by a naval historian in the 1960s. Most of the information available comes from the meticulously detailed diary kept by Alexander Graham Bell, who lived at Baddeck, and took a great interest in the hydrophone training and experiments. There is no proof he was actively assisting the RCN, but he certainly followed events closely.

Bell recorded the arrival of the flotilla on 2 September; he was delighted to discover, when he greeted Commander Jones, that he knew Jones's grandfather well. This happy note set the tone for the submarines' stay at Baddeck. There was a continuous flow of invitations between

Bell's household and the wardrooms, and at Bell's instigation the town provided entertainment and recreation for the ratings throughout their stay. Bell observed the hydrophone training from *Shearwater*, and even though it was very hush-hush he recorded everything in detail.

The courses started immediately. On 6 September 1918, Bell was clearly intrigued by the experience of being "torpedoed" by a submarine while on *Shearwater*. The evolution called for *CC2* to attack the depot ship while a patrol boat tried to locate the submarine. Bell kept a lookout for the torpedo, while others quartered the lake for a periscope. No one saw anything until the torpedo track was too close to avoid. It was a good shot, which came directly at the ship and would have hit her amidships had it not been set at a depth to pass underneath. Bell found it disconcerting to be torpedoed by a submarine that they knew was there, but could not find.

When Bell listened through the hydrophones in the afternoon, he heard a medley of submarine sounds that required interpretation. He heard the high-pitched sound of *CC2* moving underwater, the throb of a tug's engines, and other less differentiated noises from *Shearwater*'s machinery. Bell wrote that the primitive sonar could detect a submarine four miles (6.4 km) away.

Bell worked throughout September with the naval crews, experimenting with a variety of underwater detectors to improve their reception. Bell's notes strongly suggest that his involvement was planned, and that the RCN had asked him to assist.

The problems with *CC1*'s diesel engines were not entirely solved by her refit, and though she was scheduled to join her sister submarine in Baddeck on 22 October 1918, she did not. After just two months' training, *CC2* was abruptly recalled to Halifax on 31 October 1918. With only a few hours' notice, she came alongside the submarine depot on 4 November 1918. Neither submarine went to the fishing grounds to hunt U-boats.

The Admiralty then sent the boats into a care-and-maintenance routine, and ordered their crews to England. Two officers and thirty-one ratings volunteered to serve in Royal Navy submarines at this juncture, but when the Admiralty realized they were reservists, they refused them. The Armistice quickly followed, and the RCN demobilized the reservists, leaving a skeleton crew of ten regulars to decommission the boats.

While *CC1* and *CC2* returned to Halifax, a court of inquiry convened on 1 November 1918 in Sydney, Nova Scotia. One of the submarine officers had been accused of cowardice during the aftermath of the Halifax Explosion.

Gunner(T) George Brisco, RCN, who had been with *CC1* and *CC2* since August 1914, had made the accusation earlier in 1918. Brisco was an experienced electrician; Keyes and Jones regarded him highly, but he had earned his subordinates' intense dislike. He was a tough man brought up in the harsh discipline of the imperial fleet, and he enjoyed exercising his brand of authority over younger men. Two reliable sources state that he was a homosexual, who made the ratings' lives a misery if they repulsed his advances. For example, Brisco charged one young able seaman with eighteen offences during the Panama voyage – none stuck, but they nearly broke the sailor's spirit.

As the war progressed, Brisco became more and more convinced that he had been passed over for a commission from the ranks and the growing chip on his shoulder led him to a severe misjudgement. He penned his first request to become a lieutenant to Jones two weeks after the submarines arrived from Esquimalt. He wrote fluently, in a good hand, and drew attention to the impending submarine refit, which he felt he could more adequately supervise if he had an officer's status. After passing through channels, Brisco's request was denied. Miffed, but defiant, the gunner began a campaign of correspondence with no less than the director of the Naval Service himself.

By April 1918, Admiral Kingsmill was thoroughly exasperated with Brisco's attempts to pressure and threaten him and wrote that he should be "brought up with a round turn" (a round turn is a naval knot; the figure of speech is a naval term for a rebuke). Brisco's irritation and frustration increased until he decided to tender his resignation.

One morning in August Brisco's anger erupted and he presented himself, cap and resignation in hand, to Commander Jones and requested permission to speak to him. Jones inquired what was troubling him and Brisco complained that his services to the RCN had not been properly recognized. He rambled incoherently in his attempt to explain and justify his resignation; he then made an accusation of cowardice against Lieutenant Pitts, claiming he had deserted during the Halifax Explosion. Jones stopped Brisco, and called in Hanson and Pitts as witnesses to the statement. The gunner repeated his allegations, adding that he felt compelled to make them because Pitts had just been appointed to command of *CC2* and he thought he was unfit. Jones immediately charged Brisco with making false charges against Pitts and placed him under arrest pending a court martial. In the end Brisco was not court-martialled, but was charged with the lesser offence of making insinuations tending to injure the character of an officer. Before proceeding further, Jones gave Brisco the chance to retract his statements and apologize, but he refused. As Brisco had waited for eight months after the explosion to make his accusation and had recently been denied a commission, it seems likely that he was using Pitts to get back at the system.

As punishment, and in the presence of all the submarine officers, Jones logged Brisco for his conduct and expressed the RCN's complete confidence in Lieutenant Pitts. Jones also made his own addition to the ship's log: "There is no ground whatever, on which Lieut. Pitts RCNVR [sic] can be charged with improper conduct on Dec. 6th."[2] Then Jones asked for Brisco to be removed from the submarine service.

Brisco's reprimand only served to inflame him more; he persisted with his quest for "fairness" – on his terms. He twice nagged for a court martial, which he hoped would clear his name, and when his efforts were unsuccessful, discovered a regulation that allowed him to appeal directly to DNS for an investigation into Pitts's alleged cowardice. This avenue, Brisco believed, would restore his reputation. Later in the month, DNS ordered a court of inquiry into the affair.

Although the details of the inquiry are missing from the files, the conclusions are contained in a memorandum from the Naval Service headquarters to the Halifax Dockyard. The RCN wrote:

> It is regretted that the Finding of the Court of Enquiry is most inconclusive. The first paragraph is almost contradictory in that the Court finds, "the statement of Mr. Brisco is materially correct" and goes on to add that "the insinuations against Lieutenant Pitts are unjustifiable."
>
> [Brisco] is to be informed that his transfer from the submarine service was in no way a disgrace to him and no reflection on his professional conduct.[3]

Brisco was given the opportunity to rescind his resignation from the navy and he did so immediately, but he never returned to *CC1* and *CC2*. He also asked that the entry made in the log, with regard to his misconduct, be removed. It was not.

Brisco was unsatisfied with the board's findings and, because he still desperately wanted his commission, he continued to pester the RCN after he was demobbed threatening to give information to the press about the events surrounding the explosion and demanding apologies from all the officers. Of course, Brisco got nothing from the navy, as far as can be deduced from the records, but he probably received much sympathy from his cronies.

The nasty affair had no impact on Pitts's reserve career whatsoever, but certainly affected the man himself. His family members could throw no light on the episode because Pitts had never told them about it, which is not surprising. However, Pitts did demonstrate mixed feelings about his time in the first Canadian submarines: to his wife he presented a picture of enjoyment, humour and activity, but talking man to man with his nephew, Pitts made it clear that there were times he disliked the life. The incident with Brisco had undoubtedly left a very nasty taste in his mouth.

"Take off that damned coat!" growled a grim-faced, elderly man to Lt.-Commander Barney Johnson. It was a blisteringly hot and humid day when Johnson collected his new orders from the British naval attaché in Washington, D.C. Finding him seated in his underwear in front of a block of ice, Johnson quickly obeyed his suggestion.

Barney Johnson had recovered his health quickly in B.C. and declared himself fit after only two weeks of leave. In late July he reported to the Naval Service in Ottawa before travelling to the States to accept the new submarines, *H14* and *H15,* for the Admiralty.

Seated in his undershirt with his sword on the floor, Johnson put a proposition to the attaché. He had worked out a plan to retaliate against the U-boats operating around the Azores and the Canary Islands while delivering the boats to England. The attaché listened attentively and approved the plan in principle, with the condition that Johnson consult him again before he sailed. Satisfied, Johnson returned to the shipyard near Boston the same day, keen to get the sea trials started.

Johnson commanded the flotilla and *H15,* and a British lieutenant had *H14.* The boats' sea trials were bedevilled by delays, and though the submarines were commissioned in the last two weeks of August they were not ready to depart for England until November. In late October Johnson returned to Washington to get the final approval of his plan for the voyage to England and discovered that he had to report to New London, the big USN submarine base in Connecticut, for further orders.

The orders were not what Johnson wanted to hear – he was to take the flotilla to Bermuda to await further instructions. His plan to harass U-boats met serious opposition and Johnson eventually gave up the idea when he learned that the war was nearly over.

The little flotilla left New York on 9 November in appalling weather, and when the submarines reached Bermuda Johnson learned that the war had ended the day before. Commander Jones, CO of HMCS *Shearwater,* who had just arrived, offered the familiar tender's facilities to *H14* and *H15* and Johnson gratefully accepted. The two friends reminisced late into the night over many glasses of rum and caught up with three years worth of news – *H8*'s escape from the mine, *CC1* and *CC2*'s Panama Canal voyage, and *E54*'s "kill."

The Armistice caught *H14* and *H15* out and they stayed in Bermuda where they were paid off in December. Johnson, afraid that he would be forgotten there, asked to be demobilized, but the Admiralty denied his request. Mid-December 1918 found him and his crews on board the cruiser HMS *Cornwall,* sailing across the cold, grey north Atlantic, to England and Christmas at HMS *Dolphin.*

On arrival in England, Johnson was promoted to commander and put in charge of captured and surrendered U-boats before they were distributed to the Allies. It was dull work for the most part but it was alleviated by an invitation to Buckingham Palace: at last, Johnson was to receive the DSO that he had won in 1917. A proud moment, but one that he never talked about.

Johnson was demobilized in April 1919, long after most of his reserve contemporaries. However, instead of going straight home, he took his eight-week terminal leave in England, annoying both his wife and his employer, the Pilotage Authority, who did not understand his motives. Johnson found it hard to tear himself away from the submarine fraternity, so full of friendships forged in adversity; he dreaded having to be a small cog in a big wheel again; and, he simply needed more "re-entry" time.

When he got back to Vancouver, Barney Johnson did indeed find civilian life difficult. He soon chafed at his work at the Pilotage Authority, even when he became superintendent and discovered that nothing could truly replace the exhilaration of submarine command. In 1920 Johnson started a shipping business of his own – it suited his independent spirit more – and it became a success. He served his king and country again in World War II in the RCNR, but not in submarines, and lived in robust health till the age of ninety. He was buried at sea off Vancouver in 1968, mourned by his many shipmates and friends.

Twelve Canadian naval officers had joined a new elite that came of age in the First World War – the submariners. They had proved the value of their boats, and served with dedication. Johnson, the reservist, had achieved his place in the service with no formal training course of any kind and had performed as well as any regular naval officer, setting a precedent for the future. Many submariners will be remembered for their part in the birth of the Canadian Submarine Service in the CC boats in Esquimalt, and most of the Canadian submariners would have agreed with Johnson's summation: that the submarine service was a "college and a star to steer by."

Four officers who got their start in *CC1* and *CC2* remained with Royal Navy submarines after the war. Lieutenants Jock Edwards, Rupert Wood, Ronald Watson, and Roy Beech were joined by three more officers: Valentine Godfrey, Richard Oland, and Colin Donald did their basic submarine training at the end of the war, but were too late to see an operational patrol. All but Edwards were career officers and had graduated from RNCC.

Edwards earned his command in May 1919 and took over *R1* based on HMS *Vulcan* at Blyth on the northeast coast of England. He soon began to lose interest in submarines as his worries increased about the deteriorating condition of the family estate. With no money of his own to renovate it, he sensibly chose a wife who could reverse the family fortunes. He married Nora in October 1919, as he took over as officer in charge of the reserve fleet of R boats in Rosyth. Edwards remained in the navy for only five more months and resigned his temporary commission in the RCN in April 1920. He settled down on his estate without returning to Canada and became a typical country gentleman with gundogs running at his heels. Edwards served in the Royal Navy again in World War II, but not in submarines.

When Ronald Watson returned from the Mediterranean in September 1918, he took the R-class course with Edwards as well as Perisher six months later. Watson was slow to grasp the essentials at first but he rapidly improved, going to *R2* as her captain when he passed. As soon as he got some leave, Watson went to Dublin to rekindle his relationship with the beautiful Aimée whom he had met in Malta, and was successful, her sweetheart having died. They decided to marry in August 1920 in Dublin.

Though not of the same intellect as Maitland-Dougall, Watson was one of the best officers to come out of RNCC's first term of cadets. He was a sound and hard working submarine officer who showed ability all through his career. After he had driven *R2* for five months, she was mothballed, and Watson did a month of duties with the reserve Rs. Then he got the pleasure of standing by *H44* at the end of her construction, preparatory to her commissioning in March 1920. Sadly for the

Canadian, *H44* went straight into reserve at Portland and Watson barely went to sea. When the RCN unexpectedly recalled him to Canada for the recommissioning of the Canadian submarines, Watson and Aimée changed their wedding plans, choosing to marry in Halifax, surrounded by friends but not family.

Lt. Rupert Wood, RCN, who was the first lieutenant of *E38* through the Armistice to the end of 1919, moved to *H27,* and then to a group of submarines in reserve. He spent a short time in Canada, assisting in an inspection of the Canadian submarines and then returned to the RN to serve on *K8* until the fall of 1920, when he returned to Canada permanently. The RCN was gathering her own into the fold in preparation for the brief second commission of her own submarines.

Lt. William Beech, RCN, was one of only two Canadian submariners who were not called home in 1920. He became the first lieutenant of *L1,* which was bound for the Far East. They sailed with their depot ship, HMS *Titania,* in October 1919 via the Mediterranean, Suez, Ceylon, and Singapore. The voyage lasted six months, and was filled with new sights, sounds, and smells. Beech took full advantage of the experience, going ashore and exploring on foot whenever he could. His favourite pastimes included going out for dinner with friends and amateur dramatics.

In Hong Kong the submarine flotilla participated in fleet exercises and competitions before dispersing to show the flag and get away from the stifling humidity. Beech began to gain his confidence after his arrival in the Far East and he rapidly became a very good officer. He took command of *L1* in an acting capacity in September 1920 and did well, showing an ability to make good judgements and to get the job done. "I am not in this to be popular, but to do my duty," he used to say.

Lieutenant Beech did not stay on the China Station for the whole commission – the RCN brought him back to Canada in February 1921, after *L1* had gone into a brief care-and-maintenance routine. Although he had been driving *L1,* Beech was not command-qualified and he asked to do his Perisher. His request was denied, however, because by then the RCN was fighting for its existence in the face of severe cutbacks, and had been forced to get out of the submarine business.

Beech went to the surface after a stint at RNCC and continued serving in Canada and Britain. He returned to submarines very briefly in 1935 when he served as staff officer, operations, for the First Flotilla in the Mediterranean. Beech eventually retired in 1945 as a captain after commanding HMCS *Naden* in Esquimalt.

Sub-Lt. Valentine S. Godfrey, RCN, completed his SOTC ten days before the Armistice and, though he did poorly, the RN passed him. At *Dolphin*, released from the restraints of the college and home, Godfrey had begun to sample the joys of life and his fast life-style soon affected his performance.

At the beginning of 1919 he joined his first of four submarines. His record in all of them was dismal – he was often drunk, was lacking in essential knowledge, and did not do his job. By the end of 1920 Godfrey had sunk as low as he could and the RN had had enough. They shipped him back to Canada in disgrace on half pay and let the RCN deal with him in July 1921. This treatment appears to have had its effect and subsequent appraisals showed a steady improvement in young Godfrey's performance in Canadian ships. In less than a year he was making progress in leadership and command, as well as displaying gentlemanly behaviour.

It would be a great injustice to Valentine Godfrey to leave the impression that he remained a poor naval officer. He went on to have a long and distinguished career in the Canadian navy, with two mentions in dispatches and an OBE. He retired in 1952 as a commodore.

Lt. Richard H. Oland, RCN, from a prominent Nova Scotian family, became an outstanding submariner after his big ship time. Known for his congeniality, he graduated from the Naval College in Halifax in 1915 with academic honours and an armful of athletic awards. Oland finished his SOTC when peace was declared and appears to have done his sea training in several submarines in a flotilla at Portsmouth. Within four months, he was appointed first lieutenant of *R8*, relieving his fellow Canadian, Ronald Watson. *H30* followed and he served on her for nearly a year until February 1920 when the submarine was sent to the Baltic.

The renowned Captain(S) Max Horton, RN, wrote a remarkable testimony about Oland's abilities, saying that the young Canadian was the best first lieutenant in the flotilla. Oland had the gift of natural leadership, which inspires high performance and loyalty from subordinates; he was also a natural shiphandler. While Oland was working so hard, he was also courting his future wife; neither activity seems to have been to the detriment of the other.

After marrying in February 1920, Oland moved to *H51* in June for two months, and then joined *H34* at Portsmouth as her first lieutenant. He continued to perform superbly and the RN earmarked him for early command. *H34* had the distinction of being the best submarine in the Atlantic Fleet in 1921 and the RCN was quick to publicize this success, noting in the press release that Oland was largely responsible.

Despite Oland's ability to command and his superiors' strong recommendations, he never took Perisher, but remained *H34*'s Number One for two years. It seems almost inconceivable that such a good officer would not be granted an early opportunity to take the Commanding Officers' Qualifying Course, but Canada would not foot the bill, having suspended all submarine training to reduce naval spending. Oland plugged on through it all, but he must have been very disappointed.

In April of 1921 the RCN tasked Oland to recruit British ratings for the Canadian submarines, which could not be manned from within the Canadian navy. He probably would have found them easily, but the RN abruptly stopped the poaching.

At the end of 1922 the RCN reclaimed Oland, although by this time they had no submarines left in their fleet. Oland continued to serve until 1928 as a career officer and until 1930 as a reservist, when he resigned his commission. In 1941, he died suddenly in his bed, aged forty-four, two months after being decorated by King George VI with an OBE. Oland, a captain, had been back in the navy running the Naval Control of Shipping organization in Halifax.

The last Canadian officer of this era to volunteer for submarines was Colin Donald, another resident of British Columbia. "Do" (pronounced "Doe") as he was called, joined the submarine service in 1920 while a sub-lieutenant, served in the K-class submarines, and never got as far as first lieutenant. The RCN claimed him for a short period on the recommissioned submarines and by 1923 Donald's career in boats was over.

CHAPTER NINE

HMCS *CH14* AND *CH15*, 1919–1922

"Not very desirable acquisitions"[1]

The Royal Navy's submarines *H14* and *H15*, which Johnson had taken as far as Bermuda, sat in a care-and-maintenance routine for several months, and it looked as if the Admiralty was going to let them rot there. Then they came up with the novel idea of giving them to Canada as a pat on the back for all they had done over the past four years. The prime minister, Sir Robert Borden, gratefully accepted them on 7 February 1919 without apparently consulting the RCN. If he had, he would have been told that submarines were the last thing the navy wanted – they had neither the trained crews to man them nor the money to operate them.

The final blow came when the RCN learned that they had to provide crews and collect *H14* and *H15* from Bermuda at their own expense. The assistant DNS commented angrily that four submarines would be too much for the RN. Two months later, Admiral Kingsmill, DNS, informed the PM for the second time that the boats were undesirable and asked him to get the Admiralty to take them back. Borden chose not to comply with the navy's wishes because he thought the British gesture had been generous rather than expedient.

The RCN instituted delaying tactics, because they wanted to leave the boats in Bermuda until they could cope. By April, the Admiralty was getting annoyed and this sparked a third proposal to get Britain to take the boats back. Nothing came of it and *H14* and *H15* were destined for Canada and to become a millstone around the RCN's neck.

The options available to the RCN regarding their increased submarine fleet were simple. They could either keep them all in commission at an annual price of $145,000 or put any or all of them in reserve at a cost of $20,000 to $75,000 per year. Kingsmill reluctantly approved keeping the more modern Hs in commission and the CCs in reserve to maintain the training of the Canadian submariners. Shortly afterwards, DNS had a change of heart and wrote, "It is simply a waste of public money to have anything more to do with submarines at the present stage of development of Canada's Navy."[2] This memo of Kingsmill's rang the death knell of the fledgling Canadian Submarine Service, although the funeral did not actually occur for several years.

In May 1919 *H14* arrived in Halifax and, by mid-June, *H15* was on her way to Canada with a skeleton crew and Lt. George Edwardes, RNCVR, in command. The official presentation to Canada took place without ceremony after both had arrived. The submarines were renamed, in the same fashion as the first Canadian boats, by placing a "C" for Canada in front of the "H."

Edwardes, the volunteer reservist who remained in the RCN after the Armistice, inspected *CH14* and *CH15* on their arrival and reported them in good condition with a few minor defects. He gladly accepted the boring task of maintaining Canada's third and fourth submarines until the RCN recalled a regular submarine officer from Britain.

By November 1919 the RCN's predictions were proved right: they decided to lay up the four submarines. *CH14* and *CH15* were not docked to repair their defects as they should have been and a small care-and-maintenance party kept an eye on them. Just before Christmas the newer boats received a reprieve – the government decided to keep them going until they had formulated a new naval policy. The CC boats, however, remained laid up until their disposal, but *CH14* and *CH15* were to venture to sea again weekly and exercise briefly in the summer of 1921.

Canada's first submarines, *CC1* and *CC2*, reverted from the Admiralty's wartime control to that of the RCN in December 1918. They were advertised for sale in July 1920; bids eventually crept up and in October the boats were sold for scrap along with the old cruiser, HMCS *Niobe*, for $135,000. No one felt it was a good price, even though the vessels were worn out and in poor condition.

The donated submarines, *CH14* and *CH15*, emerged from their mothballs at the same time. Lt. Ronald Watson returned from England in July 1920 to take command of the flotilla, relieving Edwardes, when the RCN decided to reactivate the boats in a limited way. They were to be in commission in reserve, which meant that the submarines would go to sea once a week and practise diving once a month with a reduced crew. In reality, even this tasking proved too much for the flotilla. Finding ratings was the chief stumbling-block and the RCN attempted to procure them from England using Oland as the recruiter.

As soon as Watson realized that *CH14* and *CH15* could not go to sea with the sailors available, he concentrated on renovating the submarine shore depot. By December 1920 it was ready to accommodate the crews and to receive equipment for repairs and maintenance. A few former RN submarine ratings, who had responded to Oland's advertisements in the British newspapers before the RN stopped the recruitment, moved into the depot with the small flotilla staff. There were still too few to prepare the boats for sea, even though *CH14* and *CH15* had been docked the previous summer at Watson's behest. The batteries and engines still needed major work.

On Commissioning Day, 1 April 1921, only thirteen sailors of the nearly fifty required were present – the RCN's recruiting throughout Canada had been a failure. However, the flotilla had sufficient qualified officers as the RCN recalled them from the Royal Navy in time. In addition to Watson, Lieutenant Wood had arrived to take command of *CH14,* and Lieutenants Donald (*CH14*) and Godfrey (*CH15*) became the first lieutenants. Watson remained in command of the flotilla and took over *CH15.*

In the end, the flotilla recruited the crews themselves and managed to locate seven men with submarine experience. The remainder were landlubbers from central Canada who had never been to sea or seen a submarine. The officers trained the rookies every evening in the shore depot when the day's work was over, in much the same way as Keyes had taught the crews of *CC1* and *CC2.*

The crews laboured for over two months to make the boats operational again, reinstalling the batteries and replacing the periscopes. *CH15* was tested first in June, diving alongside initially and taking no chances with her neophyte crew. Later she submerged safely in the harbour. *CH14* was then brought up to speed and test-dived. She was operational by July. Up until then, the crews and officers had not been assigned to a particular boat but, after *CH15*'s trials, the two crews separated.

CH14 and *CH15* spent a busy summer and fall, with exercises and port visits in Canadian waters. The major event of their second commission was a combined exercise with the Army and Air Force in August 1921. This exercise simulated the defence of Halifax during a period of increasing tension and then following the outbreak of war. *CH14* and

CH15 were part of the enemy forces trying to attack the port. On the first day, the submarines were on station outside Halifax to observe shipping movements while being sought by the aircraft. The boats saw ships and aircraft but avoided detection.

"War" was declared that night and, during the second day, *CH15* attacked a "convoy" heading into Halifax. At 1605 the lookout sighted smoke and at 1630 Watson identified the "enemy." *CH15* dived and commenced an attack on a zigzagging vessel. He fired a torpedo at 1735 but missed because they were too far away. *CH15* was not detected by her target, although she had been seen by one aircraft which had been unable to alert the threatened vessel. The flotilla returned to port, satisfied with their performance, and spent the following afternoon at "make and mend," the navy's equivalent of a half-holiday.

In September, Watson set a plan in motion for the submarines to winter in Bermuda, and the navy approved it to minimize the effects of a harsh Halifax winter on the boats. The little flotilla sailed for St. George's on 21 November in company with HMS *Wisteria*, arriving six days later. The stay on the island was not demanding – the boats exercised together on week days, there were four weeks when *CH14* and *CH15* did not leave harbour at all, and another month when the boats were docked. Rupert Wood found time to marry a girl from Nova Scotia and others took in the sights and the bars. *CH14* and *CH15* returned to Halifax in April.

Within a few weeks the flotilla personnel learned that *CH14* and *CH15* were to be laid up permanently. Although the submarines had escaped the knacker's yard, the government had refused to approve the annual $143,800 to keep them operating. However, their action effectively put RCN out of the submarine game.

After a month of preparation, the boats were in immaculate condition when they were paid off in June 1922. The RCN dispersed the ratings throughout the diminishing Canadian surface fleet and sent Wood into intelligence, Godfrey to the surface, and Donald back to the RN in *K6* for six months.

Watson returned to England for a year to take the Physical and Recreational Training Officers' Course and afterwards became the first lieutenant of HMCS *Naden* in Esquimalt. Tragically, in July 1924, Watson and Aimée were drowned off Albert Head near Victoria while teaching three boy seamen to sail in a whaler. The couple were competent small boat sailors and cool-headed, but something went badly wrong and, despite their efforts to right the capsized boat, the frigid waters of the

Pacific claimed them all.[3] Only Aimée was found and she was buried in the Veterans' Cemetery at HMCS *Naden* where her grave can still be seen today. The Watsons left two orphans – Gordon, a toddler of two and a half, and Barbara, a baby of ten months.

The new director of the Naval Service, Commodore Walter Hose, RCN (Kingsmill having retired), took a great interest in *CH14* and *CH15* and hoped to get them back into commission. In 1923 Hose asked Wood to undertake a detailed inspection to estimate the work that would be needed to get them operational again. Wood's report showed how fast the boats had deteriorated in just over a year – the casings needed replacement and most of their battery cells were unserviceable. He concluded that the old CH boats would be satisfactory for training, but little else. The cost to refit *CH14* and *CH15* was $150,000.

The submarines were never revitalized – they remained snugged down, all but forgotten, for another couple of years. In February 1925 the Admiralty inquired about their condition and learned that there was little probability of their being of further service. A year later the RCN suggested disposing of *CH14* and *CH15*, along with HMCS *Aurora*. The Admiralty approved, as long as the boats were broken up and they received the proceeds of the sale. Officially the Canadian Submarine Service disbanded on 9 March 1927 when the order-in-council was signed ordering the sale of the last two boats.

Of course, the service had been effectively killed five years before. The RCN had no operational boats and had not been training any submariners with the Royal Navy since June 1922. The revival of the CH boats had been short-lived and an exercise in futility – the navy simply could not afford them, and because of that viewed them as nuisances. No senior officers could conceive of another world war only seventeen years away.

The first Canadian Submarine Service was born of desperate necessity on the eve of the Great War and *CC1* and *CC2* did stalwart duty as deterrents on the west coast of Canada. Although the rookie submariners never saw an enemy, they worked hard in primitive conditions with unreliable boats and achieved an almost impossible journey of 7,000 miles to the east coast. *CH14* and *CH15* gave a glimmer of what might be possible, but a shortage of funds extinguished it. Perhaps more important, the infant service produced several outstanding submariners for the RN's submarine operations. All were hardy, disciplined, and daring. One gave his life.

But the newly acquired Canadian submarine expertise did not end with the officers and crews. Shipbuilders in Montreal built submarines, with speed and efficiency, for Britain, Russia, and Italy; their counterparts in Vancouver built six more for Russia.

The First World War provided Canada with a legacy of knowledge to build and man submarines, but the country turned her back on it. The Canadian Submarine Service did not survive its assassination by the government in even the remotest sense. With the Canadian boats gone, the RCN made no attempt to preserve the small pool of submarine experience. They returned the qualified submariners to the surface and did not permit any to continue their careers in Royal Navy submarines. The shipyards built no more boats. When World War II broke out, the RCN had no submarines or qualified personnel available to train her burgeoning surface fleet in anti-submarine warfare. It was a monumental oversight, because the Royal Navy could not spare any boats for the bereft Canadians for two years.

However, the last word should be given to the Canadian submariners of the Great War – they led the way and set the example for the RCN's second "Silent Service." Commodore Sam Hall, RN, who commanded the British submarines, said of them all:

> Your steadiness and your grit, whilst the toll of your gallant fellows was heavy, have been beyond all praise ... You have established a magnificent record of strenuous and gallant service ... [You] leave the war with a record as proud as any.

CC1 and *CC2* at the time of their purchase in 1914. They were originally built for Chile by the Seattle Dry Dock and Construction Company.

DND/NAC PA-113254

The father of the Canadian Submarine Service, Sir Richard McBride, who as premier of British Columbia bought *CC1* and *CC2* in 1914 without federal authority.

B.C. Archives and Record Service #3273

Lt. Henry B. Pilcher, RN, suffered a nervous breakdown from the stress of authorizing the purchase of the first Canadian submarines.
B.C. Archives and Record Service #16857

Thomas A. Brown accompanied William Logan to Seattle to bring *CC1* and *CC2* to B.C. on 4 August 1914. He left an able seaman in the RNCVR and returned as a sub-lieutenant .
Brown collection

Lt. B.L. "Barney" Johnson, RNCVR, began WWI
as a civilian advising the RCN
on navigation and later became the first reservist
to command a submarine in the RN.
Vancouver City Archives

Lt. Bertram Jones, RN (right), inspected *CC1* and
CC2 before their purchase and commanded
CC2. Midshipman J.G. "Jock" Edwards, RCN,
joined *CC2* in 1914.
Pitts collection

Lt. Adrian St.V. Keyes, RN, a pioneer submariner
from Britain, was the first commanding officer of
CC1 and the flotilla.
DND/NAC E-48718

The crew of *CC2* in 1914 in Esquimalt. L to R, rear: L/Stkr. Dick Warner; Stkr. PO Roberts; LTO John Moulder; AB "Shorty" Lock; Stkr. "Simmo" Simmons; Stkr. Finmore. Middle: Stkr. "Ginger" Lee; AB Herrod; Stkr. Tom Flannigan; unknown torpedoman; LS Foreman; Stkr. Jack Sutherland. Front: ERA R. Pearson; PO G. Purvis (Coxswain); Lt. "Barney" Johnson, RNCVR (first lieutenant) with his dog; Mid. "Jock" Edwards, RCN; CERA John Hunting; ERA P. Conroy. Note: Johnson, although a reservist, is wearing the straight stripes of a regular because Esquimalt had no wavy stripes to issue.
DND/NAC PA-142539

Lt. Arthur C.S. "Panther" Pitts, RNCVR, joined *CC1* in 1915 and later commanded her.
Pitts collection

Longitudinal section of *CC1* showing the main compartments. From the stern: engine room, after battery and control room, the forward battery or accommodation space, and the fore-ends.

Control room in CC class with the search periscope raised to show detail. L to R: aft and forward hydroplane hand wheels; low pressure (LP) vent and blow manifold; LP gauge panel; helm; conning tower ladder; the door to forward battery compartment.

Ferguson collection

Fore-ends in *CC1* showing the four torpedo-tube doors (there were only two in *CC2*). On left is a cradle for a reload.

Ferguson collection

The first submariners used this apparatus for escape training in the local swimming pool and after two successful "escapes" were considered qualified.

HMCS *Shearwater*, the submarines' tender, with *CC1* and *CC2* alongside, at Esquimalt.

H6-H10 fitting out in Montreal in May/June 1915. HMS *Carnavon* is in the dry dock in the background.
Royal Navy Submarine Museum #7772

The delivery crew of *H8* in Halifax before their transatlantic passage in July 1915. Lt. B.L. Johnson, RNR (CO), is seated on the left.
Royal Navy Submarine Museum

HMS/M *H8* leaving Great Yarmouth on her first war patrol in December 1915.
Vancouver City Archives

H8 arriving in Harwich after hitting a mine in the North Sea on 22 March 1916. The explosion blew off most of her bow exposing the torpedoes' firing pistols, shattering her fore-planes, and destroying a main ballast tank and a trim tank.

The crew of *D3* (Johnson) with Sub-Lt. "Willie" Maitland-Dougall, RCN, first lieutenant (centre).

The combined crews of *CC1* and *CC2* marching in the Independence Day parade in San Diego, 4 July 1917, en route to Halifax.
Pitts collection

CC1 in the Mirafiores lock during the transit of the Panama Canal. Taken from the bridge of *CC2*, 12 August 1917.
Ferguson collection

The combined crews of *CC1* and *CC2* in Halifax after their difficult passage from the west coast, 14 October 1917. Lt. Hanson is standing on the bridge with his hands in his pockets and Lt. Pitts is on his right.
B.C. Archives and Record Service #15047

The two brothers, Hamish and Willie Maitland-Dougall, together for the last time in Sussex on 10 August 1916.

Williams collection

Lt. Ronald C. Watson, RCN, was the only Canadian submariner in the Great War to serve in the Mediterranean. He later commanded *CH15*.

Beaty collection

Gunner(T) George Brisco accused Pitts of cowardice during the Halifax Explosion of December 1917.

Detail from B.C. Archives and Record Service #15046

Sub-Lt. W.J.R. "Roy" Beech, RCN, served in RN L-class submarines on the China Station after his apprenticeship in the CC boats.

May collection

Lt. Richard H. Oland, RCN, was an outstanding early Canadian submariner who never had the chance to take Perisher.

Oland collection

Lt. Colin "Do" Donald, RCN, first lieutenant and later CO of *CH14*, 1921–22.

Ferguson collection

CH14 and *CH15* dressed overall during their first and last RCN commission, 1920–22.

Ferguson collection

The crew of *CH14* at Halifax, c. August 1921.
Young collection

Ronald and Aimée Watson perished in a boating accident in 1924. His body was never found but Aimée was buried in the Veterans' Cemetery, HMCS *Naden*, Esquimalt, B.C.
Julie H. Ferguson

HMS/M *Sealion* was the first of three S-class submarines in which Sherwood served with distinction.
Sherwood collection

The crew of *P34* in late 1942 with their Jolly Roger, which shows they had sunk four ships and two U-boats and rescued fourteen survivors (Italian). Lt. E. Keith Forbes, RCNVR, is at lower right.
Forbes collection

Near Sousse, North Africa, HMS/M *Safari* sinks (by gunfire) an Italian brigantine carrying supplies to Rommel's forces in North Africa.
Royal Navy Submarine Museum

The Canadian charioteers – Lt. C.E. (Chuck) Bonnell, RCNVR (left), and Lt. Alan Moreton, RCNVR – at Loch Erisort, Scotland, in 1942.
Ferguson collection

A chariot on the surface.
Imperial War Museum #22114

A charioteer dressed for a raid. Note the valve on the top of the helmet used for trimming, the tight elastic bands on the wrists, and bare hands.
Ferguson collection

Diagram of a Mark I human torpedo.
Janet Bell (taken from a variety of sources)

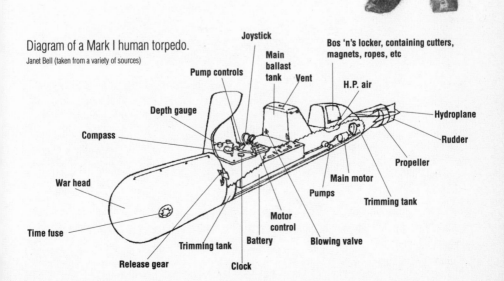

Joystick
Main ballast tank
Vent
Pump controls
Bos 'n's locker, containing cutters, magnets, ropes, etc
H.P. air
Depth gauge
Hydroplane
Compass
Rudder
Propeller
War head
Main motor
Pumps
Main motor
Trimming tank
Time fuse
Motor control
Battery
Blowing valve
Release gear
Trimming tank
Clock

The Dutch boat *O15* was the first "clockwork mouse" loaned by Britain in WWII to train the RCN's surface fleet in ASW.
Roosjen collection

LS Arthur H. Hardy, RCNVR, served as *O15*'s signalman. He is seated on the right of Princess Juliana of the Netherlands during her visit to *O15* at Pictou, N.S.
Capt. Van Oostrom Soede, RNN, collection

HMS/M *P553*, a U.S. lend-lease submarine, was used as a tame submarine in Canadian waters, August 1943.
Perry collection

Submarine officers' residence, Pictou, N.S.
E.A.D. Holmes collection

The four U-class A/S training submarines at Digby, N.S., 1945. L to R: HMS/Ms *Unseen*, *Unruffled*, *United*, and *Upright*.
McPhee collection

HMS/M *Unseen* (Cross) was seconded to the RCAF to provide ASW training to the flight crews; seen here in the Bay of Fundy in May 1945.
Royal Navy Submarine Museum

Lt. Jack A. Cross, RCNVR, while serving in *P512*, at Pictou, N.S.
Cross collection

Lt. E.A.D. "Uncle" Holmes, RNVR, in *P512*. A Canadian himself, Holmes later commanded the two U-boats which surrendered to Canadian forces.
E.A.D. Holmes collection

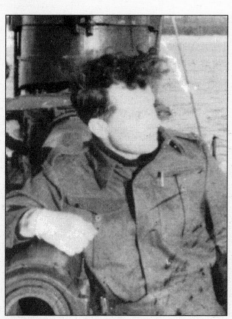

Lt. Colin W. Perry, RCNVR, in *P553* in the spring of 1943. Perry was on hand to capture a U-boat off New Brunswick.
Perry collection

Walt Disney drew an unofficial crest for HMS/M *P556* (Sherwood). The boat's nickname was the *Reluctant Dragon*.
Sherwood collection

Lt. Fred Fowler, RCNVR, on the bridge of HMS/M *Sceptre* in 1944.
Fowler collection

Lt. W. (Bill) Gilmour, RCNVR, on the Clyde in 1943 while the torpedo officer on *H33*.
Gilmour collection

Sceptre's target breaks her back after the torpedo exploded. Photographed through the periscope in the summer of 1944.
Fowler collection

Lt. Richard Blake, RCNVR, in HMS/M *Truculent* in December 1944.

Fowler collection

Lt. Fred Bunbury, RCNVR, in charge of the Shallow Water Diving Unit at Gibraltar, 1944. Although the water temperature never exceeded 15°C, the team did not wear diving suits, just the Davis Submarine Escape Apparatus and gloves.

Bunbury collection

Sub-Lt. John Gardner, RCNVR, on watch in HMS/M *Unswerving* in the Mediterranean in 1944.

Gardner collection

Lt. Johnnie Ruse, RCNVR, CO of the midget submarines *XT6*, *X21*, and *XE8*.

Ruse collection

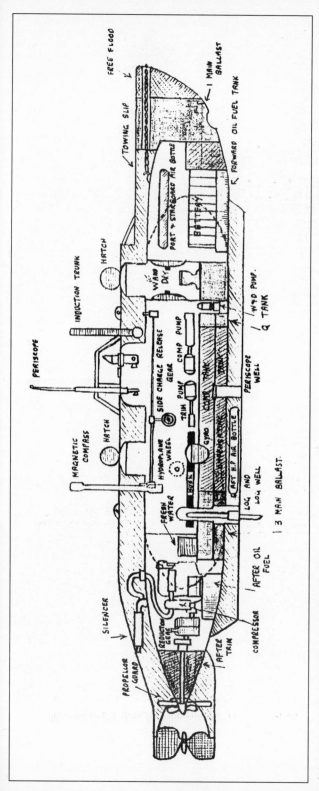

Schematic of *X20*, sister submarine to Ruse's *X21*.

An X-craft on the surface with her CO on the casing.
Ruse collection

Sherwood's command in the Far East, HMS/M *Spiteful*.
Sherwood collection

One of the T-class submarines (HMS/M *Tantalus*) at Trincomalee, Ceylon. Canadians served in this boat and others like her in the Far East during 1944–45.
Gilmour collection

Lt.-Cdr. Freddie Sherwood, DSC and bar (centre), and members of his crew of *Spiteful* after receiving their decorations from King George VI, 1945.
Sherwood collection

Lt. George L. McPhee, RCNVR.
Gardner collection

Lt. A.W. "Bud" Jorgenson, RCNVR.
Jorgenson collection

Lt. Frank P.R. Saunders, RCNVR, on watch in HMS/M *Seanymph* in Far Eastern waters.
Halladay collection

Lt. Wayne Holmes, RCNVR, on the bridge of HMS/M *Unseen*, May 1945.
W. Holmes collection

U-889 after she was commissioned into the RCN.
Thompson collection

Lt. J.R. "Rod" Johnston, RCNVR, while CO of *U-190* in 1946.
Johnston collection

U-190 after her surrender to RCN forces on 11 May 1945.
Thompson collection

The Sixth Submarine Squadron (SM6), which was in Halifax to provide the RCN with surface ASW training, August 1955. L to R: HMS/Ms *Alderney, Ambush,* and *Astute.*
DND/NAC 191817

Leading Stoker Claude "Frenchie" Gourdeau, RCN, who survived the explosion on HMS/M *Sidon* in June 1955.
Gourdeau collection

PO Laverne McLeod, RCN, lost his life in the *Sidon* explosion and was buried with full military honours at Portland cemetery in England.
Gourdeau collection

The Canadian submarine veterans of World War I on HMCS/M *Grilse* before their cruise on 20 July 1961. L to R: Lt.-Cdr. W. Wingate, RNR (CO of the original HMCS *Grilse* in 1916); *PO Fred W. Crickard, RNCVR; Cdr. C.B. Allen, RN (Ret.); Capt. L.J.M. Gauvreau, RCN (Ret.); Capt. J.C. Pratt, RCN; Chief of Staff of CANFLAGPAC; Mr. R. Tipton; *Cmdre. W.J.R. "Roy" Beech, RCN (Ret.); unknown; *LS George Gilbert, RCN (Ret.) (almost hidden); *Capt. Colin D. Donald, RCN (Ret.); *Capt. B.L. "Barney" Johnson, RCNR (Ret.); LCdr. Ed G. Gigg, RCN (CO of *Grilse*); Mr. R.J. Bower (editor of the *Victoria Colonist*); RAdm Finch-Noyes, RCN (flag officer, Pacific Coast); *Gunner(T) George Brisco, RCN (Ret.); Dr. J.P. Tully; and Capt. A.F. Peers, RCN (Ret.).

* Indicates World War I submariners.

NAC E-62075

HMCS/M *Grilse* in the Gatun locks of the Panama Canal during her voyage to Esquimalt.

DND 2-2011

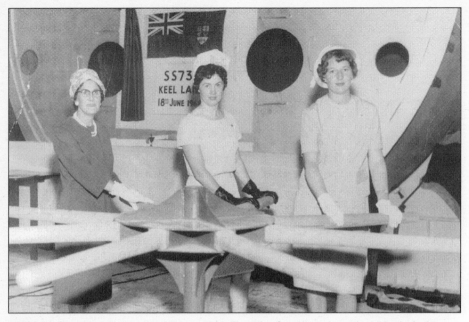

HMCS/M *Onondaga*'s keel laying, 18 June 1964. The three Canadian wives who took part in the traditional ceremony were (L to R) Mrs. Kit Bowness, Mrs. Rose Fitzgerald, and Mrs. Joan Finlay.
Bowness collection

Some of the Canadian O boat construction team entertained the Chatham staff on 1 July 1965. L to R: George Bowness (civilian staff officer), unidentified, Geoff Agnew (supply officer), Fergus Finlay (constructor), and Bill Christie (senior officer). Seated with the peacepipe, Joyce Masters (secretary).
Bowness collection

A Canadian O boat does her first test dive in the safety of the basin at HM Dockyard, Chatham.
Frawley collection

The launch of HMCS/M *Okanagan*, 17 September 1966.
Frawley collection

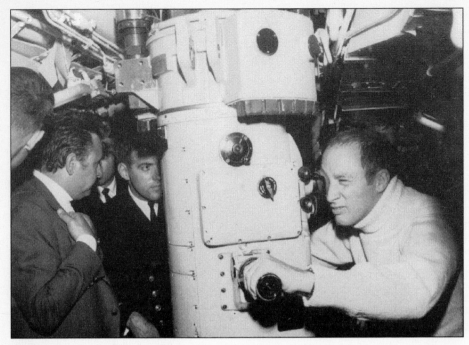

"Gee! When I grow up I want to be a submarine commander." Prime Minister Pierre Trudeau tries out *Okanagan*'s periscope after the submarine arrived in Halifax.
DND HS69-2119

Commander Ed Gigg, RCN (right), commander of the First Canadian Submarine Squadron, welcomes Lt.Cdr. Sam Tomlinson, RCN, and HMCS/M *Ojibwa* to Canada, January 1966.
Gigg collection

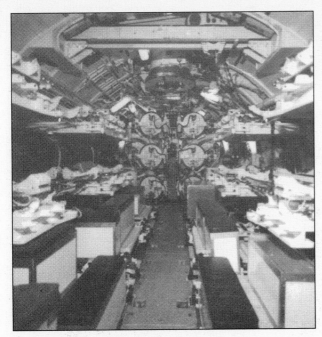

The fore-ends of HMCS/M *Okanagan* with the torpedo-tube doors clearly visible. Twenty-six bunks are squeezed in here, as well as one small locker per man.
DND #HSC86-1889

HMCS/M *Okanagan*'s wardroom – home to her eight officers – is the size of a small bedroom.
DND #ISC87-640

The control room of HMCS/M *Okanagan*, looking aft, where twenty-two people work during action stations. Centre: the search periscope (raised). Right: beyond the seated man is the trim panel and the controls for the boat's auxiliary machinery. Left: chart table, echo sounder, and underwater telephone.

Nesbit collection

The one-man diving station (right) in *Okanagan*'s control room showing the joystick, the analogue computer underneath, and related gauges. The black panel to the left is the Chief of the Watch panel (vent and blow) with the internal communication system above.

DND #IMC85-301

HMCS/M *Okanagan*'s engine room. "Bert" and "Ernie," the two Admiralty standard range V-16 supercharged diesels, are on either side.
DND HS80-435

HMCS/M *Rainbow* in 1968. She served exclusively on the west coast until 1974.
DND ECP68-276

HMCS/M *Grilse* is sunk by the U.S. Navy in 1970.
Hunt collection

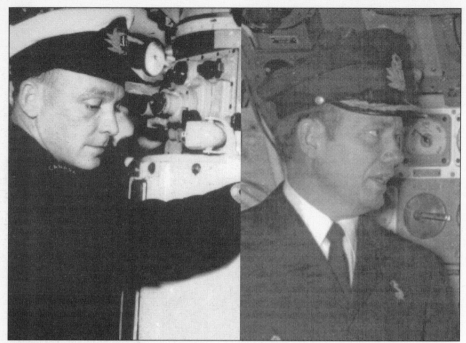

Cdr. Cliff Crow, CD (right), and Cdr. Jim Wood, CD, started the move for a submarine replacement program in the early 1970s.

Crow collection (Crow)
McFarlane collection (Wood)

RAdm C. (Chuck) Thomas, CD, when he was chief, Maritime Doctrine and Operations.

DND REP84-159

Mr. Ed J. Healey, assistant deputy minister (Matériel), during the nuclear-powered submarine acquisition program in the 1980s.

DND REPC86-129

The Hon. Perrin Beatty, MP, minister of national defence (1986–89).
DND REPC87-08

RAdm John R. Anderson, CD, chief, Submarine Acquisition, in 1987.
DND REPC87-195

The British Trafalgar-class submarine, HMS Torbay, on a marketing visit to Canada in 1988.
DND IHC87-25-2

The French nuclear-powered Saphir struts her stuff in Halifax, 1988.
DND IHC87-28-12

Ships' badges.

Drawn by Janet Bell

PART TWO
1939–1946

CANADIANS VOLUNTEER FOR SUBMARINES IN WORLD WAR II, 1940–1941

"We fought hard for last place"

The Royal Canadian Navy's unplanned expansion in the second decade of the twentieth century came about because Canada, with no naval policy, was thrust into a world war. While the war quickly gave birth to a Canadian submarine service, the lack of a naval policy killed it six short years later.

The Great War assured submarines a place in all future wars at sea, if not in all navies, by proving their offensive and defensive capabilities. Combat had sharpened submarine tactics and had improved the boats' weaponry, design, and reliability. Countermeasures were being developed, but without good sensors for the submarine hunters they lagged behind submarine development.

During the war the Canadian government had been too preoccupied with the fighting to establish a permanent naval policy, and it was not until the Imperial War Conference in May 1918 that the question was readdressed. Borden, acting as the spokesman for the leaders of the Dominions, told the British that their vision of a single navy for the Empire was out of date in light of the countries' need for increased independence. The Admiralty reluctantly relinquished their hope for an imperial fleet and sent Earl Jellicoe to the Dominions to help each formulate a post-war naval policy.

At the Armistice Canada had no certain plan to sustain the RCN, although such a plan might have kept the submarine service alive. In October 1918 Captain Walter Hose, the new director of the Naval

Service, had proposed to the government that Canada create a navy capable of preventing enemy attacks on shipping off Canadian coasts. Captain Hose recommended a force of thirty-three destroyers and four submarines. A naval committee soon diluted his requirement to six destroyers and four to eight coastal submarines, to be built at home. They did not consider anti-submarine warfare training a role for submarines.

In November 1919 Jellicoe arrived in Canada and, with the RCN's hopes pinned on him, got to work. Six weeks later he made the formal presentation of his recommendations to the Canadian Cabinet, and encouraged the ministers to formulate their naval policy quickly before the navy rusted into oblivion. Borden, ill and worried, was unenthusiastic about spending more money on the RCN.

The Naval Staff were delighted with Jellicoe's wide-ranging report,[1] which dealt with general policy as well as operational details. Regarding submarines the British admiral had recommended continuance of the Canadian Submarine Service, with more boats and a depot ship. However, Jellicoe had not calculated the capital and operating costs of the rejuvenated RCN and soon learned that he had overestimated both Canada's resolve and its ability to pay. He left for home pessimistic over the policy's chances and disillusioned with Canada.

Borden's Cabinet, reluctant to be seen expanding the navy so soon after the Armistice, decided that the caucus should consider the recommendations before they formulated anything. Three unproductive months went by, until the Tories decided to make no decision on a naval policy. The minister responsible for the navy, Ballantyne, was furious and, overreacting to this determination, swore that he would eliminate the RCN and with it the Canadian Submarine Service.

Ballantyne sadly announced the Conservative government's non-decision at the end of March 1920, and after a week of uproar softened his harsh stand by proposing a compromise for the RCN. The navy would continue along pre-war lines, with the two remaining submarines (*CH14* and *CH15*) supplemented by three extra ships donated by the Admiralty. By May Ballantyne had reduced the RCN to five hundred officers and men. The increase in submarines was never heard of again.

In the fall of 1921 Borden's government lost the federal election. Mackenzie King's Liberals, with strong support in Quebec, swept into power and inherited the naval dilemma during the Washington Conference on arms control. This multi-national conference set arms limitations for the Allied nations, which Mackenzie King translated as meaning the restriction of Canadian naval expansion.

In May 1922 King's Liberals axed the RCN – the ships were paid off and the navy became primarily a reserve force. Hose was credited with convincing the Liberal government that, if the RCN was to be tiny, Canada's maritime preparedness would have to rely on its reserves. Two destroyers were reprieved only when it was realized that the reservists needed training ships. Hose had to suspend all submarine training, disappointing those who wished to stay in the Silent Service including Lt. William Beech, who had returned from the China Station. *CH14* and *CH15* were paid off for the last time.

Canada was not the only country to attempt to blot out the horrors of the recent war by reducing her armed forces to next to nothing. Along with most Canadians, King wanted peace and isolation and had not learned the value of preparedness. His government, like Borden's, ignored the sound policy proposals prepared by Jellicoe and the RCN, preferring instead to follow the non-policy. King ignored Canada's Pacific naval requirements despite Japan's ascendancy and the previous cancellation of the Anglo-Japanese Treaty.

The Liberal government amalgamated the three services into the Department of National Defence, under one minister, following the Australian precedent. The size and clout of the militia in this new organization would certainly have overwhelmed the small RCN had it not been for the tenacity of Hose, who fiercely refused to allow any interference with the RCN by an army officer, however senior. At its lowest point in 1924, the RCN had sixty-seven officers. Reestablishment of the Canadian Submarine Service remained impossible.

Ten years after the First World War the RCN began to grow again, albeit slowly. By 1929 there were 104 officers and 792 ratings, though no glimmer of hope shone for submarines. Hose, his title changed to "Chief of Naval Staff," battled on in the early 1930s, attempting to keep his tiny fleet afloat in the sea of army officers who threatened to drown it entirely. At the same time the world threat began to shift from Japan to Germany, though few recognized it in Canada, and the naval non-policy continued. Hose had to fight with the Liberals to have the two aging destroyers replaced, but in 1930, with another Conservative government briefly in power, the RCN had two more ships built in Britain.

Hose continued to press for vessels to meet the RCN's peacetime commitments but the government would not listen. The beginnings of the Great Depression were being felt and Canada was to be especially hard hit. The government again slashed naval spending in the 1933–34 fiscal year after being told that finances could not support the three services, and the navy was the least important.[2] But the RCN hung on … just.

Hose retired in 1934 and was succeeded by Captain Percy W. Nelles, RCN. Nelles, forty-two years old when he became CNS, was a man of average intellect and limited vision; he favoured very close ties with the Royal Navy. It was this unimaginative officer who faced Mackenzie King at home and the growing threat of Nazi Germany abroad. In 1934 the RCN did briefly consider the need for a few submarines. They were quickly rejected on the grounds that boats were less efficient and less economical than destroyers. By 1938, a crisis year, Nelles controlled a fleet that barely met peacetime requirements and a supplementary reserve list of potentially useful individuals. There was still no thought of submarines.

When in 1938 the threat of war escalated, following Italy's union with the Axis and Germany's annexation of Austria, Mackenzie King expended his energy keeping Canada uninvolved rather than becoming prepared. Canada's naval policy remained nonexistent and her government's maritime defence resided largely in the Royal Navy. King's public statements on the subject consisted of reassurances – to French Canadians in particular – that he would not allow conscription or another slaughter of Canadians in Europe. His insistence that Canada would not take part in a massive war effort confused most observers. It certainly perplexed Britain, who sadly realized they could no longer rely on their senior ally.

However, when Poland was overrun, King took action despite his earlier statements and gained his Cabinet's approval to participate in the impending war. The Canadian House of Commons declared war against Germany four days after Britain had done so, and Canada entered a war as an independent nation for the first time in her history. Early wartime policies allowed expenditures for the defence of Canada only, which included minesweepers and anti-submarine vessels for the RCN, but no submarines.

In early September 1939, the RCN had two destroyers and two minesweepers at Halifax and four destroyers and two minesweepers at Esquimalt. None of them had ever trained with a submarine and only four had asdic, the forerunner of passive sonar. On the Canadian declaration of war two of the west coast destroyers weighed anchor and steamed off for the east to begin Atlantic convoy duty.

In the Great War, Canada had placed her warships under Admiralty operational control, but in World War II the RCN retained control of its

resources. Had Percy Nelles had the will and fortitude to exert the necessary pressure on the government, Canada might have been better prepared for this war, and the RCN might have done more in the early years
of the conflict; but he had not. Had the RCN had current submariners in
their ranks, they might even have had a few submarines too.

If they had been asked, the submariners would have told the policy-mak-
ers that submarines were, first and foremost, weapons of enormous strate-
gic power – even the suspicion that one might be lurking outside a naval
base was sufficient to bottle up a battle fleet. Second, they would have
said that submarines were the most economical vessel for any navy – they
had better endurance than any other warship, required no support when
on patrol, and needed only small crews. Next, the submariners would
have rebutted the argument that submarines were becoming obsolete
because of improvements in detection and the ability of aircraft to keep
them deep, thus preventing attacks. Last, they would have emphasized
the submarines' superb tactical role, their ability to interrupt the seaborne
commerce that sustains nations in peace and war, an ability demonstrated
with stark success by the U-boats twenty years before.

The spectre of unrestricted submarine warfare against commerce had
preoccupied many countries between the wars, and by 1939 international
law actually prohibited it. The Allies hoped future adversaries would stick
to the board-and-search requirements of the law, which allowed time for
crews to abandon before their ships were sunk. Most navies believed that
the law would be upheld and focused their submarines' exercises on
attacking warships and avoiding aircraft.

This hope, as well as the lack of funds, was the reason that Nelles did
not push for submarines in the fleet. His officers simply did not believe
they would ever have to torpedo merchant ships, sink enemy submarines,
or bottle up battle fleets. Furthermore, in 1936 the Department of
National Defence, including Nelles, believed that the Royal Navy alone
could and would protect the vital sea lanes across the Atlantic from surface raiders and U-boats. These assumptions meant that the RCN did not
consider the possibility that they might be called upon to supply large
numbers of convoy escorts and crews trained in anti-submarine warfare –
or that they might need "tame" submarines for training exercises.

There was a lone warning voice amongst the politicians and RCN
during these years – Ballantyne, the former minister who had nearly eliminated the RCN. He feared that in the event of war the Royal Navy might
not manage alone, and that it might be unable to come to Canada's aid in

either the Pacific or Atlantic. His anxieties were not given any credence. The total mobilized strength of the RCN in September 1939 was 397 officers and 2,276 ratings, most of whom were reservists. These numbers were the validation of all that Hose had fought for as CNS during the lean years and showed that the institution of the volunteer reserves (RCNVR) was his wisest move in developing the preparedness of an under-budgeted navy. With the start of the war naval recruiting soared; it began to pull in the next generation of Canadian submariners, though none of the volunteers knew it at the time.

During the Phoney War (September 1939 to June 1940) many naval volunteers, cooling their heels ashore, joined in the mounting criticism of Mackenzie King's limited-war policy. The PM reacted by calling a snap election for March, which returned his Liberal party with the biggest majority in Canadian history. King's timing had been lucky. The rapid fall of the European nations to Hitler's armies had not yet occurred – if it had, the result of the election might have been very different in view of King's unwillingness to get involved.

The events that precipitated the Allied evacuation at Dunkirk shocked and frightened Canadians. When Mackenzie King instituted conscription for home defence and abandoned the financial restraints of the first year, there was little outcry against his actions. King's promises to the francophones dissolved into thin air, except for one: his pledge to forbid conscription for overseas service. Millions of dollars were being spent on the war effort and the loss of Canadians in Europe was but a short step away.

As a result of the delayed commitment to the Allied effort, the Royal Canadian Navy expanded rapidly and was soon hard at work in the Atlantic, escorting the convoys of merchant ships carrying the North American war matériel to Britain. The first sixty-four corvettes were already laid down, and by 1943 Canada was providing 48 percent of the Allied escort vessels and had operational command of the northwest Atlantic. Despite this heavy ASW responsibility, the RCN gave little consideration to having a submarine service, even though the need for submarines to sink U-boats and to train the escorts quickly became apparent.

Average Canadians dreaded the prospect of war, but many were resigned to fighting it. As early as 1936, young men began to realize that war might come and they joined the Royal Canadian Naval Volunteer Reserve. They served faithfully – most of them turning up without fail for the weekly drills in their home towns, and putting in extra hours to participate in other activities. Enjoyment and pride were the motivation; challenge and comradeship the reward.

Every Canadian submariner who served in World War II was in the RCNVR, and half a dozen, foreseeing events, had enrolled early. The rest were propelled into the volunteer navy after the Nazis swept through western Europe in June 1940. None of them had considered volunteering for the Silent Service when they joined up, preferring instead to try for destroyers or aircraft carriers. When these choices became unavailable, the submarine service was fourth best, after motor torpedo boats. By 1945 only twenty-six Canadians had served in submarines in all the major theatres of the war.

The first four began their new careers after Dunkirk. James Woods of Toronto and Freddie Sherwood of Ottawa were amongst the first RCNVRs to go to England, and both had been reservists for several years.

Woods spent the summer of 1936 in Berlin and experienced Hitler at first hand. Deeply troubled after witnessing a Jew-baiting, he reacted by joining the RCNVR in 1937, aged twenty-one. Woods went to England in 1940 in the first draft of Canadian naval volunteers, hoping to serve in the American lend-lease destroyers. When the ships were delayed, Woods volunteered for submarines, deferring his desire to specialize in gunnery. Known as "J.D." to his shipmates, Woods was a "laid-back," sociable individual with a round face and a ready smile.

Just before his nineteenth birthday in 1933, Freddie Sherwood, a bank clerk, joined the RCNVR in Ottawa as a midshipman. He enrolled because it seemed the thing to do. Sherwood's confident manner and strong sense of duty and justice was saved from being too intense by his infectious good humour. He benefited greatly from his prewar service in the reserves – he earned his watch-keeping ticket and two stripes. In 1939 he longed to go to sea but was kept in command of the Ottawa Naval Reserve half company, impatiently coping with recruits. After Dunkirk, Sherwood transferred to England in the second RCN draft and had his first exposure to action in the English Channel when his troopship was attacked. He rushed on deck with only his binoculars on – they were the first thing he grabbed when a bomb interrupted his shower.

Sherwood met Woods at HMS *King Alfred,* the training establishment near Brighton; he soon earned a reputation for being as serious as Woods was relaxed. When the RN asked the course participants for two officers for the submarine service, all the Canadians present volunteered. Freddie Sherwood and Jim Woods were chosen, as they were physically fit, unmarried, and under twenty-seven years old. Following a brief period on different surface ships, Sherwood and Woods took their basic Submarine Officers' Training Course (SOTC) together in September and embarked on careers neither had expected.

These officers were the second and third volunteer reservists ever to take SOTC, which caused some distress to the regular RN types. It was not until later in the war that the VRs made up 50 percent of the students. Woods recalled that Sherwood did well on the course but Sherwood insists that they both fought hard for last place.

In 1940, the SOTC was still being held at HMS *Dolphin* at Gosport, before moving to Blyth on the northeast coast of England. *Dolphin* was the spiritual home of submariners and contained the schools, messes, accommodation, and paraphernalia of the service. In its fundamentals, the basic course differed little from the one that Maitland-Dougall attended during the First War, and, indeed, Sherwood and Woods used many of the same diagrams. A few new topics had been added, including asdic and the use of more modern attacking instruments.

The classroom course lasted six weeks (it had been sixteen weeks in peacetime) and began with a stirring introduction to submarines by the Captain(S) in charge of the training flotilla. Chief petty officers taught most of the morning classes, except engineering and communications, and brought to their lectures years of practical experience. Officer of the watch (OOW) routines, already learned, were amended for submarines – depth-keeping being one of the most important skills. OOWs were also introduced to keeping watch using the periscope. In the afternoons the budding submariners moved onto submarines alongside, either to work on the systems they had studied that morning or to go to sea. Sports were encouraged and the students played rugby or soccer before dinner to blow away the cobwebs.

By now there was a thirty-five-foot tower (tank) at *Dolphin,* which was used for the obligatory escape training. Prospective submariners viewed it with differing emotions – anticipation or alarm. Instructors exposed the trainees to the gruesome details of sinking in a submarine and then, after a gin for lunch, taught them the theory of modern escape methods and familiarized them with the Davis Submarine Escape Apparatus (DSEA). The following morning the neophytes were in the tower practising underwater escapes.

Sherwood and Woods took an examination halfway through the SOTC, and at the end. The top officer got the first choice of appointments, and so on down the list. Some of the newly qualified submariners went straight to operational boats, others received a more gradual introduction by joining training flotillas. Sherwood and Woods, being low in the standings, had no choice and went as spare officers to operational flotillas.

After Woods and Sherwood had celebrated passing their SOTC, they separated. Woods sailed to Alexandria in the Mediterranean as a spare officer based on HMS *Medway*, the famous depot ship of the First Flotilla, and later joined HMS *Parthian*, which sank a Vichy submarine.

Sherwood travelled to HMS *Elfin* at Blyth in Northumberland as a spare officer for the Sixth Flotilla operating in the North Sea. He liked the well-organized base on the bleak coast of northeast England, where everything stopped for tea and the Wrens were always finding an excuse for a party.

The Canadian quickly became the fourth hand in HMS *Sealion* whose captain was the well-known Commander Ben Bryant – a daring, feisty CO who had already earned a DSC.[3] This began a wartime partnership between Sherwood and Bryant that spanned two years, two seas, and two submarines. The friendship that developed continued until Bryant died in 1994.

The Sixth Flotilla had been reporting enemy shipping, and hunting for likely targets to sink along the Norwegian coast since April 1940 when Norway fell to the Germans. Allied submariners no longer had to board and search their targets before sinking them, much to their relief, because the British Cabinet had earlier given permission for unrestricted submarine warfare.

Sherwood's initiation into submarine life at Christmas 1940 was abrupt – foul winter weather close to the Arctic Circle, little daylight, a very demanding CO who favoured gun action, and lots of attacks. "A good introduction" is how he remembers it.

Though Sherwood, as the torpedo officer in *Sealion*, was responsible for gunnery, his stomach churned when he heard Bryant order, "Stand by for gun action!" He had never supervised the firing of the three-inch gun before. His SOTC had paid little attention to gunnery, and Sherwood's inexperience earned him a blast from Bryant, who then ordered gun drill every day, just for the Canadian's benefit.

After a couple of patrols *Sealion* moved into the Bay of Biscay to participate in Churchill's "ring of iron." This operation was designed to keep the German cruisers *Scharnhorst* and *Gneisenau* from leaving Brest, where they had been based since the fall of France. *Sealion* was ordered to report enemy warship movements, and to attack everything they sighted. They saw nothing on their first two outings and, although this inactivity bored most of the crew, Sherwood was happy to be there.

By now it was midsummer 1941, and the daylight kept *Sealion* submerged for eighteen hours at a stretch. This produced the same poor air quality as it had in WWI submarines, causing nausea and headaches among the crew. Even though trays of soda lime were provided to absorb the increased carbon dioxide, after only six hours underwater there was insufficient oxygen to keep a match burning.

In these conditions, HMS *Sealion* had a go at a U-boat, and tried to intercept the *Prinz Eugen,* but was unsuccessful on both occasions. Starting in July 1941 *Sealion* conducted several covert missions in the Bay of Biscay. They delivered supplies and men to the Resistance, collected men wishing to join the Free French forces, and rescued fugitives from the Gestapo. It was dangerous, exciting work, which occasionally turned out to be disheartening when agents failed to make the rendezvous. Sherwood admired the tough and determined Frenchmen he met, and marvelled at their courage.

Sherwood made his last patrol in *Sealion* in August 1941 when they went farther south to harry the iron-ore carriers on the Bilbao-Bayonne route. It was unsuccessful, but Sherwood had gained plenty of valuable submarine experience in a short time. He was lucky enough to have served his apprenticeship in a very happy boat, with one of the great submarine COs of the day, and he had also discovered the tremendous *esprit de corps* amongst submariners. Like his Canadian predecessors in the Great War, he was very satisfied with his decision to volunteer for submarines.

Sherwood was soon appointed first lieutenant of *L23.* His submarine career was progressing unusually fast, and he was as surprised as anyone. However, his new appointment had occurred not only because submarine losses had been heavy, but also because Bryant thought him a capable submariner who demonstrated the attributes necessary to make an outstanding one. Bryant's appraisal of his torpedo officer is worth quoting here:

An officer of outstanding zeal. Finds out things for himself and is most determined in his pursuit of knowledge, being remarkably well informed. Has excellent physique and stamina, and a happy personality which gets the very best out of his subordinates. Is well imbued with the offensive spirit.

Should make a first class submarine first lieutenant, and with further experience in navigation, has the makings of a very good commanding officer.[4]

These words undoubtedly had a lot to do with the acceleration of Sherwood's submarine career and his next promotion.

Freddie Sherwood went to his next boat, *L23,* reluctantly, because she was an ancient training boat and non-operational. The Canadian joined her in Dundee, Scotland, where he enjoyed many good parties with the attractive Scottish lasses, though without whisky, which was strictly rationed. By October 1941 Sherwood was back in familiar territory at Blyth with *L23* running for the newly relocated submarine courses. Sherwood recalled that the ratings came to them full of spit and polish and, on making a report to the officer of the watch would salute, take one step back, and fall down the periscope well. Sherwood learned to catch them before they came to serious harm, impressing on them that they could be more informal on a boat.

After a few months Sherwood returned to action in a new submarine and in a new theatre, though not with a new captain.

CHAPTER ELEVEN

CANADIANS IN THE MEDITERRANEAN, 1941–1943

"Bloody colonials"

J.D. Woods arrived in the Mediterranean in November 1940 with seventeen other submariners. He was the first Canadian to be sent there, and began his career as a spare officer in the First Flotilla in Alexandria, going out in whatever boat needed a navigator. His duties included the navigation of the submarine, the correction of all the charts carried by the boat, maintenance of the chronometers and compasses, standing watches, and the operation of the "fruit machine" during attacks.

Woods settled in during a desperate time in the Mediterranean for the Allies – the German push to invade Malta and secure North Africa was gaining momentum and causing heavy losses. The few submarines available to thwart the thrust were old and cumbersome, and the new U-class submarines had not arrived from England. Within two weeks of his arrival, Woods saw seven boats of his flotilla go to the bottom with all hands, leaving him in no doubt as to the dangerous nature of his chosen career.

In April 1941, Woods joined HMS *Parthian* as her navigating officer. She was one of the large O, P, R class of submarines designed for the China Station, and her CO was the steely-nerved Commander M.G. Rimington, RN. Under his command Woods experienced many patrols, and learned that submarines were not for him.

The young Torontonian saw the bodies of British sailors washing over the casing during the evacuation of Crete; he assisted in several daring attacks on targets alongside and at sea; he experienced the dreadful bombing of Malta when the submarines had to sit on the bottom to

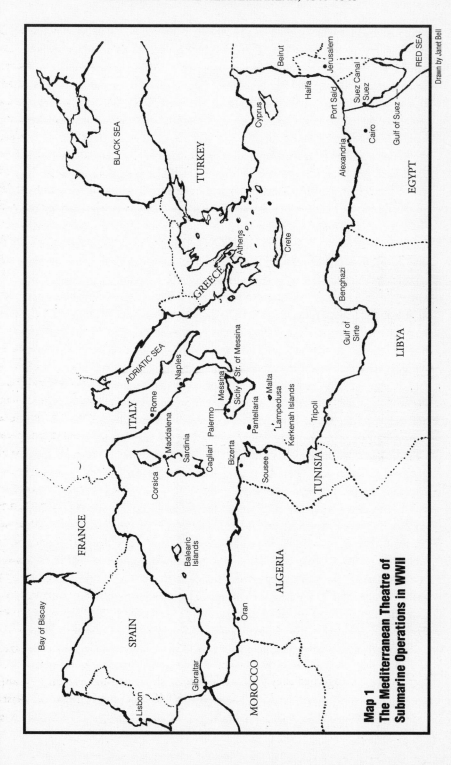

Map 1
The Mediterranean Theatre of
Submarine Operations in WWII

Drawn by Janet Bell

escape it; and he participated in the "magic carpet service" to Malta. The "magic carpets" were the First Flotilla submarines, which acted as underwater ferry boats, carrying essential supplies to Malta when the loss of Crete exacerbated the island's isolation. *Parthian* ran in and out of Malta with aviation fuel in her ballast tanks to alleviate the RAF's critical shortages. The Allied convoys were being decimated; these ferry runs enabled the aircrews to continue flying operations during the worst of the siege.

Woods plugged on in submarines, admiring his shipmates, but really wanting to get back to gunnery. Before he could, he was to be involved in one of the famous submarine attacks of the Second World War.

At the end of June 1941, when the Eighth Army was beaten back to El Alamein, *Parthian* was ordered to deal with three Vichy submarines.[1] These French boats, operating under Axis colours after the Nazis occupied France, were harassing the Allied naval forces that were in the Mediterranean supporting the failing North African campaign. Off Beirut, at 0942 on 25 June, the OOW and Woods sighted another boat on the surface at 6,000 yards (5,487 m), which was identified as one of the Vichy submarines. Their quarry was proceeding slowly on the surface on one engine. Both the Vichy and the British boats dived and *Parthian* maintained contact underwater with her adversary for three hours. The *Souffleur* eventually surfaced, and presumably thinking she was safe, let some of the crew go for a swim. At that moment *Parthian* made a difficult snap attack, firing four torpedoes at fairly long range. One hit the *Souffleur* under the conning tower, exploding in steam and smoke, and the submarine sank immediately. The French sailors who were swimming watched in horror as their boat and forty-five shipmates disappeared, then they started to swim to Beirut.

As the engagement took place within sight of Beirut and an enemy airfield, *Parthian* expected immediate retaliation. Her CO did not take the time to look for or rescue any survivors, but went deep and set a course away from the coast. When the swimmers staggered ashore, the first thing they did was to report the incident to the Axis authorities, an action which had repercussions for *Parthian*'s captain. His decision to leave the area without rescuing survivors was questioned by the Admiralty after German authorities complained. Rimington had a rough time explaining himself, but made it quite clear that he saw no survivors as he hastily departed the scene. His rapid exit was in accordance with his orders, which explicitly stated that *Parthian* must not be detected. The chances were high that she would be, operating so close to the shore.

Nearly twenty-five years later the wreck of the *Souffleur* was located by divers on the sandy bottom of the Mediterranean, broken in two just as *Parthian* reported. The Vichy submarine lies there still, unmolested.

Three nights later, while *Parthian* was charging her batteries, she encountered another Vichy submarine within two hundred yards (183 m) of her. They were so close that they could not attack with torpedoes, though *Parthian* tried to ram. *Parthian* lost contact with the enemy because of a plane jam when they dived and, after she had sorted herself out, the enemy had vanished.

Parthian was overdue for a refit, and she did no more patrols in the Mediterranean. Woods returned to England with her. During the passage he decided to quit submarines, and his superior officer agreed that he was unsuited. Jim Woods returned to general service less than a year after volunteering for the "Silent Service" and eventually got his wish to be a gunnery officer in 1942. He went on to a promotion at the end of the war to lieutenant-commander.

Keith Forbes, originally of Wolfville, Nova Scotia, has two commissioning scrolls hanging in his study in West Virginia: they show that he served in the Royal Canadian Army Supply Corps and the RCNVR during World War II. While studying mining engineering at Acadia University Forbes enrolled in the Reserve Officers' Training Program, and when war arrived before he had finished his degree, he volunteered for the army. The army failed to get him overseas, so Forbes volunteered a second time, this time for the navy, which accepted him. Temporary Acting Sub-Lieutenant Forbes, RCNVR, sailed for England in 1940 at short notice, having just enough time to buy a uniform and to have his hat christened by a seagull. His commission in the army was ignored.

Forbes spent his first weeks at *King Alfred* doing his basic officer training, which included navigation, signals, gunnery, and marching. While there Forbes opted for submarines, reasoning that after his six months' coursing, and additional time on a training boat, the war would be over. After he had volunteered Forbes began to doubt the wisdom of his choice, particularly after he saw a movie about asdic – there was a harrowing scene inside a submarine while it was being depth-charged. However, the die was cast.

After the November 1940 SOTC, Forbes joined *H44*, becoming the second Canadian to serve in her. (The first was Lt. Ronald C. Watson, RCN, who briefly commanded *H44* after the Great War.) In January 1941, the submarine was engaged in anti-submarine warfare (ASW) training for the Atlantic escorts. The boat was small, congested, and uncomfortable – "the invention of the devil," Forbes recalled.[2] Soon *H44* was reassigned to the "ring of iron" in the Bay of Biscay, along with *Sealion,* with Forbes itching for an appointment in a more modern submarine. In June 1941, he got his wish. He became the navigation officer of HMS/M *P34,* a U-class submarine under construction.

The first U-class boats were small, single-hulled submarines designed as clockwork mice to replace the old H-class. Later on it became clear that, with some improvements, they would be suitable for the Mediterranean. The U's main advantage was their fast diving time – sixteen seconds to periscope depth – but their disadvantage was an acute sensitivity to trimming which caused the submarine to break the surface at inopportune moments. U-class submarines were only 730 tons (662 tonnes) submerged, had four internal bow tubes and a twelve-pound gun, and carried four reloads. Their endurance was 4,000 miles (6,346 km) with a top speed of 12 knots on the surface and nine submerged. *P34*'s motto was *Nihil sine labore* – "Nothing without work."

P34 later became better known as *Ultimatum,* a name that was given to her after Forbes had left, but we shall use her number. The change came about when Churchill insisted that all RN submarines be given names rather than numbers, to provide a better identity and a source of pride for the crews.

P34 completed her sea trials and work-ups in the Clyde, and by mid-September 1941 she was in Malta. She joined the famous Tenth Flotilla, led by Captain George "Shrimp" Simpson, RN (SM10 [officer in charge of the flotilla]). The "Fighting Tenth," as it became known, had been officially recreated on 1 September 1941, though a flotilla of Us had been operating from Malta for nine months previously.

Forbes was the second Canadian in the Mediterranean, and the only Canadian and reservist on *P34.* He was viewed initially with some skepticism by his fellow RN officers, but Forbes liked his shipmates and soon made it clear that he admired them. He came in for some ribbing, but held his own and was quickly accepted.

When Forbes arrived, Malta was suffering from enemy bombing and lack of supplies. The air attacks caused Captain(S), Simpson, to forbid any officer to live on the submarine base in case a direct hit wiped out his entire officer corps. Forbes found himself housed in a succession of strange billets, including an old bordello and a fuel depot, most of which were sooner or later bombed into oblivion.

Records indicate that *P34*'s shake-down patrol was conducted to the southwest of Malta, but Forbes and other members of HMS/M *P34*'s crew dispute this, saying it was north of Sicily. They have endeavoured to have the official Admiralty record changed, though with no success. The second, equally uneventful patrol was off Sicily.

Forbes had to get used to the reversed night and day that his CO had instituted on operations. While submerged during daylight hours and running on their batteries, *P34*'s galley was not used in order to conserve the precious power for the motors. No one was permitted to smoke and those not on watch slept, unless an attack was in progress. At night on the surface charging the batteries, the crew was up and able to enjoy fresh air pouring down the hatch and to smoke a very welcome cigarette. The galley produced hot meals, and lunch (called dinner in the navy) was served at midnight.

Forbes saw only minor action at first; typically, *P34*'s CO did not get into his stride at once. However, early in 1942 *P34* sank her first ship, a heavily laden Italian freighter. The attack took place at the southern end of the Straits of Messina – the narrow passage between the toe of Italy and Sicily.

The New Year brought worsening bombing raids on Malta and the serious threat of a German invasion. Food and fuel dwindled as the Axis sank the convoys and the submariners' housing disappeared fast. The exhausted crews coming off patrol got little rest, and their boats got limited maintenance.

March 1942 saw *P34* sink her first enemy submarine. The Italian *Ammiraglio Millo* was carrying stores to North Africa when *P34* sighted her in the Gulf of Taranto proceeding slowly on the surface. *P34* fired four torpedoes and scored two hits, which immediately sank the target. *P34* rescued fourteen survivors before diving to avoid shore fire and one Italian officer confessed that the *Millo* had been on the surface because her captain wanted a cigarette. Simpson (SM10) commended *P34* for this attack.

When the enemy air attacks on Malta worsened and bombs started to damage the submarines in harbour, SM10 had no alternative but to have his boats spend the daylight hours on the bottom. All maintenance was done at night. After the enemy started saturation bombing in March, Simpson ordered his boats to submerge outside the harbour in daylight in the hopes of avoiding the flotilla's evacuation. This increased the strain on the crews and some COs were relieved of occasional patrols.

Forbes experienced a new CO in April 1942 when his worn-out captain was given leave. The replacement, suitably nicknamed "Basher," was a huge, indomitable man. During his only patrol in the Gulf of Taranto, *P34* was rocked by a tremendous explosion on her starboard side following a scraping sound. (Shades of Barney Johnson and *H8*.) "It was one hell of a bang!" commented one sailor. While underwater, *P34* had come in contact with the antenna of a mine. Forbes remembered:

> Internal damage was considerable. Both magnetic and gyro compasses went completely out; the larger periscope wouldn't operate; hands just popped off gauges and lay useless in the bottoms of their cases; light bulbs went; cork insulation on the hull flew like snow; a heavy metal casting under the air compressor was cracked; and the hull was dished in between the ribs on the after [starboard] side so that area looked like the skin of a very thin horse with the ribs ... visible. Later in a dockyard at Port Said the deepest indentation was measured to be 2 1/2" between the ribs. (That spoke well for good metal!)

So there they were in the dark, unable to ascertain where the submarine was, with lots of water sloshing about. Forbes wondered if the boat was on the surface, underwater, or on the bottom. He couldn't even tell if she was moving. When *P34* started rocking gently, Forbes realized that they had been blown onto the surface – a very undesirable place to be in such busy enemy waters. A couple of minutes' examination in emergency lighting showed the submarine to be reasonably watertight, so they dived. The flooding had been caused by the fore hatch lifting and reseating at the time of the explosion.

P34 turned for Malta without her sting, as the explosion had also jammed the torpedo firing mechanisms, but she was not leaking, except through the starboard stern gland where the propeller shaft went through the hull. The Tenth Flotilla staff repaired the submarine as well as they could with their limited resources during the bombing and the officers were treated to a survivors' party.

When *P34* was partially repaired, the bombing in Malta got so bad the entire flotilla evacuated. Simpson had little choice after the newly delivered Spitfires for the island's defence were destroyed by the enemy on 21 April. It was a sad day for the islanders, and a bitter one for the submariners, when the battered Tenth departed for Alexandria.

P34 went on to Port Said for further repairs. During this time Forbes was promoted, becoming her first lieutenant. While *P34* was in dry dock, Forbes persuaded the Egyptian who ran the chromium-plating shop in the yard to have the brass fittings in the boat plated. Other boats wanted to follow suit, but their number ones could not barter as well as Forbes. After the work was finished in June 1942 *P34* sailed for Alexandria, only to be evacuated a second time when Tobruk fell.

When the flotilla went to Haifa, Forbes and his shipmates took only the clothes they were wearing for the short passage, leaving the rest of their kit and belongings on their depot ship, HMS *Medway.* She was to meet them in Haifa, but she was torpedoed and sank one day out of Alexandria. The submariners lost everything and the flotilla was deprived of ninety torpedoes and all their spares and machinery. There were compensations – Haifa, on the coast of Palestine as it was then called, was a land of plenty to the submariners. They had unlimited supplies of food; fresh milk and fruit being the favourites.

Submariners soon learn to relieve their stress when they can – a habit that can result in all kinds of high-jinks. Forbes was no exception. After a run ashore with his friends, he impersonated an admiral and arranged for the duty officer to have him piped aboard their temporary depot ship, which was the commander-in-chief's flag ship. Forbes and his "flag lieutenants" came over the brow in grand style but suddenly came face to face with the C-in-C himself, who had been roused by the noise. The real admiral responded quietly, "Gentlemen, that will be all for tonight." The pranksters returned to *P34,* but sleep was elusive.

Next morning the admiral paid a surprise visit to Forbes. In *P34*'s tiny wardroom the admiral talked to the contrite number one, his two friends being ashore. Forbes, certain his career was over, was astonished when the admiral told him that he had been young once too. The great man simply asked Forbes that he refrain from that kind of activity in future. He did.

P34 was a very happy boat. Forbes and his shipmates were a well-integrated crew; they had overcome adversity together and had several successful attacks to their credit. The reliable crew had faith in their captain and the chiefs and petty officers respected their Canadian first lieutenant because he treated them with fairness and informality.

Forbes's fellow officers often kidded him about his pay – Forbes earned more than his CO. This disparity might have caused real conflict, but few Canadian submariners reported any because they handled the issue with humour, and generally banked the difference. Once in a while conflicts did arise between the Canadians and the British officers, but they were usually over Canadian volunteers out-ranking Royal Navy career officers.

After *P34* did two patrols in support of Allied convoys attempting to relieve Malta in the summer of 1942, the Tenth Flotilla returned to home base. In August a few damaged ships limped into harbour with food and enough aviation fuel to keep the fighters flying. This started to turn the war in the Mediterranean in the Allies' favour.

In September, *P34* got a second pasting off the west coast of Greece. This one was severe. She sailed with a noisy propeller shaft in company with HMS/M *Una* to intercept a southbound convoy off the west of Greece. The convoy was the most heavily defended the Allies had yet encountered in the Mediterranean – three fat merchant ships, escorted by no fewer than eleven destroyers and many aircraft. *P34*'s CO watched through the periscope as the RAF bombed the ships, and he let Forbes take a brief look too. One damaged transport came to a stop near Corfu and forty-five minutes later *P34* fired a spread of four torpedoes, one of which exploded prematurely. Forbes thought they had scored a hit when he heard a second detonation but it was an enemy bomb dropped on the torpedo tracks to alert the convoy to the submarine's presence.

The counterattack came within minutes from three destroyers using hydrophones. *P34*, with only one useable propeller, was immediately at a disadvantage and because her hydrophone (passive sonar) reception was poor, she had no idea where her assailants were. Sixty-five depth charges rocked the boat in quick succession but, fortunately, were set too shallow to be of major concern.

An hour later the hunt was taken over by one asdic destroyer. The crew of the submarine could hear every ping as the enemy searched for them. Again the depth charges rained down and this time they were very close: *P34* was straddled by four and shaken severely. The old damage to the starboard stern gland caused a heavy leak and the sea poured into the main bilges. *P34* was fighting for her life – twisting and turning, going deeper and up again, slowing down and speeding up. After ninety minutes, the pinging stopped and the submarine cautiously came up to periscope depth. On the way up the pings started again and, when the captain looked, he saw the attacker 2,500 yards (2.3 km) away heading straight for them. "270 feet!" he ordered calmly. Ten minutes later, *P34* was again straddled and the leaking, which had been tolerable before, became a torrent. The gyro toppled and the wireless telegraph (W/T) and asdic were put out of action. If the crew thought they might make it home after the last attack, they were rapidly changing their minds now.

P34 stayed deep, despite the rising water level, and altered course repeatedly in an effort to throw off their adversary. For six tense hours the submarine waited, with the crew battling the leaks. The CO dared not pump out his bilges in case the dirty water gave the hovering destroyer their position. Forbes, in charge of the trim as number one, was having a difficult time. As the water accumulated, the boat became heavy in the stern and he knew he had to move the water within the confines of the hull. Suddenly Forbes had a brain wave – he organized an old-fashioned bucket brigade using bowls and saucepans to move the water forward to re-establish the trim. He pumped out some clean seawater from the midships tanks and the boat levelled off and became more buoyant. Hope flooded the crew's hearts.

In the early evening, desperately short of oxygen, *P34* crept to periscope depth expecting to see their enemy waiting for them to surface. With a great wave of relief the captain realized the destroyer had given up and he ordered the port motor clutched in. It caught fire and *P34* had to surface. They stayed up for five minutes to clear the smoke, then submerged hurriedly. *P34* ran home on the starboard motor, surfacing only to charge her batteries at night.

After cleaning up the worst of the mess, the crew "spliced the mainbrace" (drank an extra issue of rum). Over the rum, *P34*'s captain remarked that the bloody colonials were overpaid, but "his" colonial did come up with a useful idea once in a while. Lt. Keith Forbes, RCNVR, was awarded a DSC on 29 December 1942 for his part in the incident and was decorated by King George VI in 1943, watched proudly by his father and brother-in-law.

P34 was in no shape to continue strenuous patrols and returned to England for a refit, arriving at the end of October 1942. Forbes took some leave in Canada after all his adventures, and married Betty, whom he had known for some years. Forbes's wife was already used to a relationship conducted by the unpredictable mails, and had resigned herself to continuing worry about her submariner.

Keith Forbes was one of the lucky submariners serving in the Mediterranean – he had completed thirteen consecutive patrols in a year during the worst time for losses and had survived two very close calls. Later in the war Forbes had a hand in the X-craft raid on the *Tirpitz* before leaving the silent service and finishing the war in Canadian waters.

After a couple of months in *L23*, Freddie Sherwood received his promotion to lieutenant-commander, and in January 1942 became *P211*'s first lieutenant.

P211, later named *Safari*, was the first of the new S-class and her CO was Commander Ben Bryant. A coincidence? No, not entirely. Sherwood, as a two and a half, could only serve under a submarine captain who was senior to him and there were very few such high-ranking officers in command of submarines. More important, Bryant wanted Sherwood because he knew he was good, from their *Sealion* days. Bryant welcomed Sherwood back with his comfortable Canadian drawl.[3]

The new S-class boats were stretched versions of the prewar Ss (*Sealion* was one) and were designed primarily for the Mediterranean. They were bigger than the U-class, carried a larger crew, and had six forward torpedo tubes and one in the stern. *Safari*, as we shall call *P211* from now on, had plenty of deck armament, which suited Bryant's style of warfare, but the obsolete three-inch gun was a disappointment. *Safari's* top speed was 9 knots underwater and 15 knots on the surface. Little attention had been paid to improving the habitability of these submarines – there were insufficient bunks, no air-conditioning for hot climates, and no heating for cold. Preservation of food remained primitive and fresh water was rationed to a gallon per man per day. The new Ss were designed for twenty-one-day patrols, followed by a ten-day maintenance period. Despite some drawbacks in the layout and equipment, *Safari* had a good hull and engines and was a tough boat.

Once the submarine was completed she conducted first-of-class trials and a brief work-up in the Clyde in Scotland. Submarines were in very short supply in the Mediterranean, and as soon as the new ones were safe to dive they were dispatched to Gibraltar for more work-ups.

Shortly before *Safari* sailed for the Mediterranean, Sherwood uncovered some serious discontent among his highly experienced chiefs and petty officers, many of whom had been decorated. Being the conscientious number one that he was, Sherwood undertook to determine the cause and remedy the situation. He found that the chiefs and POs were unhappy because they were about to do a second tour of duty overseas when there were others, equally qualified, who had not been abroad. *Safari's* senior rates suspected that there was a scam going on in the submarine drafting office and Sherwood immediately informed his CO.

At Requestmen (the navy's way of regularly ensuring that ratings can gain access to the commanding officer or his delegate for help) the next day, Bryant saw each man who had been adversely affected and heard the same story. He rushed to London that night and revealed his findings to the Admiral(S) (in charge of the submarine service). The investigations revealed that the drafting coxswain was indeed running a fiddle – for £10 to £25 he would provide an individual with a home billet. Admiral(S) quickly broke it up and sent the cox'n abroad with a flea in his ear. Those in *Safari* who wished to went to submarines based in home waters.

Safari sailed for Gibraltar in May 1942 with mostly new chiefs and POs, some of whom had never served on an operational boat. What they lacked in experience they made up for in enthusiasm, and on the southward passage Bryant and Sherwood made them exercise till they dropped. The crew did very well, and on their arrival in Gib the proud CO declined the proffered shake-down patrol and *Safari* went straight out to cover the June convoy to Malta. They worked from the Eighth Flotilla in Gib for nearly four months in 1942 with HMS *Maidstone* as their depot ship.

The officers and men took full advantage of the climate and amenities of Gibraltar. Although ladies were in short supply, and the Wrens were booked up with dates for weeks in advance, the submariners did not go without female company. Their rest flat for use between patrols was in the Old Naval Hospital where the "Wrennery" was also located. When the Wrens came home at curfew, after their dates, the submariners were waiting!

The situation in the Mediterranean had not turned around when *Safari* arrived, although British submarines were having an impact on the Axis seaborne supply routes to North Africa. Malta had yet to be relieved and enemy A/S patrols had proliferated, interfering with the submarines' operations. To combat the concentration of Axis A/S forces in certain important locations, the Admiralty dispersed their boats all over the Mediterranean, forcing the enemy to spread its defences thinner; the tactic worked well.

Safari's early patrols from Gibraltar were all involved with the relief of Malta and her later ones with the interdiction of Rommel's supply lines. Bryant and Sherwood left England well aware of the differences in submarine warfare in the Mediterranean and the North Sea. Boats had to operate in clear calm seas, which greatly increased their risk of detection by aircraft and surface ships; and crews had to work in unaccustomed heat, which, without dehumidifiers, increased fatigue.

While Forbes in *P34* experienced a reversed day and night at sea, Sherwood did not. *Safari* maintained a normal routine throughout her first commission. Bryant believed his crew were more alert for action, which mainly occurred in daylight, if they were up anyway. When they recharged the batteries overnight, the officers and men relaxed a little and could smoke. The tot of rum and a hot dinner were served after dark and then those who were off watch slept in fresh air. The officer of the watch and two lookouts, who did one-hour stints each, were always on the bridge ready to "hit the tit" if anything was detected approaching the submarine.

Freddie Sherwood settled into the position of first lieutenant of an operational boat well. He was the CO's right-hand man and was there to take over should anything befall his captain. As number one, or "Jimmy" to the men, Sherwood was responsible for the entire organization of the boat, while his CO concentrated on tactics. Sherwood supervised the coxswain in the allocation of duties to the crew, the cleanliness of the boat, the maintenance of discipline, and the welfare of the men. Whether in action or not, Sherwood was responsible for the trim of the submarine. This was his most critical tasking, for the submarine depended upon his skill for her safety.

"Trim" means buoyancy in submarine jargon. Boats submerge and surface by altering their buoyancy. They also maintain their horizontal balance by minute corrections in their fore and aft buoyancy. In order to be able to manoeuvre rapidly, dive, and maintain their depth accurately, the buoyancy of *Safari* had to be exactly right. For example, if the submarine was too buoyant, she would take too long to dive and could be caught on the surface by the enemy. If she was too heavy, she could plummet down into the depths out of control and be very difficult to stop. Sherwood manipulated the trim of *Safari* by adjusting the amount of water in her many trim tanks so that she was level at full buoyancy and also at neutral buoyancy when dived. He calculated mathematically how much water to put in which tanks to get it just right and then gave orders to the stoker petty officer. The trim was under constant adjustment by Sherwood or the OOW if not in action. It was constantly monitored as the displacement (weight) of the boat was always changing as stores, water, and fuel were expended and as torpedoes were fired.

Mostly Sherwood got his sums right, but not every time. Bryant got especially angry when a destroyer pounced on them and *Safari* was slow to go deep. The enemy cleared *Safari* by a few feet with the entire crew holding their breath and listening to the deafening roar of screws cutting through the water just overhead. Sherwood always endeavoured to err slightly on the heavy side with the bow down to prevent this type of scare from happening. The hydroplanes could correct a certain amount of error in the trim, but the boat had to be moving for them to do so. During avoidance manoeuvres, when the submarine was being hunted by A/S patrols, she had to be able slow down or stop, as well as surge ahead, so any errors in trim had to be minimal.

Safari's second war patrol off the east coast of Sardinia set the tone for the rest. The first sinking for a new submarine is always a memorable event and on 12 July 1942, *Safari* was blooded. In the middle of divine service a large schooner carrying timber was detected. Bryant unceremoniously ended prayers, surfaced, and attacked the vessel with the gun. The target's crew abandoned her, but *Safari*'s gun jammed before she sank forcing Bryant to finish her off with a torpedo. Four Italians were taken prisoner and surprised *Safari*'s crew by reloading the torpedoes and passing ammunition for the gun during a second unsuccessful attack. Later the Italians asked to serve on *Safari*.

In August 1942 *Safari* supported Operation PEDESTAL – the first Allied convoy to partially break through to relieve the now starving Malta. *Safari* was ordered to intercept Italian warships as they sailed from Palermo in Sicily to attack the convoy. Bryant and Sherwood watched in frustration as the big ships slipped past after the screen had forced *Safari* deep, but the next submarine in line managed to damage them, allowing four freighters and one tanker to reach Malta carrying the much-needed Spitfires, food, and fuel. *Safari* then left to go freelancing off Sardinia. They attacked all they could, bagging two coastal vessels and trying for a U-boat. The unreliable magnetic firing pistols of the torpedoes caused *Safari* to fail to sink the Italian submarine.

Bryant saw the surfaced U-boat six miles (9.7 km) away making for Cagliari in Sardinia and turned *Safari* at full speed to intercept her. He fired a broad spread of six torpedoes at long range and a poor angle hoping that one would connect. After the sixth torpedo left, *Safari*'s bow broke the surface and there was a loud explosion. Everyone but Bryant thought that they had hit the U-boat, but he realized immediately that the bang had been caused by the last torpedo detonating prematurely. A disappointed Bryant watched the enemy turn away intact, certain that the Italian CO had seen *Safari*'s two blunders: her clumsy appearance on the surface and the misfiring torpedo.

After the Italian submarine was captured during the Sicilian landings, *Safari*'s crew learned what had really happened that day. The enemy skipper of the *Bronzo* on hearing the detonation thought it was a torpedo exploding at the *end* of its run instead of at the beginning and he immediately turned towards where he thought his attacker was located. He had actually turned away from *Safari* and that was what Bryant observed. The Italian never saw the British boat break the surface. When the Italian boat was bumped, rattled, and shaken immediately afterwards, her captain erroneously thought he had collided with and sunk his adversary. He claimed it as a "kill" and was decorated for it. Later, when his boat was docked, the Italians found two huge dents in the hull where two of *Safari*'s torpedoes had hit her and failed to explode.

When the Fighting Tenth returned to Malta, *Safari* was seconded to it to make up for their losses. She arrived on 24 August. Sherwood found their new base in marked contrast to the affluence and peace of Gibraltar, but he was pleased to join such an acclaimed flotilla. Malta was still severely rationed and was being bombed on a daily basis, but the harbour was no longer the target. Food and hot water continued to be scarce. The boats ran in beer, which was rationed to one bottle per man per week. The officers and men of *Safari* were quartered in Lazaretto, an ancient leper hospital on Manoel Island in Marsamxett harbour, which was full of holes from the bombing and infested with sand fleas.

In September 1942, HMS *Safari's* first operation order from Captain(S) Simpson was simple. So simple, in fact, the staff officer of operations wrote it on a raffle ticket: "Adriatic, valid till October 11th." There was no need to give detailed orders and instructions – all shipping likely to be encountered in that area was the enemy and Bryant knew precisely what to do. He found plenty of opportunities. The patrol was typical – they shot up coastal vessels, were fired on by shore batteries, avoided A/S patrols, escorts, and aircraft, dropped dummy periscopes to make the enemy think there were lots of submarines about, and created havoc generally. A crew member made an Italian ensign and *Safari* flew it all the time on the surface from then on. They returned to Malta satisfied with their efforts – one ship sunk before breakfast, three days in a row. Once home, they were told that they were off again in four days.

Sherwood was convinced at the time that the British must have infiltrated the Italian navy, because the Tenth Flotilla's Captain(S) always seemed to know where to send his submarines to intercept the enemy. He knows now that some of this information, though not much in 1942, was obtained from Axis ENIGMA decrypts and passed on to the Captains(S) in the form of ULTRA signals.

SM10 ordered *Safari* and four U-class submarines to the north coast of Africa, near Tripoli, to attack an important and heavily escorted convoy from Naples and Palermo, which was bound for Rommel's army. This tasking was in preparation for Operation TORCH – the Allied landings in North Africa. *Safari* was the first of five submarines strung out along the anticipated track of the convoy. She missed the main body of the convoy, but the other boats successfully attacked it, sinking one freighter and one destroyer and creating great confusion. It looked as though *Safari* had missed the party, but she tore off to the south to locate any stragglers. Allied aircraft damaged the convoy further and in the early morning *Safari* found a merchant ship, the 5,400-ton (4,898-tonne)

Titania, lying stopped in rough seas and guarded by two destroyers. Bryant made a long-range attack, which failed, and then boldly went in to 1,800 yards (1.6 km) and torpedoed the wallowing ship. *Safari* avoided the escorts' spirited reprisal by hiding under a convenient layer of water (sea water of the same temperature, salinity, or density), which bounced the sound waves of the asdic back to the hunting ship without disclosing the submarine beneath it. When the five submarines returned to Malta, their Captain(S) said they had been handled with initiative and good sense, and the results certainly rattled the enemy.

The next day, 23 October 1942, saw the Eighth Army in North Africa begin its advance westward to regain Alamein and capture Benghazi. The preparations for the landings to reinforce this push would occupy *Safari* on her next outing, and see Sherwood's final patrol in the Mediterranean.

Safari was tasked first with protecting the Allied landings in North Africa (Operation TORCH: 7–8 November 1942) from units of the Italian fleet. After completing this assignment they sailed to the area east of Tripoli to again interdict Rommel's seaborne supplies.

Close to Sousse, *Safari* sank a small Italian brigantine carrying oil and barley to the Germans, after allowing the crew to abandon ship. Sherwood captured the skipper, along with his confidential books, and interrogated him while the rest of the crew rowed reluctantly ashore. The Canadian found the enemy's recognition signals for the week amongst the papers and *Safari* put them to good use.

On 14 November *Safari* received a signal that said, "Proceed with all dispatch" to the Gulf of Sirte to intercept a large merchant vessel carrying gasoline drums for Rommel's empty tanks. Normally they would have travelled in daylight submerged, but Bryant ran on the surface with the diesels running flat out, because the local recognition signals and *Safari's* makeshift Italian ensign had given him confidence. Next morning Bryant sighted his quarry and shadowed her on the surface. The enemy merchant ship became very twitchy and, when an aircraft arrived as well, Bryant had to dive. They lost the target in poor visibility but found the vessel later in the moonlight in a small desert port surrounded by what looked like E boats. Bryant cautiously closed on the surface because it was too shallow to dive, praying that they would not be detected. He fired two torpedoes at an awkward angle and the second one hit the E boats. They exploded in a sheet of flame that lit up the night like day. *Safari* had never been so exposed and unable to dive. She turned for deeper water on emergency full speed, shaking with the strain, but there was no counterattack. The E boats turned out to be lighters full of gasoline, as yet unloaded. Through the periscope Sherwood saw the trucks and tanks of Rommel's routed forces stuck on the coast road without fuel. When *Safari* returned to attack an ammunition lighter later, their original target was still burning. The lighter exploded with a remarkable bang, destroying a nearby tank, and afterwards Bryant maintained that his submarine was the first and only one to claim a tank in World War II. Satisfied, *Safari* withdrew.

On their way back to Malta, *Safari* sank a schooner and a light ship and had a spirited fight with some landing craft that surprised them on the surface. They arrived home with almost no fuel after travelling 2,800 miles (4,505 km).

By the time *Safari* ended this patrol in November 1942, the submarines in the Mediterranean had operated so effectively that 50 percent of Italian merchant tonnage was unserviceable and unable to supply Rommel's army. By December, the enemy's tanks and transport had no fuel whatsoever. The Tenth Submarine Flotilla, to which *Safari* was seconded and of which Forbes's *P34* was a part, had sunk half a million tons and damaged a quarter of a million more.

Malta was going wild at the close of November – a convoy had arrived with no losses. It was to be the first of many: after more than two years, the siege had been lifted, two weeks before the island would have been forced to surrender. As Sherwood sailed into Malta for the last time, the population were lining the ramparts and cheering their heads off. He said that it was the most incredible experience of his life – everybody on the boat was crying.

After their arrival, Bryant called his number one into his cabin to tell him that he was to return to England to do his Commanding Officers' Qualifying Course. Though Sherwood did not want to leave *Safari*, he had been wondering, along with several other VR officers, if they were going to be allowed to take Perisher. Sherwood was certainly capable of doing it, but the RN had always considered it a preserve of their career officers. However, the severe shortage of submarine COs forced the navy's hand and guaranteed the volunteers their chance. Surprisingly, the opportunity did not excite Sherwood. He wanted to remain a first lieutenant.

Sherwood had had the good fortune to serve with one of the best submarine commanders in the service during some critical operations; together they had sunk fifteen ships in the first three months of their time in the Mediterranean. HMS/M *Safari* had been constantly commended for her valour, daring, and skill by her Captain(S) and also by the Admiral(S). Britain awarded Sherwood a Distinguished Service Cross for "bravery in successful submarine patrols" on 23 March 1943. He was the second Canadian in submarines in the Second World War to be decorated, but it was not to be his last honour.

Despite his reservations about Perisher, Sherwood left *Safari* and her extroverted CO to board a flight to Gibraltar, where he spent a couple of welcome days at the rest flat. On the next leg of his journey home, the flight to England, five German JU-88s came too close for comfort, and Sherwood learned that flying in wartime was not for him. He arrived safely to start his Perisher just before Christmas.

The first Canadian submariner to lose his life in the Second World War was Hugh D.S. Russel, an English-speaking Quebecker. He was a mining surveyor when he joined the RCNVR in December 1940 for training at Royal Roads Military College; he volunteered for submarines after failing the Anti-submarine Group Control Course.

In September 1942 Russel, already a lieutenant, was posted as a spare officer to the First Flotilla in Beirut. Soon he joined the highly efficient HMS *Traveller* as her fourth hand and went straight out on his first operational patrol off the North African coast. It was an eventful introduction, with two attacks on vessels carrying supplies to Rommel, one of which sank, and a covert mission called Operation ANGLO.[4]

ANGLO turned out to be one of *Traveller*'s most dangerous operations – the evacuation of commandos from enemy territory. She had done it successfully several times before, but it was no less hazardous for all that. With brilliant moonlight illuminating *Traveller* on the surface, she cautiously approached a small bay on the Isle of Rhodes to exchange prearranged signals with the commandos. They came in so close to shore that her CO could see enemy patrols. *Traveller,* unable to dive in such shallow waters, was very vulnerable. The moon turned out to be a blessing for the commandos, who had to swim for the submarine because their dinghies had been captured. The crew would never have seen them on a black, moonless night. *Traveller* spent over two hours exposed on the surface before successfully rescuing the survivors of the raid. The boat was not seen until she withdrew, but *Traveller* was able to dive to avoid four poorly aimed depth charges from a patrol vessel. *Traveller*'s CO remarked later that the patrol's success had been miraculous.

On 28 November 1942, after a depth-charging on a previous patrol, Russel and *Traveller* sailed with a relief CO for the Gulf of Taranto as part of Operation PORTCULLIS. This was a preliminary reconnaissance of

Taranto harbour to determine the location of enemy battleships. Their findings were to be used a month later in Operation PRINCIPAL – the scheme to destroy enemy ships using human torpedoes (see next chapter). PRINCIPAL itself was so secret that even *Traveller*'s Captain(S) was unaware of the reason for this patrol.

Taranto was a difficult place to reconnoitre; her approaches were heavily defended, patrolled, and mined. HMS/M *Traveller* reported on the seaward defences of the harbour, but was never heard from again. She was the victim of either anti-submarine patrols or, more likely, a mine. Though the Italian broadcasts at the time reported a submarine was destroyed by A/S craft, the enemy records do not confirm it. Six officers and fifty-nine men were lost without trace about 4 December 1942, though Russel's mother did not hear about her son until the 12th. Ironically, the Italian warships that *Traveller* had gone to find had already left Taranto for Naples, and the planned human torpedo raid was cancelled.

CHAPTER TWELVE

THE CHARIOTEERS, 1942–1943

"Two magnificent Canadians"[1]

Two other Canadians should properly be included here, even though they were not qualified submariners. Both were men of resolute, independent dispositions, with tough physical attributes, and they chose to participate in very secret and hazardous underwater operations with the Royal Navy during WWII. Outwardly, the pair were unlikely heroes – one was a trainee accountant, the other a salesman.[2]

The aspiring accountant, Alan Moreton, sailed to England in the first draft for the RN in 1940 with J.D. Woods, having spent the Phoney War fidgeting through a boring shore job. He had joined the RCNVR before the war in Toronto, prompted by his interest in the sea and a friend's encouragement.

Another Canadian officer on the troopship was Charles (Chuck) E. Bonnell, who had commanded the Toronto Sea Cadets and at thirty was considered an elder. When the war started Bonnell cheerfully left his job in sales and maintenance, which he found confining, and looked forward to wartime opportunities for his adventurous spirit. He was separated from his wife, who lived quietly with their six-year-old daughter.

The two lieutenants completed their basic course at HMS *King Alfred* with Sherwood and Woods and served together in an armed cruiser until they were sunk off Ireland in November 1940. Both were rescued separately and Bonnell swore that he owed his life to a cheap flashlight stuck in his cap band. They subsequently went to Scotland for motor torpedo boat (MTB) training.

Bonnell and Moreton's MTB training lasted until mid-January 1941, when they parted company. Bonnell went to the Sixth MTB Flotilla at

Dover, and Moreton to a motor launch building on the River Thames, near London, and later to Lowestoft on the east coast. They both served for a year in motor torpedo boats, fast and exciting vessels that harassed enemy shipping; both took part in the rescue of survivors from the battered coastal convoys. By early 1942 Bonnell was already in command of his own MTB, had received a DSC for sinking a large enemy supply ship, and had been injured by shrapnel. Moreton's goal was to command an MTB too, and in January 1942 he achieved it, but only for a few hours.

Moreton described himself as an introvert, and more of a follower than a leader, but others saw him as an impetuous and moderately undisciplined individual. He was a tall, initially shy man, who became affable after a few beers. His most obvious characteristic was a fiercely independent spirit; it was to become his most useful asset in the dangerous job he was to undertake.

When barely unpacked at his first command in Dover, Moreton was astonished to receive an order sending him via London to HMS *Dolphin* for special duty in submarines. Both he and his CO thought it was a mistake, but upon investigation they discovered that it was not. Moreton repacked his still-folded kit and made his way within the hour to see Admiral(S) with much curiosity and some trepidation. A distinguished naval captain met Moreton and ushered him into his office. He was the admiral's chief of staff.

The captain urged Moreton to tell him about himself and it did not take long – the Canadian was preoccupied trying to figure out what this was all about. On asking why he was there, Moreton was told that the Royal Navy were about to construct "human torpedoes." It was the first Moreton had heard of this type of weapon and the captain told him not to get too concerned until he had heard more. Moreton listened attentively, becoming progressively more amazed. He then was asked if he would like to join this most secret project. Eagerly, Moreton said yes.

Without more ado, the captain took him to see Admiral(S), Admiral Sir Max Horton, VC, DSO, RN. "It was like meeting God," Moreton remembered. Admiral Horton gave Moreton a sherry and a cigarette, sat him down, asked for his background, and then said, "Do you have any questions?"

"I most certainly do," replied Moreton. "How on earth did you find my name?"

"On a list of volunteers for hazardous service."

"I don't recall ever signing something like that. But if you say so, I must have. How many of us are there?"

There was a telling pause, and then Horton quietly said, "As a matter of fact, you're the first one."

Moreton's jaw dropped.

"*Tirpitz* is the target for this operation," continued the admiral. "And there is a VC in it for those who conduct a successful attack! Do you know any other Canadians who'd be interested?"

"Yes. Chuck Bonnell and Jim Kirkpatrick, both in MTBs. They're adventurous types," Moreton replied without thinking. In front of Moreton, the admiral picked up the phone to the personnel department and told them to appoint Bonnell and Kirkpatrick to HMS *Dolphin* forthwith. Moreton recalled that he felt like an executioner, but knew his friends would like the scheme. As personnel selection proceeded, the type of individual suited for this dangerous work was often found amongst the MTB sailors. They were tough, fit, and resourceful, and many were imbued with exceptional courage.

Moreton spent the next two days in London reading all the top-secret files on the subject. He was the only volunteer to be given this privilege, a fact that until recently was still officially secret. None of the rest met Admiral(S) or were told about the precise nature of the special operations until they had begun their training.

The details that Moreton read in the classified files held him spellbound. The Italians had first developed two-man human torpedoes in the 1930s for clandestine attacks on enemy ships in port. The British paid little attention to the devices, even after the RN captured one machine, two men, and their diving suits in 1940. A year later the British began to realize their value when their battleships, HM ships *Queen Elizabeth* and *Valiant* were severely damaged in Alexandria by the same weapon. The machine was much like a large torpedo, which two men rode like a horse; it could be dived and surfaced like a submarine. The warhead, at the bow, was detachable and the divers' job was to affix it to the bottom of an enemy ship using magnets; a timing device allowed them to retreat before it blew up. Moreton closed the last file thoughtfully, temporarily bereft of his usual ebullience.

The German and Italian capital ships, which were tying up the British naval forces, could not readily be knocked out by aircraft, submarines, or surface vessels. When other, more covert, means had to be found to sink them, the Royal Navy turned to midget submarines. These were scaled-down submarines, called X-craft, which carried a crew of three or four. When their development moved too slowly, human torpedoes were chosen as an interim measure.

In February 1942 Admiral(S) ordered a prototype based on the captured Italian human torpedo, which was hastily shipped back to Britain to serve as a model. The training commander in charge of special operations, Commander W.R. Fell, RN, finished the first chariot, as they became known, in early April 1942. He fabricated this model from a tree trunk, twenty feet long and two feet (6.1 m x 0.6 m) in diameter. After the initial development by the RN, the machines were to be built by a commercial firm, and they were to be operational by late summer.

Moreton became the first member of the famous Twelfth Flotilla, although it was not called that yet. Others followed swiftly, despite the Admiralty's caution about calling for volunteers. As Fell did not want "death and glory" types, senior officers were asked to identify potential candidates for hazardous operations involving rigorous underwater training. Moreton had indeed never signed anything – he had been quietly selected. The volunteers had to be under twenty-eight years of age (Bonnell was not), confident swimmers, medically sound, and capable of becoming very fit. In addition, officers had to have previous navigational experience in small craft. The RN estimated that 50 percent of the volunteers would be rejected at the initial selection stage, and 20 percent more in training. Jim Kirkpatrick, though considered, was not allowed to leave Coastal Forces, so he did not learn that Moreton had "volunteered" him until much later.

When Moreton reported to HMS *Dolphin* he found that only one person seemed to have any knowledge of why he was there, and that was vague. Lt.-Commander Bill Shelford, RN, in charge of submarine escape training, had been told to provide him with as much diving experience as he could.

Bonnell arrived a few days later, saying to Moreton, "What sort of mess have you got me into this time?" Bonnell had willingly offered his services, even though he had only the vaguest idea of the work. Shelford remembered teaching the two tall Canadians – one night after a dive in the blacked-out submarine tank, Moreton asked him, "I suppose the next dive will be with sharks in the tank and knives?"

"Not exactly, Al," responded Shelford. "No knives."[3]

As soon as they were alone, Moreton confided his knowledge to Bonnell, who was intrigued and stimulated by the prospect. Neither Canadian realized that the odds for survival would be appalling.

Bonnell was a tall man with brown, thinning hair, and a dark, ascetic face. He had the aquiline features of a North American Indian, remembered Moreton. Everyone liked Bonnell and found him thoroughly sincere, but he was reserved and difficult to get to know well. Woods, who had sailed with Bonnell before the war, found him contradictory, sometimes wild and at other times serious. Outwardly he did not display a care in the world, but according to his closest friends Bonnell fully accepted that he might die in the war. Bonnell was far from foolish, but was always the first to attempt a risky undertaking.

By April 1942 the first batch of charioteers had trickled into HMS *Dolphin*. The volunteers were from all ranks – two from the army, one from the Royal Marines, with the majority from the navy. First, they had a rigorous medical examination for diving suitability, which Bonnell and Moreton both passed easily and then they took an intensive helmet diving course, designed to increase their underwater endurance to five hours. Later they completed submarine escape training using the Davis Submarine Escape Apparatus (DSEA).

This training could be intimidating, but it certainly weeded out those who were unsuitable. At the bottom of a tank filled with thirty-five feet (10.7 m) of water was a small watertight compartment similar to the escape compartment in a submarine. The trainees entered this dry area and put on their DSEAs. Water flooded in and crept up to their chins as the pressure inside equalized with that in the tank outside. Then the trainees opened the hatch in the deckhead and escaped to the surface, breathing through their DSEAs. The Canadians both did well, and Bonnell was clearly going to be very good. He was intensely interested in all that was going on around him, and he took charge of events and subordinates with skill. Round one was soon finished, and speculation about the team's role became intense – would they be working from submarines off enemy coasts?

Next, the prospective charioteers were guinea pigs in some crucial research. The Admiralty Experimental Diving Unit was studying the breathing apparatus and diving suits required for the chariot operations. Compressed air produced telltale bubbles that could be detected on the surface, and so oxygen rebreathers had to be used. These had a major drawback: oxygen was toxic to divers below thirty feet (9 m), causing convulsions and unconsciousness at worst, euphoria and tingling in the extremities at the least. These side effects were known as "Oxygen Pete."

The boffins, unsure what would happen if the divers went below thirty feet, did extensive experiments on the volunteers. The work was so dangerous that only two or three dives each were permitted. The charioteers suited up and were lowered into a twelve-foot-deep tank, half full of water. The pressure was then increased to simulate varying depths, while the guinea pig breathed his pure oxygen for a quarter of an hour. The subject was closely watched, and fished out as soon as he began to lose consciousness. Moreton found that he had good tolerance, much better than most, and he never blacked out.

The experiments confirmed that pure oxygen could be breathed with no ill effects down to thirty feet (9 m) – below that, shorter and shorter times could be tolerated. At fifty feet (15 m), the divers could stay down no longer than half an hour, and at ninety feet (27.4 m) only a few minutes. Their work was going to be risky, but the charioteers were not disturbed.

It was now that the remaining volunteers were officially told about the machines they would use. Most were astonished, but all were enthusiastic. The training commander also announced the first target – *Tirpitz*. No one could imagine how the chariots were going to reach the German ship, sixty miles up a heavily defended fjord, when their range was only eighteen nautical miles. Bonnell and Moreton fantasized, more seriously than not, that their delivery would be by parachute. Fell patiently discussed the idea with the Canadians, and didn't reject them as fools. This inspired Bonnell and Moreton to sport upside-down parachute insignia on their battle dress. The actual means of delivery was not revealed to the charioteers for several more months. It was probably not known to the planners themselves at this time.

When their training was finished they returned to *Dolphin* and Bonnell was given the honour of being the first to test the wooden prototype, which had no motor but could dive. The initial trial was held in a torpedo range in a tideless, sheltered corner of Portsmouth harbour at the end of April 1942.

The sun was shining when Bonnell and his partner donned their DSEA sets, with extra bottles of oxygen attached. They wore lead shoes, and life-lines secured them to a nearby motor launch. When Bonnell mounted the wooden chariot nicknamed *Cassidy* he had no idea what to expect. Fell showed him how to dive by venting the ballast tank and adjusting the planes and warned him to stay off the bottom. Bonnell tried, but *Cassidy* steadfastly refused to dive. In the end, festooned with lead weights, it finally descended to the sea bed. Later it became apparent that the chariot had been tested by Fell in fresh water and had not been readjusted for the more buoyant salt water. The motor launch towed Bonnell and his reluctant steed up and down a few times and then the first test ended. Bonnell's display of guts did much to encourage the other neophytes.

With only one chariot to work with and that by no means perfected, the charioteers had time on their hands. To prevent the lowered morale that came with inactivity, they did more helmet diving. The navy constructed a second prototype to get it the way they wanted it, and once the final changes had been incorporated a company started production.

Bonnell and Moreton worked on their diving throughout the spring of 1942; often the heavy boot of a PO instructor on their shoulders helped to persuade them to stay underwater. Their stamina increased and they learned to appreciate the outer limits of their endurance. The principle behind this method of instruction was simple – do it so often that it becomes automatic and stay under longer than you think you can. In enemy waters, the luxury of surfacing would often be impossible. The discomfort never went away, but it did become tolerable for the Canadians.

Once they reached this stage, Bonnell and Moreton found dressing in their new diving suits to be the most unpleasant part of their new job. These were made of rubberized twill, which was light and very flexible in comparison to the conventional diving suits of the day. Their one drawback was lack of durability – they could easily be punctured. First, two sets of long underwear were essential to beat the cold – one of silk next to the skin and then a thick woollen set with socks. Two assistants were needed to squeeze each charioteer into his suit. Instead of heavy metal helmets they wore flexible hoods, which were fitted to the suits with special seals. Hair came out in handfuls as the tight fitting hoods were pulled over their heads. The hinged eyepieces were left open to allow the charioteers to talk and breathe fresh air. Very tight elastic bands around the wrists prevented leaks (or so it was hoped). Two large canvas boots with lead weights came next. The dressers applied thick grease to protect the charioteers' hands as gloves were too clumsy. Weighted belts were slung around their waists.

Last, the dressers heaved two heavy tanks onto their backs, secured the harnesses, and tested the modified DSEAs. The tanks had been salvaged from downed German fighter planes and contained enough oxygen, at 1,800 to 2,000 p.s.i. (pounds per square inch) to last for seven hours. The charioteers gripped the mouthpiece firmly between their teeth, and applied a tight noseclip to prevent them breathing the air inside the helmets. The pure oxygen flowed from the tanks into the DSEA's rubber bag and the charioteers breathed it in from there through a hose and a reducing valve. A chemical in the bag absorbed their exhaled carbon dioxide.

Bonnell and Moreton always suffered from bone-chilling cold and constant leaks. The planners considered using wet suits, but rejected them as not warm enough for northern operations. All suits were meticulously maintained by professional divers.

The charioteers practised daily in the harbour. Repeatedly, they walked out from the shore on the bottom attached by a line held by their dresser. Moreton and Bonnell and their teammates learned quickly that once in the sea they had to do a trim dive – just like the manoeuvre a submarine does before a patrol. The air trapped in the suits caused them to float like corks on the surface; it had to be removed through a spring-loaded release valve on the top of their helmets. It took very fine adjustment to achieve the necessary neutral buoyancy. If the charioteers were neutrally buoyant just below the surface, as they descended further the increased pressure made them dangerously negatively buoyant. To overcome this, they passed oxygen directly into the suit via the mouthpiece, but if they puffed out too much, up they would rush, blown up like balloons. Practice and perseverance helped them achieve control. Once they caught their trim, the charioteers then ambled about on the bottom for half an hour, controlled by signals on the rope.

The Canadians were now part of a group of twenty-four officers and thirty-one men. Spirits were high, and as they became more confident they began to think the job was going to be easy. Then they had their first casualty. In excellent diving conditions, one of the most promising officers failed to surface from walking on the bottom. It was thought that Oxygen Pete euphoria had caused him to untie the rope for fun and then to fail to use his reserve tank of oxygen when the first ran out. This sobered everyone up, and the mood changed from enthusiastic fun to grim determination.

In June 1942 the training base was relocated to Loch Erisort, a remote location in the Outer Hebrides of Scotland, where security was easier to maintain and the environment was more suited to their operational requirements. HMS *Titania* became their depot ship. One team remained in Portsmouth to take delivery of the first "real" chariot, which they demonstrated to Admiral(S) (Horton) and a USN admiral. The trial went well and the success marked the achievement of Admiral Horton's objective – trained charioteers and a working machine in under three months.

On the train journey to Scotland, the rest of the charioteers let off steam. When the train was due to depart, Commander Fell found them seated underneath it, entertaining the horrified stationmaster with lewd songs and beer. At that moment, Admiral Horton came striding along the platform with a distinguished gentleman in civilian dress who was instantly surrounded by the charioteers and invited to join their party. He ignored them and walked on, while the Admiral quickly broke up the fun with his customary mild authority. Later, during a rugby match in the train's corridor, the admiral informed Fell of the identity of the VIP who had arrived with him.

"You seem to have picked the right sort of types, but I wish you would not let them attack the First Lord of the Admiralty when I am taking him to inspect the submarine flotillas in Scotland,"[4] Horton complained.

After settling into *Titania,* the First Lord of the Admiralty inspected the unruly charioteers and Horton bawled them out. The pair noticed that Moreton had one of the train conductor's buttons safety-pinned to his jacket instead of a naval button. The Canadian improvised quickly, explaining that the conductor wanted the button to send to a relative of his in Canada. Moreton still has the button, which bears the initials "LNER," the London and North Eastern Railway, and it continues to remind him of that memorable journey.

At Erisort, facilities for the project were being constructed. A jetty was built out into the remote loch and huts were erected for stores and workshops at the water's edge. The personnel lived aboard the depot ship and the chariots were kept there too. The first production chariots had not been finished, so initially the men had to share the two prototypes for exercises. Every day Bonnell and Moreton would suit up and practise submerging and diving with a "number two" while being towed up and down the loch underwater for twenty minutes at a time. High winds, which funnelled in from the sea, complicated their practice sessions. When someone else had *Cassidy,* diving training continued from a raft. It was repetitive, boring work, but vital, and was relieved when the first two production machines were delivered.

Although the chariot was shaped like a torpedo, it was a very different weapon. The two-man crew sat astride the vehicle in their self-contained diving suits, in seats like saddles. Each machine was fitted with a heavy-duty electric battery that provided power to an electric motor attached to a propeller; this drove the chariot at 3 knots for about four hours, giving it a range of twelve nautical miles. Later models had a range of eighteen nautical miles. The vehicle also had a small main ballast tank for submerging, with compressed air to blow it for surfacing, and two trimming tanks. Planes and a rudder were provided for manoeuvring and were operated with a joystick. The leader sat in front to drive and used only a clock, a compass, and a depth gauge to navigate. His number two sat behind and was responsible for their passage through obstructions using equipment stored in a locker behind him. He also had to secure the detachable 600-pound (272 kg) high-explosive warhead to the enemy's hull below the waterline.

Now that four production models were available, the training began in earnest. The teams learned to drive the chariots, to increase their endurance to six hours, to navigate in the dark underwater, and to communicate with each other. Day by day and night by night the teams worked on, ignoring the extreme discomfort. Later they learned tactics, developed methods for approaching a target and for attaching the warhead to its hull, and exercised with real battleships.

Once everyone was familiar with their own chariots, accurate navigation became the training priority. The luminous magnetic compasses were useless, because they were affected by the metal of the machines and the warhead's strong magnets, so Bonnell and Moreton used them only for taking relative bearings. As the charioteers travelled at fifteen to twenty feet (4.5 to 6 m) below the surface, where it was pitch black and silent, they had to surface every five to ten minutes for a visual check. The chariots' propensity to porpoise also made depth-keeping difficult.

Communications between the team were primitive while under way – talking being impossible. They were joined together by a life-line and used it to signal each other. One tug meant "Are you O.K.?", two tugs "Right", and three tugs "Left." The important signal was four tugs, "Emergency surface!" Moreton and his number two pressed out signals in Morse code on each other's wrists and grunted loudly if there was an acute problem developing.

Bonnell and Moreton put up with permanently swollen noses from wearing the tight nose clips for hours and with cuts and blisters in their gums from their mouthpieces rubbing. Their exposed hands became numb quickly, and when the circulation returned agony set in immediately.

Mechanical defects occurred in the chariots, unexplained things went wrong, and everyone had their share of scares. The pools of fresh water from the streams feeding the salt water loch caused the chariots to go crashing down, well past the safe depth for breathing oxygen. Bonnell and Moreton, along with most of their colleagues, suffered varying degrees of Oxygen Pete below forty feet (13 m), and everyone experienced excruciating pain in their ears. To plummet to 100 feet (30.5 m) was uncommon, but sudden smaller descents were frequent. Losing consciousness meant a hangover accompanied by headaches and depression. Several men were invalided out due to ear damage and unsuitability, but the Canadians stayed and worked on doggedly, putting up with the hardships.

Very few of the volunteers were "naturals" at the job, and for most the strain began to tell at this stage. When training was going poorly Moreton suffered from nightmares, and he was not alone. The dreams involved things going catastrophically wrong during operations. Moreton admitted they created anxiety while awake, though not enough to adversely effect his performance. The navy recognized the mounting stress and had two psychologists work unobtrusively with the charioteers.

As they progressed, Fell introduced complications into the exercises. He had the charioteers negotiating anti-submarine nets, avoiding patrols, and experimenting with various ways of attaching the huge warheads to the targets. The last was the most awkward and fraught with difficulty. It was Chuck Bonnell who discovered and demonstrated the first possible solution: he approached the target submerged, and when the chariot was well underneath he stopped and blew the ballast tank, causing the vehicle to rise and press against the hull. Unfortunately, the method only worked well when they could see. The charioteers worked together to develop each procedure from first principles and experimentation.

At the end of this training phase, the charioteers and maintenance crews were exhausted. The lack of time and constant exercising both day and night had taken its toll.

The final challenge was to perfect a means of escape for the crews after they had attached the warhead to a target. The charioteers accepted that the most likely route was ashore, even though it meant entering enemy territory. While physical fitness had been stressed throughout the training period, Fell now expanded it to incorporate more survival and commando techniques. He devised exercises, including fifteen-mile (24 km) hikes in mountainous, uninhabited terrain, and the attack and defence of a held position. None of these exercises were taken very seriously, Moreton later recalled.

The climax of this training came when the local defence forces of the area threw down the gauntlet to the men of *Titania*. It was a night never to be forgotten in Loch Erisort. The charioteers and support staff on *Titania* dreamed up some wonderful "wheezes" and "weapons." The most successful was "posting" lighted calcium flares through the mail slot of the local police station. The confusion that followed resulted in several civilian prisoners being relieved of their kilts for the remainder of the night. The charioteers declared a complete victory and the locals never dared challenge them again.

The first operation was slow in materializing, and in August 1942 the charioteers took two weeks' leave. Bonnell and Moreton spent it in London with their colleagues. When they returned to base the pace had picked up, and the first operation was being planned. Refreshed by their holiday, the Canadians worked harder than ever to be picked for the first raid on the *Tirpitz*, but first they had to prove themselves in much tougher simulated attacks than before.

The officers now selected their permanent teammates. Bonnell chose Robert Evans – a cheerful, reliable able seaman of large proportions. Moreton's number two was Malcolm R. Causer, a short and sturdy Brit with an amiable disposition. Moreton said that Causer was ideal – quite fearless and highly intelligent. The relationships that developed between the Canadians and their partners were based on trust and were very informal and relaxed.

The charioteers now discovered that they did not have to approach the target underwater at all. Trimmed well down on the surface, their low profile and dark colours could not readily be seen at night. This made navigation much easier, and they were more comfortable. This surfaced approach meant that they could not use Bonnell's method of getting under the target. The teams chose to run in at very slow speed just below the surface until they reached the waterline of the ship. The charioteers then used the securing magnets to manhandle their machines down and under the hull into the right position.

The training base then moved again, to an inland loch off Loch Cairnbawn on the mainland of northern Scotland. It was a perfect location, because it closely matched the Norwegian fjords where the German ships were tucked away, and was more sheltered than Erisort. The base at Kylesku, known as Port HHZ, was very isolated, and the only pub for miles rationed its beer. Another depot ship, HMS *Alecto*, and more than twenty small craft arrived to cope with the growing demands of the project.

The fleet lent a battleship, HMS *Howe*, as a target for the charioteers. She was anchored inshore and netted in to simulate the conditions the teams might face. The wardrooms of *Howe*, *Titania*, and *Alecto* laid sizeable wagers on the outcome of the attacks. On the first night *Howe* had the advantage, because she was expecting the attack, had her hydrophones operating, and employed a continuous motor boat patrol.

The charioteers aimed to get through the defences, place their charges, and retire undetected. Seven chariots set off at fifteen-minute intervals on their first really difficult assignment. Chuck Bonnell went third and did a textbook attack. He had no trouble fixing the warhead in a good position on the hull. His partner attached four big magnets to the ship's bottom and secured the warhead's ring to them. Bonnell then released the warhead using a lever in the chariot. His number two set the fuse and then the pair manhandled their machine clear of the target, got aboard, and started the motor. Bonnell remained dived as he worked his way through the nets without a problem and returned triumphant. The team that followed them failed.

Alan Moreton sailed fifth. From the outset, he had mechanical problems and was unable to trim the chariot satisfactorily whatever he tried. He persevered, and when he reached the last anti-torpedo net, his machine was in such a bad, bow-up attitude that he could not correct it. The team got off the chariot and manhandled it over the net undetected and established their position while a patrol passed very close. After another quick look, they proceeded on the surface. The machine's behaviour was becoming increasingly uncontrollable and Moreton had no choice but to remain surfaced alongside the target. The pair became infuriated when they were entangled in a web of fishing lines and hooks put out by the crew of the *Howe* and had to cut themselves free. However, try as he might, Causer was unable to attach the charge because they could not dive. They were so exhausted by now that they had to be content with leaving one of their securing magnets behind to prove they had actually been there. Moreton and Causer escaped on the surface, manhandling their chariot over the nets in the darkness. Moreton was disappointed with his performance, but was most encouraged that they were not detected while on the surface for so long. He said, "There were very few clean operations."

The night's score was four successes, three attacks drawn, and one failure. As the *Howe* was expecting the chariots, Fell was delighted with their overall achievement. The teams continued to practise attacks while HMS *Howe* was at their disposal and the success rate improved. Tragically, on the last night an officer died after he became unconscious under the target and this diluted their celebrations.

With that, the training course ended. The Canadians could hardly wait to tackle real operations.

In the early fall, a member of the Royal Norwegian Navy's Special Service Unit joined the charioteers. Leif Larsen had escaped Norway's occupation and was now posing as the skipper of a Norwegian fishing boat based in the Shetland Islands and gathering intelligence for Britain. Fell had recruited Larsen and his boat as the chariots' delivery system for the *Tirpitz* raid. It was not to be parachutes after all! Fell also chose the teams for the first raid. Bonnell's and Moreton's teams were selected.

A full-scale dress rehearsal took place in the middle of October 1942. The plan called for the fishing boat to carry the chariots slung underneath its hull for the ocean passage and then to tow them behind it to within three miles of the *Tirpitz*. On release the charioteers had to trim themselves and their machines before setting out alone up the fjord.

HMS *Rodney* played the part of the *Tirpitz* for the final exercise and all went well with the chariots' transport, tow, and release. In the completely dark night, Moreton travelled two and a half miles (4 km) before he could dimly see the battleship. The chariots were small enough to pass between the meshes of anti-submarine nets, but on this occasion the teams practised going over the top. The anti-torpedo nets, rather like chain mail, came next and Moreton's orders had them pulling the chariot down hand over hand and up the other side to avoid surface A/S patrols. On the surface again, Moreton took a bearing on the funnel of the *Rodney* and then very slowly began the long journey to the target. He came up frequently to renew his bearings and, much to Moreton's relief, his chariot behaved perfectly. He gently nudged the chariot against *Rodney*'s hull and, taking two magnets, Causer worked the machine under the hull. The team had a brief scare when they felt themselves being pulled towards a cooling intake, but avoided disaster with brute strength. The placement and fusing of the warhead went without a hitch, and then Moreton ordered their withdrawal. More manhandling got them clear and then he and Causer dragged their weary bodies back onto the chariot and started the motor. They got away from the target unseen, moving as fast as they could, and returned to the depot ship, triumphant.

Bonnell too was successful, though the details of his effort are unknown. Despite the crew on the battleship expecting the attack, the charioteers accomplished it without detection and, had it been real, the *Rodney* would have been on the bottom. Bonnell and Moreton, although exhausted, were too wound up to sleep and celebrated with a few drinks in the wardroom.

The Canadians were justifiably proud of their selection and performance but they endeavoured to improve further with more arduous navigational training to prepare for the operation. Then, on 24 October 1942 they sailed on the fishing boat with Leif Larsen, accompanied by *Alecto*, to the Shetland Islands where they made their final preparations. Their new base on the most northerly island was even bleaker and more isolated than Kylesku.

During this period, Bonnell and Moreton, their partners, and the other teams were briefed in detail about the raid. It was called Operation TITLE. The charioteers familiarized themselves with the topography of the fjord using an excellent hand-made model that included landmarks, obstructions, all the depths, and the *Tirpitz*. From this they chose the best place to be dropped, the courses to steer, and where to land afterwards.

The charioteers learned about their escape plan too. They were to go ashore into occupied Norway to meet the Norwegian underground, who would be responsible for getting them to neutral Sweden sixty miles (96.5 km) away. The plan sounded perilous but exciting. Even today, Moreton remembers the Norwegian challenge and passwords they were to use:

"Heil Hitler!" (said the underground).

"Hitler Heil!" (replied the charioteers).

"To hell with him!" (responded the underground).

The brand of courage demonstrated by the Norwegians involved in the raid deeply impressed the charioteers who entrusted their lives to them. Larsen and his crew were quiet and shy, yet they had done things that made the Canadians' blood run cold, and they were prepared to take enormous risks for their colleagues.

The operation was about to begin when the top brass delayed it, to wait for optimum conditions. Bonnell and Moreton could scarcely contain their impatience. The teams took a short leave to prevent an unhealthy build-up of stress and the Canadians went to Edinburgh. It was probably the only leave they could not wait to end. Before they left, Fell impressed on the teams that they had to catch special transport from Inverness back to the Shetlands at a certain time and day or they would miss the raid. Bonnell and Moreton were three hours late through a combination of carelessness and bad luck.

The Canadians were horrified by what they had done when they got to Inverness. They sought out the transport officer and asked him if a naval party had gone through. "We're in a bit of a hurry," they said, not daring to breathe a word about their destination. The officer thought for a moment and replied, "Yes, a bunch went to the Kyle of Lochalsh." The Kyle was the mainland terminus for the Isle of Skye on the west coast of Scotland and this confused Bonnell and Moreton. They were unable to contact anyone in the Shetlands and so, after some discussion, took the next train to the Kyle of Lochalsh, arriving in the early evening. The other charioteers were not there.

Dispirited and increasingly anxious, Bonnell and Moreton asked to see the commanding officer of the small base. The OOD met their request with reluctance, but eventually arranged it. "We're on an important mission and we are in the wrong place. We have to get to the Shetlands in a great hurry," they demanded. "Check with Admiral(S), and see if he can sort it out." After much foot-shuffling, the CO agreed to contact Admiral(S), but as it was a Sunday, he could not be reached. With ill-contained impatience, Bonnell and Moreton saw the CO again first thing Monday morning. He had finally got in touch with Admiral(S) who confirmed their story, and promised to try to provide an aircraft for the worried Canadians. The base CO was beginning to be impressed by his two visitors.

Bonnell and Moreton waited until after lunch, with the hours dragging by like months, only to hear that the aircraft could not be arranged, so back to Inverness they went on a freight train. After another night of waiting, they were taken to a nearby air base and flown up to the Shetlands on the morning of 28 October – the day of the raid. It was becoming apparent to the Canadians that they were cutting it rather fine.

Too fine, in fact. They were transferred to HMS *Alecto* in Lerwick harbour after she had seen the fishing boat off for Norway with Bonnell's and Moreton's substitutes. They had missed the operation by a couple of hours, but the dejection they suffered lasted much longer. "The disappointment was indescribable – a crushing blow," said Moreton. The training commander's sole comment to the tardy Canadians was "Bad luck!" There was no punishment – he just let Bonnell and Moreton wallow in the knowledge of what they had done to themselves.

As it happened, the raid they missed on the *Tirpitz* did not succeed – the chariots fell off the fishing boat and were lost before they could be launched. During the escape across Norway to Sweden, Bob Evans, Bonnell's partner, was injured by Germans when trying to evade capture. He was treated in hospital and, once fully recovered, was shot by the Nazis as a spy.

The depressed Canadians joined another group of charioteers in Loch Cairnbawn and started training for a Mediterranean raid planned for late December 1942. The method of transporting the chariots to the operational area had been improved from one small fishing boat to three large

T-class submarines. *Trooper, Thunderbolt,* and *P311* had huge containers fitted to their aftercasings to carry the chariots, but the charioteers did not get a chance to work with them until they got to Malta.

The trio of ungainly submarines sailed south first. Moreton, Bonnell, and their eighteen colleagues left later in a troopship, and at Gibraltar Moreton was hospitalized with a fever. He said goodbye as everyone else went on to meet their submarine transports and glumly reflected that nothing had gone right since he missed the train.

When the submarines and charioteers met up, they learned to work together. Tedious as it was for the larger submarines to act as ferryboats, it was to their crews' credit that no complaint was raised, and they trained hard for their new role. They exercised at night, and the submarines became adept at positioning themselves with their casings awash to allow the chariots to float free of their containers. Bonnell practised pulling his machine out, trimming it and himself, and clambering on board – none of which were easy tasks in heavy seas. The big submarines then left the charioteers to their fate.

The charioteers found life in Malta dull, and when the first operation felt slow in coming they became impatient and bored. This manifested itself in a series of escapades that culminated in an attempt to steal SM10's (Simpson) pet rabbit for their Christmas dinner! The charioteers tended to keep to themselves – it was not that they were unsociable, but rather that their ties to each other were strong and security always had to be considered. They worked hard and played hard together.

The modified submarines came under the operational control of the Experimental Submarine Unit and not Captain(S) of the Tenth Flotilla in Malta. In fact, the chariot operation was so secret that SM10 did not learn of it until a couple of days before the teams arrived. Simpson became anxious about the operation as he discovered more about it. He worried about the safety of the boats and crews that would have to support it, as well as that of the charioteers, and resented pulling his submarines off patrol for rescue duties.

After four weeks of training the teams were ready – supremely ready. Bonnell was selected for Operation PRINCIPAL and was attached to *P311.* Moreton, had he been fit for duty, would also have been in *P311*'s group. PRINCIPAL had been planned in minute detail for some months and was designed to destroy Italian warships in various ports. Initially, attacks were to be made at Taranto in Italy, Palermo and Cagliari in Sicily, and at Maddalena in northern Sardinia. Cagliari and Taranto, where Hugh Russel had lost his life in HMS/M *Traveller* gathering intelligence for PRINCIPAL, were later scrubbed when it was learned that the ports were empty. *P311* was slated for Maddalena, where two Italian cruisers were at anchor, and *Trooper* and *Thunderbolt*, with five teams, were to go to Palermo. The attacks were planned for the night of 1/2 January 1943.

The recovery schemes for the crews depended upon their objectives. Bonnell had to land after sinking his chariot south of Cape Testa, Sardinia, and then make a long trek across the island to a wooded area at the mouth of the Russu River, where *Unison* would meet him on the night of 8/9 January 1943. SM10 chose the Us for the rescue missions instead of the modified T-class, which he felt were too unwieldy and vulnerable. Simpson worried over the "very stiff schedule"[5] that Bonnell and his partner had to maintain to reach the rendezvous, but believed they could do it.

P311, with her two chariots, sailed first from Malta on 28 December. The rest left a day later. Because the containers seriously compromised the boats' seaworthiness and manoeuvrability, SM10 considered the submarines' passage through the heavily mined and patrolled Sicilian Channel and across the enemy's Palermo-Tunis convoy route as risky as the chariot operation itself. As *P311* approached the most dangerous part of the voyage on 30 December, aircraft reconnaissance indicated increased A/S patrols in the area. Mindful of his crews' welfare, Simpson ordered the submarines to wait for one day until the activity subsided, but *P311* missed his signal.

Early on 31 December 1942, *P311* reported she was clear of the minefields, but not in position to launch her chariots. She was never heard from again.

Trooper and *Thunderbolt* successfully delivered the remaining five chariots to Palermo and two teams pressed home a good attack in rough weather on the night of 2/3 January 1943. They sank a new Italian light cruiser and damaged one large transport. Two charioteers lost their lives, two were rescued, and six ended up as POWs.

Everyone on *P311* lost their lives, including Chuck Bonnell. Humming "Rule Britannia" as a signal, crew members from the rescue submarine, HMS *Unison*, examined the rendezvous on Sardinia's northwest coast and found no evidence that the charioteers had been there. Certainly no warships in Maddalena were blown up and the Admiralty believed that the chariots were never launched. Several sources speculated that *P311* was sunk by anti-submarine forces, which were particularly vigilant in that area, but enemy records show that this was not the case. The Royal Navy now believes she was sunk by a mine.

SM10 wrote immediately afterwards that, on balance, the operation was a failure, and sadly expensive. Simpson was referring to the sinkings of HMS/Ms *P311* and *Traveller* (in which a Canadian also died), the charioteers who lost their lives, and the disruption in submarine patrols that the operation caused. Others commented that alternative methods of transporting the chariots must be found because they imposed too high a risk to the Ts.

Lt. Charles (Chuck) E. Bonnell, RCNVR, DSC, never had the chance to initiate his first operational mission even though he had always been confident of success. He was remembered by everyone as an outstanding example – encouraging other charioteers to try harder and do better. That Bonnell was imbued with unyielding courage there could be no doubt. His death was officially said to have occurred on 8 January 1943, the day *Unison* found no trace of the charioteers from *P311* at the rendezvous. Alan Moreton took the news hard, knowing it could easily have been his fate too, and he missed his friend and shipmate greatly. He considers Bonnell one of Canada's bravest unsung heroes.

A saddened Moreton, back in Scotland again, began to prepare for another operation in mid-1943, but found it more and more difficult to face. Although he went to Malta a second time to reconnoitre the Sicilian beaches in preparations for the landings (Operation HUSKY) in May 1943, he did not participate except as an observer. After a further disappointment when a raid on enemy warships in Taranto was cancelled, the chariots' usefulness in the Mediterranean was over and Moreton prepared to return to Britain.

Before leaving Malta, Moreton caught sand-fly fever, which landed him in hospital again, and he began to drink. "The bloom was definitely off the rose," he remembered. On arrival in England he requested leave in Canada, which was granted on the understanding that afterwards he would return to chariots and prepare for Far Eastern operations.

While still in Canada in December 1943, Moreton requested a transfer back to the RCN – he realized he could not face any more disappointments or the heat of the tropics. The Admiralty granted his wish and Moreton served on the east coast for the rest of the war as the executive officer of HMCS *St. Boniface* on convoy duty between Halifax, St. John's, and New York. While in refit at the end of 1944 in Liverpool, Nova Scotia, Moreton met his future wife and married her after a whirlwind courtship.

The surviving Canadian charioteer was never promoted during the war because of his nonconformity and lack of operations. Moreton had not been able to take any courses in gunnery or ASW throughout his training for chariots and consequently left the RCN with only a watch-keeping certificate. He returned to Toronto to his old accounting job and remained there until he retired to Nova Scotia.

In 1945 patriotic newspaper accounts[6] about Moreton and Bonnell embarrassed Moreton as they implied that he had participated in some of the famous raids conducted by the charioteers and survived by sheer good luck. Of course, he did not, by sheer bad luck. He explained that he was inexperienced in giving interviews, that the reporter was the worse for wear with pusser rum (naval rum, reputed to be the best), and that "something got lost in the translation." As so many do, the journalist had exaggerated the facts, but he did convey that Moreton was a most gallant and determined naval officer throughout his career in chariots.

Moreton's comments, made before he died in 1993, add another perspective, "If nothing else [my service] helps to reveal the real nature of war which is full of disappointing events and fallible people."

CHAPTER THIRTEEN

THE RCN BEGS FOR SUBMARINES, 1940–1945

" … no opportunity to exercise with a submarine"

While the Canadian submarine officers were working and dying in the Mediterranean, others were about to serve in Canadian waters. This came about because of the Royal Canadian Navy's struggle to prosecute efficient anti-submarine warfare (ASW) in the North Atlantic. Many well-documented factors contributed to the ASW challenge, but the lack of a Canadian Submarine Service was a significant one, which has rarely been examined in depth. It caused the Canadian navy to co-opt one Dutch boat and to beg the Admiralty for training submarines throughout the war.

Before 1939 both naval and political opinion hindered the advances in ASW. Both camps hoped that unrestricted submarine warfare would not occur and that, if it did, enemy submarines would only pose a threat to merchant ships in coastal waters. As the tactics of the naval war quickly clarified, they differed from pre-war expectations – the battle raged in mid-ocean. Detection and prosecution of underwater targets had advanced only slightly since 1918, and though early active sonar called asdic had been developed, few had believed it would be useful in deep water. These factors combined and created an RCN that at the outbreak of war had no knowledge of the characteristics of sound propagation in Canadian waters, no scientifically developed A/S tactics for the North Atlantic, and insufficient escorts equipped with asdic.

With the onset of war there were major changes in Ottawa which also tended to make the situation worse. The naval headquarters outgrew its strength; the new Naval Board, which developed policies, and the new

Naval Staff, which acted as a think-tank, lacked members with resolve or operational experience. This caused the chief of Naval Staff, Nelles, to make most of the decisions himself, and unfortunately he was not abreast of modern ASW technology or tactics.

It was in this context that the RCN was forced to develop its ASW capability. Initially they employed small, slow patrol vessels and RCAF maritime patrols wherever enemy submarines were thought to congregate – in the approaches to major harbours and in restricted waters such as the Gulf of St. Lawrence. However, there were few enemy incursions into Canadian coastal waters, and the RCN had to come to grips with prosecuting ASW in mid-Atlantic where the U-boats ravaged the convoys. The navy did not do well – they failed to sink any enemy submarines in the first half of the war. Later, as the U-boats lost their boldness and started to attack submerged, the RCN had to raise their detection-and-attack standards even higher and again their results were dismal, even though the Allies were doing relatively well. It was not the Canadian crews' fault – collectively, they did their best.

The reasons for the Canadian failure were many and most have been exhaustively analysed and recorded. They included an unmanageable growth of the navy in ships and men, insufficient and obsolescent equipment, inadequate training, and a poor focus on the priorities at headquarters. Any one of these reasons for failure would have been serious enough, but together they proved crippling.

Part of the inadequate training can be blamed on the RCN's lack of submarines. A navy and an airforce cannot learn to be effective submarine hunters without hunting real submarines. Training submarines were vital for the development of asdic operators and ASW officers after their courses; for working up new warships, big and small; for exercising escort and support groups; for upgrading the qualifications of personnel already in the A/S trades and occupations; for training the air crews on ocean and coastal patrol duties; and for enhancing the training of the army engaged in coastal defence.

The absence of an established Canadian Submarine Service during the Second World War clearly affected the escorts' ability to score against the U-boats. In retrospect, this failure of imagination and planning seems inexcusable, though understandable in light of Canada's naval doctrine and the socio-political climate between the wars. Realizing that they were at a serious disadvantage, the RCN began the search for training submarines, but Britain was stretched to the limit and could not spare any boats during the desperate battle in the Mediterranean.

After six months of war, submarine detection training began in Halifax, using towed underwater targets – definitely a second best.[1] Area commanders began yelling for target submarines for the training base at Halifax and later at Esquimalt and St. John's, Newfoundland. And the sea-going officers began to complain about the "lack of efficiency of HMCS Ships in A/S work due to having no submarine with which to practice."[2] Naval Headquarters was at a loss over how to work up the 140 A/S vessels waiting in line until a Dutch boat fortuitously turned up in Halifax for repairs.

She was *O15* of the Royal Netherlands Navy. She had been in the Dutch West Indies when the Nazis overran the Low Countries in mid-1940, and was now under Admiralty control. The RCN saw her as the answer to their prayers. Ignoring the Admiralty's refusal to permit *O15* to stay, the Canadian navy snatched the Dutch boat and pressed her into service for ASW training as soon as her repairs were completed. After a few months the Admiralty gave in to the RCN's badgering, and *O15* became the first submarine to serve in the RCN in WWII.

By early 1941 *O15* had already been used as a target to test Canada's early radar equipment, and she was regularly exercising off Halifax with trawlers, the first of the corvettes, and minesweepers. The navy discovered that the acoustic conditions were unsuitable here for teaching the art of asdic in the summer. The warm Gulf Stream, mixing with the colder northern water, created a fifty-foot (15.2 m) layer of "mush" in the sea, which the pings from the primitive surface sonar could not penetrate. So in April 1941 the RCN moved the ASW training to Pictou, Nova Scotia, where the acoustic conditions were better, though not ideal.

In that same spring, a Canadian joined *O15*. He was a signalman, Arthur J. Hardy from Hamilton, Ontario. Hardy was a twenty-six-year-old volunteer reservist who took on the work of helping the Dutch-speaking telegraphists with English and their watches. Although the language in the boat was always Dutch, *O15* communicated in English throughout her time in Canada. Hardy was well respected and liked – "a marvellous fellow," recalled the CO. Hardy had not taken the submarine training course, nor did he ever take one, so technically speaking he was not a submariner. However, this first introduction to boats must have appealed to him because he remained in submarines for the rest of the war.

Everyday, *O15* ran out of Pictou with the two ships attached to the submarine detection school. There she gave the students a chance to see what a submarine looked like on the surface; what her periscope did to the waves; what she sounded like through the hydrophones; and most important, they learned how to locate her underwater with asdic. No exercises were conducted with aircraft at this time because the ships' companies were too inexperienced. Occasionally the work was dangerous for the submarine, with novice sailors driving the surface craft, but *O15* kept out of trouble, blessed as she was with a highly professional crew.

The Canadians did not work on Sundays, even though there was a war on, but the Dutch had no such religious scruples and were at sea seven days a week. One Canadian, who perhaps did not go to church, visited *O15* on Sundays to learn the rudiments of operating a boat. It did not take long for the Dutch CO to trust him and let him act as the foreplanesman. The young man never forgot the generosity of this action. Later, as a rear admiral, Bob Welland argued forcefully for the value of submarines as A/S platforms, and urged the government to renew the Canadian Submarine Service.

O15 provided target services and expertise to the men and ships of the RCN for two years before the Admiralty demanded her back in September 1942. During that time Princess Juliana of the Netherlands and her two young daughters, who had escaped to Canada, visited the submarine, the boat was run over by a destroyer while alongside, and a major refit had been completed. Despite the Dutch CO's impatience to return to Europe to retaliate against the Nazis for invading his country, he later admitted their work had been both necessary and worthwhile. Signalman Hardy stayed in *O15* for another year in European waters and then served on HMS/M *Sturgeon,* two more Dutch submarines, and the Free French boat, *Le Glorieux,* until the war ended. Sadly, he could not be located to contribute the rest of his story to this book.

The RCN complained furiously to the Admiralty over losing *O15*, but to no avail, and their quest for submarines escalated. After *O15*'s departure the Admiralty spared a few ancient British boats, though never enough, and Canadian submariners served in some of them. Latterly an RCNVR officer commanded one. Thirteen boats were officially employed in Canadian and Newfoundland waters during the war, but the most in use at any one time was five. Several others dropped in to assist briefly while en route from Britain to the U.S.A. for refits.

Canada, having got their hands on *O15*, then approached the neutral U.S.A. for "clockwork mice." The American navy offered four boats for three weeks, but after some thought and a strong plea to the British First Sea Lord to keep *O15*, Nelles declined them. The CNS's request ensured the retention of *O15,* but she remained the only training submarine for the armada of ASW vessels until *L27* arrived in Newfoundland in late 1941. She stayed four months before leaving for a refit. *O15,* even with *L27,* could not provide enough submarine time – at least four were needed on a long-term basis.

The RCN's refusal of the twelve submarine/weeks from the USN may have stemmed from unofficial knowledge of the lend-lease ship package that was being negotiated between the Admiralty and the United States. This included nine submarines, two of which were old boats earmarked for the RCN, and two more meant for the still-British-controlled base in Newfoundland. However, as there is no documentary evidence to support this explanation, it must remain speculative.

By early 1942, the RCN was again begging the Admiralty to increase their submarine allocation and to delay the departure of *O15* and *L27* in February for refits. The Admiralty could not accommodate either of these suggestions and for a few months the A/S schools and the escorts went without "live" training. Canada continued pleading.

When Canada officially heard of the lend-lease arrangements, they learned that four of the nine boats were for them, with the rest going to Scotland for training duties. The submarines had seen better days, having been built in 1917 and 1922, and came with insufficient spares. They were given the numbers *P512* (USS *R17*), *P514* (USS *R19*), *P553* (USS *S21*), and *P554* (USS *S22*). *P512* arrived first, in early 1942, and *P553* came in November – both were used for training around Nova Scotia and had Canadians in their officer corps. They worked not only with warships but also with coastal patrol aircraft of the RCAF and the RAF. These submarines operated in St. Margaret's Bay, near Halifax, in the winter and from the now-established base at Pictou in the summers.

Pictou had proved to be an excellent location for large scale ASW training. The local waters were sheltered and provided a good acoustic environment for the students. The town had a shipyard and ample jetty space and accommodation. The local golf club, unofficially named HMCS *Halo,* was used as the base from which a small staff administered the A/S school. HMCS *Kamloops,* a corvette, and HMCS *Swift Current,* a minesweeper, were the school's training ships. The submarine officers lived in a pleasant house overlooking the sea and used *Halo*'s officers' mess as their wardroom.

P514 went to Newfoundland in mid-May 1942 – dividing her time between St. John's and Argentia (a USN base) – after providing target training around Halifax for a couple of months. FONF (flag officer,

Newfoundland force) had suggested basing *P514* in Newfoundland before the boats were delivered, saying that she would offer a good opportunity for further ASW training of his escort groups during their twelve-day lay-overs between convoys. Sadly, *P514* lasted only one month – she was rammed in the early hours of 21 June by HMCS *Georgian*, who mistook her for a U-boat while escorting a convoy. The submarine went down with all hands. Neither *P514* nor *P554*, who replaced her in July, had Canadian officers serving in them.

To summarize the position in mid-1942: *O15* and *P512* were deployed at Pictou and Halifax, with *P514* in Newfoundland waters, shortly to be replaced by *P554*. When *O15* returned to Britain in September, *P553* joined *P512* in Halifax. Soon after this the RN withdrew the Canadian escorts from the North Atlantic for further ASW training in Britain, because of their poor record.

The submarines serving in Canadian waters came under RCN operational control and their mostly British crews were paid the higher RCN rate. By contrast, the "Newfoundland boats" remained under RN operational control with their crews on British pay scales. All the borrowed submarines were supported throughout the war by the RN staff in Washington, D.C., and a British submarine staff in Philadelphia, where the major refits were done.

As the air gap in the north Atlantic was reduced, the extra aircrews were as much in need of training with live submarines as the naval crews. For this the boats carried out different evolutions. The most important involved proceeding at periscope depth while the planes tried to bomb them with eight-and-a-half-pound (3.9 kg) break-up bombs. Sometimes they succeeded, but mostly not; though later HMS/M *Unseen* took a direct hit on her periscope, which caused a few faint hearts at headquarters to flutter and to suggest that the bombing practice be stopped. Common sense prevailed and the exercises were not curtailed despite the risks.

When the RN began to use their base in Bermuda to work up their new frigates, the Admiralty chose to take *P553* away from Halifax. This, coupled with urgently needed refits for the remaining submarines, reduced the availability of "Canadian boats" in early 1943 to unacceptable levels. Bitter competition erupted between the Newfoundland and Halifax commands when naval headquarters suggested taking the only submarine from Newfoundland to replace the Halifax boat. In the end this did not take place and instead the RCN asked the Admiralty to again reconsider the whole submarine allocation plan. The training requirements for RCN ships had become substantial. They included 145 Canadian coastal escorts, the ships of the mid- and western-ocean escort groups between convoys, and all the new RCN ships being worked up.

This overwhelming training issue prompted the first official written statement to the effect that Canada needed her own submarine service. In July 1942, the Canadian director of Anti-Submarine recommended to the new Naval Board that the RCN build six submarines for training use, reminding them of the speedy build of the H boats in the First World War. The Naval Board agreed to look into the scheme but found the shipyards fully occupied churning out corvettes. The suggestion never reached the minister of national defence because the board felt that if the expertise in submarine construction had been lost, the submariners would be demoralized by being employed solely in training boats, and the cost of the proposed submarines was prohibitive at $9 million. The director A/S, unhappy with their decision, commented that delaying six corvettes would be well worth while to improve the anti-submarine work of the "half-trained"[3] escort crews. But Nelles and the board were not going to be swayed from producing more and more surface escorts and the RCN missed the opportunity to provide the RCN with its own training submarines.

Canada then turned to the United States Navy again and asked to borrow some boats or have some built. The U.S., now a combatant, was unable to comply because her own submarines and yards were fully employed. In desperation, the A/S schools and the escort groups resorted to using towed targets once more.

Superficially, the evidence suggests a British lack of support for ASW training submarines that was high-handed and negligent. In fact, the Admiralty believed that ASW training should have priority over most operational requirements of submarines, and they did all they possibly could to aid Canada. In December 1942, the darkest hour of the war for the Allies, the Admiralty agreed that Canada needed seven target boats in order to have five at sea, and that Bermuda required four. However, they simply could not provide them. To make matters worse for the RCN in 1943, Britain decided to take another submarine away from Halifax to augment those in Bermuda. Although Canada's new vessels were being worked up there, where the base was now operated by the RCN, naval headquarters objected strenuously as their local commanders still needed all the boats they could get. In view of the state of the war, Canada seemed unlikely to get any more submarines until the situation eased, if at all, and she had to make do with what she had. Naval headquarters swallowed the bitter pill and ordered the area commanders to get on with it. The board never reconsidered their decision to continue building only corvettes, even though the lack of submarines was so severe.

The anti-submarine training facility had moved to HMCS *Cornwallis,* Nova Scotia, by February 1943, with their sea training based at Digby on the Bay of Fundy, fourteen miles (22.5 km) away. The Admiralty, knowing an additional training submarine was required by *Cornwallis,* reviewed the problem in January 1943 and concluded that four boats were needed – one for Newfoundland, two for Halifax, and one for Digby. Only three were allocated and the RN held out little hope of improvement, suggesting again that the RCN approach the USN for boats. The reason the Admiralty did this is unclear. They knew the U.S. would refuse, having been so reluctant to release their last lend-lease submarines. The RCN quickly expressed their displeasure at the review and reiterated their need.

In April 1943, *P553* and *P512* sailed for Bermuda, and *Seawolf,* which replaced *P512* in Halifax briefly, returned to Britain. As there was no submarine at Digby, this left only one – *P554* at Argentia – and hundreds more ships' companies went without training.

By mid-1943 naval headquarters in Ottawa was swamped with requests for clockwork mice. The clamour from operational commanders that reached its crescendo at this time was due in part to the U-boats' new modus operandi: they now attacked submerged, because air cover had been extended most of the way across the Atlantic. Headquarters knew only too well that the ineffective A/S operations at sea in RCN vessels were caused by inexperience, a lack of available information about the sound propagation characteristics of Canadian waters, and a lack of training. The first two problems were in hand – crews were steadily gaining experience by continued service at sea and Canadian warships were completing a bathythermographic survey. However, the third problem, the lack of training, remained insoluble without sufficient tame submarines. Requests were also coming in from the Canadian and U.S. armies, who wanted to familiarize their coastal defence personnel with submarines; from the RCAF, RAF, and the U.S. Army, whose air crews needed training in recognition and attack procedures; and, from the RCN and USN (at Argentia) who trained the huge numbers of asdic operators. In fact, although over 700 officers and 1,500 men were taking the training courses each year, the RCN was still 50 percent below their projected manning requirements for ASW. The RCN reissued towed targets.

The Allied Anti-Submarine Survey Board, led by Rear Admiral John Mansfield, RN, who had been Barney Johnson's first lieutenant in *H8*, visited Canada during 1943 to investigate the RCN's poor performance in the North Atlantic. The team was sharply critical of the low priority the Naval Board was giving to ASW training, exemplified by their decision not to build their own submarines. Their findings resulted in the formation of the Joint (RCN/RCAF) Anti-Submarine Warfare Committee, which met weekly at naval headquarters. On 26 June 1943, this committee strongly recommended that "the possibility of inaugurating a submarine branch of the RCN"[4] should be investigated. Members also pondered the possibility of using the new British midget submarines, called X-craft, as tame boats. Unimpressed, the Naval Board exhorted the committee to be more practical in its proposals to improve Canada's ASW. There the ideas died. Nelles thought it only right that the RN should supply submarines to Canada and no evidence exists to show that he ever supported the re-establishment of the Canadian Submarine Service.

The Admiralty kept doing its best to provide Nelles with boats in 1943, but they were unsuccessful. They even tried to acquire five non-operational Free French submarines for Canada, to fill the gap before several small U-class boats, which had been promised, became available. The RCN continued to badger the Admiralty until they again offered three X-craft, which were undergoing trials as targets.

This critical lack of training submarines continued late into 1943, after the war in the Mediterranean had eased and the Battle of the Atlantic had begun to turn in the Allies' favour. ASW had become an underwater game of hide-and-seek where the skills of the asdic operators and the tactics of the escort COs had to be very, very good to be successful. The state of operational readiness demanded could only be reached by sea training with live boats.

When *P554* in Argentia left for a refit in mid-1943 she was not replaced, which left the RCN with no clockwork mice at all for some months. Later *L23*, Sherwood's old boat, was delayed by a collision in New York harbour, and the Admiralty released two more old L-class submarines – *L26* and *L27* (for the second time). *L27* arrived in the fall of 1943 and worked out of Halifax in December, along with *P553* which had returned from Bermuda. *L26* came out of refit in February 1944 and went to Halifax where she was put out of commission by a battery explosion.

The age of these borrowed submarines took their toll on available submarine training days. Their maintenance and repairs substantially reduced their sea time, because in Canada they were deprived of their usual spares and maintenance personnel. For example, no dockyard, workshops, or stores existed at Digby so any equipment needing repair or maintenance had to go by train to Halifax 140 miles (226 km) away. Inoperable periscopes had to go to Philadelphia, and supplies took six months to arrive after being requisitioned. Several measures were taken to improve this situation and Canadian dockyards did their best, but were inexperienced with submarines.

By late fall of 1943, the RCN had three submarines and was expecting a fourth. *P553* was operating from Halifax and Pictou, and *Seawolf* was back at Digby. *L23* arrived fresh from her repairs in October and provided target duties at Halifax and Digby, while *L26* and *L27* were refitting. By Christmas, *L27* and *P554* had finished their refits and were operating with *P553* in St. Margaret's Bay. *Seawolf,* now in Bermuda, assisted with the increase in Canadian escorts working-up there, although the RCN had asked for her back. No target submarine operated from Newfoundland in the winter of 1943/44 until *L23* was released from Digby in February.

All the serviceable ASW training submarines were working hard six days a week, with several escorts, motor launches, and aircraft simulating the hunt. The ships depth-charged and pinged the submarines all day long and occasionally gave them the chance to practise attacks at the end of the day. A typical night exercise involved ten escorts and seven motor launches. Although many senior naval officers from Ottawa, Halifax, and St. John's were asked to come and observe the efforts and successes of the Canadian and British submariners, few accepted the invitation. Admiral Murray, the flag officer, Atlantic Coast, was the notable exception.

In late 1943, the Admiralty acknowledged that Canada needed seven training boats and had only five, not all of which were serviceable. They now planned to allocate captured Italian boats to Bermuda, instead of the Free French submarines, which would release boats for the RCN before the promised U-class submarines arrived. They also announced that they could provide six X-craft for use as training targets for £90,000 and deliver them in April 1944. This offer caused a flurry of activity in Ottawa.

The Naval Board cautiously agreed to look at this scheme, having declined a similar one, as a means of establishing a small, non-operational Canadian submarine service. The Naval Staff enthusiastically recommended it, asking that the personnel for the first crews leave immediately for training in Britain. But Nelles delayed committing himself because he was concerned about logistics. Finally he was satisfied, and the board approved the recommendation for a "submarine branch for A/S Training ... and that six 'X.T.' craft ... be procured."[5] Almost at once the proposal ran into difficulties. Only fifty officers and men were required to crew the midgets and to provide shore support, and the board decreed that the numbers were too few to justify the effort and expenditure of implementing a submarine branch for the RCN. So, on 7 March 1944, Nelles refused the Admiralty's offer, letting another chance to develop a modest Canadian submarine service slip away.

Shortly after these decisions were made, the minister of national defence fired Nelles for his poor performance and his lack of communication with and understanding of his operational commands.

When the RCN learned that *P553* and *P554* were to be paid off in mid-1944, they expected the worst, but as it turned out the loss did not hurt ASW training off Halifax as much as they had imagined. Because of chronic breakdowns, the submarines had performed inconsistently for some time, and fewer ships were being trained in Canadian waters. In fact, the RCN had, of their own choice, sent *L26* and *L27* down to Bermuda in May 1944, before *Unseen* arrived in July for Digby. The rest of the promised U-class submarines arrived from Britain in the late summer of 1944. HMS/Ms *Upright, United,* and *Unruffled* were distributed between Canadian waters and Bermuda. *Unseen* was handed over to the RCAF in December and fitted with a mock U-boat schnorkel to assist in radar detection exercises. The Admiralty gave *L26* and *L27* to the RCN in November 1944 to be sunk as bottom targets, and *L23* stayed at Digby until the war's end.

It was only in the last year of the war that Canadian researchers had begun to understand the acoustic properties of the sea off the east coast and in the Gulf of St. Lawrence. The first steps in the research of underwater sound propagation were taken in 1943 when a bathythermographic survey was done in the Gulf. A similar survey was done in 1944 in the approaches to Halifax harbour. "The researchers were amazed by what they found."[6] They discovered that the sea was made up of distinct layers of water of different salinity and temperature and that these layers could reflect the beam of asdic allowing submarines to hide underneath them with impunity. Earlier in the war the Admiralty and the RCN were unaware of the dangerous possibilities of these conditions, which the escorts faced.

At the close of 1944, with the European war winding down, the RCN and the Admiralty turned their attention to the Pacific. The RCN hoped to allocate one submarine on the west coast while maintaining two on the east coast; however, the Admiralty unofficially offered five more boats if they could be manned by Canadians. As the RCN had only twenty-odd submariners, most of whom were overseas, and all of whom were officers, they did not accept the offer, even though they badly needed the boats for the future. In April 1945 Canada had a change of heart and asked the Admiralty if they would consider developing RCN crews to man the RN-lent submarines, but it came too late. Canada ended up with no boats at all.

The arrangements for the Canadian clockwork mice continued more or less the same, before and after the European peace in May 1945, with three submarines at Digby for *Cornwallis* (*Seawolf, Upright,* and *L23*), two in Bermuda (*United* and *Unruffled*) and one for the RCAF (*Unseen*). HMS/M *Searover* briefly added her weight to the ASW training in April, but was never officially allocated.

The submarine detection schools were now getting enough practice with tame boats, but the escort groups still were not. For example, in the two and a half months since its formation, Escort Group 28 had had only two days' training with a submarine and some of the ships in the group had never trained together. When headquarters ordered EG-28 to locate and destroy *U190* which had sunk HMCS *Esquimalt* off Halifax, they failed. Other groups were going to sea having had "no opportunity ... to exercise with a submarine"7 at all, even at this late stage. Suddenly, probably as a result of EG-28's failure to retaliate successfully against *U190,* the RCN provided more submarine time for the operational groups, which continued until Japan surrendered.

The lack of training submarines was Canada's fault, though a few tried to lay the blame at the Admiralty's door. Nelles, the chief of Naval Staff, and the Naval Board were the chief culprits. Throughout the war they persisted in their belief that the mother country was responsible for the provision of training boats and that operations always took priority over training. Even when confronted with the evidence and an opportunity halfway through the war to rectify the situation, Nelles took the position that a submarine service was not essential to the RCN.

If the Canadian government and navy had seen fit to foster the expertise of the officers and men of the embryo Canadian submarine service that had been developed in the First War and had kept *CH14* and *CH15* in reserve, this debacle might have been avoided or at least minimized. Although old, the Canadian H boats could have been pressed into service as tame boats in the early days of the war, just as their sisters had been in Britain. To have expected *CH14* and *CH15* to remain in commission for ASW training before WWII would have been unrealistic – the vision of the senior RCN officers was not broad enough and the economy not sturdy enough. During the war, the RCN's fixation on building more and more surface escorts and their inability to come to grips with the priority of training prevented the construction of six training submarines.

The Royal Canadian Navy learned their ASW training lesson the hard way and a few senior officers were determined to have submarines in the future peacetime fleet. In early 1945, after Nelles had been relieved, and during the planning for the post-war navy, the RCN asked the Admiralty for one boat for the east coast to continue the instruction of asdic operators and ASW ships. This belated realization and the willingness to rectify the previous errors heralded the birth of the modern Canadian submarine service – some would say, the true beginning of the Canadian submarine service. The earlier foray into a submarine branch by the RCN in WWI was really an accident – very short-lived, and hardly worthy of the name, though it did produce some noteworthy submariners.

Several Canadians served in the target submarines used by the RCN. Most had volunteered in the second half of the war hoping to see action and felt let down when their postings turned out to be considerably less exciting than their colleagues' in operational boats.[8]

Jack A. Cross from Montreal, a quiet, comfortable man to know, became the respected commanding officer of *Unseen*. He was fairly tall and stockily built, and his square, often smiling face was topped off with slightly thinning brown hair. Cross joined the RCNVR in 1940 and took his SOTC in January 1942, after deciding that he had had enough of being a sitting duck for a German torpedo in a surface ship. After two months as a spare officer at HMS *Dolphin*, Sub-Lieutenant Cross joined *P512* in Pictou as her fourth hand to learn his new trade. During his eighteen months in her, Cross was promoted and worked his way up to first lieutenant of the boat.

Another submarine officer, who had been born in Canada but was living in England when war broke out, joined Cross on *P512* in June 1942. Edward A.D. Holmes had already got substantial submarine experience under his belt before he took his SOTC, having served as a liaison officer in the Dutch *O21* in the Mediterranean where he experienced attacks on Italian convoys and the sinking of a U-boat. Holmes was awarded the Netherlands Bronze Cross in June 1942 for his valour, skill, endurance, and devotion to duty. As soon as he joined *P512*, her British CO nicknamed him "Uncle" because he was the eldest on board. Holmes and Cross soon became good friends and when Holmes got married in 1943 to a Canadian, he asked Cross to be his best man.

P512 was the first lend-lease submarine to be assigned to Canadian ASW training. The boat was very old, displaced 680 tons (616.8 tonnes) and had internal main ballast tanks. She could dive up to 200 feet (61 m) and proceed at 13.5 knots on the surface and 10.5 knots submerged. The ship's company comprised four officers and twenty-nine men. *P512* worked out of Pictou and Holmes found it a tedious job sailing each morning into the Northumberland Strait and running prescribed courses at set depths while the trainee asdic operators endeavoured to locate them. Rarely was the submarine allowed to depart from this strict routine and employ evasive tactics of its own. Cross and Holmes remember lots of paperwork, though for two days they assisted the RCAF in making an instructional film on submarine recognition, as well as a movie called "Freighters under Fire" in which *P512* played the part of a U-boat.

The British CO, Lt. John Ogle, RN, gave Holmes and Cross plenty of opportunities to learn ship handling and they practised coming alongside, entering and leaving harbour, and driving the boat on the surface. Ogle returned to England after becoming engaged to Cross's sister, and in April 1943 Holmes also left *P512* to go to *P553*, initially as her torpedo officer, and later as first lieutenant. Cross remained in *P512* as her number one while she was ping-running for the Allied escorts at Bermuda, but by October 1943 he was standing by HMS/M *Vigorous* with her CO. The captain turned out to be none other than John Ogle, his future brother-in-law.

While on *P553* Holmes met Colin Perry, another Canadian submariner, and together with their captain, Lt. "Rocky" Hill, RNR, they operated out of Halifax through the winter of 1942/43. The crew put up with most uncomfortable living conditions. *P553* was unable to come alongside after the daily exercises, but had to anchor off the shore in St. Margaret's Bay. There was no pleasant house to accommodate them, as there had been in Pictou and they lived on board the submarine. When the sea froze in early 1943 the ship's company was miserable but was given no respite. At the beginning of June, *P553* returned to Pictou to continue the work in better acoustic conditions until the winter, but by now Holmes had left.

Perry was the only RCNVR officer who had not volunteered for submarines – he had actually been drafted into the Silent Service while serving on an escort trawler, HMS *Valse*, at Leith in Scotland. Perry believed it was a mistake, but as he had no objections he never questioned it. Perry completed his SOTC in August 1942 and immediately returned to Canada on leave. Afterwards he joined *P553* in Halifax and became her navigator for six months. Perry, though shy and very young, did an excellent job and was promoted to lieutenant.

In September 1943 Perry experienced one of the few exciting events that occurred during the service of the Canadian training submarines. While *P553* was in Pictou, he and the CO were involved in an attempt to take over a U-boat. Using a German double agent, the Canadian authorities planned to entice *U536* into rescuing some captured German submariners who were organizing an escape from Grand-Linge POW camp, south of Montreal.

The RCN asked "Rocky" Hill, the CO of *P553*, to choose a good site for the rendezvous between the U-boat and the POWs. He picked the Baie des Chaleurs in New Brunswick. The army assisted in setting up a camp containing the necessary equipment near the Maisonette lighthouse two weeks before the rescue attempt. Initially Hill and Perry were to replace some of the German escapers, get on board the U-boat, and then capture it. Later the RCN abandoned this scheme as too dangerous and substituted a safer plan of locate-and-destroy.

On the night of 26 September 1943, Perry and his CO were prepared for almost anything to happen. They sat waiting in the lighthouse, playing cards with the interpreter and the officer in charge of the operation. The night before, officials had captured a lone German POW. He was the only one to escape from the camp before the tunnel to freedom collapsed.

Soon the mobile radar picked up the first indication of a possible target on the surface. It soon disappeared – the submarine had dived. The shore party reported this to the RCN surface ships hovering outside the bay and they began to hunt. Hill and Perry waited, unable to contribute much to the proceedings. After twenty-four hours without success, the RCN called off the search. The submariners were furious – they wanted the U-boat hunted to exhaustion – even if it took forty-eight hours. Glumly, they packed up and returned to Pictou and their more mundane duties.

What had happened was this. The U-boat CO had become suspicious of the communications from the "POWs" on shore and the amount of naval activity in the isolated bay, and decided to withdraw without completing his mission. (He was unaware that the prisoners' escape had failed.) To avoid the continuous A/S patrols, the U-boat went to the bot-

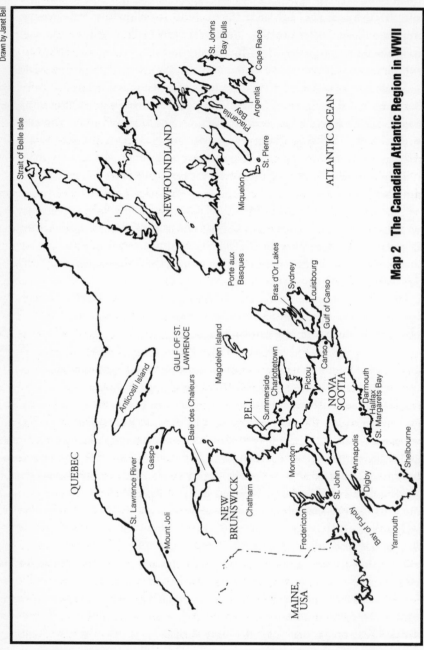

Drawn by Janet Bell

Map 2 The Canadian Atlantic Region in WWII

tom and lay doggo for a day in very shallow water. The RCN never found them despite many attempts. When the A/S activity ceased a day later, the U-boat crept out of the bay barely underwater and escaped. She was not the expected *U536* – that one had been sunk on her way to rescue her countrymen and Doenitz diverted another.

Holmes, after nine months on *P553*, rejoined *P512* in Bermuda in November 1943 to relieve Cross as her first lieutenant. The boat's routine was similar to that in Canadian waters, except that she operated in company with USN boats and trained both American and Canadian surface ships. The officers spent their off-duty time socializing and sightseeing – the real war seemed far away.

Holmes remained with *P512* until she was returned to the USN in the fall of 1944. He then became the first lieutenant of HMS/M *Seawolf*, which was completing a refit. Holmes returned to Digby in *Seawolf* where she operated as a clockwork mouse for the A/S school until the war ended, and she was scrapped. He narrowly missed serving with another Canadian in *Seawolf* – Arthur Walkley survived only one year in submarines before requesting a return to General Service.

Perry returned to England briefly after his time in *P553* and completed the only operational patrol of his career in HMS/M *Taku* off Norway at the end of 1943. It was uneventful, except for appalling weather. Perry then became the first lieutenant of *L23* in February 1944 for nine months while she was working in Newfoundland and Digby. His record showed that he also served for a month in *L26* while she was prepared for paying off, but Perry denies this.

In November 1944, Perry joined up with Cross as the first lieutenant of HMS/M *Unseen* and stayed with her until after the European war ended. Perry decided not to volunteer for the Pacific war, was demobilized soon after Japan capitulated, and returned to Montreal with his wife and young baby. He still lives there in retirement.

Cross, in the meantime, was back in England with *Vigorous*. After her work-ups, *Vigorous* sailed from Britain in June 1944 to Malta. The Germans were retreating from the Mediterranean and *Vigorous*'s flotilla was employed in the interdiction of vessels engaged in the enemy evacuation of Crete and other islands. Cross experienced several sinkings and his first depth-charge attack during *Vigorous*'s first three war patrols and then had to tear himself away to do his Perisher. He was sorry to leave Ogle and his first operational boat, but was keen to have his own command. His course lasted ten weeks and he suffered the same trials and emotions as all Perishers. Cross passed and was appointed as CO of HMS/M

Unseen which was in Digby running for the RCAF. Cross took over the submarine on 15 April 1945 following two months' leave.

Three other RCNVRs were amongst *Unseen*'s officers at various times during her Canadian commission (July 1944 to October 1945) and all but one served as her first lieutenant. They included volunteer reserve Lieutenants George McPhee, Colin Perry, and Wayne Holmes (not "Uncle"). McPhee and W. Holmes had joined the RCNVR in mid-1941 and late 1942 respectively as seamen. Later they received their commissions, went to the U.K., and volunteered for submarines. McPhee joined *Unseen* from a Far East boat and Holmes, a bank clerk in civilian life, came from service in home waters and from *Seawolf* in refit. All the rest of the officers and men in *Unseen* were British, except for one A/S rating who was replaced by an unidentified RCN petty officer for the rest of the commission. McPhee recalled Jack Cross as one of the very best COs he had ever served under. He said, "the crew ... thought he walked on water."9 W. Holmes agreed.

CHAPTER FOURTEEN

CANADIANS IN EUROPEAN WATERS, 1943

"We think you should dive for Canada!"[1]

The ultimate objective for most submarine officers is to pass the Commanding Officers' Qualifying Course, known as Perisher. However Lt.-Commander Freddie Sherwood, RCNVR, was different – he wanted to remain a submarine first lieutenant, believing he was better suited to that position.[2] But the Royal Navy would not permit it and loaded the Canadian on a historic Perisher in December 1942. Sherwood's course was the first to accept volunteer reservists. The other VR to be selected was Lt.-Commander Ted Young, RNVR, and he and Sherwood soon became firm friends.

Early in the war the RN had shortened Perisher from fifteen weeks to seven, but in January 1943 had to lengthen it to nine to add high-speed screened and night attacks at Scapa Flow. The course still taught the fine art of periscope attack, as it did in 1917, but the equipment and tactics had evolved.

Sherwood joined the five other hopefuls for the dry land phase of Perisher at HMS *Dolphin*. Every day after breakfast they walked briskly along the sea road to the "Attack Trainer." This submarine simulator was arranged on two floors of the school and allowed the trainees to make mistakes while attacking targets without endangering a real submarine. On the top floor was the plotting room where their instructor, known as "Teacher," set up the attack scenarios and surveyed the trainees' progress. Wrens operated the simulator's machinery and plotted the attack. Down below was a mock-up of a submarine control room, with a fixed, short-ened periscope. The top of it poked out into the room above and was covered by an inverted marmalade tin when not in use.

Upstairs Teacher used a travelling turntable to simulate attacks. He would select a ship or submarine from shelves filled with scale models and place it on the turntable. Downstairs, the student whose turn it was to be "CO" waited nervously for all to be readied. Around him, his fellow Perishers prepared to act as his attack team as if they were at sea. When all was ready above, the duty CO yelled "Start the attack! Up periscope!" and a Wren whipped off the marmalade tin. Teacher and the Perishers started their stopwatches and the model target was sent down tracks towards the periscope, turning to simulate the change in relative bearing. A student might see a U-boat or the *Scharnhorst* heading straight for him. "It was very realistic," remembered Sherwood. The periscope provided only sections of Teacher's changing scenes, which the students had to piece together mentally – a difficult skill. While Teacher continuously altered the plot, the duty "CO" concentrated on manoeuvring his boat into the best position for firing the torpedoes.

Learning how to attack the target successfully and avoid being rammed was the objective of these intense three weeks. Day after day, for hour after hour, the Perishers took turns as "CO," practising simple attacks with a single target while keeping a steady course, and later progressing to dealing with several zigzagging ships. When a student left the periscope up too long, or delayed going deep, the team upstairs took great delight in stamping on the steel floor to indicate that the submarine had been rammed, bombed, or depth-charged. The sounds were "pretty frightening," said Sherwood.

After each attack the students trooped upstairs for their debriefing. Their efforts could be either exhilarating or devastating. After a bad day, Perishers were often despondent, knowing that they were practising textbook attacks in perfect conditions. They knew only too well that they would have to contend with much worse at sea. However, as the weeks went by all of the students improved, and most began to feel confident. The next phase was conducted at sea, in a real submarine with real targets. Sherwood and his coursemates stayed in the pleasant resort of Rothesay on the Clyde and were ferried out daily to HMS *Cyclops,* the depot ship of the training flotilla. The Perisher boat turned out to be Sherwood's old *Sealion.*

Sherwood was evaluated on his ability to lead, to make snap decisions under pressure, to show creative tactics, to display safe handling of his submarine, and to conduct effective attacks. Each Perisher acted as duty "CO" for a whole day, with his colleagues assisting him as they had done in the Attack Trainer.

The prospect of the first attack at sea filled the Perishers with acute uncertainty, but once it was under way they were too busy to worry. Teacher kept an eye on everything through the search periscope and was ready to step in if it became necessary. On occasion it did, and he would hit the klaxon to make the submarine go deep. It was a moment all the students dreaded because it indicated that they had made an error in judgment. The attacks began simply and developed towards the end of the sea phase into complicated multiple-target affairs, with escorts screening them. Often one or all of the ships would alter course unexpectedly. Teacher then added night attacks, which compounded the strain. At the end of the course the Perishers were wrung dry.

Sherwood did not pass on his first attempt, and Teacher ordered him to repeat the sea phase. This was most unusual: failures were never given a second chance and were returned to General Service forthwith. Sherwood joined the next class for another gruelling three weeks at sea. This course was the first to go to Scapa Flow and exercise with some fast, modern warships, which provided them with more realistic targets. Everyone found the speed bewildering initially, especially in the confined waters of the Flow, but quickly became accustomed to it. It was exciting, heady stuff and a valuable experience for them all.

Sherwood passed this time, and his Teacher remarked, "We came to the conclusion that you would be no danger to yourself or to the enemy. We think you should dive for Canada!"[3] And so Sherwood, a reservist, became the first Canadian submarine commanding officer of the Second World War, and the first and only one to take two Perishers.

Sherwood chose to go straight to his new command after Perisher, instead of taking leave. He had been given a training submarine, *P556*, an ancient lend-lease American boat that had seen better days. Their first assignment was to the Seventh Flotilla in Scotland for target duties. Once there *P556* joined another American S boat, commanded by his friend, and fellow Perisher, Ted Young. Young's boat had earned the nickname *State Express*, but the old *P556*, a chronic sufferer of machinery breakdowns, became known as the *Reluctant Dragon*.

The new COs found their role as clockwork mice tedious. Every morning before dawn they slipped from the depot ship and made their way out to the exercise area. They ran up and down submerged for two hours, surfaced, and repeated the whole performance again and again for the trainee A/S ships. Later on, *P556* joined the famous ocean escort work-up base at Tobermory in Scotland and at last she was able to act like a real submarine. It was excellent practice for the crew, and was to stand Sherwood in good stead for his next command.

In June 1943 came the message Sherwood most wanted to hear – he was to take over a new, operational submarine. As she was still building and Sherwood was overdue for a long leave, he decided to go home. The RN could not secure transportation for him, so he did it himself. With the help of good friends, the RCAF, and Canada House, a USAAF flight took him as far as New York. Sherwood spent his time in Ottawa savouring the prospect of his new submarine.

Keith Forbes, who had had an exciting time as the first lieutenant of *P34* in the Mediterranean, returned early from his honeymoon in Canada to stand by HMS/M *Stoic* during the latter part of her construction. He stayed only long enough for her trials, work-ups, and one uneventful shakedown patrol off northern Norway. In July 1943 Forbes was posted to HMS/M *Sea Nymph,* operating from Holy Loch in Scotland. This turned out to be a very stimulating appointment.

After a quiet first patrol in the Bay of Biscay,[4] *Sea Nymph* had some unusual modifications made to her stern. Forbes watched in consternation as the dockyard mateys drilled a huge hole through the pressure hull and inserted a wide-bore pipe near the steering mechanism – with no explanation. Later he learned that *Sea Nymph,* along with five other submarines, had been selected to tow six midget submarines to Norway for a raid on three big German warships tucked away in Altenfjord, including the *Tirpitz.*

After the failure of the chariots to reach their objective, the first X-craft were quickly brought to operational readiness, and by the late summer of 1943 they were considered capable of mounting the attack. The X-craft carried two monster mines called "side cargoes." These contained two tonnes of sensitive explosive, which could be released individually from the control room to fall directly under a target's hull. Their fuses could be pre-set to allow as much as thirty-six hours for the X-craft to clear the area. Occasionally limpet mines replaced the huge side cargoes, but these had to be manually placed on the target by the crew's diver.

With her sister submarines and depot ship, *Sea Nymph* sailed immediately after her modification to Loch Cairnbawn in Scotland, where they were paired up with their X-craft – *Sea Nymph* got *X8.* These six submarines represented almost the entire operational submarine strength in home waters at that time and demonstrates how important the objective was to the war.

One visit to an X-craft was enough for Forbes – he thought they were the invention of the devil. He also thought *X8*'s crew were "maniacs" to spend their time in such cramped conditions and to face such peril. For the *Tirpitz* raid the midgets faced a five-day passage of a thousand miles (1600 km) under tow and then sixty miles (96 km) under their own power up the heavily defended fjord to their targets, using different crews.

The wide-bore pipe that had been fitted to *Sea Nymph* was, of course, for the 600-foot (183 m) towing line. It was a five-and-a-half inch (14 cm) nylon or hemp hawser, containing three telephone cables. The planners hoped that one of the three would remain intact during the passage to provide communication between the two vessels. The parent boats could tow the X-craft either on the surface or dived.

Planners gave the big submarines only five days to master towing the X-craft and exchanging the passage and attack crews. Neither was an easy task – the X-craft porpoised up and down continually, the tows broke, and communication was unreliable. The practice sessions were rushed, because the raid had to take place around the fall equinox to ensure there was enough of both darkness and daylight above the Arctic Circle where the targets lay. If they missed the opportunity, the raid would have been delayed six months.

The parent submarines and their charges left Cairnbawn for Norway on 11 September 1943 after testing the communication system and the towline release. *Sea Nymph* travelled on the surface as much as possible so that she could maintain a good speed of advance. The passage was perilous – dreadful gales, glassy calms, minefields and rocks were all too possible, and enemy aircraft and A/S patrols had increased in their operational area since the expulsion of the Germans from North Africa and Sicily.

Operation SOURCE had been supplied with intelligence from Russian air reconnaissance and the German Enigma. This continued to be updated during *Sea Nymph*'s long journey. A stream of signals kept the attack crew informed of exactly where the German ships were located. *X8* was to attack the *Lutzow*, the German pocket battleship.

The first two days were uneventful, mainly because the weather was kind to them. *X8* carefully maintained a depth of about forty feet (13 m) below *Sea Nymph*, which ran at 12 knots. Several times a day they both slowed down to allow the midget to surface and ventilate. This was a dangerous manoeuvre in rough seas due to the small freeboard (between waterline and the casing) of the X-craft. However, Forbes had already had difficulties.

Soon after their departure, *Sea Nymph* lost telephone communication with their charge. The nylon tow, chosen over hemp by the X-craft CO, had stretched much more than anticipated and broken all the telephone wires inside. They continued the journey, but because they were unable to warn *X8* of dives or slowdowns, the midget sometimes plummeted to the limit of the tow, with her crew compensating as best they could. When both submarines were on the surface for *X8*'s ventilation periods they resorted to signal lamps for communication. It was a worrying and fatiguing time for both sides – in fact, Forbes got almost no sleep throughout the operation. He learned to catnap when and where he could.

As dawn broke, on the third morning, Forbes was on watch on the bridge and he looked "for the zillionth time" at the tow line. This time he noticed that the tow line was running along the surface like a ribbon, instead of disappearing into the depths. With growing horror, he realized that *X8* had gone. How? When? Why? screamed through his mind. He knew that it must have happened at some point after the last ventilation period – approximately five hours ago. That meant *X8* could have been lost forty miles (64 km) back – it was a lot of ocean to search. *Sea Nymph* turned around and began to look without breaking radio silence.

The tow had actually parted two hours previously. *X8* immediately surfaced to look for *Sea Nymph*, but try as they might, they could not locate their big sister. Visibility was good, but *X8*'s low profile and the rough seas made their task harder. For his part, Forbes had posted extra lookouts on *Sea Nymph* to find their lost charge and to warn of enemy air attacks. They were within sight of Norway.

As the hours stretched out, it looked more and more unlikely that the crew of *Sea Nymph* would find their "special friend." *X8* was eventually found, by accident, at 1700 by *Stubborn*, who signalled Admiral(S) with her position. *X8* stayed with her new sister for a while, but lost contact during the night. On receipt of an Admiralty message *Sea Nymph* altered course to rescue their charge. When she arrived the next morning at the rendezvous there was no *X8*. It later turned out that she had been steering 146 degrees instead of 046 and it took the rest of the day for *Sea Nymph* to locate her, even after talking to *Stubborn*. *X8* was found thirty-six hours after the tow parted.

As *Sea Nymph* approached, the X-craft thought she was a U-boat and desperately tried to dive but without success. It was not until Forbes banged on the midget's hatch with a wrench that they realized their parent had come back for them. Although everyone was exhausted, they were also happy to be back on track. The spare wire tow line was cheerfully rigged and "Look out, *Tirpitz*, here we come!" resounded throughout *Sea Nymph*.

The weather began to deteriorate. That meant the submarines could stay on the surface free from the fear of air attack, but then *X8* began to list to starboard and have difficulties with her trim. *X8*'s attack CO heard the hiss of escaping air and deduced that the starboard buoyancy chambers of her huge mine were leaking, and it would drag *X8* down with it if it sank. There was nothing for it but to jettison it. The crew set the weapon to "safe," so that it would not detonate, and let it go. Despite their precautions it blew up fifteen minutes, startling the crew on *Sea Nymph,* who were, of course, unaware of the action taken by *X8*.

By now the increasingly nasty weather exacerbated the troubles of the tiny submarine, and the other explosive charge began to take on water and to bang against the hull. After much deliberation, *X8*'s attack CO decided that it too must go. Disappointment was intense in both boats when they surfaced to ventilate and the word was passed. This time they decided to set the fuse for two hours.

Just short of the appointed time, when the two boats should have been miles away, the charge detonated and damaged the midget submarine. The explosion flooded her wet and dry compartment, broke some pipes, and rendered her incapable of diving. Weary, cold, and miserable, *X8*'s CO realized that their situation would jeopardize the rest of the operation; sadly, he decided he had no choice but to scuttle the boat. However, the weather was so bad this could not be accomplished immediately. A day later, after dark and in towering seas, *Sea Nymph* managed to recover the attack crew, and both crews watched as *X8* was quickly swamped and made her last journey to the bottom. Forbes still remembers that night well – everyone was numb with cold, soaked to the skin, and scared.

After the anticlimax, *Sea Nymph*'s crew rehashed the events over and over again and realized they neither failed nor lost anyone, and in fact they had learned a lot. They concluded that the problems could have been avoided or solved earlier if they had spent more time exercising together at sea before sailing for Norway – the shortcomings of the synthetic towline being a prime example. *Sea Nymph* headed home after standing by to assist in the recovery of any X-craft that returned from the raid.

The four remaining X-craft pressed home a successful attack on the *Tirpitz.* The crews of *X6* and *X7* managed to deposit their explosives under the hull before being captured. They were on board at the time of the tremendous explosion, anxiously looking at their watches, but came to no harm. The "Beast," as Churchill had nicknamed the battleship, was blown nearly six feet (2 m) out of the water, took on a list to port, and started leaking oil.

Irremediable defects prevented *X10* from reaching her target, and *X5* was lost about one mile from the target. No one could determine if *X5* had dropped her mines in position or not. All the towing submarines returned safely to Lerwick, including *Sea Nymph* and Forbes. For the Canadian, the raid that had started with such promise and excitement was the most miserable, exhausting, and frustrating operation of the war.

Operation SOURCE turned out better than anyone realized at the time. Although *Tirpitz* did not sink after *X6*'s and *X7*'s mines exploded, the German battleship was unable to threaten the northern Allied convoys again. It took seven months to repair her hull, machinery, and armaments sufficiently for her to be towed to drydock. On that passage the *Tirpitz* was further damaged by Allied air attacks.

In late 1943, two months after the X-craft raid, Forbes took his Perisher. He did well in the "Attack Teacher" and went up to Scotland confident he would pass the sea phase. All went well for him until one black and foggy night when the Perishers were taking it in turns attacking their target ship using radar on the surface. When Forbes's turn came, HMS/M *Proteus* collided with the target. The Teacher had demanded that he conduct the attack from the information that the radar was supplying, even though it was visually apparent to Forbes that he was on a very real collision course with the target. Teacher refused to let Forbes take avoiding action, and as *Proteus*'s CO did not step in, the result was inevitable. Two other Canadians remember that night – George McPhee was on the bridge and Rod Johnston was down below when they heard and felt the enormous crash.

The Perisher target suffered such severe damage that she was beached and *Proteus* never sailed again – her bow cap was smashed and the damage extended aft to the torpedo tube doors. Forbes left submarines forever, effective that moment, and the submarine's captain was relieved of command. Forbes was neither called to testify nor given the results of the subsequent court of inquiry. The findings could not be located in the British records, even after an extensive search.

It was a distressing end to Forbes's very promising submarine career. He said, "There was nothing like serving in submarines."[5] A year after his disastrous Perisher, Forbes returned to Canada and commanded one of the ships used by the A/S training school at HMCS *Cornwallis*. Later he prepared corvette crews for the surrender of the U-boats at the end of the war.

CHAPTER FIFTEEN

CANADIANS IN EUROPEAN WATERS, 1943–1944

"Go away and think about it"

Sixteen other volunteer reserve officers became submariners, and like those that went before them, they came from every sort of background. They served in British submarines in all the major theatres of operations, as well as in ASW training boats in Canada and Bermuda. Three Canadian submariners earned their dolphins in 1942, nine in 1943, and four more in 1944.[1]

Bill Gilmour and "Hank" Hunter took the same SOTC in April 1942. Hunter was a U.S. citizen working in an advertising job in Quebec when the Dunkirk evacuation propelled him into the RCNVR. He declined an offer to join the USN when the States entered the war, preferring to remain in the RCN.

Gilmour joined the Naval Reserve at HMCS *Discovery* in Vancouver during his second year at UBC and his naïveté led his shipmates to nickname him "Junior." His interest in submarines began in Halifax when he visited the Free French submarine *Surcouf,* which was being used as a stop-gap convoy escort early in the war. Gilmour transferred to the Royal Navy in the summer of 1942, and immediately volunteered for the Silent Service. Gilmour's fellow submariners held him in high regard – he did his job quietly and efficiently and was blessed with an ability to get along with everyone.

Both Gilmour's and Hunter's first postings were to training flotillas in Scotland in H boats. Gilmour did well, becoming first lieutenant of *H33* after two months, but Hunter was less motivated. Gilmour then joined HMS/M *Syrtis (P241)* for her trials, as her fourth hand, and experienced a few uneventful anti-submarine patrols off Norway and in the

Bay of Biscay. In October 1943 he became the first of five Canadians to serve on *Truculent* based in Scotland; later, having been promoted to lieutenant, Gilmour sailed for Ceylon. On arrival in January 1944 he contracted dengue fever, a tropical disease, and had to be hospitalized.

Hunter, meanwhile, worked on *P58* for a while as her junior officer before moving to HMS/M *Torbay* in 1943 for six months. Before he left her, *Torbay* had engaged the enemy numerous times in the Aegean and participated in the invasion of Sicily. His CO commented after one particularly hectic patrol that the crew was continually kept on the jump. *Torbay*'s CO was pleased with Hunter's performance, which improved after a shaky start. Hunter had proved himself under rigorous operational conditions, but saw no more action after leaving *Torbay*. He was first lieutenant for a short time in both HMS/Ms *Tribune* and *Thrasher* before becoming the second Canadian to join *Truculent*.

Hunter enjoyed the company of two other enthusiastic Canadian submariners in *Truculent* – Dick Blake and Fred Fowler. This was not an exciting time for them – no patrols, only a brutal passage to Philadelphia for a refit. They suffered gale-force winds and monstrous seas all the way across, which damaged the boat but not the crew, and caused navigation to be a matter of guesswork and bad language, according to the CO. Hunter left the boat in February 1945, and did not go back to submarines.

Fred Fowler was the only Canadian submariner who was able to provide the author with a contemporary account of his wartime submarine experiences – his mother had kept his many letters home. From New Brunswick, Fowler sailed to England in the same troopship as Sherwood *et al.,* but served in destroyers for three years before switching his allegiance to submarines. The young Canadian regarded Sherwood as his mentor, explaining that he always used to do a sales job for the Silent Service whenever they met. When Fowler found himself in an unhappy ship in Canadian waters, he experienced diving in one of the Canadian A/S training boats, and recalled Sherwood's words. Fowler came ashore, immediately volunteered for the submarine service, and was accepted. He was a most likeable man, keen and energetic, with a good sense of fun; he fitted into the Royal Navy wardrooms with ease. Fowler relished serving in submarines – he likened it to playing "cowboys and Indians." The New Brunswicker served with considerable distinction in his first boat, HMS/M *Sceptre,* as her navigator and later as the torpedo officer.

The submarine had already earned the sobriquet "Bring 'em back alive" *Sceptre* when Fowler joined her. For most of 1944 they patrolled in the dangerous waters off Norway and he wrote, "This navigation racket will either make me or break me." Fowler was referring to his constantly broken sleep and the quantity of paperwork that he had to do. *Sceptre* saw a lot of action, sank many transports, and attacked a U-boat.

They operated in bad weather that never seemed to end. Fowler suffered badly from seasickness in the gales, and had to tie himself to the bridge to avoid being washed overboard. "A couple of times found [me] hanging on and standing in cold [water] up to my waist," wrote the Canadian. "The Ursula suit is not completely waterproof ... at the end of two hours you find yourself quite damp and cold" (an understatement). Fowler rarely undressed except to don dry underwear, and always slept fully clothed. Despite the grumbles, he enjoyed the life and wrote that he had never been bored since he had opted for submarines. He also found that he had little opportunity to spend his salary – his bank account grew nicely. He was able to increase the allotment to his family, and even invest. The food parcels from home were treats that Fowler shared in the wardroom – the chocolates were the most prized. "I don't think [the Britishers] have seen chocolates like that since '40 at least," remarked Fowler when he thanked his mother.

Sceptre completed two special operations with the X-craft flotilla, seven months after *Sea Nymph*'s experiences. Fowler's first X-craft operation (GUIDANCE), in April 1944, was notable because they had to restrain themselves from attacking a U-boat that passed close by on the day of the raid. Fowler likened the incident to "a man in the desert who, when it began to rain soup, found himself with only a fork!" *Sceptre* became the first boat to recover her midget submarine and bring it home safely to be used again. They had towed *X24* to Bergen, Norway, to destroy a huge floating dock used for U-boats. By mistake the midget sank a large merchant ship lying alongside it but the team's achievement was recognized by their colleagues as the two boats came home to their cheers.

Summer found *Sceptre* in the Bay of Biscay off northern Spain shooting up all the ships she could find, and nearly causing an international incident. It was often quite difficult to identify the targets as neutrals or German ore carriers. When *Sceptre*'s torpedoes missed a German vessel and sank the ship behind, which was showing her navigation lights, the CO thought they might be in trouble. Two days later, off San Sebastian, *Sceptre* attacked a berthed ship and, after the torpedoes had been fired, realized they were in a neutral anchorage. This time the CO was sure they were in trouble. The attack added yet another bar to *Sceptre*'s Jolly Roger but unfortunately killed a Spaniard on a neutral ship. Luckily, the

Spanish chose to pursue neither incident, mainly because both ships that were sunk turned out to be German.

In September and October 1944 Fowler's CO credited him with much of the submarine's success, including a second successful operation (HECKLE) with *X24*. The midget succeeded in destroying the floating dock at Bergen that had been missed in an earlier raid, and also damaged two merchant ships. Fowler earned two Mentions in Dispatches for his

> ... outstanding efficiency, courage, and devotion to duty in seven patrols in HMS *Sceptre* during which 2 successful special operations have been carried out and 9 enemy supply ships have been sunk and one damaged. Lieut. Fowler has, during most of this time, been the Torpedo Officer and during attacks keeps the plot. The success of the attacks has been in great measure due to his efficiency, a fact which was particularly reported in HMS *Sceptre*'s Tenth Patrol Report. By his efficiency and unfailing devotion to duty he has been an inspiration to the whole crew.[2]

Fowler eventually left *Sceptre* when she went into refit in December 1944, and was sad to go because the wardroom had been close-knit and fun, with a reputation for success. *Sceptre*'s officers were also sorry to lose their "colonial." Fowler's adventurous spirit and his sense of the ridiculous had made him a welcome member of *Sceptre*'s company.

In December 1944 Fowler joined HMS/M *Truculent,* meeting Dick Blake and the only American in the RCNVR, "Hank" Hunter. Hunter introduced the Canucks to rum and Coke, and on arrival in Philadelphia, they tried mixing them themselves. "It wasn't until the third round [that] we discovered they were pouring doubles ... !"

Fowler left *Truculent* in February 1945 and became first lieutenant in *United,* which was one of the Canadian training submarines operating in Digby and Bermuda. Fowler had a much quieter time of it than he was used to. Two days after VE Day he took the opportunity in Bermuda to marry his fiancée, Kate. They both returned to New Brunswick after his demobilization in September and Fowler rejoined his father's insurance business.

Dick Blake, who met Fowler on *Truculent,* was another Canadian who served in both British and Mediterranean waters. He was a tall, personable student of mathematics and physics at McMaster University when he joined the RCNVR as a seaman. Nearly fifty years later, Blake commented that he did it because most of his friends had. "I certainly didn't understand the issues or the underlying political, economic, and social problems, but I did feel I should do something for my country."

After getting his commission, Blake served in corvettes and destroyers for two years. During escort duty on the Gibraltar run he started to consider the submarine service. Blake wasted no time in applying when a message arrived on board requesting volunteers. He says frankly, "My motives were not heroic, but rather I was intrigued by the technical challenge" – not surprising in view of his interest in engineering. Blake also liked the independence submarines enjoyed; he hoped to have a chance to serve in other theatres of the war.

According to Blake his SOTC was "intense, exciting and professional." At the end of 1943, Blake went to HMS/M *Truant* in Scotland as her navigator for a year. *Truant* worked off the Norwegian coast, usually as one in a line of submarines laid out to intercept the *Tirpitz* if she attempted to break out of Altenfjord. She never did. During this period Blake's brother, a decorated bomber pilot, was shot down and killed. It was a shock to Blake, and it sobered him. "It gave me a great deal to think about," he wrote.

Blake reluctantly sailed with *Truant* for the Far East, but severe mechanical problems caused her to turn around at Malta. Blake was relieved – he did not like heat. During the six weeks spent in Malta, *Truant*'s two junior officers drew lots to see who would go on which patrols in the S-class submarines based there. Blake saw minor action around Crete and in the Aegean, but cannot remember in which boat. He returned with *Truant* to the U.K. in September 1944.

When *Truant*'s CO moved to *Truculent,* he asked Blake to go to Philadelphia with him as his navigator. They joined the boat at Aberdeen, Scotland, and much to Blake's delight he found Hunter and Fowler on board. The appalling Atlantic weather they encountered was made worse for Blake because his wife was at sea too – on a troopship corkscrewing viciously to the south of them. Blake became *Truculent*'s first lieutenant when they arrived at Philadelphia.

Blake remained with *Truculent* until her post-refit trials and work-ups were complete in July 1945. Anxious to get back to university in September, he became the first RCNVR submariner to be demobilized, but at the last minute, the RCN changed their minds and decided he should take one of the surrendered U-boats on its publicity cruise. Blake had already been issued his travel warrant, and he left for Hamilton immediately, using the warrant and expecting to be hauled back unceremoniously. However, he heard nothing. In 1948 Blake graduated from McMaster in mechanical engineering, believing it to be more useful than pure math and physics, and joined the Naval Research Establishment, where he worked on the development of variable depth sonar, among other projects.

Two Canadians who served briefly in submarines were Fred Bunbury and Ted Cayley. Little is known about Cayley, as he could not be located, but he volunteered in 1943 and served in HMS/S *Trespasser* for an unremarkable year. As the war ended, Cayley became sick and was later invalided out of the RCN. Bunbury served for two years in the British Submarine Service at the end of the war, but he only spent five months in a submarine. He was another Canadian who opted for "special duties" of the most hazardous kind, though he was to become neither a charioteer nor a midget submariner.

Bunbury was a young English-speaking Quebecker from La Tuque who was working as a chemist in the textile industry when war was declared. He confessed that he joined the RCNVR for the travel and adventure, though he also felt that he ought to "do his bit." Bunbury followed a family tradition of naval service that coincidentally provided a link with William Maitland-Dougall, who lost his life in *D3* in 1918. Both their ancestors served on the vessel that took Napoleon into exile on St. Helena.

After serving in a cruiser that was torpedoed twice at the height of the Mediterranean war, Bunbury became fed up with surface warfare and volunteered for submarines. After successfully completing his SOTC in 1943 he spent a short time as navigator in *H32*, in a training flotilla at Londonderry, then went to HMS/M *Strongbow*, a new boat. At the end of work-ups, Bunbury reported difficulties with his vision which the doctor diagnosed as eyestrain. The condition cleared up, but the doctor thought it likely to recur, and this prognosis precluded further service in submarines. A very disappointed Bunbury trudged back to the Admiralty for new instructions.

Bunbury was sent for an interview with the captain responsible for special duty personnel. In a scene reminiscent of Moreton's chariot recruitment, the captain told the Canadian that there was a vacancy in Gibraltar that was closely related to submarines, but that it had to be filled by a volunteer. Bunbury asked for more information before handing himself over.

"Have you ever heard of limpets?" asked the captain. He was referring to limpet mines, which were planted on the hulls of ships.

"Yes, sir."

"Well, we are having trouble with them at Gib. The job involves
searching the bottoms of merchant ships assembling for convoys. The
ships are searched for limpets by a small party of shallow water divers
using the Davis Submarine Escape Apparatus. You would be in charge of
this unit," explained the four-ring captain.

"But I've had no experience in mine disposal, sir," interjected Bunbury.

"Don't worry about that. The search party's duty is only to locate
limpets. Others get rid of them."

Bunbury was apprehensive, and felt that he could not in all con-
science make a decision of this magnitude after such a short interview.
His emotions must have been obvious to the captain, who inquired, "Are
you married? Do you have any next of kin?"

"No, sir, and my parents are dead," responded Bunbury weakly.

"Go away and think about it. Come back to see me tomorrow with
your decision. You are under no pressure to accept. Remember, this is
highly confidential and you must not discuss it with anyone." Bunbury
put aside his plan to consult with a friend, and before he left asked if he
might practise his submarine escape procedures again at *Dolphin*.

Bunbury spent the evening "walking the streets of London with no
one to talk to except total strangers I met on the frequent stops in pubs
for a reassuring drink to give me courage. I went over all the reasons why
I should decline to go and yet I knew all the time that I was going to accept."

Next morning Bunbury accepted the appointment. The captain's
response was, "Good. I knew you would, and incidentally, old boy, the
DSEA tank at *Dolphin* is closed for maintenance. There will not be an
opportunity for you to do a refresher course." Bunbury learned there
would be no turnover from Lieutenant Crabbe, the officer he was replacing in the Shallow Water Diving Unit, as he and his second string had
already left the unit. (In the 1950s Crabbe became known after his body
was discovered underneath a Russian cruiser.)

"We want you in Gibraltar right away. Good luck!" said the captain
to a breathless Bunbury, who rushed off to pack.

He was in Gib within the week and started his new duties immediately. Bunbury had a lot to learn – the first thing was that the second-in-
command, who had "left" the team, had in fact lost his life during an
operation. It was that old devil, Oxygen Pete, which had caused so many
casualties amongst the charioteers. Bunbury gritted his teeth, determined

to display confidence to his men, who had been badly shaken. The team of one petty officer and four seamen, none of whom were submariners, were all volunteers and very young. They and their new CO stuck with the unit until the end of the war.

Bunbury soon learned the two-man procedure for searching merchantmen for limpets. The divers first visited the vessel's master and asked for weighted lines to be put over both sides of the ship as far as the bilge keel, then shinnied down the ropes to the water. Pausing for breath and giving their aching muscles a rest, the divers donned their DSEA, and continued down underwater until they felt the bilge keel. Here they released the ropes and made their way aft, feeling for mines. At the end of the bilge keel, the divers swam to the rudder and screws to inspect them. At no time did they work in pairs, have a rope attached to them, or have any means of communication with the surface or each other. When the search was over, the divers surfaced in a state of near exhaustion and hypothermia, to be picked up by their launch. Although the water was about 10 to 15 degrees Celsius, Bunbury and his teammates wore only swim suits, and gloves to prevent their hands being ripped to shreds by the barnacles. The toxic effects of breathing pure oxygen were taken into account at all times; Bunbury never allowed any search to exceed ten minutes, and he always dived with his men.

The Shallow Water Diving Unit worked for the remainder of 1944 to the end of the European war without incident, and without finding any limpet mines. Each dive was thorough and sometimes quite hectic. Once a convoy of eighteen ships had to be searched in a single night following an intelligence tip. Bunbury remembered, "Diving at night was exceptionally hazardous and ... frightening. Although the diver had a powerful waterproof flashlight, once submerged he had absolutely no sense of direction or depth if he was swept by the tide beyond his light's ability to pick out the ship's hull. It was impossible to know whether one was sinking or rising." Bunbury believes their activities deterred the German and Italian agents from further mining attempts.

After VE Day the teams in Gibraltar were quickly disbanded. Bunbury married a WRNS officer, and he and his wife returned to Canada. Later, they were transferred back to England, where Bunbury now lives in retirement.

A latecomer to the Mediterranean was John Gardner, who did his SOTC with several other Canadians in early 1944. A classmate remembered him: "He was rather unique. He had all of the qualifications ... to succeed in almost any field."[3] Gardner was a lanky Newfoundlander, highly intelligent and very personable. "We all liked [him], because he was humble, sincere, and down to earth."

Gardner joined HMS/M *Unswerving*'s all volunteer reservists wardroom at Malta just before her second war patrol and he remained with this spirited submarine until after VE Day. As her most junior officer, Gardner had no bunk, did no watches, and was very seasick. He soon earned his watch-keeping certificate, took his place on the roster, and stopped being seasick.

Although the Germans were retreating in the Mediterranean, they fought to the last man for the Greek islands. *Unswerving* saw a great deal of action. Gardner got his baptism immediately when they sank five caiques and were strenuously depth-charged by eleven escorts during an abortive attack on a convoy. Gardner became *Unswerving*'s navigator, was promoted to lieutenant, and took seven German prisoners from two armed patrol vessels which they had sunk by gun action. The Newfoundlander found it exhilarating to be a young man just out of school and navigating a submarine. "To do it now would be very different," he acknowledges.

Unswerving's patrols continued to be busy and they rarely came up empty-handed. However, as targets became scarcer following the German evacuation of the islands, *Unswerving* sank only one tanker on her last patrol in October 1944. However, this sinking earned the submarine a place in history – the 1,900-ton (1,723 tonne) *Bertha* was the last ship to be sunk in the Mediterranean in World War II.

By November Gardner's war was essentially over. *Unswerving*, taking a well-earned rest from patrols, acted as a communication ship for the army, which was engaged in preventing a civil war between various Greek factions in the Aegean. The ship's company lived on board and Gardner, not being in signals, had time to explore the islands.

Unswerving returned to Britain in the spring of 1945 for decommissioning, and Gardner went on leave in Canada. Afterwards he spent three months as first lieutenant in HMS/M *Upright* based at Digby and, although his record does not show it, commanded *U-889*, one of the surrendered U-boats, for three days.

Gardner resumed his university studies in metallurgy after demobilization and later worked for Alcan Aluminum, mainly in Europe. He is now retired and divides his time between winter in rural Quebec and summer on his ketch, *Annie J*, in Nova Scotia.

CHAPTER SIXTEEN

A CANADIAN COMMANDS AN X-CRAFT, 1944

"Terra firma, terra firma. The more firmer, the less terror"[1]

Another Canadian, who was not technically a submariner, became an X-craft commanding officer. He joined the midget submarines of the Twelfth Submarine Flotilla in 1944 after three years on North Atlantic convoy duty in corvettes (as an executive officer) and destroyers.[2]

When war broke out, Johnnie C. Ruse was in his last year of high school and his bush pilot father, hoping to delay the inevitable, refused to allow his son to join up until he had graduated. Ruse longed to follow in his footsteps and, motivated as never before, matriculated in three months. He decided the best way to flight training was to enrol in the RCN and quickly transfer to the RN, but he remained stuck in Canada. Though Ruse eventually got to England (in late 1943), he never flew a plane. He joined the staff of the Commodore(D [Defence]), Western Approaches, as an instructor teaching escort personnel how to capture and neutralize U-boats and their crews. This year-long job entailed spending time in HMS/M *Strategem,* where Ruse discovered an affinity for submarines and volunteered for the Silent Service. His applications were continually turned down, so he tried for "special and hazardous service" instead, which he guessed was probably X-craft, the midget submarines. By now twenty-three years old, Ruse considered that his confidence, daring, and determination would be useful in the midget submarines.

Both the CO of *Strategem* and Commodore(D) recommended Ruse and he set off for a series of selection interviews with Admiral(S)'s staff in London. The ideal character type for X-craft had traits similar to those of the charioteers. They had to be young enough to thrive on danger, but also mature enough to be strongly determined to succeed when things went wrong.

The meetings went well and Ruse was chosen to go to the training establishment, HMS *Varbel*. Its location and *raison d'être* were so secret Ruse set off in September 1944 knowing neither his destination nor the type of work he was to undertake. *Varbel* turned out to be on the Firth of Clyde in Scotland where the training of personnel and the trials and work-ups of the X-craft were done.

HMS *Varbel* actually consisted of two bases - *Varbel I* and *Varbel II*. When Ruse arrived in Port Bannatyne on the eastern shore of the Isle of Bute, he could see *Varbel I*, a former hotel, high on a hill behind the fishing village. The surroundings looked bleak as Ruse trudged up the very steep road to the base. Panting at the top, he stopped to rest and turned to see the anchorage below him, but could not see the exercise area. Very shortly, Ruse visited the advanced base, *Varbel II*, at the head of the loch. This was an attractive shooting lodge, located in an oasis of lush, green, low-lying land amongst the steep, rocky hillsides that kept the loch in deep shadows. It was here that the sea training was done.

Ruse entered *Varbel I* for the first time and confidently introduced himself to the captain in command of the base. The CO went through the Canadian's experience and immediately placed him on the roster of spare COs for the training boat, *XT6*. He exempted Ruse from the classroom training usually given to new volunteers because of his time in *Strategem*.

Even though Ruse had suspected he would be joining X-craft, and had imagined what they would be like, his first impression took his breath away. Surfaced, *XT6* could barely be seen above the water because of its low freeboard. She looked too small to be a working submarine: at fifty feet (15 m) long and seven feet (2 m) wide, she displaced thirty-four tons (31 tonnes). Down below the usable space was less – thirty-five by five feet (11 by 1.5 m) – and the dim lighting, the maze of instruments, pipelines, valves and gauges, and the lack of headroom made Ruse wonder if he could ever command one effectively. His mind whirled around, trying to absorb it all.

Subsequent trips clarified the layout for Ruse and, as the X-craft operated in an identical manner to a full-size submarine, he quickly got the hang of it. The forward compartment contained the battery of 112 cells, which drove the boat underwater at 2 knots for about eighty miles (130 km) and at 6 knots in short bursts. The diving lock-out, known as the "wet and dry" compartment, was amidships; it was flooded up to enable the diver in the crew to exit underwater to cut through nets and other obstacles. This space served as the crew's escape compartment and also housed the single head. The aft compartment contained everything else – the controls, compasses, trim valves, periscope, pumps, engine, and electric motor. It served as the control room as well, with one miniature periscope. The single diesel engine, identical to those in London's double-decker buses, was squeezed in so tight the engineer had difficulty working on it. This provided a maximum surface speed of 6.5 knots and an average range of 1,000 miles (1,609 km). X-craft could remain dived for twenty-four hours without replenishing their air supply, but the atmosphere rapidly deteriorated. Condensation was their main enemy: it caused repeated short circuits in the electrical equipment. Ruse and his crew spent hours keeping everything dry. Ruse's training focused on the acquisition of technical efficiency – a vital necessity to survival and successful operations. Acclimatization to discomfort and high risks did not appear on the list of objectives. Ruse began with the "hands-on" training. As a student CO under supervision, he not only learned the skills of conning and diving such a small submarine, but also how to operate the systems and machinery. Escape training was done in the loch, rather than *Dolphin*'s tank, and was more unpleasant.

With a crew of only four, everyone had to do everything. Ruse's primary task as CO was navigation, and precision was imperative to get under the target. He also helped out with the cleaning of the boat, and often cooked. His first lieutenant was responsible for depth-keeping and trimming, and the diver handled the steering. If he was busy cutting through nets, number one took over from him. The engineer was the fourth member of the crew. The manoeuvrability and control of the X-craft underwater were outstanding – they could hover, go astern, and move vertically up and down with no headway – which no full-size submarine could do.

Ruse worked hard and enthusiastically and was soon chosen by a spare crew to be their captain. This unusual method of appointment was used because the attack teams worked better with COs they trusted and respected. Ruse remained in *XT6* for a few months perfecting his attack skills and then took command of *X21*, an operational boat, to prepare for upcoming raids.

By 1944 each X-craft had three crews – one for the attack and two for the passage to the target – and all were trained identically in case they had to replace each other. However, during training, the passage crews were additionally responsible for the preparation of the X-craft for the next day's exercises. From sun-up to sun-down the training of the *X21*'s three crews was relentless. Nothing was left to chance – they practised navigation, net cutting, manoeuvring under a target, and avoiding patrols.

The Canadian CO became used to working on his hands and knees – the control room was scarcely larger than a small closet with headroom of five feet (1.5 m) – though he could stand to use the periscope. Ruse was unable to stretch his arms out without hitting equipment or his shipmates. He prepared many surprisingly good meals in these conditions in the carpenter's "glue pot" which served as a double boiler and supplied his crew with endless cups of sweet tea. There was no time for Ruse to sleep during exercises, and though a bunk was provided he never used it.

The conditions the crews endured would have been intolerable to most people, but men like Ruse thrived on the challenge. The crews' isolation and their high achievement levels bred a strong *esprit de corps* and the competition to outdo each other at sea and ashore was fierce. They let off steam regularly either in the mess at *Varbel,* in local pubs, or at their rented flat in London. Ruse thought his fellow officers were full of crazy, eccentric ideas and brimming with energy – four of them soon earned Victoria Crosses.

Ruse's training intensified and rumours surfaced that crew selection for another raid on the *Tirpitz* was imminent. Their depot ship, HMS *Bonaventure,* moved the teams to a new location where planners laid out courses that simulated obstacles, and the trainees were sent on mock patrols as if they were on the raid itself. Ruse ran the gauntlet of minefields, shore batteries, destroyers, and anti-submarine and anti-torpedo nets. The most difficult skill to master was being towed underwater at 12 knots behind a big submarine – *X21* porpoised continually through a depth of 100 feet (30 m) of water. This oscillation was normal and soon Ruse learned to recognize a good up or down and when to make adjustments. The vigilance required was exhausting. Every six hours, the tiny boat surfaced to "guff through," or run the engine for ten minutes, pulling fresh air in through the induction mast.

Most attack exercises were three-day affairs and the Twelfth Submarine Flotilla often used the battleship HMS *Malaya* as a target. The crews never slept and had to take Benzedrine tablets to stay alert. Once the X-craft was in the right position the attack crew replaced the passage crew, the tow was released, and the boat began the run up to the target at periscope depth, usually at night. When they were about 300 yards (275 m) from their quarry the X-craft dived deeper to get below the hull of the target. Completely blind, the COs manoeuvred their boats underneath the ship at less than one knot. This task was always tricky, but became easier with practice. After the fuse was set, the 2,000-pound (900 kg) explosive charges were released, and the X-craft started the dangerous withdrawal to meet her sister submarine about a day later. The attack and passage crews were exhausted at the end of an exercise, and frequently dissatisfied with their performances.

After three severely depressed submariners had committed suicide following unsuccessful practice attacks, sentries were posted outside the officers' cabins on their return. This controversial routine was not welcomed by the X-craft crews. They saw the troubled individuals not as trying to get out of the job the easy way, but as men who feared that they might let their shipmates down if they continued and decided to ensure that they would not. The pressures and stresses were enormous on such young shoulders, and as they learned more about the raid on the *Tirpitz* everyone began to show signs of strain. Ruse began to experience a recurring nightmare. He found himself trapped under the target, unable to decide whether to release the charges and be blown up with them or to withdraw. The crews never discussed this manifestation of pressure, and, indeed, Ruse did not realize until years later that his colleagues, including Moreton, the charioteer, experienced similar reactions.

After all the preparation, the planned raid on the *Tirpitz* was cancelled and Ruse suffered intense disappointment. The navy sidelined the X20s for use as training platforms for Far Eastern operations and their crews reacted by driving them beyond their limits. Pressure dents became a status symbol, recalled Ruse. He took *X21* down to 400 feet (120 m) on several occasions but the creaks and groans from the pressure hull, designed for a maximum depth of only 300 feet (90 m), worried him sufficiently to prevent him going deeper. An American observer reportedly was scared witless by Ruse's antics – Ruse had perfected an airless surface from 200 feet (60 m), which blew *X21* right out of the water like a breaching whale.

Ruse waited patiently to get a new operational X-craft to replace the aging *X21,* and in the spring of 1945 he heard that he was to go and stand by *XE8*. He was elated. She was one of the newer, improved models, designed especially for Far Eastern operations. *XE8* was eighteen inches (46 cm) longer than the earlier midgets, and could accommodate more stowage, a small refrigerator, and an air-conditioning unit to make the crew more comfortable in the tropics. She also had three hydraulic arms on the upper deck, which enabled the X-craft to snug up underneath the hull of a target when slightly positively buoyant and deploy the side cargoes (mines) more accurately. Stronger tow-ropes and more durable telephone links to the towing submarines were provided, following the experience gained in earlier raids.

When *XE8* was completed, the manufacturer presented Ruse with a visitors' book, suitably inscribed: "The fewer the men, the greater share of honour." *XE8* was loaded onto a flatcar and camouflaged as a motor torpedo boat for transportation to Scotland. Once they arrived at the sea *XE8* was unloaded, commissioned, and launched on Easter Sunday, 2 April. She was aptly named *Expunger,* though the same could not be said of her nickname – "Screwball." Her motto was *Hoc super omnia* – "This above all" – and the crest, designed by the first passage CO, depicted a ferocious Malay tiger taking a bite out of a Japanese battleship.

The trials and work-ups of *XE8* and her crew began at *Varbel* immediately. Ruse re-instituted the efficient routines that he had established in *X21*. Early on, *XE8* did her deep dive to 300 feet (90 m) attached to a strong hawser from a diving vessel, and then the crew settled down to test every piece of machinery and equipment exhaustively. The last and definitely the most rewarding item in their preparations was to achieve operational readiness. By now the base was a hive of activity from dawn till dusk and well into the night – at its busiest, *Varbel* had twenty-four X-craft in training.

The first batch of XEs were shipped off to the Far East in February 1945, but Ruse's *XE8* was scheduled to go later with a second group. Training intensified and excitement mounted in anticipation of their first operation. *XE8*'s work-ups went very well and the crew was psychologically ready. However, the war was drawing to its close, and before Ruse and *XE8* could be deployed the operation was cancelled. Ruse sank into a depression that lasted a long time: "I couldn't even go back to the boat again. I sent someone down to bring my personal gear back." Ruse never saw *XE8* again and did not finish her work-ups. "All my time, energy, and commitment had been wasted," he said. Ruse left his midget submarine on 14 April and the decision to pay off HMS *Varbel* was made soon afterwards.

However, *XE8* did not go into reserve, as two of her sisters did, but was handed over to another CO. The final decision to cancel the departure of the second batch of XEs had not, in fact, been made; it had simply been delayed for a month. Ruse knew nothing of this, nor did he know that as early as November 1944 the Admiralty had decided to close *Varbel* once the second XEs had been worked-up. Ruse accepted the cancellation of the plan as final, and concluded it was pointless to stay.

Varbel was decommissioned on 15 May 1945, never to reopen, and the final decision to cancel the departure of the second batch of XEs for the Far East was made on 25 May 1945, long after Ruse had left the flotilla. *XE8* and her sisters went into immediate reserve on 31 May 1945 with the Fifth Submarine Flotilla at HMS *Dolphin*. *XE8* was later taken out of reserve in February 1949 and made operational again for a few years. In 1954, on her way to the scrapyard, *XE8* slipped her tow and sank off Portland. There she lay for over twenty years before being located by divers and raised in 1976. She is now being restored and will be on display at HM Dockyard Chatham museum.

The Admiralty considered Ruse for the job of submarine instruction officer in Newfoundland, but Admiral(S) disappointed Ruse by saying he was unsuitable as he was not a submariner. Instead the Canadian went on a torpedo course, and spent most of his time in a pub, too miserable to participate. He was finally appointed to HMCS *Ontario* as her torpedo officer. She was a former British cruiser, commissioned into the RCN, and Ruse sailed in her to Hong Kong. He did not see any action in *Ontario* either as she arrived in the Far East too late.

It was in Hong Kong that Ruse began to come to terms with his disappointments. He witnessed the release of Allied prisoners of war whom the Japanese had captured. "It was a most dreadful shock," he remembered, and realized imprisonment would have been a likely fate for him too, if he had been caught in those waters. Ruse came back to Canada in March 1946 in *Ontario* and was demobilized. He rejoined the Royal Canadian Navy as a lieutenant-commander during the Korean War on a short service commission, but never went overseas or back to submarines. Later Ruse went up to the Arctic in the icebreaker, HMCS *Labrador*, and was involved in the preparation of the beaches for the DEW Line supply landings. After leaving the RCN for the second time, he went into private industry in Ontario, where he still lives, though now in retirement.

Johnny Ruse has always regretted that he was not allowed to join the submarine service. He still looks upon his friend Freddie Fowler, of *Sceptre*, with kindly envy. Ruse had not passed his SOTC and so was technically not a submariner – but if he was not one in theory, he very definitely was one in practice. Work in X-craft was hazardous, exciting, and demanding, and had brought out the best in him. He enjoyed his time in Scotland with all the other young and dedicated officers, and despite the enormous disappointments Ruse remembers the experience with much affection and pride. He returns to the reunions of the Twelfth Submarine Flotilla regularly.

CHAPTER SEVENTEEN

CANADIANS IN FAR EASTERN WATERS, 1944

"If that was a seagull, it lays pretty big eggs!"

Nine Canadian officers served in British submarines in the Eastern Fleet, operating from Ceylon and Western Australia during the last two years of WWII. Some were experienced submariners and have been mentioned before; others were newcomers to the service. None came to the Pacific theatre until 1944, when more and more boats were allocated to it, and the submarine war was being fought by the Allies with increasing strength and success.

The Far East had no submarines from 1939 until the fall of Singapore, then only two from late 1941 to August 1943, and for the same reason that the RCN had been denied ASW training boats – there were not enough to go round. HMS/Ms *Trusty* and *Truant* sailed from Britain in the fall of 1941, but when Japan invaded Singapore they were driven to relocate briefly in northeastern Java. By March 1942 the Japanese had driven these submarines back to Trincomalee, Ceylon, where they managed only three patrols every two months. Initially, because of inadequate intelligence, *Trusty* and *Truant* were used almost exclusively to alert the Allies to enemy incursions into the Indian Ocean through the Straits of Malacca. By the time more submarines began to arrive, the Japanese had occupied vast territories in the region, and were threatening Australia.

In March 1942 the Admiralty appointed a commander-in-chief, Ceylon, to fill the vacuum caused by the Allied military collapse in the area and also dispatched a submarine depot ship to Trincomalee. July 1943 saw six submarines arrive in Ceylon and these heralded a steady stream of boats from October onward. This was made possible by the Italian naval surrender, which had released Allied boats from the Mediterranean and allowed the Admiralty to redeploy all the new and refitted S- and T-class boats to the Far East. Soon twenty submarines formed two flotillas in Ceylon, the Fourth and the Eighth, and two more depot ships, HM Ships *Adamant* and *Maidstone,* arrived. This increase permitted regular patrols of more enemy shipping routes and attacks on Japanese naval units and supply ships.

By mid-1944 there were twenty-six British submarines in the Far East, a sufficiently high number to split the force. The Eighth Flotilla joined the U.S. 7th Fleet in Australia at Fremantle. The Second (newly formed) and the Fourth Flotilla remained in Ceylon.

The Eighth Flotilla and HMS *Maidstone* arrived in Fremantle in early September 1944 to a big welcome. The British boats were more effective than the larger U.S. fleet submarines in the shallow coastal waters of the southwestern Pacific. The S boats were earmarked for the Java Sea and the T boats for the South China Sea, farther north. The flotilla came under operational control of an American – the Commander, Submarines, U.S. 7th Fleet, headquartered at Perth, just north of the base at Fremantle.

The first Canadian to arrive in Trincomalee was Lt.-Commander Freddie Sherwood, DSC, RCNVR, in command of a new S-class submarine, HMS/M *Spiteful.* After his long leave in Canada, Sherwood stood by her construction, had Bryant's modified periscope from *Safari* fitted, and recruited the officers he wanted from *P556.* A nasty dockside battery explosion and high noise levels delayed their acceptance trials. Work-ups ended in Scapa Flow with a proud Sherwood entertaining his brother to a day at sea. While showing off to him a little, he ran *Spiteful* up and over the Barrel of Butter, an inshore shoal, which made the crew nervous of his ability to command.

Spiteful made her first shake-down patrol in December 1943 off the Norwegian coast with the objective of locating and destroying U-boats. There were rough seas that shook the crew's tummies loose, but no enemy boats were seen. The new sailors found their energy quickly sapped by the submarine's wicked motion on the surface and the bone-chilling cold. They were too busy surviving these conditions to be over-concerned by the enemy aircraft that continually bothered them.[1]

In early 1944, the Admiralty confirmed their departure for the Far East and Sherwood gave the ship's company leave while *Spiteful* was modified for her long patrols in the tropics. At the end of February *Spiteful* sailed from the Clyde crammed to the deckheads with extra gear and stores. She went through the Mediterranean, where they repainted the boat in the eastern colours of pale blue-green, through Suez, and on into the stifling heat of the Red Sea. They arrived at Trinco on 20 April better acclimated to the difficult conditions they would be enduring. The crew found Ceylon full of intriguing sights, sounds, and smells.

The ship's company was relieved to come alongside "Mother *Maidstone*," their comfortable and roomy depot ship, and Sherwood met Commander Tony Miers, VC, DSO, RN, commander of SM8. Miers's firm friendship with Canadian submariners originated here and lasted until his death in 1984. He was a spirited disciplinarian, but staunchly devoted to his crews.

Within a month *Spiteful* left on her first war patrol off the Andamans, a chain of islands in the Bay of Bengal, 750 miles (1,200 km) east of India. Sherwood's objective was to sink Japanese supply ships, preferably tankers, though he was also allowed to attack local junks that were carrying Axis cargo. The latter proved risky in areas of frequent A/S patrols, as the junks had to be boarded first. After an eight-day passage *Spiteful* reached her billet, and Sherwood searched assiduously for targets, to no avail. On their last day on station he decided to shoot up the Japanese military installations in Port Blair, a former penal colony. Sherwood calculated they would have only ten minutes to succeed before an enemy aircraft based on the island put them deep.

In mid-afternoon on 1 June 1944, *Spiteful* surfaced and had the first round off in twenty-five seconds. It fell short but the next two scored hits. After unjamming the gun, they fired nine more rounds, seven of which hit the governor's house and barracks before the lookouts reported an aircraft. *Spiteful* hurriedly withdrew at periscope depth, then went deep and altered course, losing the plane easily. *Spiteful* returned to Trincomalee on the surface, as was the routine.

Most of the COs were young and inexperienced, and the different operational conditions in the Far East posed challenges for them that worried their Captain(S) constantly. Their billets were in waters that were sometimes too shallow for submarines, and strewn with shoals, small islands, and narrow channels where an enemy could hide. The submarines could not manoeuvre safely in such places and navigation was a nightmare. To make it even more difficult, the Axis used small, shallow-drafted transports, which clung to the shorelines in the knowledge that torpedoes did not work very well in such situations. However, it was in the submarines' favour that the warm tropical sea had distinct temperature layers, which allowed them to hide more easily from enemy asdic. *Spiteful* carefully determined the location and depth of the layers every day.

Spiteful's company also had to contend with the climate. The heat and humidity were extreme, causing the crew to sweat profusely. They got rid of their underpants and shorts which rubbed their skin raw and instead wore towels like sarongs. With fresh water rationed, the crew could wash their hands and faces only once a day and their bodies every second or third day. It is surprising that more sickness did not occur – prickly heat and boils were the most frequent reason for being on sick parade, but these never prevented their sufferers from standing their watches. Cases of severe dehydration were rare, but collapse from heat stroke was common. *Spiteful*'s crew did not succumb to either. However, they all suffered from short tempers, and there were some nasty blow-ups. These were usually allowed to run their course to ventilate the severe stress that built up on long patrols.

Spiteful's sailors took a while to trust their Canadian captain, whom for obvious reasons they called "Fender." His reservist's wavy stripes, his brush with the shoal, and two Perishers diminished their confidence, and his "upbringing" with guns in *Sealion* and *Safari* generated skepticism. However, this latter experience was ideal for Pacific submarine warfare and Sherwood, like all COs before him, worked hard to earn their respect. As they got to know their CO better, the sailors were relieved to discover he was not "medal hungry." *Spiteful*'s cox'n said that by the time the first Far Eastern patrol was over the ratings began to trust Sherwood and believed he might get them home.

Spiteful spent three weeks in harbour between patrols preparing for her next outing. Sherwood ensured that his crew got ten days' leave each. The junior ranks could choose between going to a rest camp in the suburbs of Colombo or to a tea plantation. Neither was ideal: Colombo cost too much, with the better bars and restaurants off limits, and the plantations were boring. While they worked on *Spiteful* in Trinco the ratings' beer and shore leave were restricted, and as a result Ceylon was unpopular. It was different for the officers – they could afford Colombo's night spots if that was their preference, but the relaxation provided by a quiet plantation also had its attractions. Trinco offered them opportunities to swim, picnic, and sail, often with the flotillas' Wrens.

Spiteful's second patrol began on 21 June 1944. They headed for the Malacca Strait, which separates Sumatra from Malaya. Sherwood found

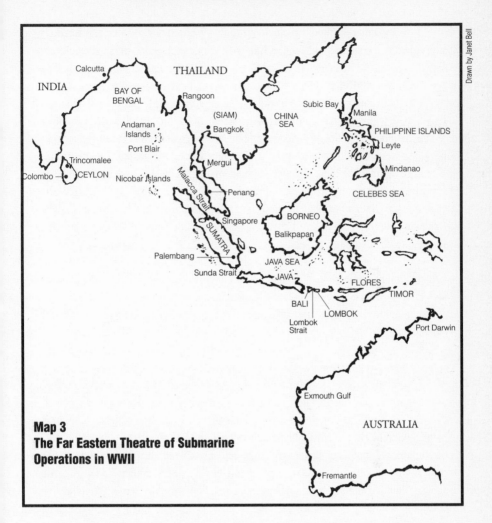

Drawn by Janet Bell

Map 3
The Far Eastern Theatre of Submarine
Operations in WWII

glassy seas, mirages, and almost no water at its northern end. These and the featureless coastline presented his navigator with substantial problems. Constantly anxious, Sherwood used only the small attack periscope and hardly slept.

"Aircraft red, twenty-five to fifty-six hundred yards," reported the radar operator as a convoy of small vessels retaliated after a surface attack from *Spiteful.*

"There it is!" yelled the signalman, beside Sherwood on the bridge. The CO pulled the plug, retiring with no score.

"Are you sure that was an aeroplane you saw? Are you sure it wasn't a seagull?" he asked his signalman once in the control room. Then there was a reverberating crash.

The lookout looked up and replied, "Well, sir, if it was a seagull, it lays pretty big eggs!"[2] *Spiteful* had some cork shaken loose and a few lights went out, but her worst damage was jammed steering. After it was repaired, Sherwood surfaced cautiously to find his targets had vanished.

On *Spiteful*'s return to Ceylon, Sherwood took some well-earned leave, and went off to Colombo with a fellow CO where he met a cypher Wren called Mary on a blind date. Sherwood insists that he had to compete for her attention, and that there were other interested submariners, but according to Mary, the others had no chance: she had eyes only for Freddie. They spent their next few dates discussing everything but submarines, as Mary wanted to take Sherwood's mind off his work. Then, because *Spiteful* was in the flotilla that was spun off to Australia, they did not see each other for months.

Spiteful was the first boat in the Eighth Flotilla to sail for Fremantle, and she did a patrol en route. When the rest of the submarines left Trincomalee, their depot ship headed straight to Australia to arrive ahead of them.

Sherwood took his submarine northwest of Sumatra for ten dull days, and afterwards conducted a reconnaissance of Christmas Island, a phosphate mining centre lying southwest of Java. *Spiteful* briefly shelled and hit some fuel tanks there, and was accurately fired on from the shore. She dived hurriedly and withdrew, having achieved her objective. It was on this patrol that *Spiteful* crossed the equator for the first time. The rest of their passage was quiet, apart from an unplanned deep dive when three out of four inlet valves were inadvertently left open. Sherwood's prompt action saved the boat and convinced the crew that he was a trustworthy CO.

The presence of the American submarines in Fremantle caused some dissatisfaction in the British boats. The size and comfortable living conditions of the American boats generated envy in the hearts of *Spiteful*'s sailors and embarrassed her officers. However, the British submarines had one major advantage over their American cousins – they could operate in shallower, more restricted waters, which compensated for the disparity to some degree.

The Australians welcomed *Spiteful*'s crew into their homes and many spent their ten-day leave as guests of these hospitable people. The matches were usually good, but when they turned out poorly Sherwood would "recall" the crew member. If the ratings preferred not to stay with a family, they went to a seaside hotel south of Perth. Sherwood often stayed at a sheep station upcountry with his friend and fellow Perisher, Ted Young of HMS/M *Storm*. The owners treated them like their own sons, and the two weary COs relaxed by riding, shooting rabbits, and walking for miles every day. However, Sherwood soon tired of the standard fare of Western Australia. "Damned mutton," he complained.[3]

Spiteful's ratings thought Australia was "sheer heaven." Gone was the feeling they had endured in Ceylon's stratified society, that they were not good enough. Here society was classless and the local beer came in huge, three-pint bottles. There was an over-abundance of food and parties, the girls were beautiful, the weather was perfect, there was no blackout, and rental cars were readily available.

In October 1944 the Americans invaded the Philippines. The flotillas' hopes ran high that a more forward submarine base would be set up there in early 1945 to provide easier access into the South China Sea, which had more targets. The Fourth and Eighth Flotillas were earmarked for the Philippines, but the move was delayed and *Spiteful* continued to operate from Fremantle.

Soon Sherwood and his submarine were off to spend thirty-four days west of the Sunda Strait, which lies between Sumatra and Java, hoping to intercept enemy shipping as it steamed into the Indian Ocean. The submarine was stored for thirty-five days, with two weeks of emergency rations. The provisions took up every nook and cranny of the submarine – even the passageways were "decked" with them, reducing the already limited headroom by eighteen inches (46 cm).

Spiteful was unlucky this time out, saw little, and attacked nothing. They plotted a Japanese minefield and returned to Christmas Island. *Spiteful*'s engines acted up on the way home; they covered the last 500 miles (800 km) at 4 knots, which won them the record for the longest patrol in the flotilla to date. Boredom was ever-present on the long passages to and from the patrol areas, and the sailors passed the time by playing uckers, liar dice, and cribbage. Favourite books were read more than once.

On arrival home *Spiteful* took on a fifth officer for training. Lt. Bob Fennell, RCNVR, a Canadian from Toronto, had a penchant for parties and fast cars. He transferred to the RN in mid-1943 and served in a destroyer on the Murmansk run for a few months before the dreadful conditions prompted him to volunteer for submarines. Fennell went straight out to the Far East after his SOTC, worked briefly as a spare officer in Trincomalee, then sailed with the Eighth to Fremantle.

On 16 November, with Fennell on board, *Spiteful* headed to the Macassar Strait to hunt for Japanese supply ships. The boat refuelled at

Darwin, where the inhabitants had recently been bombed by the Japanese, then threaded her way northwards through the islands to spend two weeks on station without once seeing a target. Then they sank a 200-ton (181-tonne) coaster with gunfire after the ship ignored *Spiteful*'s signals to stop. Fennell unwisely took credit for this successful gun action when in fact Sherwood and the first lieutenant had told him what orders to give the gun crew.

Sherwood believes that ULTRA signals were responsible for leading them to their next target. These signals to the submarines were so secret that the COs were forbidden to mention them in their patrol reports. Sherwood sighted a small convoy just where he was told it would be, north of Bali: it consisted of one escort and two merchantmen. He chose to attack the third ship, which turned out to be the smaller, but by the time Sherwood realized his mistake, it was too late to change horses. He fired six torpedoes at a very difficult angle and they all missed. The escort retaliated with eighteen depth-charges, but *Spiteful* took refuge between two density layers and escaped.

Afterwards Sherwood turned his boat for home, taking her south through the Lombok Strait east of Bali. This stretch of water was a challenge for every submarine CO – besides the fact that it was actively defended by Japanese destroyers and shore batteries, it had seven-knot tides. Sherwood successfully took *Spiteful* through, going with the tide on the surface on a moonless night. He found it hard to believe the echo-sounder, which read 200 feet (61 m) when the submarine was going like an express train through white water – "A most terrifying experience."[4]

The torpedoes *Spiteful* fired on this patrol were the first she had expended in six months, and Sherwood's reports began to indicate his frustration over their unproductive months in the Far East. He was not alone – many other submarines had small bags too. *Spiteful* returned to Fremantle in time for Christmas 1944 after thirty-eight days at sea.

In the New Year of 1945, *Spiteful* did her last Far East patrol. They went to the South China Sea, the first S boat to do so, with two objectives – to destroy enemy shipping and to act as a rescue boat for Allied air crews who might be shot down during an air strike on Singapore. *SM8* cautioned the Canadian CO not to venture too far east and get tangled up in uncharted minefields. The passage to their patrol area took two weeks and as soon as they arrived Sherwood heard a mayday. *Spiteful* searched for five days with no success and then chased a large warship into the mined area. Sherwood quickly withdrew when it became too risky.

Then suddenly *Spiteful* was homeward bound, her last and longest patrol over. She had covered 6,873 miles (11,058 km) in thirty-seven days, spending only twelve and a half days on station. The average patrol for the S-class was twenty-eight days in the southwest Pacific, and *Spiteful* had topped it on every occasion. They went back to Australia like a horse to its stable, without bothering to refuel at Exmouth Gulf.

Once in home port Sherwood again indicated his disappointment that they had not more to show for their arduous patrols. His Captain(S) thought otherwise, remarking upon the Canadian's patience and fortitude during the poor hunting; on his good leadership, which had in large measure maintained the morale of his crew; and on the thoroughly conscientious and painstaking manner in which he had conducted his Far East deployment. The USN commander of submarines also threw in some accolades of his own. He wrote, "This submarine and her gallant [CO] have invariably performed their ... duties in a smart, seamanlike and aggressive manner. Congratulations!"[5]

At Fremantle *Spiteful* landed her torpedoes and ammunition, which were too scarce to take home, and took on gin and beer to compensate for the weight loss. The beer, packed in colossal bags, went into an auxiliary ballast tank and the gin was stowed in the ammunition racks. In the middle of March 1945, *Spiteful* pointed her weary bow towards Ceylon and made a quiet passage across the Indian Ocean. After a brief period of leave during which Sherwood was reunited with Mary, they continued home. The beer, which Sherwood had paid for, was drunk while alongside on the voyage and cost the sailors a nickel for three bottles.

Fennell left *Spiteful* to spend two months in HMS/M *Voracious,* a British A/S training boat working with the Australian navy. He then fell ill, remaining on sick leave until he was demobbed in October 1945. Fennell later settled in Australia and lived in the south in Walkerville.

When *Spiteful* was between Port Said and Malta, victory in Europe was declared and the submariners celebrated their survival by splicing the mainbrace. Released from anxiety about attacks, they stopped every afternoon to have a swim in the Mediterranean. *Spiteful* finally came alongside at Devonport on 2 June and one sailor's diary noted, "Greenery, lovely; weather, bloody!"[6] *Spiteful* was home, bringing with her a healthy and happy ship's company. Sherwood noted that they had no VD, no crimes, no leave-breakers, "no nothing." *Spiteful* went into refit in Plymouth soon after her arrival and Sherwood learned that he had been awarded a Bar to his DSC for gallant services in Far East war patrols.

After a leave in Canada and the completion of the refit, Sherwood took *Spiteful* to HMS *Dolphin* where she was placed in reserve. Later she became *Sirene* in the French navy, and ultimately was scrapped in 1963 in Britain.

During the refit, Sherwood expropriated *Spiteful*'s wheel as a memento of his service in submarines, having replaced it with another, and proposed to Mary. She accepted, and they have lived in Ottawa ever since. *Spiteful*'s wheel became a coffee table and has pride of place in Sherwood's study, along with an oil painting of his favorite submarine.

Sherwood was the only Canadian to command a submarine in the Far East. The others became navigators, torpedo officers, and junior hands. Some of them missed the action entirely, while others were in the thick of it.

Bob Fahrig from Manitoba waited six months to be loaded onto his SOTC in 1943, following two years in the British coastal forces. In January 1944, having sailed out to Trincomalee on HMS *Adamant,* he joined HMS/M *Trespasser* (*P312*) for six months as her navigator. He experienced several special operations, most of which were unsuccessful, and saw few targets. *Trespasser* returned to Britain in June for a refit, and Lt. Ted Cayley, RCNVR, replaced Fahrig.

Fahrig served for the next year in HMS/M *Sportsman* (*P229*) – first in Scotland in a training flotilla and then in Philadelphia during her refit. The boat was modified for the Far East, but she was never needed. Back in Britain Fahrig became the first lieutenant of the surrendered *U-2326* and later of *Saga* before returning to Canada in October 1945 for discharge. Fahrig remarked afterwards, "It's not an easy life by any means, but I wouldn't switch to anything else."[7]

The T-class submarines of the Royal Navy were first constructed in 1938; they were bigger and better suited to conditions in the Far East than the S-class had been. *Tradewind* was one of the improved T-class, begun in 1941. She was five feet (1.5 m) longer than her predecessors, and fifty-five feet (16.8 m) longer than the S-class. There were eight torpedo tubes in the bow and three in the stern and one four-inch gun on the forward casing. In comparison, *Spiteful* had only seven torpedo tubes and a three-inch gun. In the Far East the Ts carried a crew of sixty-two and the Ss, forty-eight. However the performance of the two classes was similar. Though they were larger and had greater endurance, the T boats only provided a marginal improvement in living conditions and they were no better equipped to cope with the heat and humidity of the tropics than the S-class. Fans moved the sodden air about the boat, but the air-conditioners did little to improve the habitability, and consequently they were usually turned off.

November 1943 found six Canadians on the same SOTC at Blyth, four of whom were to serve in the Far East, though not in the same submarines. They were Ed Gigg, Bud Jorgenson, George McPhee, and Frank Saunders. In the sixties, twenty years after his war experience, Gigg was to play a significant role in re-establishing the Canadian Submarine Service.

Among the quartet who served in the Far East was George McPhee, a Chrysler employee from Windsor, Ontario. A youngster in 1941, he joined the RCNVR as a rating and was commissioned two years later. McPhee's submarine service began in HMS/M *Proteus* and he was on the bridge when Keith Forbes had his altercation with the target – "It was an exciting night," he remembered. One month followed in HMS/M *Varangian* (*P61*), a training boat, then McPhee sailed for Ceylon. He joined Bill Gilmour from B.C. in HMS/M *Tantalus* (*P318*) in August 1944, for one patrol.

Bill Gilmour, it will be remembered, was hospitalized when he reached Ceylon in January 1944, but he had recovered sufficiently by May to become the navigator in *Tantalus*. He did two patrols before McPhee joined him. The first was a multi-purpose mission in the Malacca Strait – they laid some mines, sank a coaster with the gun, and did a special operation. Gilmour's second outing took place in July when he had his first taste of a counter-attack after *Tantalus* attacked an escorted convoy. They also engaged a Japanese U-boat but failed to sink her. After *Tantalus* returned safely to Trincomalee, McPhee arrived and Gilmour had the pleasure of a fellow Canadian's company. McPhee remembered that Bill Gilmour was fun ashore and serious at sea.

On 25 August 1944 *Tantalus* sailed for Fremantle, doing a patrol in the Malacca Straits en route, with a relief CO, Lt. J. Nash, RN. He was nicknamed "Rash Nash" and attacked everything he saw with gusto. *Tantalus* was constantly harried by aircraft and was either bombed or depth-charged every day on station. Nash's report of one enemy attack shows what Gilmour and McPhee experienced. The submarine "had been severely shaken and a number of lights and electrical instruments smashed and small fittings carried away ... The most serious defects were two hull valves which had jumped off their seatings and were ... leaking,"[8] causing a flood aft and restricting their diving. Eventually the leaks were stopped, but the submarine was stuck in a peculiar bow-up attitude which could not be corrected. This did not deter Nash from completing the patrol.

In Fremantle, McPhee left *Tantalus* to become a spare officer for three months because he was unable to cope with the humidity on patrol. His knowledge of American automobiles made him indispensable to Commander Miers, and also saved his life, though not in the accepted sense. Miers was frustrated with the defective brakes on his Dodge, which apparently could not be fixed and he gave McPhee an offer he could not refuse, "Get my car fixed and I will give you a driver's licence for Australia." McPhee made friends with the warrant officer in charge of the U.S. maintenance depot and had the brakes repaired in no time, with new tires thrown in as a bonus. Miers, properly grateful, presented McPhee with the licence, which he still treasures.

When orders arrived for McPhee to return to the U.K. on HMS *Otis,* Miers cancelled the transfer. He wanted to retain his mechanic, who was also to become the chaperone for his fiancée. McPhee spent many an hour in the Dodge keeping Patricia company, while Miers finished his work before their dates. He was not trusted sufficiently to be left entirely alone with her, and so another officer acted as the chaperone's chaperone. A month after *Otis* had sailed, without the Canadian, Miers could keep McPhee no longer and sent him home on the damaged *Rover* in early 1945. On arrival in Trincomalee, McPhee learned that *Otis* was missing. "I was in a state of shock for days," he wrote.

McPhee met up with Gardner in Malta as *Rover* plodded to Philadelphia for her repairs. Once in the U.S. he was given leave in Canada, and made plans to marry, anticipating an extension. It was not to be. The European peace was declared and McPhee received an early recall to assist with the surrendering U-boats. He postponed his wedding and ended up in *Unseen* until she left Canada, at which point he was demobbed. McPhee's freedom lasted as long as the ferry ride to Saint John, N.B. where he was retrieved by the RCN on the jetty. Back he went to Halifax, to one of the surrendered U-boats. McPhee returned to Chrysler Canada after the war and stayed with the company until he retired in 1979 as manager of personnel administration. The day after his retirement, he began a new career, graduating in 1982 with a master's degree in divinity; he is now an ordained minister of the United Church of Canada. In 1990, McPhee looked back on his submarine service: "I was privileged to serve with some rather outstanding young men."

After McPhee went ashore, Gilmour stayed in *Tantalus* for one more patrol in the South China Sea in October 1944. It was a marathon. He remembered the difficulties that the Lombok Strait presented – "I used to bust myself to get an accurate fix as late ... as I could so we could position ourselves at the entrance ... as expeditiously as possible" for the dead-reckoning submerged run.

Tantalus encountered many targets on this patrol, including an enemy submarine, but only sank two, suffering a severe depth-charge attack in the process. At the end of the patrol, *Tantalus* stopped at a small island to pick up a party of agents who had mounted a courageous attack from a captured junk on shipping in Singapore Roads. Operation RIMAU was a fruitless effort – they determined that the commandos had been on the island about two weeks before, but now there was no sign of them. The Japanese had ambushed the agents as they returned and either captured or killed them.

Gilmour suffered discomfort during this patrol, but was unaware that he was ill again, with pneumonia and pulmonary tuberculosis. These ended his submarine career. He remained in the RCN while he recovered in a sanitarium in Western Australia, then was sent home to Canada for extensive chest surgery. Gilmour was invalided out of the service in 1946 and went back to university to finish his degree. He was called to the bar in 1952, choosing to practise in the Okanagan Valley of B.C., and later led the Liberal party of British Columbia. Gilmour felt that his time in the Silent Service was probably the happiest in his life, and certainly the most colourful. "I enjoyed submarines and found them a challenge. I was most impressed by the calibre of the officers and men with whom I served in the Royal Navy," commented Gilmour forty-five years later.

A Vancouver-born Canadian who was living in South Africa came to submarines by a circuitous route. Arthur "Bud" Jorgensen had tried to join the South African air force while doing a commerce degree at Johannesburg University, but because he had not graduated he was turned down. He jumped on a tramp steamer and headed for Vancouver in the hope that the RCAF would accept him for pilot training. On arrival in Canada in late 1942 Jorgensen was refused a second time. Disappointed, he joined the RCNVR as a rating. By May 1943 he was an officer on his way to England and the RN, with no definite ideas about which branch to enter.

Jorgensen chose submarines after meeting some submariners at a RN golf tournament and admiring their camaraderie. After SOTC, Jorgensen was appointed to HMS/M *Otus,* a training submarine, in Durban, South Africa, as her torpedo officer. After that he went to Trincomalee and served as a spare officer in the Second Flotilla. He did one operational patrol on *Trident*. In May 1945 he was posted to HMS/M *Shakespeare* to supplement her crew following the boat's near destruction off the Andaman Islands.[9] Jorgensen helped to prepare her to limp back to England for repairs and then went to Fremantle as a spare. After VJ Day Jorgensen returned to Ottawa for demobilization and spent the rest of his life as a successful businessman in South Africa.

Frank Saunders met his future wife at Blyth during the "Canadian" SOTC at the end of 1943. Joan was the daughter of a local doctor and remembers being attracted by the warm personality of the blond, blue-eyed man from Saskatchewan. Saunders, eager for a front-line job, had volunteered to serve in aircraft carriers, but was sent to submarines.

Saunders and Joan were parted at the end of SOTC when Saunders joined a training flotilla in Scotland. He was not impressed with his first submarine – *H32* leaked a lot and was infested with rats, who nibbled on everything including a precious letter from Joan. Two months later, Saunders served briefly as the third hand in HMS/M *Vitality,*[10] which was undergoing major repairs, but left her after the shake-down patrol. In December 1944, Saunders married Joan when he learned he was going to the Far East.

Saunders joined Forbes's old boat, HMS/M *Seanymph,* and after a quiet shake-down patrol off the Orkney Islands, they sailed on 12 March 1945, leaving Joan behind. Joan began to receive letters from her husband, often out of order, all of them filled with his incurable optimism and good humour. At Port Said Saunders became acting first lieutenant when the previous one was discharged for alcoholism. At Trincomalee, Saunders left *Seanymph* before she went on to the Philippines. He was transferred to HMS/M *Rorqual* in June, but as there were no further mine-laying requirements in the Far East they returned to England. Saunders got home to Joan safe and sound, having seen no action at all.

Sadly, Frank Saunders was killed in a car accident in 1969 at the age of forty-six, just a year after retiring from the Royal Canadian Navy with the rank of lieutenant-commander. He was deeply mourned by all who knew him, including the Boy Scout movement and Big Brothers of British Columbia, for whom he had worked with distinction.

Ed Gigg was the youngest of ten children from North Bay, Ontario. He joined the RCNVR in 1942, as soon as he was old enough. While still a seaman he volunteered for submarines, but was not accepted until he had completed officer training in late 1943. Gigg said that he was welcomed into the British submarine service as a dumb colonial boy, because they were so short of officers. He scraped through his SOTC and was appointed to HMS/M *Oberon* while she was under repair. Before she was finished he became the navigator in HMS/M *Uther.* Gigg enjoyed his four months in this training boat, but longed to serve in an operational submarine. In July 1944, Gigg got his wish and flew to Ceylon as a spare officer for the Fourth Flotilla. During his first breakfast on HMS *Adamant* he found himself aching to be an "insider," but knew he had to wait until he was actually appointed to a submarine. Gigg soon joined HMS/M *Tradewind.* Initially he suffered badly from prickly heat, and underwent the standard treatment of being painted with gentian violet.

Gigg considered himself fortunate to be in *Tradewind*: she was commanded by a submarine captain of considerable repute, Lt.-Commander S. Maydon, RN, whom Gigg liked and whose methodical approach everyone respected. The Canadian experienced much action while based in Ceylon which included a few very hazardous special operations (some of which were unsuccessful), many sinkings, and one tragedy, the details of which were not fully known until after the war.

The tragedy occurred on 18 September 1944, when *Tradewind* torpedoed and sank a large escorted transport, without knowing the content of her holds. The *Junyo Maru* was carrying 2,000 Allied prisoners of war and 3,500 Indonesian coolies to prison and labour camps. Her Japanese crew commandeered all the lifeboats and a British survivor recalled their treatment when they tried to climb into the boats. Their frenzied captors were "slashing with their swords ... many [in the sea] lost their hands, many had neck wounds which were fatal."[11] Forty-four hundred people died that afternoon and only 1,100 were rescued by the Axis escort vessels.

Two days before Christmas 1944, *Tradewind* arrived in Fremantle. Australia did for the crew all that it had done for *Spiteful*'s. On his first afternoon ashore Gigg joined some other officers and went to visit the sick Bill Gilmour, who needed cheering up. They left beer under his bed so that he could better celebrate the festive season in hospital. On Christmas Eve, Gigg attended a party where his Australian hosts did everything they could to make the submariners feel at home, including giving them small gifts. As a replete Gigg wandered back to the depot ship in his shirtsleeves, he realized how much he was missing the cold, snowy nights of Ontario, his family, and their old, familiar traditions.

Tradewind's patrols from Australia in the New Year of 1945 were notable for the depth-charge attacks they sustained and sailed away from, as well as a new CO. "Rash Nash" presented quite a contrast to Maydon's methodical style of command. His "gung-ho" approach stirred different reactions in the crew but, as Gigg concluded, "both were successful, for we survived."

The reprisals *Tradewind* suffered all followed attacks on small escorted convoys, and were difficult to evade because the waters were so shallow. The submarine wiggled out of trouble when she could, or waited silently on the bottom forty-five feet down, while the enemy pinged away and dropped depth charges all around. Although the worst damage *Tradewind* sustained was broken glass, everyone expected more from the proximity of the explosions. Sometimes the hunters simply failed to detect them – twice they ran right over the boat and missed her, and when *Tradewind* got stuck on the bottom and blew her main ballast to get loose, they must have been blind as well as deaf.

Tradewind's last patrol in the Far East was her longest, at fifty-two days, and she became the first Allied boat to operate in the shallow Gulf of Siam, the big horseshoe-shaped area south of what is now Thailand. *Tradewind* sailed in March 1945, hopeful of an overabundance of targets because the area had not been patrolled in eighteen months, but for nearly four weeks, she encountered nothing. When the crew became despondent, Nash extended the long patrol and *Tradewind* managed to sink two junks, one tug, and one small coaster before she had to leave for Fremantle. She arrived in Australia to the news of victory in Europe and a commendation from her Captain(S).

Gigg sailed back to England in *Tradewind* and returned to Canada for a well-deserved leave during which his request to join the RCN was approved. He received his permanent commission in September 1945, retroactive to May. The RCN assured Gigg that he could remain in submarines and return to *Tradewind* in refit. When he arrived in the U.K. the RCN ordered him to *Crusader,* a destroyer building on Clydeside, which had been loaned to the RCN. Gigg's protests fell on deaf ears, and he had to be content only with dreams of returning to the submarine service and being able to take his Perisher "in due course." This took longer than Gigg anticipated and he became a Fleet Air Arm pilot in the interim. It was not until 1950 that he was able to return to his beloved submarines.

The last Canadian officer to undergo basic submarine training in World War II was Edwin P. Love. Little is known about his experiences as he could not be located. He was serving in the Canadian Officers' Training Corps at the University of Alberta when he joined the RCNVR in January 1943, aged twenty-one. After his SOTC in 1944, Love went out to Colombo as a spare officer and then, at the end of January 1945, joined HMS/M *Visigoth,* a training boat, as her navigator. Her cox'n recalls Love sporting a revolver on his hip and being teased unmercifully by the crew who thought he came from the Wild West. Love remained with *Visigoth* when she moved to Trincomalee in March 1945, but does not appear to have done any operational patrols.

Canadian submariners distinguished themselves during the conflict of 1939–45 in every theatre and every conceivable type of operation. Four of the twenty-seven officers were decorated, one twice. They all served with great determination and skill and a few did so with conspicuous gallantry. Everyone is listed and remembered on the Honour Roll of the Canadian Submarine Service, which is carefully kept by the First Canadian Submarine Squadron in Halifax.

Canadians serving on Royal Navy submarines in the Mediterranean in the first half of the war helped sink over one million tonnes of enemy shipping, and these activities were instrumental in starving Rommel's forces into retreat in North Africa. These submariners experienced some of the worst depth-charge attacks of the war, and continuously risked their lives in minefields. Relief did not come to them on return to port either – they endured limited food, no hot water, broken sleep, and constant bombing.

Other Canadian submariners did stouthearted service in home and Canadian waters. One was a first lieutenant in a submarine that towed the X-craft to the *Tirpitz*, on their first daring raid. Others provided the vital ASW training for the surface vessels of the RN and RCN. For these men there was no exciting action, no satisfaction in sinking a U-boat or in rescuing agents from enemy territory. There were no decorations, no survivors' parties – nothing but boring routines. However, their commitment was no less important or impressive than that of their colleagues.

The nine volunteer reserve Canadians who served in the Far East did so with resolve and tenacity, enduring frightful humidity, heat, and fatigue in Royal Navy submarines that were not designed for the climate. Some saw no targets, while others were called upon to fight for their lives in spirited enemy attacks. Others still participated in sinking enemy shipping by gunfire and torpedo, as well as experiencing the danger of vital special operations. The Far East submarines operated as submarines should – entirely alone, with almost complete freedom of action, and were unsupported for very long patrols. Few submarines were lost in this theatre and all the Canadians survived.

The three Canadian officers who served in chariots and X-craft successfully completed the most rigorous, uncomfortable, and hazardous service that could be imagined. Two of them – Moreton and Bonell – were considered among the best in their field.

It had been a long war and the weary Canadian submariners wended their way home with relief in their hearts and uncertainty in their heads. Most were young men who had not been established in careers when they volunteered and now faced the difficult prospect of choosing what to do next. They were all irrevocably changed by their experiences of the past five years, and only Ed Gigg had made a definite choice. His decision to make the navy his career kept the submarine flame alive in the RCN. Just.

Only two submariners, out of twenty-seven, did not return from the Second World War – Lt. Chuck Bonnell, DSC, RCNVR, the charioteer; and Lt. Hugh Russel, RCNVR, of HMS/M *Traveller*. Both were involved with Operation PRINCIPAL and were lost at sea in the Mediterranean.

CHAPTER EIGHTEEN

THE "CANADIAN" U-BOATS, 1945

Operation ADIEU

As a result of Operation ADIEU, the Royal Canadian Navy acquired two German U-boats as part of her fleet – *U-889* for six months and *U-190* for over two years – and five Canadian submariners served in them.[1]

By March 1945 the Allied navies were planning for the end of the war at sea and their opinions varied as to how the U-boats should be handled. The Admiralty wanted all the enemy submarines to return to Germany, be made non-operational, and then sailed to the United Kingdom. By contrast the United States Navy insisted upon having the U-boats in their operational areas for themselves. Discussions lengthened as the parties endeavoured to find common ground. Canada was not represented, but appeared to be content with the Admiralty's position and communications. By the end of April, Ottawa learned that U-boats would be instructed to proceed to the nearest Allied port following Germany's capitulation

Britain expected that up to one hundred and sixty enemy boats might surrender in their waters. The RCN hoped to bag five or six in her Atlantic zone and identified two "surrender points" in the northwest Atlantic. The USN believed that most of the U-boat COs would scuttle their commands and, indeed, that was the original German plan. A special Tripartite Naval Commission was formed to decide the disposition of the surrendered U-boats. It was composed of two representatives each from the U.K., the U.S.A., and the U.S.S.R. Their task was to allocate all enemy-surrendered vessels, including U-boats, to the Allied navies. The Allies also prepared for the U-boat warfare to continue for two to four months after the declaration of peace, perpetuated by crews who either refused to surrender or failed to receive the signals.

In readiness for the surrender the RCN withdrew two officers and six ratings on 1 May 1945 from the training submarines operating in Canadian waters. None were Canadians. These individuals formed two U-boat reception teams – one in Shelburne, Nova Scotia, and one in Newfoundland. That same day, the Admiralty signalled to the U-boats in German:

> Surface immediately and remain surfaced.
> Report immediately in plain language your position ...
> Fly a large black flag ... by day.
> Burn navigation lights by night.
> ... refrain from scuttling or ... damaging your U-boat.[2]

Nothing happened. Enemy submarines did not pop up all over the ocean, and by 4 May they still hadn't. Hitler's successor, Doenitz, wanting none of his U-boats to fall into Allied hands, had ordered all of them to cease hostilities and come home. A few outward bound U-boats altered course and began to make their way back to Germany, but most bided their time.

The German High Command signed the unconditional surrender that ended the European conflict on 9 May 1945 after Doenitz had scrapped his plan to recover his U-boats, offering them in exchange for better conditions for his defeated citizens. He ordered his submarines to surface and report their positions in plain language every eight hours, while laying a course for the nearest Allied port. In dribs and drabs, the U-boats complied, now that Germany had officially capitulated. Meanwhile, the Admiralty had signalled the Allies to implement Operation ADIEU – the process for managing the U-boats.

Anticipating some useful public relations, the Canadian minister of national defence removed all security precautions surrounding the surrender of enemy submarines. He ordered full assistance for the media to cover the event and even encouraged reporters to interview the German crews.

By 10 May eighteen U-boats had surrendered, and position reports had been received from eight more. Three were in Canadian waters. *U-190* was 500 miles (804.5 km) east of Cape Race and *U-889* was 250 miles (402.3 km) southeast of Flemish Cap. The third, *U-805*, off Newfoundland, was claimed by the Americans.

U-889 was the first enemy submarine to capitulate to Canadian forces. On 10 May, an RCAF Liberator's sighting report caused the RCN to divert two minesweepers from a convoy to the U-boat's position. They approached cautiously but *U-889* gave no trouble. High seas prevented the boat being boarded, so she followed the sweepers *Rockcliffe* and *Dunvegan* towards Shelburne, Nova Scotia. Later the frigates *Buckingham* and *Inch Arran* took over and safely delivered their charge into port on 13 May.

The press outnumbered the RCN officials at *U-889*'s official surrender at Whistle Buoy, seven miles off Shelburne, and every camera clicked as a sailor raised the white ensign on the enemy boat. Then half the German crew brought *U-889* into Shelburne and joined their shipmates in detention, where the press interviewed them that evening. The U-boat's CO was separated from his crew.

The RCN were delighted with their catch because *U-889* was a type IXC U-boat which had been used for experimental work before undertaking her first patrol off Halifax. When the crew of the U-boat was transported to prison camps, the RCN allowed the captain and six others to remain behind to assist the special submarine team in evaluating the surrendered boat. They began the inventory of the submarine immediately.

HMCS *Victoriaville* (a frigate) and HMCS *Thorlock* (a corvette) intercepted *U-190* after she reported on 11 May. The surrender took place just before midnight (GMT) when a party from *Thorlock* boarded her. They found that the German crew had prepared their boat in accordance with the orders and had no intentions of scuttling her. At 0001 GMT on 12 May 1945, the white ensign fluttered from *U-190*'s mast. *Victoriaville* took the U-boat's crew off soon afterwards and the submarine's CO signed a makeshift deed of unconditional surrender, a copy of which can be seen in the Canadian War Museum in Ottawa. *U-190* was taken to Bay Bulls, Newfoundland, where she arrived on 14 May. It was apt that *U-190* had fallen into Canadian hands, because her last victim had been the minesweeper, HMCS *Esquimalt,* which she sank on 16 April 1945 near Halifax with the loss of thirty-nine men. *U-190*'s crew was taken to Halifax and held up for public display before being handed over to the military for interrogation.

U-190 and *U-889* were the only two U-boats to surrender to Canadian forces out of the expected six. Both were in Halifax and ready to go to sea again when they were commissioned into the RCN on 1 June.

After destoring, the RCN team rigorously examined the German boats and prepared detailed reports for the Admiralty, the USN, and the Canadian CNS. The cipher equipment was stripped out of *U-889* and shipped to the Canadian signal school at St.-Hyacinthe and her acoustic torpedoes and other weapons were removed for analysis. The team found *U-190* in a "definitely unsanitary state"[3] and she had to be fumigated. The RCN had difficulty manning the two boats and decided to get *U-889* to sea first for her early evaluation trials. They supplemented *U-190* with individuals from *L23* and *Seawolf* after these were paid off later in June.

By July the RCN had appointed "Uncle" Holmes, the first lieutenant of *Seawolf*, as the senior submarine officer for the two boats, and gave him command of *U-889* even though he had not taken Perisher. Holmes caught the tail end of *U-889*'s evaluation trials, which had lasted seven weeks. While the U-boat's weapons and equipment continued to be analysed ashore, Holmes took *U-889* on a publicity cruise so Canadians could "ooh and aah" at her. The U-boat visited ten eastern Canadian ports where VIPs only were allowed down below. The general public had to make do with wandering about the casing and peering down the hatches because of their predilection for stealing vital pieces of equipment for souvenirs. *U-889* made this cruise with a minimum crew, many of whom had never been on a submarine before, so no diving was permitted.

Meanwhile in Washington the Tripartite Naval Commission considered the fate of the Canadian U-boats. The RCN asked that *U-889* be allocated to Canada because the sea trials on her acoustic torpedoes had not begun and "Canada leads the RN and USN in this field."[4] *U-190* was offered to anyone as she was old and of less value.

Holmes reluctantly transferred to the non-operational *U-190* when a qualified Canadian submarine CO became available. Jack Cross relieved Holmes when his previous command, *Unseen,* returned to the U.K. He had been on his way to Montreal to get married when he heard of his appointment and he regretfully delayed his wedding. In the event, the postponement was unnecessary – Cross commanded *U-889* for only three weeks before demobilization. Lt. Rod Johnston, RCNVR, relieved him and became the longest-serving Canadian in the U-boats.

U-889's first lieutenant and navigator also arrived with Cross from *Unseen*. Both were Canadian: the new number one was the other Holmes (Wayne), and the third hand was George McPhee. The ratings in *U-889* were mostly RCNVR, and none were submarine qualified. The RCN thought this manning was adequate for the proposed surface torpedo trials.

Lt. Wayne Holmes, RCNVR, had passed his SOTC in July 1944 (one of the last Canadians to do so), and spent his submarine career in anti-submarine training boats in England, Bermuda, and Canada. He had already served in HMS/Ms *Unrivalled, Upright, United, Seawolf,* and *Unseen* when he returned to England to head for the Far East. When Holmes arrived, just after VE Day, his appointment was cancelled and the RN sent him instead to Lisahally in Northern Ireland, just downriver from Londonderry. Here Holmes assisted with nearly eighty surrendered U-boats of all classes, serving briefly with a part-German crew in a cargo-carrying U-boat. He returned to Canada in the fall, hoping to be demobbed and to join his recent bride. Instead he joined *U-889.*

Preparations continued on *U-889*'s acoustic torpedoes and their sea trials were planned for November 1945. Whether they took place is unclear in the records, but it is unlikely that they did for the RCN conducted many trials during the next year, though not in *U-889.*

In December, despite the RCN's wishes, the Tripartite Naval Commission allocated *U-889* to the United States. Surprisingly, the Canadian navy did not object to the decision, and in January 1946 the German U-boat was towed to New Hampshire after six months of service with the RCN. Rod Johnston, Wayne Holmes, and George McPhee went with her.

Then RCN directed their attention to the U-boat they had spurned – *U-190* was in a care-and-maintenance routine with a crew of nine. In early 1946 Johnston took over from "Uncle" Holmes and began to prepare her for the acoustic torpedo trials, previously scheduled for *U-889,* in Bedford Basin.

Rod Johnston had been in submarines since November 1943 but had never seen a torpedo fired in action. He had been easily persuaded to volunteer for submarines and spent four months navigating HMS/M *Una* at Tobermory while he was attached to a training flotilla. Johnston did one uneventful patrol off Norway, and his last memory of *Una* was practising submerged beachings on England's northwest coast. By August 1944, he was enjoying Bermuda as *Upright*'s navigator when he met Wayne Holmes who was in *United.* Johnston became the fifth Canadian to serve in *Truculent,* relieving Dick Blake, her number one, in February 1945. After hurriedly marrying his childhood sweetheart in April, he sailed *Truculent* back to the U.K. after her refit for the Far East, but neither *Truculent* nor Johnston went out to Ceylon.

Johnston returned to Canada with Wayne Holmes in November, both eager to see their wives after six months away. They were astonished therefore, having already been discharged at *Cornwallis,* to be met off the ferry at Saint John, New Brunswick, and asked to return to the RCN to take over *U-889* first and then *U-190.* Both agreed, though reluctantly. Like all the other Canadian U-boat commanding officers, except Cross, Johnston had not taken Perisher.

On their return from delivering *U-889,* Wayne Holmes was finally demobbed and McPhee and Johnston moved to *U-190.* Day after day they fired and recovered the acoustic torpedoes while aircraft took photographs. Work continued from January through the summer with the Naval Research Establishment, but McPhee soon left for civvy street. At the end of 1946, the trials were completed, but Johnston stayed well into 1947.

The RCN seriously considered disposing of U-190 at this point, but did little to bring it about. The old U-boat began to deteriorate rapidly, and in July 1947 the decision was finally taken to pay her off. Johnston saw no future in hanging around any longer and was pleased to be demobbed. Because his wife was expecting their first child, he did not return to university, instead taking a sales job. Two years later, Johnston was back in the RCN as an intelligence officer. He served both at sea and ashore as a straight-striper until 1967. Johnston still feels disappointed that he did not see action in submarines and that he did not get to the Far East. However, he enjoyed his submarine life and remembered the tremendous comradeship the service brought with it. "We were all in it together," he said.

When the RCN thought *U-190* was likely to sink alongside, they decided to use her for target practice. They scheduled Operation SCUPPERED for 21 October 1947, a date filled with meaning. It marks Trafalgar Day – the long-revered anniversary of Nelson's great victory in 1805.

A skeleton crew trimmed *U-190* on an even keel, lashed her rudder amidships, plugged her hull penetrations with wood so she would sink, and painted her casing with bright yellow and red stripes. "*U-190* will be in all respects ready for destruction" by 17 October, announced the officer in charge of the ship reserve.[5] The surface units of the RCN, as well as naval aircraft of 883 and 826 Squadrons, had practised hard for the event, shelling and bombing dummy targets for days.

U-190 was towed into position at 1030 on Trafalgar Day and was left to wallow in the swell. The RCN had chosen the location for Operation

SCUPPERED with an eye to history. The U-boat was drifting over the spot where she had torpedoed and sunk HMCS *Esquimalt* in 1945. The RCAF had the first runs on the target and they were so accurate that they left little for the ships to shell. *U-190* lifted her bows to the sky after the first rocket attack and slid quickly to the bottom.

To say that the surrendered U-boats *U-190* and *U-889* were part of the Canadian Submarine Service is stretching a point, though several historians have tried. The navy used the U-boats solely for publicity purposes and for some serious study to advance Canada's knowledge of their erstwhile enemy. There was never any intention of maintaining either of them as a part of the navy's postwar fleet.

PART THREE
1946 to the Present

CHAPTER NINETEEN

CANADA RENTS SUBMARINES, 1946–1959

" … no intention of establishing a submarine arm
in the Royal Canadian Navy"[1]

As peace settled over the world in 1945, Canadians found that war had changed them, and their country. The survivors and those who had served at home had become more sophisticated and less isolationist and the nation's industrial base was stronger and more diverse. Canada had earned respect as an independent nation, and her voice began to count in global affairs and the emerging Commonwealth. The first postwar election in June 1945 returned the Liberal government, but not Prime Minister Mackenzie King.

The effect of the Second World War on the Royal Canadian Navy was equally profound. Having become the third largest navy in the world, the RCN desired a large blue-water peacetime fleet and in 1945 submitted a grandiose scheme that included five U-class submarines to the government. Cabinet refused it, stating that Canada required coastal defence only as the country would soon be a part of a collective western security arrangement. The RCN's plans dissolved overnight, and with them the hope of getting their own boats.

In the end it was the government's yearning to increase Canada's voice abroad, not any national maritime strategy, that led to the re-establishment of the Canadian Submarine Service. Canada enthusiastically embraced the idea of the North Atlantic Treaty Organization (NATO), recognizing that to expand her overseas influence, she would be wise to contribute a vital element of defence to the Allies. This realization resulted in the Canadian armed forces specializing in anti-submarine warfare (ASW) and owning submarines.

However, Canadian-owned submarines would not materialize for another sixteen years. Immediately after the war, and the denial of their "grand plan," the RCN had to suspend all ASW training until 1946.[2] When the training resumed, the RCN set a precedent by renting a boat, HMS/M *Token,* from Britain. She served on the east coast from August to November 1946, with the RCN paying her operating expenses.

In 1947 the RCN reconsidered their need for ASW training submarines, correctly predicting the advent of nuclear-powered submarines and recognizing that they could not possibly counter this new threat, as well as to meet Canada's future obligations as an ASW specialist, without boats of their own. The RCN concluded that they required a submarine all year round. On requesting a boat for 1947 from the Admiralty, the RCN were disappointed to learn that they would have HMS/M *Alliance* for only two months while she was en route to the Pacific. Peeved, Canada refused *Alliance* and asked the USN for one submarine for the east coast for a year and another for the west coast, on a periodic basis.

Although the United States Navy replied to Canada with a resounding yes, the RCN discovered that the Americans could only supply one boat for two weeks each quarter on the east coast and less for the west. It was not what the RCN expected and Canada returned to the Royal Navy, cap in hand. HMS/M *Artemis* came for two months at a rental of $10,000. After this lesson, the RCN included the cost of renting a full-time "clockwork mouse" in their budget.

The RCN was moderately successful in renting submarines during the next few years and British boats provided up to six months ASW training a year for $41,300. The RCAF were able to benefit by the training opportunities that were now available to them, and requested more time, but their demand could not be met. USN submarines were used though only for short, irregular periods on the west coast.

As the decade closed Canada announced its first defence policy since WWII. It reflected the nation's membership in NATO – in future, Canada and her allies would face the threat of an increasingly aggressive Soviet Union. The government confirmed the RCN's ASW role and gave them a ceiling of 9,047 men and 19 percent of the defence budget.

The beginning of the fifties heralded an escalation in requests for the use of training submarines in the RCN, which made impossible demands on the single boat. For example, a projection for 1952 and 1953 showed that three submarines were needed to provide the 725 submarine training days per year on the east coast and 240 on the west coast. Additionally,

A/S equipment under development in Canada required a live submarine to provide the extensive testing needed. Even so, the RCN had to make do with the use of a boat for only six months a year until 1953, at which point even that became unavailable because of the growth of the RN's own ASW training program, and the Korean War. This development precipitated a clamour from Canadian air force and naval officers who worried about the RCN's ability to meet their ASW commitments to NATO in peacetime, to say nothing of wartime.

As much as a Canadian Submarine Service was needed, it was still out of the question. The RCN was struggling too hard, both politically and financially, to get into a battle with a government that believed a new naval branch was inappropriate. The navy remained the impecunious cousin of the army and air force; they had to trade off naval expansion against soaring personnel costs, which also denied them the chance to train submariners for the future.

Despite the heavy odds against them, in 1952 the RCN began preliminary work on a plan to show the politicians why a Canadian submarine service was necessary, based on the premise of independence in ASW training. Unfortunately, any proposed submarine branch had to start from scratch, and manning presented a bigger hurdle than acquiring boats. There were no qualified Canadians left in submarines except Ed Gigg. He was, by now, the first lieutenant of HMS/M *Alderney*, having finally returned to the RN submarine service in 1950 after an interlude as an RCN pilot. Gigg took his Perisher in December 1952, which positioned him well to command a Canadian submarine when or if any materialized. Gigg had no idea if they ever would, but his transfer back to Ottawa in 1953, after commanding HMS/M *Selene*, allowed him to be closer to the planning process.

Over the next two years the RCN developed its arguments for a Canadian submarine service. Besides the quantified need of five submarines in peacetime and eleven in wartime, they emphasized that rental boats would have to be returned to their country of origin in an emergency. Most of the senior naval officers supported the concept, though the increasing naval air requirements caused a few to balk, fearing that aircraft procurement would suffer if Canada acquired submarines.

Regrettably, this initial RCN study on re-establishing the Canadian Submarine Service was ill-prepared and the navy shelved it, setting up a special committee in April 1953 to prepare a better case. When news of their work got out, the Conservative opposition questioned the minister of national defence who answered, " ... it would be spreading our resources very thinly"[3] to have a submarine service. He was content with rental boats.

By July 1953 the committee had presented their conclusions to the naval staff. This time the study effectively justified the immediate need for a Canadian submarine service and provided suggestions on how to achieve it. The figures showed there was a shortfall of 700 submarine days in 1953, which would rise to 910 by 1955. When translated into actual submarines that meant the RCN needed 3.5 boats immediately and 4.5 more in two years. Controversially, the team suggested that the service should have an operational as well as a training branch. The study ended by recommending that the RCN buy the two U-class submarines that had recently been offered by the Admiralty, and man them with a nucleus of RN personnel until RCN submariners could be trained.

The naval staff disliked the proposal and refused to approve it until the old, cheaper arrangement of "renting" submarines was included, despite the advice of the British flag officer, Submarines (FOSM). Early in 1954 CNS, Vice-Admiral E. Mainguy, OBE, CD, presented the rewritten proposal for a new Canadian submarine service to the minister of national defence, Brooke Claxton. The minister was shocked at the idea and complained, it was "the first...I have received...on this subject."[4] Admiral Mainguy finally persuaded Claxton to support the concept by saying that it was no more expensive to buy submarines than to rent them and that manning them did not mean the RCN would have to expand.

However, once Claxton presented the proposal to the Cabinet defence committee for approval, it failed. The committee found the idea of a Canadian submarine service very undesirable and demanded that the RCN continue to rent boats. Although the RCN continued to seek the renewal of the Canadian Submarine Service, the Liberal government remained intransigent.

RCN negotiations for rental submarines proceeded with the Admiralty during 1954 and soon the idea of renting a squadron emerged. To achieve it the RCN agreed to inject two hundred officers and men into the British submarine service to sweeten the deal. Many believe this was done to form a cadre of qualified Canadian submariners for use in future Canadian submarines. However, the preserved documents do not support this theory – the personnel offer was merely a bargaining chip to rent a whole British submarine squadron. On 12 November 1954, the press announced the formation of the Royal Navy's Sixth Submarine Squadron for service in Canadian waters. The release said, "The new arrangement will provide the opportunity for officers and men of Canada's anti-submarine navy to obtain first-hand experience in submarines, thus acquainting them with techniques which, in time of war, they may have to encounter."[5] *On the surface* was left unsaid, but it was implied. These were techniques the navy would "encounter," not "employ."

What did Canada and her navy get in the end? The contract, known as the Heads of Agreement, provided three submarines permanently on station in Halifax for four years. This gave the RCN two and a half serviceable boats on the east coast year round at an annual price of $645,000, rising with inflation, plus the cost of two dockings. The submarines were A-class boats – bigger, faster, and able to dive deeper than the older Us – and were manned by Brits. In return the RN got two hundred Canadian officers and men to supplement their submarine branch, whom FOSM promised to try to post to the Sixth Squadron.

Just two weeks after the contract was signed the first of three drafts of submarine volunteers flew to the U.K. from Montreal. Many went for a change and some simply wished to experience England. Eighty more ratings followed after Christmas and four officers and thirty-eight men left on 24 January 1955. All were surprised by the austerity in the RN.

On 4 April 1955 the Royal Navy's Sixth Submarine Squadron officially came to life in Halifax when HMS/M *Astute* slipped alongside. She was given a rousing welcome, and after the speeches the media toured the boat. The RN personnel were delighted with Canada, the living conditions, and their pay increase, which matched their incomes to those of their Canadian peers. The second submarine, HMS/M *Ambush,* arrived on 27 May and the last one, HMS/M *Alderney,* came in July. By now, the Royal Navy had named the submarine depot in Halifax HMS *Ambrose* after the famous depot ship of WWI and had chosen their motto, "Out of the depths, we are here."

The submarines' routine in Canadian waters involved seven weeks at sea, followed by one week alongside for maintenance and a semi-annual docking. The Sixth Submarine Squadron (SM6) worked flat out from the beginning. During the first nine months of operation, the submarines participated in fleet and RCAF exercises, major NATO exercises, Canadian research, ship work-ups, and personnel training. The three boats steamed 44,000 miles (70,800 km) and spent 321 days at sea. The RCN was delighted with the early results of the cooperative scheme, despite needing 40 percent more ASW training time, and soon set aside all thoughts of gaining submarine independence. FOSM kept his promise – by the fall of

1956, eighty-nine Canadian officers and men were serving in SM6 and those still in England were permitted to take their families over. Meanwhile, the training drafts of RCN officers and men were studying at the submarine school in England at HMS *Dolphin*. Although everyone had been told what to expect in postwar England, life in the RN came as a shock. The men's quarters were clean, but very spartan, and had no central heating. There was snow at the bottom of the bunks in the mornings, remembered one sailor and another remarked that they never managed to warm up because the classrooms were no better than the barracks. The Canadians were always hungry too – the RN rations were much less than they got on Canadian ships. Their grumbles led the British petty officers to conclude that the Canadians were soft, but the RN ratings knew that was unfair.

All the draftees found the classroom courses demanding. The ratings learned about submarine construction and layout, how to dive and surface, and the use of diesels and main motors. Every day all day they listened to lectures, watched instructional movies, copied detailed diagrams, and pored over working models. At night, many gave up the lure of a pint and buried their heads in their notes. They took the three-day escape training, which some enjoyed and a few hated. Later the students spent a week studying the systems of a real submarine alongside, preparatory to going to sea for three days. This cruise was the climax of their training course and the ratings operated the boat under the close supervision of its real crew. They experienced their first dives, dummy torpedo attacks and gun actions, and they conducted countless exercises – man overboard, equipment failures, flooding, fires, etc. Exhausted but more confident, the trainees returned to the classroom for a review before they took written and oral final examinations. By now the students had thoroughly absorbed the fundamental submarine rule – every man must do his duty quickly, quietly, and conscientiously, and report his actions to the control room. Most passed their exams and went to operational submarines or to spare flotilla crews, but they all knew they had to consolidate their knowledge by working. Those ratings who required specialist courses for their trades took them before being posted to a boat.

The officers, meanwhile, were doing much the same, though in greater detail and with a different emphasis. The Submarine Officers' Training Course lasted for six months, followed by extensive exams. Periscope routines and trimming the boat were some of the additional topics for study. They also took familiarization cruises and escape training.

For the officers, HMS *Dolphin* was an experience in itself. Located in an old fort, the home of the British submarine service was on the Gosport side of Portsmouth's harbour entrance. The officers' cabins were small but adequate, though icy cold and damp in winter. The wardroom, by contrast, was spectacular. Every new officer entering it could not help but feel the history and tradition. The huge paintings of famous naval battles and the figurehead jutting proudly into the room from the centre of the minstrel's gallery made them aware they were in hallowed halls, inhabited by the ghosts of legendary submariners. Newcomers were not accepted readily into the most exclusive club in the world and the Canadians initially felt left out. They quickly discovered they had to earn their acceptance.

In 1955 a Canadian sub-lieutenant under training in England paused to enjoy a June morning.[6] Berchem was on the bridge of HMS/M *Springer* in Portland harbour just before he sailed on his first cruise to Kiel, Germany. His submarine was the outboard boat in a trot of three attached to "Mother" *Maidstone,* with *Sidon* sandwiched between *Springer* and a Danish submarine. At 0830 the young man was startled from his reverie by the sound of a dull whoosh, followed by a puff of thick, white smoke from *Sidon*'s bow. Then he saw a cloud of smoke and debris shoot out of her conning tower. As he ducked below the bridge rail, he heard muffled cries and remembered with horror that four or five Canadians were members of *Sidon*'s crew. Berchem could not react as *Springer* quickly let go all her lines and backed hurriedly away from the scene. As they left, he faintly heard the pipe on the depot ship: "Emergency parties to muster!"

Sidon had experimental torpedoes on board, which were fuelled with high-test peroxide, an unstable and dangerous material. They had been loaded three nights before in readiness for sailing the next morning for test firing, but fog had postponed their departure. Instead of unloading the torpedoes in accordance with regulations, *Sidon* left them in their racks in the forward stowage compartment with the crew monitoring them carefully.

On the morning of 16 June 1955, the fog cleared and *Sidon* prepared to sail to the firing range after *Springer* had left for Kiel. Down below, the Canadian submariners were at their posts. Leading Stoker Claude "Frenchie" Gourdeau and PO Sam Jennings were in the engine room and an able seaman was on the casing. *Sidon*'s new draftee, Petty Officer 2nd Class Laverne McLeod was having a cup of tea in the forward accommodation space while awaiting his assignment from the cox'n. The other Canadian, PO1 "Spud" Gregory, was in the fore-ends where it was a hive of activity.

The torpedoes were being loaded into their tubes. The starboard torpedo was a quarter way in as Gregory turned to make his way aft to the heads; one minute later it exploded, with such violence that debris was expelled forward, out into the sea, and aft throughout the boat.

In the engine room the air blast bent Gourdeau double while electrical short-circuits flashed and crackled around him. All the lights went out and the compartment filled with smoke. Gourdeau and the electrician-on-watch ran into the after-ends and closed the watertight door behind them, clipping it shut. "I was not really frightened," he remembered, "because we were alongside and on the surface. I knew we should be able to escape through the after hatch."[7] Gourdeau could not find the big hammer for knocking the clips off the escape hatch and had to use a steel bar instead. It took him nearly ten minutes to open the hatch and during this time he noticed that *Sidon* was going down by the bow. After releasing the hatch, he cautiously opened the door to the engine room and helped several choking and injured sailors to safety, including Jennings and Gregory, whose call of nature had been interrupted. Then Gourdeau hoisted himself onto the casing and into fresh air. The CO asked him if there was anyone else left below. "I don't think so," replied the Canadian and then asked, "Shall I close the engine room hatch, sir?"[8] Getting no reply from the distracted captain, Gourdeau left it open and made his way aboard the *Maidstone*. The four Canadians drew together for support. They were alive, but worried. What had happened to the fifth of their group? Where was McLeod, the new PO?

In the forward compartment of the submarine, the force of the blast had wrenched off both the bow cap and the rear torpedo tube door and sent searing flames and toxic fumes aft. The forward accommodation space and the wardroom were demolished and debris piled up outside the control room forming an impenetrable barrier to rescuers. Water poured in through the torpedo tube, causing the alteration in trim that Gourdeau had noticed and contaminating the batteries, which released chlorine into the already poisonous environment. Rescue efforts began immediately but were hampered by the barrier of debris and the toxic atmosphere. Personnel used DSEA sets to try to reach the personnel in the torpedo compartment but these proved unequal to the task. Later investigators discovered that their efforts had in any case been in vain – the sailors forward of the control room were all dead anyway, killed instantaneously by the explosion. *Sidon* sank twenty-five minutes after the bang taking fourteen victims down with her, including Laverne McLeod and the brave squadron medical officer. He was the only one not killed by the explosion; he died from asphyxiation while attempting the rescue. Eight crew members were injured.

Petty Officer Second Class Laverne D. Mcleod, RCN, was twenty-four years old when *Sidon* blew up, and had served the shortest submarine appointment on record – one hour. He died instantly when a piece of debris fractured his skull as he sipped his tea. McLeod was the fourth Canadian to lose his life in submarines, but the first in peacetime. It was sheer luck that "Spud" Gregory had not died too – his visit to the heads had saved his life.

About ten days later *Sidon* was salvaged and beached at Portland. Gourdeau volunteered to help with the gruesome task of retrieving the bodies of the victims, all of whom, including McLeod, were buried with full military honours in the cemetery at Portland. Gourdeau and Jennings were reassigned to HMS/M *Scorcher* which was completing a refit and *Sidon*'s hull was sunk as a bottom target after the equipment was removed.

By mid-1955 the Royal Canadian Navy was approaching its peacetime strength of 20,000, and the new Liberal minister of national defence continued the refrain that Canada had no intention of establishing a submarine arm.[9] The government continued to restrict defence spending harshly, which eroded Canada's naval commitment to NATO and compromised the politicians' influence abroad. In this same year the navy yet again reactivated the proposal for the "acquisition of an RCN submarine branch, [and the] building and refitting of ... 7 or 8 submarines."[10] Soon, however, the advent of the nuclear-powered submarine put a whole new spin on the issue.

When the Conservatives came to power unexpectedly in mid-1957, the RCN's hopes rose. The new minister of national defence, Major-General George Pearkes, VC, CB, DSO, MC, had little choice but to re-establish the Canadian Submarine Service after the RN stated that they could no longer guarantee three boats for the Sixth Submarine Squadron and that Canada had to man SM6 themselves. By 1958 Pearkes was publicly acknowledging that he was considering building submarines in Canada as the RCN now had enough qualified personnel to man three. (This was the first recognition of the unintentional bonus of the Heads of Agreement contract – qualified Canadian submariners.) These officers and men were unashamedly used by the navy as a lever to gain Tory approval for a submarine branch. The clincher came when the USN offered the RCN a boat from their reserve fleet for the cost of reactivation only.

By the end of 1958, a clear picture of the costs of either buying or renting a U.S. or British diesel/electric submarine emerged and in March 1959 the RCN opted to accept the USN's offer of one unmodernized fleet boat, estimating the cost at between $1.6 million and $3.6 million. Though slow and without a snorkel, this submarine had two advantages – it would not be recalled in an emergency and Canadian submariners would gain experience in a U.S. boat as a prelude to acquiring their own, based on U.S. designs.

It took a while for the decision to pass through the normal channels for comment and approval, but in mid-1959 the Treasury Board agreed to the expenditure. The price wavered for a while but finally settled at the bargain price of $887,000 for five years, which included the activation, modifications, spares, torpedoes, and personnel training.

On 8 January 1960 the Tory Cabinet approved the scheme and Canada was set to inaugurate her second submarine service in nearly forty years. This time it was a more deliberate act than the unplanned acquisition of the primitive CC boats in World War I. The RCN decided to deploy the "new" submarine on the west coast while seeking another U.S. boat for Halifax. They prematurely forecast the end of their anti-submarine warfare training woes – one submarine down and nine to go!

Although the $2.3 million in the 1961–62 estimates for the loan of a second U.S. submarine had been approved, the chief of naval staff delayed its acquisition until he had a firm decision on building boats in Canada. The ensuing wait caused the RCN to lose the USS *Tigrone,* one of the few suitable reserve submarines left.

The renewal of the Canadian Submarine Service did not mean the RCN could end the Heads of Agreement contract. They still needed a minimum of three boats on the east coast to tide them over until their own submarine service evolved. The contract was due for renewal and negotiations began poorly with the Admiralty in a position of strength – they knew they had Canada over a barrel. First, they asked the RCN to pay for and undertake all the refits of the Canadian As in Canada, to which the RCN replied, "Impossible!"[11] A year later, still at an impasse, the RN added the cost of the three As' modernizations as well. Although this major upgrade would result in better targets, Canada was most reluctant to pay the piper.

The Admiralty itself was not entirely to blame for the stalemate. It was under severe pressure from the British government to stop giving a quarter of its submarine resources away to Commonwealth navies, and to encourage them to develop their own submarine services, something the RCN had been vainly attempting to do. The RN's reduction of SM6 in February 1960 to one boat and the stalled negotiations forced the RCN to reconsider doing the As' refits in Canada. After some scratching of heads, they put the refit costs ($1.34 million) into the 1960–61 naval estimates supported by the minister of national defence.

In June 1960 the chief of naval staff met his opposite number at the Admiralty. The meeting was a tough one – at least, tough for Canada. The Admiralty stood by its position that the initial agreement had been more than generous to the RCN by paying the capital costs and most of SM6's operating expenses and that the renewal contract would have to be more equitable. The CNS made the mistake of reminding the admiral that, to preserve the right to recall the submarines in an emergency, they had agreed to pay for refits. The First Sea Lord sharply told CNS that the recall provision was because they owned the boats. CNS left no better off than when he had arrived.

It took another year for the two parties to renew the Heads of Agreement contract. In the end, the RCN paid for the contentious refits but they were done in Britain because the cost was a million dollars less than doing them in Canada. The RN paid for the aging As' modernizations, but the cost of other alterations was split equally. The new price tag was over $3 million per annum for two and a half training submarines, representing an increase of about $1.4 million each year.

CHAPTER TWENTY

THE NUCLEAR-POWERED SUBMARINE ACQUISITION, 1960–1962

A leap of faith!

While the RCN pursued a variety of interim solutions to the problem of the lack of ASW training boats, something momentous was afoot in the world of submarines. Nuclear power as an underwater propulsion system was revolutionizing naval thinking, planning, procurement, and tactics because it allowed submarines to be independent of air – they no longer had to surface to replenish their batteries. This feature made them virtually undetectable, gave them sustained high speed, and had a significant impact on the RCN's submarine acquisition process in the 1960s.

After the Americans launched the world's first nuclear-powered submarine, USS *Nautilus,* in January 1954, the RCN began to investigate the technology[1] with half an eye on its use for a new Canadian submarine service. In August 1957 a few senior RCN officers sailed in USS *Seawolf* and she took their breath away. She was big – 4,200 tons (3,809 tonnes) submerged – and her crew of ninety-five lived in comfort. She could operate at 720 feet (220 m) and carried twenty-six torpedoes for her six bow tubes. The Canadians learned that in addition to the three American nuclear-powered submarines (SSNs) already at sea the USN had five building and planned to lay down seven more in 1958. Britain was also about to take the plunge.

The RCN's confidence in acquiring submarines grew when the minister of national defence announced in December 1957 that no further naval shipbuilding would take place until the navy had decided on the type of nuclear-powered vessels they wanted. The navy's first study into nuclear-powered submarines began less than a month later and they signed the first of several agreements to exchange marine reactor information with the U.S. a month after that. The study found that SSNs were now a better, cheaper, and less vulnerable ASW platform than surface ships, which, if espoused by the RCN, would shift their traditional view of submarines away from training and usurp the surface vessels' predominance in ASW.

However, from training boats to the "leading edge" of offensive submarines was a huge leap, and the chasm to be crossed yawned wide and deep not only for the politicians but for the navy too. No one was asked to jump over it in 1958.

The Naval Staff reviewed the possibility of acquiring SSNs in March and decided that Canada had indeed got a requirement for them, recommending that they be included in the 1960–61 estimates. Lt.-Commander Gigg, the only submariner present at the meeting, was filled with hope. Subsequently the CNS, Vice-Admiral Harold G. DeWolf, RCN, DSO, DSC, stated unequivocally that the Canadian navy had no intention of acquiring any more diesel/electric submarines.

To show his serious intent DeWolf constituted the Nuclear Submarine Survey Team (NSST), to consolidate the information previously gathered and to clarify and cost the whole project, including its infrastructure and personnel requirements. The team of fourteen, led by Rear Admiral(Engineering) B. Spencer, began its deliberations in September 1958 and submitted its final report in June 1959, confidently expecting the government's decision a year later.

Vice-Admiral DeWolf went public in an interview in May 1958. The resulting articles[2] were eye-openers for the population in general and the Canadian shipbuilding industry in particular. He declared, "Nuclear submarines will ... make up half of Canada's fleet,"[3] but explained that construction in Canada would not start for two years. He did not provide a cost of an SSN, but the papers estimated it to be $50 million. DeWolf justified this expense by citing the possible presence of Soviet submarines in the Arctic and the RCN's urgent need of A/S training boats. Media commentary acknowledged that there might be a role for Canadian SSNs, but suggested that the RCN should start with conventional boats instead. The press took up a refrain that would become familiar, even in the 1980s – the expense "stagger[s] the imagination."[4]

To signal their seriousness about building SSNs, the RCN sent four officers to the British Reactor School. Others left soon afterwards for

AECL's new school at Chalk River. More were shipped off to USN operational submarine billets for training. One of these officers, Jim Wood, who swore he had never volunteered for submarines, eventually became Maritime Commander, after initiating the 1980s' submarine acquisition.

Soon the projected costs for an SSN looked alarmingly high to the NSST's leader. Spencer took his figures to the Cabinet defence committee three times in six months, in case the government wanted to abandon the study. The minister of national defence reacted cautiously, but allowed the work to continue. After this reassurance, the Americans granted Canada every assistance they could for one year. The legendary Admiral H. Rickover, father of the USN nuclear submarine program, was even in favour of doing a direct infusion of the technology into Canada. However, once the deadline passed with no Canadian decision, Rickover slammed the doors shut, and they never reopened.

In May 1959 Britain laid her first SSN keel, while the Canadian government became more alarmed at their own temerity in believing they could do it too. Several senior officers felt the buffet of government anxiety, and wrote strong representations to CNS to bolster his resolve. All stated that it was essential that a nuclear Canadian submarine service be established forthwith, otherwise ASW efficiency would fall seriously during the next decade. DeWolf agreed with them, but would soon retire.

The NSST delivered their final report on time in June and it was an impressive 200 pages. The team recommended the American *Skipjack*-class submarine and presented two options for acquiring five boats. The boats could be bought from the U.S.A. for $52.5 million each, or Canada could build her own for $65 million each. The Naval Board disagreed that Canada could build one boat every four years, believing as the shipyards did, that it would take six to eight years, and that the unit price would be more like $80 million in the end. The NSST predicted the associated costs of the project at about $28 million and an annual operating cost of $2.16 million/SSN. Despite the anxiety over expense and construction time, the Naval Board recommended to the chiefs of staff that SSNs be included in the 1960–61 naval estimates.

By mid-August the NSST had disbanded and the expertise regrouped into the Nuclear Submarine Project Group, in preparation for the political go-ahead. The team consisted of two sections – the Marine Reactor Group, under the engineer-in-chief, which was responsible for the nuclear system and sub-systems only and the submarine group, under the naval constructor-in-chief, which looked after everything else, including the hull, weapons, and other systems.

However by the fall of 1959, the navy's resolve to acquire nuclear-powered submarines started to weaken. The first indication came when RCN asked the British flag officer, Submarines (FOSM) whether conventional submarines might not continue to be useful operationally; the second was the replacement of the determined DeWolf by Vice-Admiral H.S. Rayner, RCN, DSC, CD.

Rayner soon presented a memo to the defence minister justifying an offensive Canadian submarine service and asking for twelve SSNs, but he also offered a way out if the government thought SSNs were too expensive. The comparative costing showed that each diesel boat would be about $54 million cheaper than each "nuke." In the final sentence, CNS asked for approval of conventional submarines if SSNs were denied. This alternative, which was quite unsolicited, drained the strength from the proposal.

In January 1960, the Cabinet defence committee (CDC) approved the modified proposal in principle but deferred the choice of boats until March. The RCN's second submission further weakened their position by leaning heavily towards diesel/electric submarines and dropping the number of boats to six or eight. When the CDC demanded more information about conventional submarines, the RCN formed the Conventional Submarine Survey Committee (CSSC) to provide it. CSSC recommended two boats – the British Oberons if cost was the priority and the American Barbels if suitability to requirements and Canadian production were more important. They recommended six submarines for the east coast and three for the west.

By August, CNS and the other chiefs of staff had given up on "nukes" entirely, discarded the Oberons, and came out in favour of the immediate construction of six Barbels in Canada at a total cost of $170 million, trading off six proposed escort vessels. This price was more than twice the projected cost of six Oberons built offshore.

The American Barbels' design, developed in 1955 (the Oberon design was from 1946), was overwhelmingly superior to the O boats. It incorporated the tear-drop hull, which provided increased submerged manoeuvrability and higher speeds (see Table 1) and, best of all, could accommodate the most up-to-date sonar. The price was the catch, however. If Canada was going to extend herself to acquire Barbels, there was a very good argument for paying the extra to get SSNs. This fact was not lost on the politicians who considered the third revision of the proposal in September.

Table 1
A Comparison of the Barbel- and Oberon-Class Submarines

	BARBEL	OBERON
DESIGN ERA	1955	1946
HULL FORM	Tear-drop	Conventional
MAX. SUBMERGED SPEED	23 knots	16 knots
MAX. SNORT SPEED	14 knots	12.5 knots
MAX. SURFACE SPEED	15 knots	15 knots
MAX. DIVED TIME @ 3 knots	102 hours	96 hours
TACTICAL DIAMETER (manoeuvrability)	200 yards	440 yards
TEST DEPTH	700 feet	625 feet
CAVITATION SPEED @ 300 feet	18.5 knots	15 knots
ENDURANCE (10 knots on surface)	14,000 miles	10,000 miles
DISPLACEMENT (submerged)	2894 tons	2408 tons
LENGTH OVERALL	219 feet	295 feet
BEAM	27 feet	26.5 feet
TORPEDOES	6 x 21"	8 x 21"
OFFICERS	8	7
MEN	77	61
COST PER SUBMARINE	$22 million	$11 million

When the defence committee noted that the six Barbels could be afforded only at the expense of six new surface ships, they imposed two conditions for approval. First, and most important, the RCN had to gain the consent of NATO's Supreme Allied Commander, Atlantic, (SACLANT) to replace some of Canada's NATO-tagged surface ships with submarines. Second, they wanted yet more information on other diesel boats that might suit.

The second condition brought the Oberons back into the discussion despite the fact that they did not meet the stated operational requirements. By October, Rayner was suggesting two options – first, that six Barbels could be built in Canada; second, that six Oberons (built offshore) and four ASW frigates could be acquired for the same price. CNS told his minister that the first scheme would be better for NATO and the second would be good for both NATO and Canada. CNS supported the

Barbels, adding that the all-American content would be easier to maintain and replace than the unique British equipment, especially in wartime. Harkness, minister of national defence, began to lean towards the Barbels. His resolve was strengthened by SACLANT approving the replacement of RCN surface ships in NATO with submarines and requesting that Canada provide nine submarines to NATO by 1966.

Archival material shows that the RCN did not utilize the NATO force requirement of nine operational boats from Canada to bolster their January 1961 submission to the CDC. Was it possible that they had little inclination to do so because, if they had, their fleet's balance would have shifted away from their beloved surface ships?

On 7 March 1961, the proposal to acquire six Barbels reached Cabinet and five weeks later Prime Minister Diefenbaker announced that no decision had been made. He disliked President Kennedy, and Canada's deteriorating relations with the U.S. probably made him reluctant to endorse the American option when the price and delivery dates of the Oberons were so appealing.

The Canadian navy worked on the preparations for construction of the Barbels during the spring and early summer as if the acquisition were decided. The U.S. shipyards modified their design to Canadian requirements and the RCN chose the submarines' equipment and finished the work schedule. Meanwhile the Canadian shipyards lobbied hard in Ottawa and the press reported that the government intended to order the Barbels.[5]

In August 1961, Diefenbaker's vacillations and his antics over the U.S. Bomarc missiles caused the Americans to withdraw their Barbels offer. This caused the government to revert to a training-submarines-only mentality, which, combined with the availability of the British Oberons, seemed to leave the RCN with no choice but to go back to the RN.

Meanwhile the sources of submarines for Canada to rent in the interim were drying up. The U.S.A. was not building any more conventional boats, and their conventional boats in reserve were becoming more unsuitable every day; and the British were increasingly reluctant to release any more of theirs to Canada. At this point, the Heads of Agreement contract for the Sixth Submarine Squadron was renewed for four years, but with the condition that Canada make alternative arrangements. The Admiralty seemed to be forcing Canada into buying British.

In March 1962, the Cabinet defence committee finally recommended that three Oberons be bought from Britain (a reduction of three), and eight general-purpose frigates be built in Canada (an increase of four). A timely indication from the RN that an Oberon might be available for early delivery, with two more to follow shortly thereafter, swayed the committee. The surface mentality prevailed.

That same month the Tory Cabinet approved the proposal for three Oberons, as long as defence contracts would be forth-coming from Britain to offset the purchase. The few Canadian submariners who were going to have to live with the choice heartily disliked it, and for many others the tardy decision was second best. In April, with the contract unsigned because of difficulties negotiating the offsetting purchases, Harkness announced the Oberon acquisition in the House of Commons, as part of a $300 million expansion for the navy. He justified the decision to build them offshore by showing that three submarines could be had for the price of one home-built boat.

But the issue of nuclear-powered boats would not go away, partly because Cabinet had not ruled it out. The mounting disappointment with the Oberon choice and the RCN's uncertainty over whether their submarine requirement was for operations or training created the 1962 Submarine Committee. This body, formed only three weeks after the announcement of the plan to buy the Oberons, was to study the navy's operational requirements for submarines.

During this review, Gigg was kept out of headquarters in case his opinions scuttled the Oberon purchase. He was saying, among other things, that if new diesel/electric boats were bought they would provide the government with an excuse not to buy SSNs. He turned out to be correct.

Commodore R.P. Welland, RCN, the assistant chief of Naval Staff and a strong proponent of operational submarines, chaired the 1962 Submarine Committee (as a young lieutenant, he had spent his wartime Sundays on the Dutch boat, O15). Welland's team re-examined the RCN's overall submarine requirements, reviewed the reports of the Nuclear Submarine Survey Team and the Conventional Submarine Survey Committee, brought their costings up to date and reconsidered the contract for the Sixth Squadron. The most important result of their first meeting was the realization that the government would only approve a submarine program that demonstrated operational tasks that only submarines could perform.

The report of the 1962 Submarine Committee proved that the navy did have operational requirements that only submarines could fulfil, as well as training commitments that could not be honoured without submarines. The RCN needed high-performance submarines to respond to the Soviet submarine threat with effective ASW in all Canadian zones of responsibility, including the Arctic. Furthermore, they felt they had to set an SSN to catch an SSN, especially if it was under the ice. The report said nine boats were the minimum required (twelve would be better) initially, to provide seven for the Atlantic and two for Pacific. These boats needed long endurance, sustained high speed, full ASW detection, tracking and classification equipment, and a weapons system that would be effective against all comers. The committee chose the expensive and sophisticated U.S. nuclear-powered Thresher-class as the only boat that could meet these criteria. They wanted the boats built in Canada, at an estimated cost of $400 million spread over ten years. For the interim, the committee proposed acquiring three Oberons and three A-class submarines and continuing SM6.

The committee's recommendations never reached the Naval Board. After the policy committee concluded that the report was flawed, the British First Sea Lord arrived and dangled the half-built HMS/M *Ocelot* in their faces. The 1962 report was buried on a dusty shelf, and the hopes for Canadian nuclear-powered submarines were over for another twenty-five years.

The outcome of this attempt to re-establish a realistic Canadian submarine service may have been predictable years before but hope had kept the prospect alive. Once the procurement reached the political arena, the massive amount of dollars involved paralysed the ministers. It was the idea of operational submarines, not nuclear power, that offended many. For their part the RCN had failed to present a firm, united front on the subject, and their strong desire, after so much delay, to have anything at all that operated underwater clouded their resolve to hold out for SSNs or the Barbels. (Three USN Barbels were operational until the mid-70s in the Pacific, and two were still in service as "clockwork mice" in July 1990.) One other factor was also involved in the debacle, though it was never overt: it was the apprehension in the hearts of some of the senior officers responsible for the procurement. They feared that submarines were superseding surface vessels in importance.

In September 1962 the Conservative Cabinet postponed the Oberon acquisition, because Britain had been slow to participate in the offset purchases demanded by the contract. The RCN morosely decided they had better buy three old and by now very unsuitable A boats from the Royal Navy, despite a strong plea from the senior Canadian submariner, Ed Gigg, to keep all the borrowed/bought boats from one country, i.e., the U.S.A. Before anything was done, the Tories self-destructed in the federal election of April 1963. Lester Pearson's Liberals formed a minority government, and the new prime minister appointed Paul Hellyer as the minister of national defence.

The leap of faith to offensive nuclear-powered submarines had not been taken. The politicians' anxieties and the RCN's disorganization caused Canada to miss the best, if not the only, opportunity for giving Canada a realistic submarine service.

CHAPTER TWENTY-ONE

THE REBIRTH OF THE CANADIAN SUBMARINE SERVICE, 1961

A second wind

On 20 July 1961, eleven aging gentlemen joined a knot of younger men who were gathering on a jetty in Esquimalt in the early morning sunshine. They were no longer spry, but their eyes sparkled with scarcely contained excitement. Each had been invited by the RCN to celebrate an unusual event and Rear Admiral E.W. Finch-Noyes, RCN, flag officer, Pacific Coast, cheerfully welcomed them.

Among the visitors were Barney Johnson, sharp as a tack at eighty-three; "Roy" Beech, a former snotty from the CC boats who had also served in China; and Colin Donald, who had commanded *CH14*. Representing the ratings of that era were George Brisco, who left the CCs after accusing Pitts of cowardice; George Gilbert, a torpedoman; and Fred Crickard, who had been a young able seaman on *CC2*. These six men had been invited to inspect the newly arrived submarine that signified the rebirth of the Canadian Submarine Service. Initially they were quiet, drinking in the moment, and privately remembering other boats of nearly fifty years ago. Johnson may have remembered his shipmate, Maitland-Dougall, who had lost his life commanding D3 – Willie would have enjoyed this occasion too.

The new submarine was HMCS/M *Grilse* and the visitors' reveries were interrupted by the invitation to board her. Gently and carefully, petty officers helped their guests down the hatch of the submarine and into the control room. The strong smell of diesel fuel instantly took them back to their time in submarines, but *Grilse* herself was a surprise. Her sheer size was overwhelming; the equipment was sophisticated and some of it unfamiliar; and the improvement in living conditions was staggering. Their eyes darted everywhere; thoughts began to tumble over each other; questioning gathered speed; and soon recollections started to well up from forgotten depths of memory. The former submariners began to enjoy themselves.

As Lt.-Commander E. Gigg, RCN, the CO of *Grilse,* began the routine for leaving harbour, the veterans stood quietly on the periphery of the control room, watching every move. The terminology used was American as the *Grilse* was a former U.S. boat, but the sequence was much the same as it had been for them. When *Grilse* reached deep water, she dived and altered course towards the open Pacific. Each visitor spent several minutes looking through the periscope, marvelling at its technology. Soon they were spread out through the submarine, examining everything closely – each visitor with his own guide. The crew of the *Grilse* delighted in explaining the details of the equipment to the old-timers who responded with keen interest and sharp questions.

The sophisticated attack instruments in *Grilse* caught the attention of the former officers – in *CC1* and *CC2* the captain had had little to assist him but a primitive periscope and good eye. *Grilse* could fire a torpedo from more than 5,000 yards (4,500 m) with a reasonable chance of success, but the old boats had to get as close as 700 yards (640 m) to hope to score. *Grilse* had four huge diesels and an auxiliary, and there was no cage of white mice in her control room.

Four hours later, the visit ended and Finch-Noyes met the veterans on the jetty to find out what they thought of the new boat. "Her personnel are evidently well trained and enthusiastic," commented Johnson, and the submarine was "on the top line."[1] All appreciated that they had been honoured by their modern counterparts in a unique way by this special invitation, and expressed their thanks.

When the RCN acquired *Grilse* in 1960 the acquisition did not conflict with their move towards nuclear-powered submarines (SSNs). They considered the loan of diesel/electric boats (SSKs) from the U.S. reserve fleet an essential but temporary measure, until the proposed SSNs were commissioned. After Cabinet approval, the U.S. Congress ratified the loan of a U.S. boat in May 1960. The renewable five-year agreement cost Canada $1,764,000 for reactivation and modifications,[2] and the RCN estimated $292,000 for annual operating expenses and $1.3 million for a refit.

Lt.-Commander Ed Gigg, RCN, and three non-submariners chose USS *Burrfish* from ten boats in the U.S. reserve fleet at the end of 1959, and her reactivation began in October 1960. *Burrfish* was a Gato-Balao-class fleet boat which had been designed for the war in the Pacific and later converted to a radar picket boat. She had also been updated to a GUPPY (Greater Underwater Propulsive Power) with more powerful batteries.

The RCN put Ed Gigg in charge of manning and reactivating *Burrfish* (renamed *Grilse*) before the agreement was signed with the U.S.A. Although he was the senior RCN submariner and had commanded the British boats *Selene* and *Tally Ho,* his appointment as the submarine's commanding officer was not confirmed until nearly a year after her selection. His six officers and seventy-two men trained during the boat's preparation.

Once Gigg was named commanding officer, Lt. John Rodocanachi, RCN, was made the executive officer (XO). He had transferred from the Royal Navy in 1957, following time as the first lieutenant of the Sixth Submarine Squadron and HMS *Astute*. Rodocanachi was short, very personable and well respected. On arrival, he spent hours crawling about the bowels of the submarine to acquaint himself with the boat.

Neither Gigg nor his XO had any experience in American boats so they took the American Commanding Officers' Course together in the fall of 1960. The other five officers knew U.S. submarines much better – they had all passed the U.S. SOTC and had served in U.S. boats as a product of the SSN acquisition project. They joined *Grilse* in March 1961. Training of the ratings also began in the fall of 1960 at New London, Connecticut, where they took their basic submarine course.

When the ratings joined *Grilse* in April, life was cramped. The new crew worked alongside their American counterparts for three months, with the USN captain in command. The CO and XO learned to give orders in American, and to follow unfamiliar procedures that caused Gigg some difficulties. For example, "Hard-a-port!" became "Full left rudder!"

On a warm cloudy afternoon on 11 May 1961, HMCS/M *Grilse* was commissioned into the RCN. The traditional, colourful ceremony dramatically marked the long-awaited revival of the Canadian Submarine Service with bunting, music, and speeches. About three hundred people attended the proceedings, including political and naval dignitaries of the two countries. *Grilse* was the third RCN vessel to use the name and the choice caused the RCNSA training sloop to give it up, becoming *Goldcrest.*

The Canadian destroyers *Terra Nova* and *Chaudiere* accompanied by the RCN band, provided the backdrop to the ceremony. The commissioning pennant of USS *Burrfish* was hauled down to the strains of the U.S. National Anthem and the American crew marched off to "Anchors Aweigh." Then Mr. J.P. Sévigny, the associate minister of defence, signed the transfer papers and his wife renamed the submarine with the familiar words: "I name this ship *Grilse*. May God bless her and all those who sail in her." In his speech Vice-Admiral Rayner, RCN, CNS, said, "This is a red-letter day for the Royal Canadian Navy because the commissioning of the HMCS *Grilse* marks the re-establishment of a submarine component in our navy after a lapse of nearly forty years."[3] After the commissioning service Gigg ordered, "Commission *Grilse*! Coxswain pipe!" and the pennant and Canadian ensign were raised. The executive officer gave the order, "Man the *Grilse*!" and the crew marched aboard to "Heart of Oak." The Canadian CO came last, and was piped aboard his submarine for the first time.

Grilse was 311 feet (95 m) long with a submerged displacement of 2,425 tons (2,199 tonnes). Her surfaced speed was 20 knots and she could maintain 10 knots underwater for short periods. Her cruising range was 12,000 miles (19,308 km) and her operating depth was 400 feet (120 m). *Grilse* had four torpedo tubes in the bow, and modern radio, radar, and sonar equipment. Down below *Grilse* was palatial in comparison to anything the sailors had experienced previously. Each crew member had a bunk and the officers all had cabins separate from the wardroom. Best of all, two water distillers produced 1,000 gallons (3,785 l) of fresh water a day allowing the crew to shower twice a week at sea.

After one month of work-ups and maintenance, Gigg reported, *Grilse* "slipped with almost impolite eagerness"[4] and sailed for home on 19 June 1961 while her USN friends lined the jetties and cheered. On the voyage Gigg had to contend with his feisty U.S.-trained officers, who could not resist teasing his British ways and inexperience with a U.S. boat. At 1100 on 14 July 1961, *Grilse* arrived in Esquimalt and Gigg signalled, "Have surrendered to [the Fourth Canadian Escort Squadron] and am proceeding to harbour under escort."[5] The return home was joyous for the sailors, many of whom had been away for six months. A month later the veteran submariners from the First War visited *Grilse* and were shortly followed by the minister of national defence.

On arrival, *Grilse*'s first maintenance period created strained relations between Gigg and the dockyard. Gigg, enthusiastic to show the submarine's economy and independence to headquarters, had his crew do the work. The dockyard staff, who had worked hard to train and prepare for

Grilse's arrival, construed Gigg's choice as a lack of confidence in their abilities and the misunderstanding lasted for months.

As soon as the work was complete, *Grilse* began her work for Pacific Command. She became the clockwork mouse for the ASW training of all the west coast ships, the flight crews of 407 Squadron and some of the U.S. naval aviators. The submarine participated in joint RCN/RCAF tactical exercises as well as larger U.S./Canadian exercises off San Diego and Pearl Harbor. *Grilse* was the target for the personnel undergoing A/S training in the fleet school at Esquimalt, and she worked with the Pacific Naval Laboratory in their research and development of ASW equipment and weapons. *Grilse* was at sea more than 50 percent of the time. The crew grew more efficient and an excellent *esprit de corps* built up. This was partly because they were the only submarine on the west coast and partly because their success had been achieved by prolonged effort and close teamwork.

Despite the sea-time, *Grilse* had a lower attrition rate in her crew than any other ship in the RCN at that time. The few new recruits who did join *Grilse* did their entire submarine qualification process on board, using a scheme developed by Gigg. Gigg had advocated this system because as long as there was only one Canadian submarine, it was the cheapest route.

Gigg was also responsible for having an insignia designed and approved to show that *Grilse*'s sailors were submariners. He did not want them to wear another country's badge, which many tended to do even though it was forbidden. The insignia for the submariners was a scarlet heraldic dolphin worn above the left cuff.

In her inaugural year *Grilse* spent 205 days at sea, steamed nearly 30,000 miles (48,270), and dived 329 times. *Grilse* had her first interim docking in August 1962 and the dockyard mateys were closely supervised by Gigg's crew. This period also brought changes to the officers – Rodo went ashore and "Rusty" McKay became XO. Gigg remained the commanding officer of *Grilse* until December 1962, when Lt.-Commander George McMorris, RCN, relieved him. The outgoing captain wrote, "I have spent the happiest period of my service life in this submarine with a fine crew."[6] Gigg joined the staff of the director Naval Ship Requirements in Ottawa, and made a nuisance of himself at every opportunity advocating SSNs.

After Gigg left, *Grilse*'s routine did not change much. She continued with her role of ASW training, did several cruises both long and short, participated in multi-national exercises and saw many submariners trained and officers rotated. The Esquimalt dockyard did *Grilse*'s refits and took the many challenges in their stride – relations between the submarine and the dockyard, at last, were cordial.

The drawback of serving in a tame submarine for officers was the lack of operational experience, which significantly reduced their chances of passing Perisher. One Canadian remembers his embarrassment when asked how many attacks he had done. Most on his Perisher were able to answer between eighteen and twenty-seven, but he had to reply, "None." In his previous year in *Grilse*, not one torpedo was fired, no mines were laid, no covert operations were conducted, and no attacks were practised. This not only caused difficulty in qualifying commanding officers, but also produced less realistic anti-submarine training for the Canadian forces.

"You'll never guess what is up here,"[7] relayed the watch, when a young soldier reported for duty in *Grilse* in the spring of 1968. It was a first. When *Grilse* needed a second "doc" for her cruise to Japan, Gary Sandecock, an army medical assistant from the National Defence Medical Centre in Ottawa was appointed. The crew treated the "pongo" (army man) with reticence initially, but did show him around the submarine. The captain, Lt.-Commander Maurice Tate, RCN, gave Sandecock simple duties and later rotated him through all the departments of the submarine which hastened the crew's acceptance of this "brown thing" (the army uniform he wore was brown). The cruise was such a unique experience for Sandecock that he kept a diary. It is probably the only existing detailed record of life on a Canadian submarine from an outsider's point of view, and as such has a historical as well as a personal value – one can only hope that it will be preserved.[8]

En route to Hawaii Sandecock got used to a torpedo as a bunk-mate and learned to use a sextant. He saw the ocean change colour from milky grey to light blue. He learned the routines of a submarine at sea and experienced the teamwork. He noticed the close comradeship amongst the submariners and began to envy it. The crew initiated Sandecock into the delights of free ascent in the escape tank at Pearl Harbour. He did not like it. "… A unique experience," was all he could croak out afterwards.

Once in Japan, *Grilse* participated in exercises with the Japanese and American navies and her crew played their teams at softball. Sandecock enjoyed the bars, geisha houses, restaurants, and shops with the crew just like any tourist, and when *Grilse* returned to Esquimalt Sandecock was touched to find the submariners had truly accepted him into their special fraternity. Later on he enjoyed repeating the experience in another Canadian submarine. Sandecock was the first soldier ever to serve in a submarine and later became the only pongo accepted for membership in the Submariners' Old Comrades Association – a singular honour.

Grilse was soon to end her usefulness. The RCN planned to refit her and continue her target services for the west coast fleet, but a shortage of funds and three new submarines intervened.

If the RCN thought that the new Liberal government of Lester B. Pearson would expedite the postponed Oberon acquisition, they were wrong, and they quickly had to make contingency plans. On taking office in 1963 Hellyer, the new MND, halted work on all major defence contracts, while he reconsidered them in light of an increasing deficit. On three occasions the navy unsuccessfully pressed the Cabinet to conclude the Oberon agreement, while quietly revisiting SSNs and deciding to acquire more U.S. diesel/electric boats in the interim.[9]

"It never ceases to amaze me how many people say they believe we should get USN submarines as an interim programme and start building our own nuclear propulsion submarines, yet continue to write about getting Oberons as if they were the best solution," wrote Ed Gigg in frustration.[10] The assistant CNS, Welland, agreed and said that Canada must not end up with a mixed bag of submarines (RN and USN), which would bring with them tiresome logistical and personnel training problems. However, the pressure of 2,000 submarine training days in 1963 did nothing to promote the RCN's objectivity at this stage – it was quickly becoming a case of any submarine.

In October Hellyer convinced the RCN that they had lost all hope of acquiring submarines when he publicly denied that he was discussing submarines with Britain, and cancelled the frigate program. The minister then caught the navy hopping when he called for a review of Canadian ASW and their recommendations for the most suitable ASW platforms.

On 5 November 1963 the small Canadian Submarine Service, certain of their imminent demise, got their reprieve. The Cabinet finally approved three of the six Oberons from Britain. Apparently, when Hellyer paid his first official call on the British minister of defence, he got his counterpart to sell the three boats for $11 million each on a handshake. It is difficult to pinpoint the deals made at this ministerial meeting to secure the Oberons because they were verbal. But deals there were. One was probably Canada's payment for the modernization of one of SM6's A boats.

"These submarines will be used *primarily* (author's italics) for train-ing purposes, but are also fully operational as A/S weapons systems," announced the minister of national defence firmly.[11] He also said that the O boats would become part of the Canadian contribution to NATO, as agreed with SACLANT earlier. The government did not mention the second batch of three submarines, and they were never heard of again.

The predictable uproar from the shipyards and their unions followed DND's announcement. Canadian Vickers, who had stood to gain so much, responded with "profound shock"[12] to the news, predicting large-scale unemployment in their yard. However, they avoided lay-offs by building sections of SSN hulls for the USN. Hellyer was unrepentant, pointing out that the O boats were merely filling the gap before SSNs could be built at home and that they had to be built offshore to hasten the process. The Canadian submariners were disappointed in the choice – most favoured the American SSKs. Gigg again forecast that the three Oberons would become the government's excuse to buy no more sub-marines of any kind.

Canada, having already lost HMS/M *Ocelot* and by now also *Opportune*, was offered another hull by Britain, HMS/M *Onyx*. With relief, the RCN accepted her, to regain some of the lost time, and they did so knowing that it meant all three boats would be built by the naval dockyard at Chatham instead of by a commercial yard. This change denied Canada a fixed-price contract, because by law Her Majesty's Dockyards can make neither a profit nor a loss.

The first submarine was scheduled to arrive in late 1965, the next two in 1967 and 1968. All three needed modifying to meet Canadian requirements, so it was fortunate that *Onyx* was not so far along in her construction as to preclude this. The design changes included enlarge-ment of the "snort" de-icer, a different weapons fit, a larger air-condition-ing unit, a better active sonar, and some different communication equip-ment. The RCN briefly considered alterations for operating under the ice, but rejected the idea.

The contract negotiations with Britain concluded at the end of 1963; a final price of $40 million was agreed on, excluding torpedoes, which was $7 million more than Canada had expected to spend. The short Canadian letter of intent, sent to the British ministry of defence (MOD) along with the down payment of $100,000, turned out to be the final written contract – no other, at least, could be found in the archives. Details on spare parts, logistical life support, and other components were missing. Canada made the first progress payment of $12 million in early

1964. So that *Onyx* could be launched in the spring with her Canadian name, Indian names were chosen for the three new Canadian submarines – *Ojibwa, Onondaga,* and *Okanagan.*

The RCN dispatched a team to Chatham in July 1964 to oversee the entire construction project. Specialists in engineering, naval construction, electrical engineering, and supply were included, under a senior officer. To fill the gaps in the letter of intent to the British MOD, DND's procurement department began to work out a more detailed agreement.

When the Heads of Agreement contract for the Sixth Submarine Squadron lapsed again, in June 1963, the RCN renewed it, because the Oberons would not arrive for several years. The Admiralty drove another hard bargain – they demanded an additional $214,000 and required Canada to pay not only the refit costs of one A, but also the full modernization costs. Although Hellyer had guaranteed this, the RCN were irritated with the condition because SM6 had been drawing stores from the RCN throughout their time in Halifax and neither returning nor paying for them. The report of the ensuing investigation could not be found in the records, so the remedy, if any was found, is not known. SM6's three As were scheduled to return to Britain in November 1964, April 1966, and June 1967, prior to each new Oberon's delivery. In fact, the last A boat left Halifax in May 1966.

After scuttling the frigate program and approving the submarine purchase, the politically ambitious Hellyer began to show his true colours to the Canadian defence establishment. The theme of his White Paper on Defence in the spring of 1964 was the preservation of peace, but the policy created an uproar with its the plan to unify the three armed services. The references to submarines were lost in the indignation over unification, but the White Paper did mention that the navy would further study the possibility of building nuclear-powered submarines, and would replace *Grilse* on the west coast with another diesel/electric boat.

With a defence policy geared to peace and the primary reason for the RCN's need of submarines stated to be ASW training, the SSNs were a lost cause from the outset. Try as they might, the RCN could not justify the acquisition of two or three nuclear-powered submarines to run about as clockwork mice. A new naval study showed that, with only 11 percent of ASW training time needing high performance SSNs, a conventional submarine service made more sense and SSNs could be borrowed from Britain or the United States. Had the Canadian foreign policy, and therefore the defence policy, been different, there might have been something on which to hang the SSNs.

Cabinet approved Hellyer's defence policy in the fall of 1966. The bill passed into law in April 1967, and unification of the Canadian Armed Forces occurred on 1 February 1968, transforming the Royal Canadian Navy into Maritime Command. By now the senior naval officers who had opposed the scheme had fallen to Hellyer's axe, and many of the rank and file had left the forces of their own accord. Those that stayed in swallowed hard and climbed into the green uniforms that became the laughingstock of the world's navies. For the Canadian Submarine Service, the taste of unification was less bitter: they were looking forward to three new boats and were never much interested in uniforms anyway.

Two other events, minor in comparison with the Oberon acquisition, affected the small submarine service in the '60s. In August 1964 qualified Canadian submarine officers were granted the right to wear their own distinctive "dolphins." Someone with a sense of history chose the date of authorization – it was exactly fifty years to the day that *CC1* and *CC2* had sailed into Esquimalt harbour to form the Canadian Submarine Service.

The second event happened a year later, when the Ensign flown by all warships was replaced by the new Canadian flag. On 15 February 1965 the old Ensign was lowered for the last time on HMCS/M *Grilse*, Canada's only submarine, with a sense of loss. This feeling was mingled with a sense of hope and pride when the new Maple Leaf was raised immediately afterwards.

CHAPTER TWENTY-TWO

THE CANADIAN O BOATS

"I name this ship ..."

The Canadian navy now had to manage a submarine service with boats of two nationalities. Welland's earlier predictions of difficulties in the logistic, personnel, and training spheres were already coming to pass in the design and construction phases of the new Oberons. They would intensify as the first boat was commissioned.

For example, the RCN wanted torpedoes of a different diameter than those used by the RN; the British light bulb sockets would not take North American light bulbs; the British electrical equipment and machinery did not meet the RCN standards; and spares had to be brought across the Atlantic at considerable expense. In addition, when the RCN moved the galley forward of the control room to get more room for sonar equipment in the second two boats, three bunks were lost, which resulted in an accommodation crisis – there was nowhere to put the trainees. It looked as if the RCN would have to accept "hot bunking." Although this sharing of a bunk by two men (when one was on watch, the other would be sleeping) was never officially acknowledged, it certainly occurred. As the construction got under way it seemed that the critics of the Oberon program had been correct – the problems were partially dealt with and were certainly lived with, but they never went away completely.

Just before the Canadian team arrived in Britain to oversee the Oberons' construction, the first boat was launched. Formerly *Onyx, SS72* was christened HMCS/M *Ojibwa* (pronounced O-JIB-WAY) on 24 February 1964 by Lady Patricia Miers, who wrote that she was greatly honoured to be chosen. The choice, however, was criticized by some who were unaware of the connection between her husband, Rear Admiral Sir Anthony Miers, VC, KBE, CB, DSO, RN, and the Canadian submariners who served under him in Trincomalee and Fremantle during World War II. After the launch the Mierses rekindled their warm friendship with a new generation of Canadian submariners and it lasted another twenty years.

HMCS/M *Ojibwa* was only a shell of a submarine when she slid down the ways. The pressure hull had been welded together in sections, and a few pieces of equipment that were too big to go in through the hatches were "end-loaded." Swarms of highly skilled workers began the fitting-out, the most complex phase of the submarine's construction, in the dockyard's non-tidal basin. Shipwrights, plumbers, welders, and electricians started the work, and later pipefitters, joiners, coppersmiths, and upholsterers took over; and these were but a few of the trades involved. The process lasted about eighteen months.

The Canadian Naval Submarine Technical Representative and his small team officially began their work at Chatham on 12 March 1964, led by Captain William B. Christie, RCN. Christie had been part of the Nuclear Submarine Survey Team, and although not a submariner, he was well experienced in warship construction. Christie's team was responsible for all technical and contractual matters regarding the O boats.

With *Ojibwa* launched, intense preparations were under way to start the second submarine. "We worked cruelly hard,"[1] remembered the OWL (operations, weapons and electrical officer). He bore the brunt of the decision to increase the Canadian content of the submarines and to use the smaller but more reliable U.S. Mark 37 torpedoes. The design changes and increased Canadian content escalated the price of the submarines significantly; however, the navy persuaded the government to foot the bill. The price now stood at $51.4 million, $18.4 million over the original quote.

In June 1964, while *Ojibwa* was being fitted out, the keel of the second Canadian submarine, *Onondaga,* was laid following a year of preparatory work. Several wives (of whom three were Canadian) of the shipbuilding staff participated in the traditional ceremony. Led by the admiral's wife the ladies manned a huge capstan, which rolled a prefabricated circular section of the pressure hull weighing several tons into place on its construction berth.[2]

Afterwards, ten circular frames of *Onondaga*'s hull were welded together, forward and aft of the section laid at the ceremony; then the specially shaped bow and stern pieces were added. When the steel plates had been wrapped around the frame and the external tanks added, *Onondaga* began to look like a submarine. She was launched after the casing, bridge, and fin had been fitted. This phase of the construction took about fifteen months. On 6 June 1965 the third and final keel was laid for *SS74,* HMCS/M *Okanagan,* with the usual ceremony. The build was three months behind schedule but under budget – Canada had shaved $2.3 million off the last estimate.

As HMCS/M *Ojibwa* approached completion in the summer of 1965, most of her officers and key ratings had arrived, including her commanding officer, Lt.-Commander Sam G. Tomlinson, RCN, who was considered the best submarine driver and tactician the RCN had ever had. They were to be with her for the next nine months participating in the submarine's trials and completion program and her commissioning.

The third week of September 1965 was designated "Canada Week" at the Chatham dockyard; thousands of guests attended *Ojibwa's* commissioning on the 23rd and *Onondaga's* launching on the 25th. Hellyer complained in his book, *Damn the Torpedoes* (McClelland & Stewart 1990), that the British showed "incredible insensitivity" in failing to invite high-ranking Canadians to *Ojibwa's* commissioning, not playing "O Canada," and not flying the Maple Leaf. To set the record straight: four Canadian warships and their crews attended; the Canadian high commissioner to Britain, Mr. Lionel Chevrier, was the guest of honour; Canadian flags flew everywhere; the champagne was from Niagara; and several Ojibwa Indians participated.

Under Tomlinson's outstanding ship-handling, *Ojibwa* had one of the best submarine work-ups and inspections in twenty years. However, all was not well. The ratings' jobs had changed, following the introduction of the operator/maintainer system into the RCN, and this caused serious discontent among the British-trained men who found themselves expected to do unfamiliar tasks with no transition training. On *Ojibwa's* arrival in Halifax, over half the crew requested a transfer to General Service. It was an astoundingly high percentage, which worried the new squadron commander and his superiors.

Five months later on 17 September 1966 the final Canadian submarine, HMCS/M *Okanagan,* was launched by Mme. Monique Cadieux, wife of the Canadian associate minister of national defence. *Onondaga* was commissioned on 22 June 1967 in Canada's Centennial year and twelve months later it was *Okanagan's* turn to be brought into the fold, on a cold and rainy June day, with Lt.-Commander Nigel Frawley in command. The First Canadian Submarine Squadron was now complete and *Okanagan* soon joined her two sisters in operations and exercises. By now SM6 had gone home, never to return.

The First Canadian Submarine Squadron officially came to life on 22 April 1966, with Gigg in command, three months after *Ojibwa*'s arrival in Halifax. Gigg, surprised and thrilled to be chosen, set about making the Canadian Submarine Service the best in the world and brought the operation of the First Canadian Submarine Squadron into line with the rest of the fleet. He established a watch system of four hours on and eight off and advocated living aboard in foreign ports. Gigg supported Tomlinson in his decision to have the senior rates stand duty watches in harbour to ensure there were enough to take the boats to sea in an emergency. He also chose to follow the USN's submarine training system with its formalized on-the-job-training (OJT) package, because he believed that it produced better submariners than the RN method, and most important, that it would resolve the problem of having to man submarines of two nationalities.

It was these new policies of Gigg's, combined with Tomlinson's difficulty understanding his crew's complaints, that exacerbated the dissension in *Ojibwa*. The senior ratings found themselves doing two duty watches in five in port and the junior rates one in three, which (compared with one in eleven in destroyers) they considered excessive. The men also sorely missed the privilege of shore accommodation in foreign ports after their discomfort at sea in the Oberons. When the crew learned that the old hands had to requalify using the new OJT section of the training program, they rebelled, feeling it was not only an imposition but also an insult. To resolve the discontent Rear Admiral Landymore talked with his disenchanted submariners on his first official visit to *Ojibwa*. After hearing their grievances, he changed the harbour duty watch system on the spot and promised to review the other issues. In fairness to Gigg, the new OJT scheme was well-intentioned and designed, if poorly implemented, and it was supported by his officers.

Tomlinson's problems with personnel culminated in his being relieved of command. Later he ruefully remarked, "*Ojibwa* was the most unhappy period in my naval career" and would say no more.[3] Tomlinson had been in the unenviable position of having to implement Gigg's policies, as well as oversee the crew's uprooting from the "good life" in Britain. Afterwards he served as the squadron's operations officer for a few months, and then left submarines forever.

What did Canada get for her $50 million plus? In 1968 the Oberons were among the best diesel/electric boats in the world. However, they were outclassed in every respect but quietness by the faster, air-independent nuclear-powered submarines. In fact it was the O boats' low noise propagation that kept them competitive longer than anyone expected. The layout of the new submarines was very much like the WWI boats, because basic physics had not changed, but their equipment and sensors had improved beyond imagination.

A civilian's guided tour of HMCS *Okanagan* will help the reader understand what Canada had bought. A member of the crew meets the visitors at the brow and guides them through the forward entry hatch and down a vertical ladder to the deck of the cafeteria. Immediately their nostrils are assailed by the strong smell of diesel fuel and they notice the quiet, broken only by a few voices and the occasional clang of some maintenance work. Their eyes take in a monochrome world of grey, white, and black and a vast array of instruments, pipes, wires, and equipment. Moving seems unwise, in case they touch something they should not. A young sub-lieutenant, detailed off as the visitors' guide, is encouraging. "Let's start in the fore-ends," he suggests, and leads the way, unconsciously bending his lanky form this way and that to avoid things.

Standing in the forward torpedo room, the officer points, "Those are the inner doors of the six bow torpedo tubes. The pressure hull ends about halfway down the tubes and beyond that is the bowcap with the outer torpedo doors. Twenty-six bunks are squeezed in here among the reload torpedoes." Thin wires, strung fore and aft, allow curtains to be pulled across each bunk in an attempt at privacy. Small boxes, about two cubic feet, line the walkway through the middle. They are lockers, one for each sailor's possessions – submariners' mementos have to be small. Their suit bags go under the mattresses. Spare gear for the torpedoes is stored in an overflowing trench towards the outside. The forward escape hatch and an angled torpedo loading hatch are above.

Turning round and retracing their steps aft, the tour pauses in the forward accommodation space. This consists of the chiefs' and petty officers' mess with twelve bunks, *Okanagan*'s small cafeteria, and rows and rows of bunks, known as "coffins," stacked three high. To starboard is the stainless steel galley, which is scarcely bigger than a closet. One of the cooks sticks his head out and says proudly, "I cook for sixty-nine people in here and don't do any walking!" There are two ovens, a deep fryer, and hot plates.

"Where's the dishwasher?" someone asks.

"They're over there."

"Where?"

"Those two guys at the far table!" The cook laughs.

"What do you do with your garbage?" inquires another.

"We crush all the cans into pellets in a compactor and use them to weigh down the gash [garbage] bags which go out of the ejector."

"Where do you store your food?"

"Well, under your feet are all our dry goods." The cook pulls up a trapdoor. "It's filled to the deckhead if we are going away for a long time, though stowed in such a way that those valves can be reached in an emergency."

The visitors scramble through another watertight door and are introduced to the cox'n who is just emerging from his cabin – the "goatshed" – which he shares with the CERA. The space is so small, a guest asks, "How can you live in there?"

"We had the human rights people down here," replied the cox'n. "Their response was the same. They couldn't believe we would put up with it!" However, the goatshed does provide a measure of privacy for the two most senior NCOs on board.

Moving further aft the visitors see the wardroom pantry, three more bunks alongside the gangway, and the wardroom. This is "home" for the officers and is the size of a small bedroom. Here eight officers eat, sleep, do all their paper work, entertain, and relax. Bunks pull out from the built-in couches, and one tiny closet and eight small drawers provide storage.

The tour peers into the ship's office, which is another marvel in miniaturization where the scribe processes the flood of paper generated by the submarine. In 1968 it had a typewriter and a photocopier, though today a computer and a printer are *de rigueur.* "The daily newspaper is published here," says the officer.

Moving on, the guests step over a deep coaming (a raised lip to keep water out) and enter the control room – the nerve centre of the *Okanagan.* It lies amidships directly below the fin, and uses up the full width of the submarine. It seems quite large after the confined areas further forward, but it is only the size of an average living room. Here twenty-two personnel work when the submarine is at action stations. It is crammed with equipment – hundreds of dials, two periscopes, the sonar room, the chart table, the engineering control panel, and the diving station, to name a few. On the port side is the one-man control station, which is similar to the controls of an aircraft, complete with a joystick. Someone says so. Their guide says, "Yes, well the submarine flies in three dimensions too. We even have an auto-pilot! This is the depth gauge (equivalent to the altimeter), the inclinometer (turn and bank indicator), and the compass. Push the stick forward and the submarine goes down and pull it back and she rises. These are the engine telegraphs and this is the chief of the watch panel which controls the diving and surfacing of the boat, and trimming."

"Flooding and emptying the ballast tanks?"

"Yes. We call it venting and blowing."

"Why are some of the handles missing?"

"The tanks are being used for fuel or dirty water and it prevents mistakes. This panel is used to blow the trim and Q tanks. Q is a small tank, which is flooded in an emergency to dive extra fast. The other two panels control the submarine's auxiliary machinery and move water around in the trim tanks to change the submarine's attitude."

The group sees, on the starboard side of the control room, more instruments, the underwater telephone, the chart table, navigational aids, the fire control panel, and the sonar room. It is into this small space that *Okanagan*'s five sonars feed their vital information. Three skilled sonarmen are on watch at sea at all times, rising to six at action stations. "Later I'll introduce you to the operations officer and he can explain the sonars to you," says the officer.

In the centre of the control room, just aft of the ladder to the bridge, are the search and attack periscopes. The attack periscope is small to lessen detection and is the preserve of the captain. The search periscope is used by the OOW and others for checking the surface and for navigation. It is bigger and has binocular vision. "Would you like to look through it?" asks the guide. It comes up and he flips the handles down. "You can change the magnification, like this, and you can turn it through 360 degrees if you walk around."

At the after end of the control room on the port side are the heads. They are as small as those in commercial aircraft. Further aft is the radio office, closed to all but authorized personnel for security reasons, and the captain's cabin. "Close to all the action!" comments the guide.

"But it's scarcely bigger than a powder room!"

"Oh, it's not that bad and it is a lot better than I put up with! See, he has a fold-down sink, a fold-down desk, some cupboards, and a bunk." The visitors realize that it is a quiet place for the CO to call his own, used for thought, the interminable paper work, and relaxation. It is the only privacy afforded anyone on the submarine, except in the heads.

The visitors pass a ladder going down below. "That leads to the radar room and the auxiliary machinery space. We'll go down later," says their guide. Through another watertight door they enter the engine room, which takes up 30 percent of the space inside the pressure hull. It is oppressively warm and humid. "We've just charged our batteries," the sub-lieutenant explains. He introduces Bert and Ernie, the two massive diesel engines. "They are really generators, because unlike the earlier submarine diesels, these in *Okanagan* are not able to drive the boat directly but feed electricity to the batteries."

"How fast can you go?"

"The O boats can do nearly 18 knots on the surface and 12.5 knots when snorting. This is the ballast pump which brings sea water into the tanks, these are the water distillers and these two are air compressors. We use high-pressure air to blow the water out of the ballast tanks to surface and low-pressure air to complete the emptying of the ballast tanks on the surface. Our distillers make twenty-five gallons of fresh water every hour – it's not much."

Further aft again they enter the motor room, which contains all the controls for running the double armature main motors. These lie beneath the deck and are coupled to the two propeller shafts. "The four motors can be used separately, in series, or in parallel, which enables a wide range of power for manoeuvring the boat," explains the officer.

The last watertight compartment in the stern, the "after-ends" where twenty-one stokers (today called engineers) and cooks live, has two stern torpedo tubes. The visitors see another miniature office for the CERA and a small machine shop.

On the way forward again, the officer responds to another question, "Where is the battery?"

"One is under your feet, the other is under the forward accommodation space. It consists of two groups of 224 cells and can drive the submarine at 16 knots for very short periods and at lower speeds for longer. *Okanagan* has a nominal cruising range of 10,000 miles and can stay at sea for ninety days. She can carry thirty reload torpedoes and dive to more than 600 feet."

"Other than the battery, what else is down below? I saw a ladder going down from the control room."

"Ah, yes, I forgot. The auxiliary machinery space is there." They go down into a very cramped area. In it is the equipment that transforms the direct current from the batteries into alternating current to run all the boat's electrical and electronic equipment. Two high-capacity air-conditioning units and the hydraulic system that operates the masts, main vents, exhaust valves, steering gear, and hydroplanes are here.

"Anything else?" someone inquires.

"The radar and electronic surveillance rooms are below the control room, as well as the fresh vegetable locker."

"Do you have freezers?"

"We couldn't do without them! They're below too. Speaking of refreshments, would you like a drink?"

"Yes, please!" And they return to the wardroom.

Now everyone has a gin-and-tonic, and the subject changes to the sensors of the *Okanagan* and the sub-lieutenant turns the visitors over to the expert. "Sonar works like an underwater radar. It is an electronic means of acquiring targets and avoiding attackers. We have five, although our underwater telephones are for communication only," the Ops-O begins.

"Why so many?"

"They do different jobs, all of which provide us with vital information. Some are passive and one is active; some tell us the range and bearing of a target, others its speed; some are used for long-range detection and others for short-range work."

"Do you want to know about our torpedoes?" asks another young man, obviously the torpedo officer.

"Yes, but after I find out how far away the *Okanagan* can hear a ship."

"Classified, I'm afraid!" says the Ops O. "Over to you, Torps."

"*Okanagan* carries Mark 37 acoustic homing torpedoes. They are nineteen inches in diameter and about eighteen feet long. They are driven by an electric battery, are wire-guided, and have passive/active sonar in their noses," explains the officer. (In the 1970s, the Mark 37 torpedoes were converted to an Otto fuel propulsion system.)

"Another drink?"

"No, thank you. Can we see the bridge?"

"OK, but only after you've signed our guest book." Their guide produces a large, well-thumbed, leather-bound book. "You may like to see who has been here before you – Pierre Trudeau, Leo Cadieux, Admiral Sir Anthony, and Lady Miers. It's quite a collection!"

The visitors scramble up the ladder in the control room, through the lower and upper hatches and into the fresh air. "That feels good!" The bridge is small and high. It is designed for the OOW and two lookouts and has a compass repeater, a klaxon alarm button, and a voice pipe to communicate with the control room. Nothing is projecting up from the fin but there are seven openings aft of the bridge. "From front to back, these holes allow the search and attack periscopes, the radar mast, the electronic surveillance mast, the snort induction and exhaust, and the communication mast to be raised. This is the underwater telephone transceiver."

"Cold and wet up here, I should think."

"It certainly can be. The lookouts spend an hour on watch up here. Any more and their concentration falters. The OOWs do two hours. It feels wonderful to go below for hot soup." The guests return to the casing and the visit ends. The visitors come away with a great deal of respect for the men who, not only go down to the sea in ships, but also go down under it – in boats.

The Canadian navy acquired another American submarine in 1968, bringing the total to five. The procurement began when *Grilse* arrived in 1961 and was an on-again, off-again process, overshadowed by the more important question of which submarines should replace the Sixth Squadron.

Even though 1961 marked the RCN's largest requirement for training submarines, they had not planned on adding another American boat, now that they had *Grilse* on the west coast. However, the United States Navy forced them to consider it by offering Canada USS *Tigrone,* one of their few suitable remaining submarines. It was a take-it-or-leave-it offer, which Canada chose to leave, hoping instead to get two older U.S. boats later to tide them over until her own submarines could be built. The navy's refusal of *Tigrone* ushered in several years of inaction on the problem of the short-term lack of target boats. One reason for this paralysis was the navy's reluctance to approach the government for money for another submarine or two while they were already having difficulty negotiating to build six.

The next look at the subject surfaced at the beginning of the O boats' construction, when *Grilse*'s five-year contract was coming up for renewal. At headquarters' request, Gigg wrote a discussion paper,[4] which considered several alternatives to *Grilse,* including a high-performance submarine or a fourth O boat (now priced at $17 million). In the end, he recommended retaining and refitting *Grilse* for $1 million.

However, the navy kept the option open for another O boat, despite the cost, while at the same time learning that there would be no suitable American submarines available until 1970 unless Canada was willing to pay $14.5 million to modernize an older type. This put the RCN between a rock and a hard place, as they did not have enough money in the 1968–69 naval budget to cover either option. By August the Canadian navy was angling for a used O boat. However, this scheme failed too.

In the end *Grilse* had her major $1.2 million refit in early 1967 and no other submarine was acquired until after all the O boats arrived in Halifax and *Grilse* was back at sea. In 1968, the navy was surprised to learn that a U.S. submarine was available at a price they could afford. USS *Argonaut* was a Tench-class GUPPY, which had just gone into reserve after a three-year deployment in the Mediterranean. The Americans gave Canada six weeks to decide.

The Tench-class had been derived from the Gato-Balao-class of fleet boats, and when first built, *Argonaut* was nearly identical with *Grilse*. However, she had received numerous conversions and modernizations since her only war patrol in 1945, and had greater endurance and performance, more modern detection gear, and a stream-lined fin. In the fall of 1968 Rodocanachi went down to Norfolk, Virginia, accompanied by two others to inspect her. Although they found *Argonaut* in a superficially deplorable condition, her hull was sound and they decided she would suffice.

Instead of renting *Argonaut,* the navy chose to buy the hull for $153,000 and modernize her in Esquimalt for $2.5 million. Some of the officers and men who had manned *Grilse* flew down to Norfolk in mid-November 1968 to prepare the submarine for the voyage to Esquimalt. They were shocked when they saw what Canada had bought – there were tons of rotted food in the storerooms, the heads leaked, only one of the four diesels worked, and the electrical generator was unserviceable. This "new-to-you" submarine (*SS75*) was renamed HMCS/M *Rainbow* and quietly commissioned into the Canadian navy on 2 December 1968.

Rainbow staggered home on two engines and caught fire twice on the way. As if that were not enough, the new submarine was refused entry into her home port – someone had forgotten to pay the sales tax and customs duty. The $12,000 was rustled up and *Rainbow* steamed in to a salute from the admiral. Her modernization took eight months, and after work-ups *Rainbow* assumed the same role as *Grilse*. Her more modern sonars delighted the submariners and made her a more worthy adversary for the air and surface units of Maritime Command (Pacific).

After *Rainbow* arrived, *Grilse* never sailed again for the Canadian navy, even though there were two years to run on her second contract and she had been refitted. As the navy had managed to get *Rainbow* by convincing the politicians that the older submarine was unsafe, *Grilse* languished alongside. Some of her more modern gear was transferred to *Rainbow* during her modernization, but had to be returned when the American auditors reminded Canada that *Grilse* had to be operational when she reverted to the USN. In September 1969 *Grilse* went back home to be used for target practice and now rests on the bottom of the Pacific west of San Francisco, fully equipped.

Grilse had provided value for money as a tame submarine and had the honour of restarting the Canadian Submarine Service after a gap of nearly fifty years. She re-established the tradition, initiated a rebirth of pride in submarines, and provided a necessary example of what a submarine could do to the top brass and politicians in Ottawa. If it had not been for *Grilse,* the navy would have found it even more difficult than it was to acquire three new operational submarines in the 1960s.

Rainbow served in the Canadian navy for six years, keeping the Pacific ASW forces on their toes and also training many new Canadian submariners. These were the baby-boomers, several of whom went on to command the new O boats. *Rainbow* earned her share of glowing accolades and even a mention in a Russian newspaper following her "sinking" of a U.S. carrier bound for Vietnam. Her crew got up to the usual pranks: for example, in 1974 they "acquired" a rather obscene statue from Prince Rupert. The town, keen to divest themselves of this embarrassing item, heaved a sigh of relief when the submarine sailed with "Freddie" secured to the casing. The crew painted Freddie black, dressed him in a submarine sweater, and awarded him his Dolphins. When some surface officers tried to steal him, *Rainbow* donated him to HMCS *Naden*'s wardroom in the hopes of better protection. The Princess Patricia Canadian Light Infantry managed to snatch Freddie when the submariners were not looking and took him with them to Cyprus, where a Norwegian contingent made off with him. Freddie's whereabouts now are uncertain, but rumour has it that he is residing temporarily in Finland.

HMCS/M *Rainbow* was decommissioned on 31 December 1974, only six years after she was bought, to the dismay of many. Once the submarine presence was lost on the west coast, they predicted it would be almost impossible to restore. Officially, *Rainbow* was a casualty of the severe fuel crisis and the fiscal restraint of the Liberal government, but her noisiness and the need of an expensive refit also hastened her demise. Although she was declared surplus, effective December 1974, Maritime Command chose to lay her up early without deciding on her final disposition, hoping that if the economy improved they could perhaps recommission her.

Over two years later the aging submarine was towed to Portland, Oregon, where she was broken up for $213,687 of metal. As foreseen, *Rainbow* turned out to be the last Canadian submarine to serve on the west coast, despite the increasing strategic importance of the Pacific.

CHAPTER TWENTY-THREE

SELECTION AND TRAINING OF CANADIAN SUBMARINERS

So you want to be a submariner?

Canadian submariners are a different breed – different from other sailors, very different from the man in the street, and different in their training. They are tougher, too. They have had to be to survive in a navy that has traditionally rated submarines as secondary to surface vessels, even in anti-submarine warfare. For years they have fought for recognition, endeavoured to educate the fleet, and have had to earn their spurs over and over again. Mostly in isolation, the officers and men have maintained their belief in themselves and their boats until a change occurred in how they were viewed by senior officers and government. When their tenacity and dedication finally began to pay off, their submarines were past their prime.

In their early years, Canada's fully operational O-class submarines were used almost exclusively as target boats. It was not until 1981 that Maritime Command actually tasked a Canadian submarine with an operational patrol. The primary role for Canada's Oberon-class submarines has evolved: from ASW training to the surveillance of shipping, on and below the surface. In peacetime it means participation in operational patrols and covert missions, as well as national and international exercises. If international tensions rise, Canada's submarines are earmarked to intensify their surveillance of shipping in the Canadian zone of the Atlantic. In outright war, their increased surveillance role would continue, but the Os could also join the NATO submarine pool for use as hunter/killers, if the Canadian government approves.

With three boats surveillance can only be achieved intermittently in Canada's assigned Atlantic area[1] and not at all in the Pacific. Many find this lack of coverage foolish beyond belief, especially as Vancouver handles 70 percent of all Canada's seaborne trade, but others support the *status quo*, claiming that Canada needs only the *capability* of responding to incursions. However, providing a 100 percent submarine presence in both oceans has been and remains financially daunting.

As surveillance slowly superseded training, the boats' employment took on a more operational emphasis. Needless to say, that did not happen overnight. Slowly, very slowly, the submariners convinced the navy that the use of their boats as ASW platforms in their own right was an inevitable and important development. This halting advance was not helped by the squadron commander's lack of clout in the Canadian navy – most other navies considered their submarine services important enough to have an admiral in charge. In the mid-1980s, the traditional Canadian resistance to submarines dissipated after the Maritime Commanders Vice-Admiral Jim Wood, CD, and Vice-Admiral Chuck Thomas, CD, took the firm stance that if any component in the above-the-sea, on-the-sea, and under-the-sea approach to ASW was lacking, the navy could not properly do its job.

It took the 1987 proposal for nuclear-powered submarines to briefly end the inequity of the Canadian submarine squadron commander's rank – Thomas raised it from commander to captain. A small gain, but it meant that the incumbent was at least equal to the surface squadron commanders with whom he had to compete for personnel and operations that would benefit the squadron. However, the advantage was short-lived – after the SSN acquisition was cancelled, the position was downgraded to commander, again relegating submarines to secondary importance.

A typical "year" for Canadian submariners is fifteen months, measured between their boats' dockings, and their peacetime operational cycle is sixteen weeks – ten at sea, four alongside in routine maintenance, and two of minor work-ups before being deployed again. When the Os were relatively new there was no spare crew, and the personnel spent twice as much time at sea (up to 250 days a year) as the destroyers' crews; but in 1988 the submarine sea time was capped to ease the strain. For submarines themselves, and for each crew member, there is now a limit of 150 sea days a year (187.5 between dockings), which includes time in foreign ports. The squadron strictly adheres to this regulation and only the Maritime Commander can change it.

Certain events take place in the submariners' year. Following each docking the boat works-up and participates in a torpedo certification at the firing range off St. Croix in the U.S. Virgin Islands. Then boat and crew are either deployed to Britain or the Caribbean for international exercises and/or do an independent operational patrol of 30–50 days in the "Canadian" Atlantic, the details of which are classified. (The squadron conducts one patrol every eighteen months.) After that their remaining sea days are mostly spent locally, exercising with the surface fleet and maritime patrol aircraft. "The [ships' and planes'] jobs are to find the submarines and our job is to show them they can't!" says a former squadron commander.[2] One boat also conducts the new Submarine Officers' Continuation Training Course twice a year, which provides coaching and practice for future Perishers. When these activities are added up, the submariners' calendar of 150 sea days each year is all too short, and the squadron is often hard put to it to keep within the time limits and still meet MARCOM's demands.

Manning the Oberons has never been easy for the squadron, because they have had to manage without a spare crew. (The RN had one spare crew for every 2.5 Os.) Gigg, who has often been blamed for this policy, never fully supported it, as he believed the complements of the new boats were too small to absorb the inevitable personnel shortages caused by sick leave, courses, and other unforeseeable difficulties. Over the years this lack has meant that to keep boats at sea squadron shore staff and crew members had to be juggled from submarine to submarine (cross-decking) to fill the gaps. At one point the shortage was so bad that as a boat came alongside her crew would pack their sea bags, walk down the jetty to another submarine, climb on board, fire her up, and go straight back to sea, losing their leave and time at home. The situation is now vastly improved but cross-decking still occurs every so often, even though there is a pool of personnel earmarked for sea duty in squadron shore billets.

When a lack of submarine volunteers compounded the manning shortage in the 1980s, the squadron faced a crisis – find more personnel, or tie up the boats. To avoid the latter they allowed untrained sailors to go to sea, but it was an unpopular as well as an unsafe solution to the problem. To remedy it Maritime Command decided to conscript officers and men into the Canadian Submarine Service, effective 1 January 1986, as well as continuing the volunteer entry route. The new policy allowed them to post any military personnel into submarines as long as they were male, medically fit, and had an acceptable English-language profile. This meant that in trades or military occupations where the squadron was undermanned they could simply commandeer the manpower they needed. Contrary to gloomy forecasts that conscripts would dilute the elite spirit of the Canadian Submarine Service, it turned out that the policy had the opposite effect – many of those pressed into service caught the addiction and later volunteered to remain in submarines. However, by 1990, without much prospect of new submarines, Maritime Command had to take further steps to ensure that a sufficient number of officers were entering the service. Now officers can be conscripted, or can volunteer for submarines *before* they have earned their surface bridge watchkeeping tickets.

With the perennial manpower shortage and a retention rate of about 50 percent after five years, the squadron aggressively recruits officers and men from coast to coast, visiting the military colleges, the shore establishments, and even the ships. One squadron commander, wanting to entice the grass roots to submarines, developed a summer course for sea cadets.

It is impossible to describe a "typical" modern Canadian submariner, for there is no such creature, but as a group they are undoubtedly a unique breed. Examination of this uniqueness is the best way to paint a composite portrait of them because it forms the true essence of the service.

"Canadian submariners are first-rate, aggressive and innovative," wrote a British authority in 1988.[3] So far so good – but, having quoted that, perhaps it is better to begin with a self-portrait. Using the pseudonym "Pantera Rosada" (the Pink Panther), a famous Canadian submariner wrote an article in 1985 that will help the reader gain a few insights.

Rosada says that Canadian submariners consider themselves objects of curiosity, occasional derision, and (they hope) a certain respect. They are clannish and proud, easily able to recognize another of their kind across a crowded room, and tend to organize themselves into groups. These organizations are filled with pleasantly potty individuals who believe they will one day rule the world, citing as examples submariners who are now taskforce commanders, or are in charge of whole navies. Rosada notes that a Canadian submariner's pride reaches its peak over his dolphin badge: "Provided he is equipped with Canada flashes and a Dolphin, the remainder [of his uniform] could be purple-striped pyjamas."[4]

On the more serious side, Rosada explains that Canadian submariners see themselves as superb professionals. This stems from the concentrated and closely orchestrated team effort that it takes to safely conduct the daily routines in a submarine, to say nothing of attacks. For example, if the entire crew of a minesweeper fell asleep at the same time their vessel would continue to float; if only a couple of key submariners fell asleep, their boat would sink – it is amazing how professional people can be when their safety is at stake.

Rosada also explores the paranoia exhibited exclusively by Canadian submariners. He believes there are three reasons for it: Canada's emphasis on surface ASW, which has led submariners to be viewed as the "enemy"; the fact that they have only three submarines, which has put them into a minority position; and the mistaken belief that the squadron is a threat to other projects. Although Rosada's article is an irreverent look at modern Canadian submariners, it clearly delineates the concerns that lie closest to their hearts.

A description of Canada's submariners would not be complete without an outsider's appraisal, if only to put their outrageous opinions of themselves in perspective. The combined qualities of self-reliance, innovation, stability, adaptability, aggressiveness, and compatibility that characterized the successful Canadian submariner fifty years ago are just as necessary today. However, a sailor aspiring to a trade such as sonar or radar now needs, in addition, the intelligence and skills to master the sophisticated technologies found in modern submarine systems.

For the first twenty-five years of the modern Canadian Submarine Service, those who served did so entirely voluntarily, and it was rarely the individual's first choice. Many of the men chose submarines for a change – the training and experience were good, the travel varied, and the responsibilities and challenges greater. The inducement of a hundred or so dollars extra per month in submarine pay was the primary drawing-card for some, but not many, and the informality on board appealed to others. Many officers had had their initial aspirations in the navy foiled and were attracted by the prospect of early command. A few, only a very few, regretted their choice. The vast majority got hooked in short order.

And an addiction it is. You only have to sit with a bunch of submariners to realize what their service means to them. They may grumble and groan, but they are bursting with pride to be a part of it. Their talk quickly veers to submarines and anecdotes follow fast and furious. Their sense of humour is wicked. Eyes gleam, voices become animated and their world closes in around them. Their strong comradeship develops from working closely together, sharing the same hardships, knowing their jobs, and relying on shipmates whom they respect. The outsider soon realizes that this is a closed and happy fraternity. He may envy it but he cannot join.

Submariners do not think they are the best, they *know*, with deep and utter conviction, that they are the best. Their belief is not surprising when their training and service are examined. Submariners are worked, tested, schooled, tested again, made to escape from 100 feet (30.5 m) underwater, tested again, pressurized, frozen, locked up, nearly drowned, gassed, and tested some more. And that is just the start – they still have to go to sea to earn their Dolphins. They suffer the indignity of being SPUTs (surface pukes under training) on their first boat and then they must study, practise, be tested, study some more, be tested again until they can identify everything in the submarine, respond to every conceivable emergency correctly, and do their own jobs to perfection. On their next submarine, the newly qualified submariners are worked even harder, in an area so small they sometimes wonder how they can breathe. They may share their bunks with a torpedo and sleep in clothes that they may not have a chance to change in three weeks. They have itchy growths of beard and all they get for a shower is a "bird-bath." If they can take it, it is small wonder that submariners *know* they are the best.

If pushed to think of something negative about serving in submarines most submariners mention fatigue as the most trying aspect of their life at sea. For submariners' families, though, the negative effects can be more pronounced. All naval families cope with separation, but submarine officers' wives also have to accept their husbands' utter dedication to their careers. This focus is visceral and total – for an ambitious officer to move continually towards a successful Perisher, it has to be. Some wives find it hard to play second fiddle to a boat and an ambition, but they do it because they must. Divorce is common in the Canadian Submarine Service, but no more so than in the general population.

Sadly, submarines are becoming an unrealistic career option in the 1990s. By the end of the decade there may be no submarines left for men to serve in or for officers to command. Even before the O boats entered their senior years, any officer choosing a submarine career knew that he could not stay in it until his retirement, as he might in other countries. Many former Canadian submarine captains leave the navy after their "drive" but those who remain move on to shore jobs, command of a destroyer, perhaps later command of the squadron. After that, anything goes, even flag rank. However, very few submariners reach the exalted rank where they can truly influence procurement and operations. The men, by comparison, can serve in submarines for their whole career, but not many do because their career progression in the Canadian navy is based upon the surface fleet. Even though submariners assume more responsibilities earlier, no one gets promoted faster than their surface cousins – the same time in rank, the same courses, etc., still apply.

Canadian submariners have to be English-speaking males, of any age. It is one of the few situations in which the Charter of Rights is not contravened, because when certain ships were designated French-speaking units the boats simply did not happen to be chosen. French Canadians have been under-represented in the submarine service – few have volunteered – but they can and do serve in them as long as their English-language profile meets the required standard. To date only one francophone, Commander J.A.Y. Plante, CD, has commanded a Canadian submarine; he went on to become the squadron commander.

Canada's submarines remain the only all-male preserve in the navy. When the ships, trades, and occupations were opened to women, and the possibility of females serving in submarines was investigated, the officials discovered that the boats were unsuitable even for the men who were already there. It quickly became a non-issue. There is an old story that says it all – a sailor wrote to Agriculture Canada, describing the dimensions and living conditions in the fore-ends and asked their experts how many pigs could be kept there. "Only three pigs could exist in those conditions," came the reply.

Nowadays men and officers can volunteer for submarines at any age, but officers are warned that the older they are, the smaller is their chance of becoming a commanding officer. This is not discrimination, but is based on performance statistics – submarine officers reach their peak for command in their late twenties and early thirties.

Submariners' lives at sea can be hectic or boring. There is not much in between. When they are not sleeping or on watch, they engage in all sorts of activities to pass the time. They enjoy bridge, cribbage, Scrabble, Monopoly, uckers, and chess, and messes challenge each other to tournaments, which are hotly contested. Some, for whom games do not appeal, write or draw for the submarine's newspaper. Others prefer model-building and all appreciate the current movies specially provided for them – *Das Boot* was a great favourite. Some commanding officers keep personal logs – collections of messages, photos, drawings, etc. – which essentially become a record of their time in command.

Most submarines have a newspaper, which is a combination of gossip sheet, information bulletin, and critical review. The captains act as editors-in-chief, ensuring that the special tone of the paper is maintained; without exception they are irreverent, funny, and rude. One captain opened his inaugural edition by asking for "almost anything including dits, yarns, lies, cartoons, quizzes, contests, character assassinations (within reason) or whatever else you can think of."[5] He was swamped. The papers are distributed at sea and are usually shredded before coming alongside.

One memorable outcome of off-watch time was the numerical DOL-PHIN CODE, completed by the officers of HMCS/M *Okanagan* in July 1976. The code was designed to abbreviate electronic communication from Canadian submarines, and to make their sometimes very rude signals more acceptable. The Canadian submariners achieved a world first, but they based their DOLPHIN CODE shamelessly on the better-known FALCON CODE of the aviators. The flyboys' code had been in use for several years and the submariners were at the short end of it frequently. They retaliated by using it themselves, for lack of anything better, but longed for a code of their own.

A few examples include:

5 = I was unaware that medical standards had been revised.
You must be as blind as a bat.
12 = I am surfaced (surfacing) because:
a. I must make repairs
b. I wish to bail out water
c. Your chances of locating me are negligible otherwise.
d. I wish to barbecue the next meal.
17 = It is difficult to believe that you and I are operating in the same ocean.
32 = If you're so good, why aren't you in submarines?

Since the Canadian submarines started using it, the DOLPHIN CODE has been adopted by most Western submarine services. It was used in the Falklands war by the Brits, and the Soviets were presented with a copy in 1986 by Captain(N)* Keith Nesbit, CD, the CO who started the whole idea. Rumour has it that the Russians are beginning to use it, and Nesbit can't wait for the day when DOLPHIN 67.E comes through the ether for a Canadian submarine. (67.E means "RPC for sarnies and sludge," which translates into "Request the pleasure of your company for sandwiches and beer.")

Today the Canadian submarine training of officers and men is a mixture of home-grown and British courses. The non-commissioned members

---

* The (N) designation differentiates the naval ranks from those in the army, which are lower.

continue to do their basic classroom course at the Fleet School in Halifax, followed by their submarine qualification at sea (on-the-job training, or OJT), which remains much as Gigg introduced it in 1966. The only difference today is the addition of the conscripts. After the basic course most who pass go straight to sea for their OJT; a few who need specialist courses go to England first, and may also do their escape training there, though now it can be done in Halifax. The OJT lasts an average of six months and concentrates on safety and then on the details of each department. Every SPUT has a "sea daddy": an experienced submariner who helps him through his practical training. At the end of the qualification time he receives the coveted Dolphins, and even for a conscript it is a moment of deep satisfaction.

There is no doubt that the first few months in a submarine are different for the volunteer and the conscript. It is a time of challenge and excitement for those who chose the life but a tough adjustment for the conscripts, who miss going onto the upper deck for some fresh air, loathe the wicked motion of a submarine on the surface in heavy weather, and find they can never get away from people, the smells, and the discomfort. Wise sea daddies assist the SPUTs over this hump and the conscripts who are sensible reserve judgement.

All submariners based on the east coast did their escape training in England until 1991. They generally took it after the classroom phase of submarine training, but sometimes during their OJT. Now Canada does her own wet escape training in Halifax. The after-ends of *Olympus*, the harbour training boat acquired from the RN in 1989, were converted to enable the after escape tower to be flooded. This "at-home" solution does not permit pressurizing the water, but it saves money and the submariners get regular refreshers.

In the early decades Canadian submarine officers, unlike the men, took the classroom phase of their basic training (SOTC) with the Royal Navy. In 1981 that changed and a Canadian SOTC was established at the Fleet School (Halifax), as a hedge against the day when the RN closed their diesel/electric training facilities. The course lasts sixteen weeks and there are usually six to ten volunteer and conscript trainees. Before their OJT the SOTC officers do two more essential courses – on torpedoes and on the submarines' fire control system.

The demanding officers' OJT lasts between six and twelve months. Two months' is devoted to the complicated task of trimming the submarine, and even after that phase is completed the trainees will not be left alone for long – the ability to cope with emergencies while on the trim takes longer. They also learn to keep watch with the periscope, or on the surface with only a gyro, a lookout, and a microphone to aid them. They feel very much alone on the bridge, but they quickly learn that with their seamen's eyes, and common sense, they can keep their boat safe without much technology. Several more months of study and practice routines in the various compartments of the submarine follow and then the new submarine officers proudly put up their dolphins and are ceremoniously thrown over the side.

Any specialist courses that are required are taken with the RN after the officers have earned their dolphins, in contrast to the men's training progression, in which they are taken first. The Canadian navy has neither the money nor the numbers of officers to warrant setting up its own courses. And then, there is Perisher ...

CHAPTER TWENTY-FOUR

COMMANDING OFFICERS' QUALIFYING COURSE

Pass or Perish!

Perisher, the Royal Navy Submarine Commanding Officers' Qualifying Course, remains the ultimate goal of all Canadian submarine officers except engineers who are ineligible. It is what they live for, dream about, and prepare for throughout their careers. When they are not talking about their sports cars and sweethearts over a beer in the squadron wardroom, they are talking about Perisher.

Perisher has endured without a break since the inaugural course in September 1917, which was probably attended by a Canadian – Lt. Willie Maitland-Dougall, RCN. Although the course has lengthened over the years, and now reflects the modern equipment and the advent of nuclear-powered submarines, it still teaches the art and science of submerged attack. Today's Perisher also expects the potential captain to be able to conduct all types of operations in every conceivable circumstance in war and peace, all the while safeguarding his boat. Last but definitely not least, Perisher examines the officers' leadership skills.

Time magazine called Perisher the most expensive and most difficult course in the world. The Royal Navy did not dispute the reporter's estimate of $2.3 million per candidate, which was made several years ago, though Canada actually pays $365,000 per student (1990 dollars). The higher figure includes the overheads of several surface ships and submarines used during the sea phases. A prospective surface-ship captain takes no equivalent training to prepare him for, or to prove him worthy of, his command. There is nothing else quite like Perisher, though TOP GUN, for U.S. naval fighter pilots, has some similarities.

Every Canadian submarine officer aspires to early command. From the first day he joins the squadron a young officer works single-mindedly towards Perisher. He thinks about it an inordinate amount of his time. It becomes the be-all and end-all to his existence, and he listens in awe to older officers' tales of *their* Perishers. He knows his Perisher will be the greatest challenge he will ever face. He knows that he will learn his own outer limits, his weaknesses, and his strengths as never before. He knows that if he passes it will be the greatest personal triumph of his life. Everything hinges on it – his submarine career, his self-esteem, his reputation. Everything to lose and everything to gain. Pass or perish!

There are many recipes for preparation for Perisher – almost as many as there are candidates. Some do little besides utilizing their sea time, others practise mental arithmetic endlessly, and still more work on visualizing attacks. The build-up to the course peaks when an officer reaches second-in-command (XO). He holds this position in a Canadian submarine for two years, and if he has an accommodating CO he gets to handle the boat and practise attacks. This is really the key to success. If he measures up, the aspiring CO will be recommended for Perisher by his captain. If the squadron commander agrees with the analysis, a place on a future Perisher is booked for him.

The First Canadian Submarine Squadron attempts to be very selective in the matter of whom they send on Perisher, but the very small number of qualified officers has often meant that all XOs were sent. Failure is very expensive, not only for the country, but also for the squadron, and it is devastating for the officer – he will never serve at sea in submarines again, and it may restrict his advancement in other branches of the navy. He will always bear the stigma of a "failed Perisher."

Though the media have on occasion screamed that Canada has more Perisher failures than other countries, it is not true. Canadians have averaged a 60 percent pass rate, the same as everyone else's. What makes a run of failures difficult in a small squadron is that the shortage of qualified COs is felt more acutely than in the larger submarine services. In the '80s the squadron began a formal effort to give its officers better preparation for Perisher, after four students in a row failed and one quit in mid-course.

The ensuing investigation found two major reasons for the failures. First, the Canadian officers did not have enough operational experience, and the XOs were not getting sufficient hands-on attack practice. Second, the squadron commanders were unable to make an accurate judgement on the readiness of the potential Perishers – they generally observed them during normal submarine routines rather than while attacking. Thus the decision to load an XO on Perisher had begun to be based more on seniority than merit.

The main result of the inquiry was the implementation of the Submarine Officers' Continuation Training (SOCT), which began in the spring of 1988. The course, known as "mini-Perisher," takes place twice a year and provides the officers with their essential attacking practice. All senior sub-lieutenants and above participate, six at a time, and an officer will take the course six to eight times before he faces Perisher itself. It is held on an operational boat, at sea, and the surface fleet provides target services as requested by the squadron. As in the real thing, there is a "Teacher" (the squadron commander) who teaches and drills the participants, and maintains safety when inexperience endangers the submarine. The SOCT never approaches the difficulty of Perisher, but rather focuses on the development of an officer's eye, his ability to form accurate mental images of what is occurring on the surface, his mental agility, and his attacking drill.

The Submarine Officers' Continuation Training already has a growing reputation – the word from the Royal Navy Teachers, whose opinion is the one that counts, is that the Canadians are now the best-prepared officers taking Perisher. The British, Australian, and Dutch navies each want to observe the course to see for themselves what is making the Canadians so successful.

An aspiring submarine CO with about ten years of submarine time leaves the First Canadian Submarine Squadron to take his Perisher with much less anxiety these days. In fact, since the introduction of SOCT, every Canadian who has gone on Perisher has passed. But even in the '90s, however good a submarine officer appears to be, he can still fail – there is no surefire method of predicting the outcome.

So what is this legendary course like? The best way to describe it is to follow the experiences of a fictitious twenty-nine-year-old lieutenant as he takes his Perisher in the mid-1980s. "Scott Melton" volunteered for service in Canadian submarines immediately after graduation from military college nine years ago. He is clever, full of energy, and very proud of his achievements in his career. He has the blessing of his CO and the squadron commander, who both feel he will do well. Scott also has an understanding wife who will not see him for six months.

On arrival at the British submarine headquarters near London, Scott joins eleven other officers from NATO and foreign navies, with whom he will train. They meet their two Teachers who will guide, teach, and judge them throughout the course and listen to FOSM's words of welcome and warning. The young officers attend an informal dinner with their Teachers that evening and both sides size one another up in an atmosphere of palpable tension. From the moment he arrived, Scott has been under observation. Night and day, at sea and in port, working and playing, stressed and even while relaxing, the Perisher is watched; he knows it, and must try not to be intimidated. But Scott knows he is not in competition with his fellow students – he merely has to meet the standard, but what a standard! The Teachers encourage the Perishers to work together and develop close relationships, which provide support and help each candidate do his best. The first dinner starts the process.

The pressure is on Scott and the others immediately – some of it is self-inflicted, but the rest is deliberately applied by Teacher. One thing is certain, it is unrelenting. Dismissal can occur at any time and most Perishers admit to feeling, at least once during the course, that they are bound to fail. Scott even heard one student acknowledge it on the first night. The Canadian, in contrast, kept silent, not wanting to display a lack of confidence.

The Royal Navy's Commanding Officers' Qualifying Course is divided into two distinct phases during its six-month span – a safety phase and an operational phase – both of which use simulators and real submarines. The safety phase comes first and concentrates on instilling the practised routines that protect the submarine and her crew during torpedo attacks, as well as honing the attacking skills of each student. The operational phase teaches submarine tactics – the art of conducting covert missions and working as a member of an ASW team.

The twelve officers form two groups, each with one Teacher, and the work begins at *Dolphin* in the south of England or at Faslane in Scotland. The safety weeks begin in the submarine simulators known as attack teachers. In these working mock-ups of a submarine's control room the Perishers can make mistakes and learn from them with no dire effects. The simulators are highly computerized and are manned in the same way as a real submarine control room, with Perishers in supporting roles when they are not at the periscope. The computer simulates the boat's controls and systems, including sonar, while at the same time presenting a real-time image of ships in the periscope. Even though the attack teachers are familiar to the aspiring COs, the first morning with Teacher watching brings damp palms. The Perishers spend several weeks doing attack after attack here, turn and turn about.

They begin with a series of single-ship torpedo attacks, which take about fifteen minutes each to develop and conclude. The student has to manoeuvre the submarine into a firing position and fire the torpedo, while remaining safe and anticipating the actions of the ship, which may be trying to elude or attack him. It is a time of tension, frantic activity, and total concentration, which leaves each student drained. After the first few days of this the future COs are circumspect – all have been advised politely, criticized publicly, and yelled at by Teacher. Occasionally, they have been encouraged. All have made mistakes that they would prefer to forget. Every evening Teacher debriefs each on the day's activities and discusses progress. Scott is finding that his self-criticism, essential for his continuing improvement, is developing. He feels he has a long way to go before he can be sure of passing. The Canadian is surprised how low he gets when he makes a bad attack at the end of the day; he is anxious to combat the depression so that it will not affect his performance next day. He discovers that the others have the same feelings, which makes Scott feel a little better.

Later, in the simulator phase, Teacher increases the complexity of the attacks until a student is managing up to four ships at a time – one of which might be coming straight at the submarine at 30 knots, with the others weaving around him. Several things are certain – the targets are always unpredictable, the mental gymnastics to calculate ranges and speeds instantaneously are continuous, the constant timed looks through the periscope never let up, the requirement to plan a good torpedo firing is paramount, and the calculation of when to go deep if a ship turns towards him must always be accurate. There is little room for error and it adds up to superior effort. Sometimes the activity and concentration so involves a student that he forgets to fire his torpedoes. Scott has not had this happen to him yet, but he understands how it can.

By now the Perishers are working well together, and drawing much closer to one another. They bolster each other up when they get low, congratulate one another after good attacks, and help when necessary. Scott finds he can talk about his feelings more openly now, without fear of censure or shame. The first stage is almost over and Scott is still on the course; however, he still remains unsure if he has what it takes to finish it. One non-English-speaking candidate has already gone because he could not cope with the language.

And then there were five.

The multi-ship attacks that bring the simulator phase to a close are unlikely to be encountered in modern-day submarine warfare, and Teacher has to remind his charges that they do them as a way to prove that they are capable of safe command. And a Perisher who knows he can cope with four ships will derive much confidence from the knowledge. Scott is just relieved he is still on his feet.

The embryo submarine captains now continue the safety weeks at sea. The two groups join up again in Scotland, where they will all "command" a submarine and conduct rotating attacks. Boisterous conversation breaks out between the students as they make the sea crossing to the Isle of Arran in the Clyde to their hotel. They all catch a glimpse of the two Perisher boats which will be their workplace, but when one of the frigates that will be running for them heaves into view, the discussion peters out. Each man contemplates the next hurdle – they all know that the time of clear computer images in the periscope of the simulator is behind them.

For the next three weeks, the Perishers put in gruelling sixteen-hour days. On the first day at sea no one derives any comfort from the warm familiarity of the O boat. Scott is desperately nervous, and later all agree that the first at-sea attack is the worst. Teacher chooses one frigate of the four he has at his disposal for the first attacks and stations himself at the search periscope, where he controls everything. It is now that Teacher begins to show his particular strengths for the job – which include vigilance, patience, understanding, and diplomacy. He endeavours to draw the best out of each student and only extricates them from danger at the last minute so they can experience most of the consequences of their mistakes.

The students closet themselves in the goatshed while they wait for Teacher to prepare the first attack. All are demonstrating symptoms of acute anxiety – silence, chain-smoking, throwing up, or talking incessantly. Scott is withdrawn and pale, fidgeting with his stopwatch hung around his neck – oblivious of his surroundings. The Perishers still work as an attack team during each other's performances, as they did in the simulator, except that the one who has the next attack endures the wait alone.

The Perisher who is acting as CO is not appraised solely on his attacking performance, as he was in the simulator. Now he manoeuvres the boat in and out of harbour, dives and surfaces, directs the crew, avoids detection, and presses home torpedo attacks – all the while keeping his boat safe. In all but fact, he is the captain. It is his ability to handle this multiplicity of tasks under fierce pressure and scrutiny that Teacher evaluates. A brilliant attacker will not pass Perisher if he does not gain the crew's confidence, or if he sails into danger.

Scott Melton waits for his first turn at sea. The hour seems both interminable and instantaneous. Then he steps into the control room trying to conceal his nervous shakes. Above all Scott knows he must act confidently. He survives his first "real" Perisher attack, not brilliantly but not badly either. "Thank heavens that's over. I feel better now. I think I could do another," he says to no one in particular. He gulps down scalding coffee as he goes through the details of his attack. He will not feel nauseated again.

The student captains do about four attacks each day, a rugged total of twenty for their Teacher, who takes part in each one. He debriefs the Perishers after each attack, while the frigates make a run for the other Perisher boat. Teacher is aware that some students are shaping up well and others are struggling a little. One is doing poorly.

As the long, hard days move along, Teacher adds ships. The Perishers are now juggling three or even four frigates, along with the local fishing boats and ferries. Many students leave it too late to go deep to avoid being run over; they suffer the ignominy of Teacher intervening and yelling "Flood Q!" Always a black mark. Scott cringes at the memory of his misjudgment. But slowly he is improving, feeling more sure of himself and sounding more like a real submarine captain. He finds he can rely on his mental calculations and his visualization of the surface with accuracy and certainty. However, putting the periscope segments together in the mind's eye is proving almost impossible for one Perisher. Scott recognizes his colleague's increasing strain but his attempts to help are rebuffed.

Then Scott has a bad day and it ends with a simply awful attack, probably the worst he has done so far at sea. All his assurance deserts him and he blindly stumbles into the goatshed to be alone with his frustration. He is sure that Teacher will dismiss him and he cringes when he recalls how failed Perishers are treated. Submariners are always uncertain about how to approach one of their own who did not make the grade. It is rather like a death.

Scott does not hear the first summons from Teacher. When he does, he jumps up and puts on his hat. In the captain's cabin, Teacher sits slumped over the tiny table, a glass of whisky at his elbow. His face is solemn.

"You sent for me, sir?" Scott mumbles.

"Yes, come in and sit down. I'm sure you know why."

"It's the end, isn't it?" blurts the Canadian, wondering how he is going to take it.

"No, no, not at all," Teacher says gently. "I thought you could do with some encouragement. Attacks like your last one happen to all of us just when we think we've got it in the bag." He pours a good dollop of whisky into an awaiting glass. Scott savours it – it is the finest malt.

"I appreciate your understanding, but why did I make such a hash of it just when I was beginning to feel OK?"

"It is for the very reason that you were beginning to rest on your laurels a bit that your concentration relaxed. I want you to know that I believe if you go on improving as you have been you will make a fine submarine CO."

"Thanks, sir!" replies a much relieved Scott, and he returns to the goatshed smiling broadly.

A week before the safety phase ends, the students throw a traditional mess dinner for the officers of the two Perisher boats, to thank them for their support. Though the course is not over and one failure has occurred, this dinner is given early so that the students are still together – during the final week the failures will have left, minutes after they are told. A lone piper leads the diners into the dining room for an excellent meal, speeches, and much drunken frivolity. No one is in bed before 0300 and they are not expected back at sea until Monday morning.

The Perishers start the final week with a series of highly complex attacks, which will essentially make or break them as future submarine captains. By Tuesday it is clear that Scott's friend will not meet the standard, however much practice he gets – he is unable to visualize the surface, is getting irritable, and worst of all is often dangerous. Meanwhile, Scott is going from strength to strength, having conducted a series of well-executed, difficult attacks. He is sure he will pass now and his eyes have a sparkle they did not have earlier in the course. That night the hotel's Perisher bar is unusually empty as the anxiety over failure mounts – the students, however confident they are about their own performances, cannot face their failing friends.

On Thursday Teacher gives the failing student most of the attacks to do in the morning, but it does not help; Teacher is continually extricating the boat from danger. Eventually the real captain surfaces the submarine while Teacher calls the student into his cabin. Teacher's own steward hovers outside. A few minutes later, Teacher, the student, and the steward march down to the main hatch and climb the ladder to the casing. Sadly, Teacher bids his student farewell, feeling he has failed too. The student and steward, with a comforting bottle of whisky in his pocket, climb into a waiting launch. The experienced NCO stays with the student, comforts him, collects his already packed baggage from the hotel, and sees him home. The departure of a failed Perisher does not always happen like this – it depends on Teacher. Sometimes the students may take a farewell glass of malt together in the wardroom and see their friend off on the casing.

And then there were four.

The rest of the Perishers expected the loss of their fellow student, but it is still a shock. There, but for the grace of God, go I ... , thinks Scott, who finds that the pleasure in his own sure success is tinged with genuine sadness. The Perisher bar is full again that night and the patrons have to shout to make themselves heard.

At the end of the next day Teacher formally tells the remaining students that they have met the standard and opens a bottle of champagne to celebrate. The new COs are reluctant to show their intense delight because they still have not finished Perisher, only passed the safety phase. Now they are facing more classroom, simulator, and submarine time, which will be just as demanding as the first half, but their new-found confidence makes it less intimidating. The first thing Scott does when he gets ashore is to phone his wife. Second, he gets blind drunk. Then he sleeps.

In the operational phase of Perisher, now that the students have proved they can handle a submarine expertly and safely, they concentrate on tactics. Submarines must attack not only ships but also other submarines, and they conduct covert operations that include photography, reconnaissance, and personnel transfers in and out of hostile territory. Combined ASW operations with surface ships and aircraft are also part of any submarine's repertoire. During this phase the students command a submarine for twenty-four-hour periods, plan and execute operations, lead the ship's company and administer the boat's needs. The time is more realistic and the Perishers have fewer rules to follow, which allows their own creativity to emerge. Scott finds himself looking forward to this phase: he is more relaxed. He has three good friends on whom he can rely when the going gets tough, and most of all he has his wonderful new confidence. He believes that there is little that will surprise him.

However, during the first sea-week of this phase another student fails. This time the removal is dramatic. The student is lifted off by helicopter, a shattered and a deeply disappointed man. Scott is upset – he did not expect this one – and it severely bruises his colleagues too, until Teacher reminds them to get on with the job.

And then there were three.

For the last week, the submarine has been "at war" with a couple of frigates and aircraft, and the Perishers are revelling in the competition. The remaining three are tired, more tired than they can ever recall. Sleep comes only in occasional catnaps and Scott wonders if fatigue can be terminal. They keep one step ahead of the ASW forces arrayed against them, lay mines, photograph a hostile destroyer underwater, and enter some small bays to do reconnaissance. At last the final day of the course dawns – they are to land and later pick up four commandos near an enemy beach, which is heavily patrolled. The Canadian will do the recovery.

Scott takes over command in the early hours of the morning and looks through the periscope. "What a filthy night!" he announces to the control room. He can see so little in the murk that the pick-up of the commandos will have to be done using sonar. The Canadian makes a cautious approach to the rendezvous and waits at periscope depth – the commandos are late. Why don't they come? At last something is heard in the sonar room and Scott leaps to the periscope. He knows where they should be, but cannot see them. Scott has to be certain before he surfaces. Again he strains to locate them and again he fails. Another Perisher has a look – no luck either. Teacher tells them to look again and then offers the Canadian the larger search periscope, saying, "Look dead astern!" Scott can just make them out, right where they should be. He safely surfaces the submarine, recovers the commandos and is deep again within ten minutes. Scott's Perisher is over.

Teacher invites the three successful Perishers into the wardroom for a celebration. It is handshakes all round and huge wide grins. This time the students do not repress their feelings – they have triumphed. Messages, which they all plan to retrieve for framing, go out to their respective navies announcing their success. Teacher announces the Perishers' future commands – Scott has HMCS/M *Okanagan*. The new COs toast their Teacher and thank him profusely. They know that they will turn to him for advice over the years and that he will always hold a special place in their hearts.

As the Perisher boat heads to Faslane during the rest of the night, the students sleep. They arrive just as the sky is lightening, in time for the final ritual. This is a breakfast in the old tradition with porridge, eggs and bacon, venison and quail, and all the trimmings. It is followed at 0900 with port; plenty of port. Then Lieutenant(N) Scott Melton, the new Canadian submarine commanding officer, phones his wife with the news, tells her he loves her and falls into bed.

Scott returns to the First Canadian Submarine Squadron with his honour intact. He is now a member of a very elite group: he can hold court in the wardroom and tell *his* stories to the beardless "subbies" who hang on his every word. Scott will take over *Okanagan* in a matter of weeks. He cannot wait to be piped aboard his own boat – it will be the second proudest moment of his life.

Perisher has changed significantly since the mid-'80s, though this account does not detract from the layman's understanding of the newer course. The Royal Navy's emphasis now is on nuclear-powered boats, having reduced their diesel/electric fleet and eliminated O boats. The safety weeks are almost entirely conducted in the Attack Trainer, now renamed the Command Team Trainer, and the Perishers experience one week at sea. It is not only the expense that has made this alteration necessary, but also the nature of submarine warfare itself, which is now much more submarine versus submarine. The tactical phase has also seen its sea time first curtailed and then eliminated.

The First Canadian Submarine Squadron is reluctantly looking at alternatives to the British Perisher, because it is now almost exclusively geared for SSN/SSBN command. If the government decides to replace the O boats the navy may choose to develop its own Perisher and the Submarine Continuation Training course, though it was not begun for this reason, will provide a stepping stone towards this fundamental change in tradition.

CHAPTER TWENTY-FIVE

REJUVENATING THE O BOATS, 1980–1986

… of SOUP and teeth and spare tires

The Canadian Submarine Service never grew, even during the Cold War when submarines became the primary ASW platform and other navies embraced them as vital capital ships. The resulting imbalance in the modern Canadian navy was more puzzling still, in view of the country's reliance on sea lines of communication, her North American and NATO commitments, and the immense length of her coastline. Though the navy was unsuccessful in acquiring more boats, the squadron eventually became more operational, though not because of the above demands or a changing maritime strategy. The reason was partly squadron pressure but mostly, ironically enough, the fact that the submarines' progressive obsolescence reduced their value as effective clockwork mice – which released them from serving the fleet. The Canadian Oberons' aging and the delay in their replacement made a major upgrade necessary, to keep them and their weapons effective.

The Canadian navy made repeated attempts to acquire more submarines during the next decade. When the Trudeau government axed the second batch of three Oberons in 1968, the navy pressed for one more for the west coast. Britain refused to build Canada another O, but did offer a much older *Porpoise*-class submarine, which the navy declined. The next attempt occurred in 1974 after *Rainbow* was decommissioned. Two submariners (Commanders Jim Wood and Cliff Crow) at NDHQ tried for another U.S. boat, but their effort was stymied by senior officers who felt the money should be held for a future replacement program. The earmarked funds disappeared into general use shortly afterwards.

Wood and Crow, who had each commanded an O boat and who would become squadron commanders, carried the flame alone through the mid-'70s eventually trying again in a proposal to acquire ten to twelve boats. This shocked the surface-oriented navy, but the pair's continued determination paid off – the proposal was finally incorporated in the long-term plan for the Canadian Armed Forces. If Wood and Crow had not persisted, the navy probably would not have considered submarines at all.

Next came some unsolicited offers for a west coast submarine. Perhaps hearing of Wood and Crow's work, the Americans made a low-level initiative to sell used Barbels to Canada. It failed to get to first base. Then in 1978 Britain offered Canada a "new-to-you" Oberon, which needed modernization. This scheme looked very hopeful for a while, especially after Treasury Board approved the funds. However CDS, General R.M Withers, CMM, CD, decided against it at the last moment, echoing his predecessor that the $11.25 million to upgrade the O would be better spent on a replacement program. In retrospect, his decision appears questionable, but probably felt right at the time. Finally, the French offered Canada a nuclear-powered submarine for $50 million. The navy apparently discussed the proposal with some seriousness, but the logistics of operating a sole SSN must have invalidated the offer. After this the Canadian navy made no further attempts to procure a fourth submarine for the west coast – their eyes were by now firmly focused on a new and larger submarine fleet for the future.

By the end of the '70s the navy realized that they would have to finesse *Ojibwa, Onondaga,* and *Okanagan* into old age. The boats were unable to operate effectively because of their out-dated equipment, poor torpedoes, and incipient lack of spares. Submarines deteriorate in two significant ways. The pressure hulls wear out slowly but inexorably, with very grim consequences if they are not watched closely; and the equipment and weapons become outdated quickly as technology accelerates, though the process is unlikely to sink the boat.

Submariners take their pressure hulls very seriously – the steel has to be free from all fatigue and the hull has to be perfectly circular. The Canadian hulls are regularly checked and the frequency of examinations increases as the boats grow older. In 1990 the submarines met all the requirements for safe diving, but when their hulls fail any of the tests, they will not be allowed to dive so deeply again or at all. This is expected to occur in the 1990s.

By 1980 the O boats' original analogue equipment was hampering the submarines' capabilities – the fire control system was obsolete as early as 1975, their sensors were seriously limiting their detection skills, and the Mark 37C torpedoes were increasingly unreliable and hard to maintain. Spare parts, which had to come from England, were becoming scarce and more expensive. Something had to be done. The ambitious modernization program was called SOUP (the Submarine Operational Up-date Program), the weapons update was not named, and the scheme for ensuring an ongoing supply of spares was to become known as the Logistic Support Agreement (LSA).

The preparations for SOUP began in 1978 and the program was approved in February 1979. Crow actually wrote the SOUP proposal for four submarines, not three, as the acquisition of the used Oberon had looked so certain. The program aimed to make the submarines useful and competitive again but could not extend their lifespan. The boats were SOUPed up during their mid-life refits in the 1980s.

The vacuum tube fire control system was replaced by a state-of-the-art digital Singer Librascope Mark 1 from the U.S.A. The navy purchased four of these and used the last one, originally destined for the fourth boat, in the attack trainer ashore. This very sophisticated system not only provides target tracking and control of torpedo firings, but also gives the command team a display of tactical information, all of which is controlled by a real-time computer.

The sonar suite was extensively upgraded, though replacement of the active sonar had to wait until more money was available. A Sperry micropuffs passive ranging sonar, which can determine a target's range, bearing, course, and speed, was installed under the upper casing on the pressure hull. This system can track up to four targets simultaneously, giving continuous updates on their status, which are fed directly into the new fire-control system for an attack solution. The data from the long-range passive sonar (which has not been replaced) and the periscope can also be fed into the new fire-control system. The old short-range passive sonar, the 719, was removed.

During SOUP all three submarines were wired to receive the American Mark 48 torpedoes, which were a separate procurement. Other purchases included a new gyro, SATNAV (Satellite Navigation), a Doppler log, new radio and internal communications systems, new underwater telephones, and high-endurance batteries. SOUP also provided the search periscope with an image intensifier, which allows remarkable night vision and the attack periscope with a low-light television recording capability. The navy also established a new Submarine Operational Support Centre in the Fleet School at Halifax to train personnel on the new equipment.

The three mid-life refits and SOUP took one submarine away from operations continuously from 1980 to 1986. *Ojibwa*, being the first built, was the first to undergo modernization. Her mid-life refit was already under way in 1979 when word came to crank up the pace to include SOUP which ran concurrently. *Okanagan* was the last to be finished in 1986. In the end SOUP came in on time and on budget ($45 million), even though there had been considerable inflation over the course of the program.

The results of SOUP, were gratifying. The submariners, delighted with the new systems, stayed in longer and volunteers increased. The upgrade slowed down the submarines' deterioration from an equipment point of view, and if the hulls can take it, they should be able to operate into the late '90s. Whether they will remain effective that long is another question altogether.[1]

For years the Canadian Submarine Service had been dissatisfied with its outdated Mark 37C torpedoes, originally purchased from the United States as a cheap, standardized NATO weapon. The government was reluctant to endorse their replacement because they did not want a costly modification made to aging boats when new ones were on the horizon. After a long tussle, Cabinet finally approved the American Mark 48 torpedoes for the O boats in February 1985, on the understanding that they were really for the new submarines whose acquisition program was under way.

The torpedo program, at $125 million, was much more expensive than SOUP because each Mark 48 cost $1.2 million. The price included the weapons themselves and the alterations to the submarines, but not the facilities to maintain the costly beasts. Those required an additional $18 million and were incorporated into the submarine replacement program. As the Os had originally been built for long, 21-inch (53 cm) torpedoes, they were not difficult to modify.

The Mark 48s, coupled with SOUP, have given the old Oberons longer, sharper teeth and have made them a force to be reckoned with once more. The new wire-guided weapons are nineteen feet long, weigh 3,480 pounds (1,578.5 kg) each, and have nearly four times the explosive power of the Mark 37s, sinking ships by exploding beneath them and breaking their backs. The 48s are impulse-fired and can run 50 km at 55 knots, at depths of about 3,000 feet (915 m). Each O boat carries up to fourteen of them, six in the tubes and about eight reloads. Interestingly, the first Mark 48 was fired by HMCS/M *Rainbow* in 1969 at the Nanoose range on Vancouver Island.

As the new submarine replacement program remains undecided, the maintenance facility for the new Mark 48 torpedoes in Canada has not been established. The squadron have their new weapons stored and maintained in the United States.

The other pressing problem for the squadron was that of spare parts for the Oberons. As the boats aged the cost of maintaining them rose exponentially and the price of spare parts soared when the Royal Navy decided to phase out their O boats in 1987. Canada had not negotiated a support contract with the British ministry of defence at the time of the Oberon purchase, though why they did not remains a mystery. In the late '80s the navy determined the technical and engineering requirements needed to keep the Os operational for another decade. The findings were not encouraging, but an unexpected offer helped them out of a tight spot.

When Margaret Thatcher privatized the supply department of the British ministry of defence, they offered Canada spares at a secure price until 1997. The renewable Logistic Support Agreement was signed in 1989. At the same time Britain sold HMS *Olympus* to Canada as a harbour training vessel. The LSA turned out to be inadequate and in 1992 the navy bought HMS/M *Osiris* to cannibalize at a bargain price of $180,000. She arrived in 22,050 pieces in 1993.

CHAPTER TWENTY-SIX

REPLACING THE O BOATS, 1983–1987

"Only consider diesel / electric boats ..."

Although submarines to replace the aging Oberons were in the long-term plan for the Canadian navy, the struggle to raise their priority and to gain governmental approval was long and painful. The process lurched along, sometimes on and sometimes off, causing wide mood swings in the submariners and the defence community. Unbelievably, the undertaking went on for more than a decade, changed horses twice in mid-stream, and was still undecided when this book went to press. The submarine acquisition program exacted its toll on personnel at all levels too – they have come, gone and come back to it; retired, resigned, and been fired from it; and even got promoted over it.

The Canadian Submarine Acquisition Program (CASAP) really began in the early 1980s, though it was as yet unofficial, unsupported, and unnamed. Wood, now a rear admiral, drove it carefully but hard, safe in the knowledge that new submarines were in the long-term plan for the navy and that no one had stopped him so far. Indeed CDS had given his tacit approval by quietly cautioning Wood to only consider diesel/electric submarines because nuclear-propelled boats would never be politically acceptable. Wood's back-room team prepared the "Future Submarine Study," which recommended eight to twelve submarines with under-ice capabilities. The report garnered little support and so Wood resolved to push harder. He announced that he wanted Cabinet approval of the program within a year.

The headlong rush to Cabinet was gruelling and not without difficulties as departments disputed costing, the acquisition methodology, and even the submarine requirements themselves. The small team also talked with the Australian submarine service who were replacing their Oberons, hoping that knowledge, time, and cost-savings might accrue if they collaborated. This joint venture proposal was incorporated into the final Cabinet document, which recommended that Canada acquire diesel/electric submarines, twelve if possible but no less than four, most of which would be built at home at a price of about $6 billion. Remember that figure!

However the proposal did not reach Cabinet for another two years. Roadblock after roadblock was put in its way, mostly by the navy itself. It seemed to the submariners that Wood's second-in-command, Commodore Chuck Thomas, CD, was reluctant to support the program and the assistant deputy minister (ADM) (Matériel), John Killick, actually obstructed it. For example, it was not until June 1983 that Thomas finally allowed staff to be dedicated to the program and set up a special submarine section in his department. This long-awaited move was crucial for the project's official recognition and clout. Bytown mess served a lot of beer that night and the toast was "CASAP!"

Three other events in May 1983 had also helped to secure CASAP's position. First, the Aussies delivered copies of their submarine Statement of Requirement and their Request for Tender, as well as an official invitation for Canada to observe their design evaluation process. Second, Thomas and Killick went to bat for CASAP, who thought they could not accept the RAN's offer and asked DCDS for $100,000 from his project development fund. Third, the report of the sub-committee on National Defence of the Standing Senate Committee on Foreign Affairs, titled *Canada's Maritime Defence,* was released. It suggested that "Canada [should acquire] seventeen submarines; ten [being] the absolute minimum,"[1] to balance the fleet and enhance their ASW capability.

Just before Wood left Ottawa to become Maritime Commander he signed the enabling Memorandum of Understanding for cooperation between Australia and Canada. And, although he had not got the submarine acquisition to Cabinet, he was satisfied that he had significantly improved and secured its place on DND's project priority list. It is also safe to say that without Wood's advocacy and determination the Canadian submarine replacement program would have languished in the shadows. CASAP naively anticipated calm seas from now on.

The second half of 1983 brought much activity to CASAP – they were preparing for the Australian trip, fine-tuning their documentation for CDS, MND, Cabinet, and the Treasury Board and starting to find out which Canadian companies were capable of building which sub-marines. But after the team arrived in Australia, Killick, through whom all plans had to pass, suddenly told CASAP to hold off for nine months. He was not going to have CASAP approach industry without Cabinet approval or have a premature submarine submission jeopardize the new frigate program.

The delay made for a very difficult time in Australia. Initially the Aussies did not make the Canadians welcome, and later Killick's edict increased their reluctance to share their material. Later the team gained invaluable information about submarine designers/builders and their boats and learned several important lessons, which resulted in Canada's refusal to collaborate with the RAN any further. Their surprising decision was upheld in December 1985, when after several investigations the RAN was proven guilty of collusion with two firms by rigging their evaluation process.

When the team got back from Australia in early 1984 they felt they could choose Canada's next submarine without further ado, but CASAP was determined not to fall into the same trap. Its focus, after declining "bulk discounts" with the RAN, was to get its own acquisition program, now standing at twelve to sixteen boats, past CDS and through Cabinet.

After the Conservative party won the Canadian general election in September 1984, CASAP waited with bated breath to see how the new government would affect it. Then all at once DND gave the go-ahead – but for only four boats, with the rest to follow. (DND thought the politicians would choke on the higher numbers.) By December CASAP's morale was high – it had its first funding and had moved into offices of its own. CASAP cranked up their pace.

At this stage CASAP was moving the project towards realization with little attention from politicians or the media. The majority of Canada's population was also still unaware of the acquisition, but would not be so much longer. CASAP welcomed a new leader at the beginning of 1985, Captain(N) Dent Harrison, CD. He was a submariner and an engineer who was respected for his hard work, experience, and integrity. He reported directly to Rear Admiral Ed Healey, CD (chief, Engineering and Maintenance [CEM]), and through him to Killick.

By now CASAP was ready for Cabinet, and as its funds were dwindling it needed to present its proposal quickly, and send it on to Treasury Board. The inevitable delay came this time from Commodore John R. Anderson, CD (Thomas's deputy), who later was to play such a key role in the program. He asked for an air-independent propulsion (AIP) retrofit to be added to the Statement of Requirement to provide the proposed boats with under-ice capability. Once the SOR was rewritten CASAP then had to persuade the tough new defence minister, Eric Nielsen, of the proposal's merit, so that he would willingly and effectively sponsor it through Cabinet. But, try as it might, CASAP could not get Nielsen to read its submission – Thomas had convinced the MND that other naval procurement had higher priority. In the end CASAP resorted to slipping the documents into Nielsen's briefcase as he left for his summer vacation in 1985. It may appear that Thomas was lukewarm towards the submarine program, but he has always denied it, explaining that naval programs must be done in stages to be successful, and indeed, the facts show that Thomas nursed major project after major project through the political hoops to implementation. He was soon to support CASAP with spirit.

Besieged by submarine sales pitches, CASAP attended only two that significantly influenced the acquisition program – one from the French navy and one from a Canadian firm. The French navy's engineering chief, in Ottawa to discuss general procurement, quietly offered Canada a diesel/electric version of their small Rubis-class SSN. However, Healey became intrigued by the Rubis's unusual nuclear reactor, which made the French SSN cost little more than modern conventionals; he wondered if this meant that Canada could aspire to SSNs. Harrison, on the other hand, was fired up by a proposal from Energy Conversion Systems Inc. (ECS) of Ottawa to put a marine version of the Slow-poke (low-power) nuclear reactor into diesel/electric boats for use under the ice.

Meanwhile Nielsen read CASAP's brief on holiday, and became immediately and personally interested in the project. He scheduled a briefing for 28 August 1985 and Harrison gave an inspired presentation while a group including chief of Defence Staff Theriault, Killick, Healey, and Thomas listened intently. The half-hour presentation stretched to two because of Nielsen's penetrating questions. "[He] was a breath of fresh air," Thomas remembered.

Near the end, Nielsen interrupted, "Was nothing prepared on nuclear-powered submarines?"

"Minister, all we give you is the art of the affordable," jumped in Theriault, the CDS.

Nielsen pointed a finger at him and rejoined, "That's my decision, not yours!" Theriault subsided.

At the end of the briefing Nielsen promised that he would seek Cabinet approval for four diesel/electric submarines no later than mid-October.

The CASAP team left the minister's office both bewildered and exhilarated – suddenly they had a minister who wanted to do something about the Canadian Submarine Service. Had the political will changed? Should they continue to work on the conventional acquisition? Would Canada really, seriously, look at SSNs? Healey certainly thought so, but few in CASAP did. Shortly afterwards, the high priority of Nielsen's Nuclear Submarine Option Study (NSOS) into the feasibility of Canada building and operating "nukes" forced them to reconsider their opinions. NSOS's work was done quietly, so that the competitors for the SSK contract would not find out – they did, of course, but not for some time.

On 11 October 1985, Nielsen kept his word and signed the memorandum to Cabinet for four SSKs. He wanted no delay to occur in this program in case SSNs were found to be impossible for Canada as they had been in the 1960s. Cabinet approved the conventional acquisition and CASAP moved to the next stage. In contrast to previous good-news days, Bytown Mess did not run out of beer – CASAP worried about the future of the diesel program.

Nielsen's ministerial colleagues were not overjoyed about the pre-feasibility study into nuclear-powered submarines. Michael Wilson opposed SSNs on financial grounds and Joe Clark positively hated them because he believed SSNs would upset the balance of power between NATO and the Warsaw Pact. The objections raised by both men presented formidable obstacles to be overcome if Canada was ever to aspire to SSNs.

Major naval procurement usually follows three steps. DND calls for an unfunded "request for proposal" (RFP) from interested companies, and after evaluation of their submissions awards the funded "project definition" (PD) contract to two (preferably) of them. The construction contract goes to the firm that produces the best PD. The diesel/electric submarine project had an additional phase at the beginning called "source qualification," which allowed the navy to find out which Canadian companies were capable of building which submarines. CASAP planned to issue the Requests for Source Qualification (RFSQs) in mid-1986, giving the firms six months to respond, and then to call for the RFPs in April 1987. This timeline allowed construction to start in 1988/89 and the first of class to commission in 1994.

The prospect of such a plum contract galvanized interested Canadian companies into a bustle of negotiations between themselves, the European designers/builders who were not allowed to compete in their own right, and the equipment manufacturers. Seven consortia emerged, comprising fifteen Canadian firms, which collectively spent millions of dollars preparing their submissions. They were told by Healey, now in Killick's old job, that they must identify the best submarine designs and combat-control systems in their RFSQs. When CASAP and other experts objected to this on the ground that Canada might end up with the wrong boat or wrong combat-control system, Healey held firm, explaining that his decision would protect the navy from cost overruns in a program of such high technical risk. CASAP also imposed a condition – the submarines had to be proven, i.e., either at sea, on order by another navy, or under construction.

There were seven available diesel/electric submarines from which the potential Canadian contractors could choose. They were the British Upholder; the Dutch Walrus (most expensive); the French diesel/electric version of their Rubis-class SSN; the German TR 1700 and IKL 2000; the Italian Sauro Super 90; the Swedish Type A47/1.

Four designs did not qualify. The French conventional Rubis class, the German IKL 2000, and the Swedish Type A 47/1 were unproven and the Italians disposed of their own bid by failing to comply with DND's deadlines. Table 2 compares the specifications of the remaining three contenders (costing about $2 billion for four) and the small French SSN.

Table 2
A Comparison of Three of the 1986 Diesel/Electric Submarines with the Small French Nuclear-Powered Submarine (Rubis)[2]

	Rubis	Tr 1700	Upholder	Walrus
Submerged Displacement	2,670	2,350	2,438	2,800
Length (Metres)	72	66	70	68
Hull Diameter (Metres)	7.6	7.6	7.6	8.6
Torpedo Tubes	4	6	6	4
Reload Weapons	14	14	14	16
Unrefuelled Range (nm)	Unlimited	15,500	8,000	10,000
Max. Speed (Knots)	25	25+	20	20
Endurance (Days At Sea)	70+	70	49	49 (?)
Battery (No. Of Cells)	None	960	480	480
Diving Depth (Metres)	300	300	200+	300+
Crew	66	32	46	45

Prior to CASAP's notable briefing to Nielsen, the newly elected Tories undertook a comprehensive defence review, and Thomas took such good steps to protect the submarine project that the requirement increased again to eight and survived a cost-cutting revision. The review was to form the basis of the first White Paper on Defence since 1971, which the Tories hoped would revitalize the armed forces so Canada could regain a louder voice abroad. A lesser priority, though touted as the main one, was the recovery of control over Canadian sovereignty, especially in the Arctic. CASAP nervously wondered if the White Paper would secure their position.

The review sparked an interest in the press and the submarine program got its first copy in both specialist magazines and daily newspapers. Speculation centred on the number of submarines Canada would purchase, whether the government was serious about Arctic sovereignty, and if it was, whether the boats would be nuclear-powered. The stories petered out because the journalists had no idea just how serious the minister of national defence was about SSNs.

However, the Nuclear Submarine Option Study was gathering steam and helped to delay the White Paper. Just before CASAP distributed its Request for Source Qualifications, the press started reporting that the navy was going to have to choose between the second and/or third batch of six frigates and SSNs because Canada could not afford both. The potential prime contractors put the items down to speculation, reassured by the new minister of national defence, Perrin Beatty, publicly announcing in July 1986 the acquisition of four diesel/electric submarines with initial funding of $49 million.

CASAP distributed the RFSQs on time, and evaluated the seven resulting submissions with regard to operational requirements, engineering, combat systems, and logistic and financial considerations. All respondents named the three designs rumoured to be CASAP's selection – British Upholder, the Dutch Walrus, and the German TR 1700 – and were allegedly chosen to receive the RFPs. The potential consortia began working on the next phase in the acquisition process, but soon were wondering why no official announcement had been made identifying the successful firms.

By now the trickle of press items on the possibility of Canada changing to nuclear-powered submarines had increased to a flood. The consortia's anxiety grew with the government's growing preoccupation with northern sovereignty, because they stood to lose millions of dollars if SSNs became the submarine of choice. The press reports reached a crescendo in April 1987 and DND had still not made the RFP announcement. "If a white paper on defence – the first in 15 years – fails to chart a nuclear course for Canada's navy, naval planners in Ottawa and Washington and submarine builders in Britain and France will eat their pocket calculators," opened the Report on Business in the *Globe and Mail* on Monday, 6 April.[3] CASAP was about to become an item, a big item.

When the ADM (Mat.) told CASAP (without giving a reason) not to issue the RFPs for the diesel/electric program the staff knew exactly what was up – Canada was going to change horses in mid-stride. Realization hit the consortia soon afterwards when, with no explanation, their RFPs failed to arrive. Several sources maintained that the potential contractors had been officially told of the switch to SSNs in April, two months before the White Paper was announced, but as CASAP itself was not warned this was unlikely.

On 6 June 1987 Captain(N) Harrison, CASAP's project manager, sat in the gallery of the House of Commons to hear the contents of DND's White Paper. When he heard the minister of national defence, Perrin Beatty, announce that Canada was going to build twelve nuclear-powered submarines, Harrison was bitterly disappointed. He said, "After working so long and hard on the SSKs, we were nearly ready to go and had every indication that eight new conventional submarines would soon be a reality for Canada."

The nation, the navy, the First Canadian Submarine Squadron, and many others around the world were stunned by the news. The initial, emotional reaction of the submariners was one of delight. It lasted about ten seconds – then common sense prevailed and everyone realized it could never happen.

Could it?

CHAPTER TWENTY-SEVEN

THE NUCLEAR-POWERED SUBMARINE ACQUISITION, 1985–1987

"From a '62 Volkswagen to an '88 Porsche"

The dynamics that drove the Canadian decision to acquire twelve nuclear-powered submarines were varied and sometimes unexpected. They revolved around personalities, skilfully manipulated facts, assumptions, and politics. Initially, the adoption of SSNs stemmed from the curiosity of Eric Nielsen, the minister of national defence in 1985. Later the project took on a life of its own, sped on its way by the navy's powerful desire. The report of Nielsen's Nuclear Submarine Option Study (NSOS) undoubtedly shaped the Tories' White Paper on Defence but, more than that, many believed that the new policy was developed *solely* to justify the SSNs.

The Nuclear Submarine Option Study was done quickly, without all the facts, and with such ambition that it could not be taken as a definitive analysis. Indeed, Nielsen intended it to be only a preliminary report on various aspects of the question: whether any country would be willing to transfer its nuclear technology to Canada, whether Canada could afford SSNs; and whether there was a suitable submarine available. Even so, at the end of 1986 Healey and Thomas's belief in NSOS's findings was so encouraging that Beatty ordered the inclusion of SSNs in the draft of the Tory defence policy. The study indicated that Canada could build twelve British or French nuclear-powered submarines for about $5 billion. Exclusive of infrastructure (another $3 billion), this sum would be spent over several years and could be cost-neutral if the third batch of frigates was scrapped.

A vitally important result of the NSOS, and a less well-known one, was the articulation of the three-ocean concept of defence, which enabled the navy to unify and to demand tasking and equipment to handle the huge naval responsibilities it implied. It also gave Beatty exactly what he needed to justify SSNs politically. The heightened Arctic responsibility, previously acknowledged but impossible to fulfil, was reinforced by recent foreign intrusions into polar waters that Canada believed were hers. Later Thomas was unable to explain why the three-ocean approach had not been used before when it was so obvious. Was it that the threat from the Arctic was insufficient? Or was it that money shortages had prevented the navy from pursuing it?

The three-ocean policy may have navigated the SSNs through the political seas, but it was also partly to blame for the SSNs foundering on the public shore. The electorate came to the conclusion that DND had developed the concept solely to justify the SSNs; after all, the Atlantic, Pacific, and Arctic oceans had always been there. Had they not always required protection? If previous governments had ever shown concern about the responsibility, even though they could not meet it, the public cynicism about the idea might have been less.

As Beatty's support grew, Healey, Thomas, and Fowler, ADM (Policy), began to treat the NSOS report as definitive rather than as a feasibility study. In retirement Healey admitted the data were sketchy, but still felt they had been sufficient to proceed. The ambitious Beatty trusted the trio's judgement when he included SSNs in the defence policy, but had the sense to include two submarine project options in the White Paper he presented to the Cabinet committees. One had SSNs and the other SSKs, though the cost, to the year 2010, was shown to be nearly equal. The SSNs caused ministerial squabbles and opposition, even though they were cost-neutral – it was simply the thought of "nukes" that spooked them.

Beatty was up against ministers like Michael Wilson (Finance) and Joe Clark (External Affairs). Wilson felt unable to justify such huge spending to the population when he was wrestling the deficit, and Clark hated the idea so much he even attempted to get his Committee on Foreign Affairs and Defence to reach a negative consensus on the inclusion of SSNs in the policy. He was unable to achieve this and observers allege that Prime Minister Mulroney acted swiftly to change his attitude. In the end, Beatty stick-handled the new defence plan through Cabinet too, using sovereignty protection, public opinion polls,[1] and the carrot of a more influential voice in world councils to gain its acceptance. The press did not report the ministers' anxiety over the White Paper until after Cabinet approved it. A month before Beatty announced it to the country, ministers started preparing the public by stating that nuclear-powered submarines were the only means of protecting Canada's northern sovereignty.

After Beatty himself said publicly that Canada was thinking of buying twelve SSNs, many newspapers ran special features on the subject, and correctly identified the British Trafalgar and French Rubis as likely contenders. More cautious, the *Globe and Mail*[2] alleged that the Cabinet had only agreed to support DND's procurement plans in principle. Foreign reaction to the speculation was muted, though independent American analysts expressed anxiety about Canada asserting her rights in the Arctic where USN submarines had reigned supreme for thirty years.

Perrin Beatty presented his eagerly anticipated defence policy, entitled Challenge and Commitment, to the House of Commons on 5 June 1987. It was very different from the last Liberal policy of 1971, stressing the three-ocean responsibility and putting Canada's own defence requirements ahead of those of NATO or North America. The plan did restate Canada's traditional security policy elements and ASW specialization. Beatty reminded Canadians that the Arctic was now the essential operating area for submarines.

It escaped no one on that historic Friday that the navy was the major beneficiary, with six more frigates, twelve nuclear-powered submarines, an underwater surveillance system for the Arctic, and new shipborne helicopters. Beatty estimated the total cost of upgrading the Canadian forces at about $200 billion spread over fifteen years, which was the equivalent of a 2 to 3 percent increase in the annual defence budgets. (Later the SSN program was spread over twenty-seven years.) As expected, the third batch of patrol frigates was lost. Beatty justified these cuts by showing that the frigates and conventional submarines would cost about the same as twelve SSNs, but would cause a significant loss in capability.

It was the intention of the government and the navy to use the SSNs solely for ASW but the policy failed to clarify this important point. The omission became another obstacle to the public's understanding of the new plan.

Canada's preoccupation with her sovereignty increased in the 1980s, nudged along by politicians of every stripe, until it became the perfect foundation stone on which to build the '87 White Paper and the ideal Canadian hook on which to hang SSNs. Although many believed that

Pacific defence was the more urgent issue, protection of Arctic sovereignty became the vehicle by which the Tories and DND attempted to sell the new defence policy to Canadians.

The government capitalized on the strong emotions that the Arctic elicits in Canadians who proudly believe it belongs to them. The Tories told the people that they could not protect their birthright with a few Rangers armed with a 1-800 phone number to Ottawa and occasional maritime air patrols. The Tories emphasized that Canadians should be NATO's northern expert because Canada had the longest Arctic coastline of any NATO nation, had the greatest Arctic landmass of any NATO nation, and lay between the superpowers of the U.S.A. and the USSR. The Tories confessed to the population that they did not know who was intruding into "their" Arctic and violating "their" Northwest Passage.

After that all the Tories had to do to convince the electorate, or so they thought, was to bring the only warship capable of operating in the north into the equation. The SSNs would, they said, develop Canada into NATO's northern expert, protect Canadian sovereignty in the Arctic, and as a bonus defend the northern Pacific. The new boats would also provide some muscle to the government's claim that the Northwest Passage was Canadian, although the U.S.A., for one, used it as if it were international waters. However, the picture was, in truth, infinitely more complicated. Was the Soviet threat real? How big was it? How many and whose boats used the Arctic waters that Canada claimed as her own? Which dollar figures were accurate? Shouldn't Canadians have a peace dividend? Could DND and the politicians be trusted?

In the 1980s the Soviets dominated the northern ocean – 60 percent (126) of their submarines were based above the Arctic Circle, with a new one launched every five weeks. By contrast, NATO had no submarine bases in the Arctic and focused their efforts on northwestern Europe. With the Greenland-Iceland-U.K. (GIUK) gap effectively closed by the Allies, the Soviets were forced to find and use another route for their SSNs to reach the shipping lanes in the Atlantic. The alternative was to transit through the Canadian-claimed waters of the Arctic archipelago, and out into the Canadian Atlantic between Greenland and Canada. The GIUK gap closure also caused the Soviets to develop SSBN (missile-launching submarines) sanctuaries under the ice where their boats would be safe from air and surface attack and could launch missiles capable of reaching western targets. Canada was especially vulnerable to these Soviet strategies, although DND admitted that they had no firm evidence of Soviet activity in the Canadian-claimed Arctic. If tension escalated or war broke out Canada could field nothing to engage the Soviet boats in the Arctic and only had three aging diesel submarines to interdict them as they arrived in the Canadian Atlantic zone.

DND also knew that the Americans, whose Arctic interests were different from Canada's, used Canadian-claimed Arctic waters when they transited the ice cap from either east or west. Though hardly an enemy threat in the military sense, the U.S. insistence on using the Northwest Passage as if it were international waters provoked the politicians, and they began to want to exert control where they previously had none. The navy was only too happy to oblige as they had been tasked with Arctic protection and had never had anything to do it with. "Frigates and aircraft do terribly under the ice!" pointed out one former submarine squadron commander.[3]

Reaction to the Conservatives' 1987 White Paper on Defence came fast and furious, with either ecstatic support or vituperative opposition.

The navy was thrilled – even the loss of the third batch of frigates could not wipe the grin off its face – though privately Jim Wood, Maritime Commander, wondered if they had been too greedy. Thomas, who succeeded Wood, said, "We have moved from a ceremonial navy to an operational one"[4] and ended up with most of the credit. Even the submariners were under the impression that he had been the prime mover.

The submariners chortled, "It's like going from a '62 Volkswagen to an '88 Porsche."[5] When the euphoria wore off, they worried that the prospect was too good to be true but their hopes strengthened as the program progressed. The SSNs meant that the Canadian Submarine Service would go from being the navy's second-class citizen to being in the front line – and the only ones in the Arctic front line at that! Other advantages would be reliable boats, a submarine presence in the Pacific, less recruiting problems, and a whopping challenge. Endless hot water for showers was much anticipated, though hardly fundamental. "It will spoil people," grumbled one whiskered chief.[6]

By and large, NATO welcomed Canada's increased effort against the Soviet submarine threat from the north, but the Americans were less happy about Canada's plans. Although officially they made polite supportive statements, they had reacted adversely to the prospect of Canada interfering with their Arctic submarine operations. The U.S. submarine service, muzzled by President Reagan, was privately appalled – they wanted to remove the British Trafalgar from contention so Canada could not get its hands on "their" nuclear technology, but most of all they wished to prevent their northern neighbour getting SSNs at all. The British submarine service was also lukewarm to the idea, though for other reasons. They worried that their construction program would suffer if Canada selected the Trafalgar. However, the Thatcher government was elated at the prospect of a major overseas submarine sale.

The Canadian opposition parties' antagonism to Beatty's White Paper was predictable. "A dangerous proposal ... [which] is going to send the wrong signal to the Russians," said the Liberals.[7] In fact, the Grits mistakenly favoured reliance on the obsolete air defence system for Arctic protection, along with a fixed surveillance system under the ocean. The New Democrats opposed the whole policy and again flirted with the expensive idea of making Canada neutral. Both political parties questioned the submarine's price-tag and gave the electorate the impression that the SSNs would take $8 billion from general revenue rather than from funds already allocated to DND for the next fifteen years.

Canadian defence commentators supported the forces' upgrade in general and the SSN program in particular, saying that the boats would allow Canada to defend her sovereignty in all three oceans and to pull her weight in NATO. Most Canadians agreed that Canada needed to protect her Arctic territorial waters and to improve her naval forces, but they could not agree about the SSN component. The word "nuclear" frightened many who believed the submarines would carry nuclear weapons or spread radioactivity.

In contrast, the peace movement in Canada was in a state of shrieking shock. Their reaction revolved around the offensive nature of submarines and the use of nuclear power.

The speed with which the Canadian nuclear-powered submarine program took off from the gate was astounding and probably unequalled by any previous DND procurement. Healey and Thomas were determined to get the first Canadian SSN laid down in 1991, four years away, and Beatty ran interference for them. A third player, Rear Admiral J.R. Anderson, CD, soon joined the project, who would prove crucial to the acquisition's outcome. Everyone watched the acceleration of the SSN program with concern and something approaching awe.

The nuclear-powered submarine acquisition did not require parliamentary approval to proceed – the special powers of the National Defence Act obviated that – but it did need the Cabinet's blessing and DND hoped to secure that by the end of 1987. The first indicator of the new political will was Beatty's cancellation of the diesel/electric program.

This made many in CASAP, including Harrison, afraid the navy might be left with no boats at all if the government or its successor cancelled the controversial program.

Healey, as ADM (Mat.), automatically became the SSN project leader. He created a new department, led by Commodore Ed Bowkett, CD. The submarine engineering and maintenance department was made responsible for the construction of the whole submarine, the SSN fleet's infrastructure and "all things nuclear." The CASAP project team amalgamated with the NSOS group and began the work to select a submarine design. The British remained cool to the Canadian advances and the French still burned hot, but the rules had changed. Harrison, during his visit to France and Britain after the announcement that Canada would build SSNs, found that for the first time his hosts far outranked him.

The most urgent item on the acquisition agenda in the summer of '87 was to get the Americans to release data on their submarine reactor, used in the Trafalgar, so that a design selection could be made by Christmas. At meetings in Washington to secure the technology transfer Beatty, Healey, Bowkett, and Thomas were told in no uncertain terms by U.S. defence department and submarine service officials that Canada was incapable of managing a nuclear-powered submarine project. The humiliated Canadians returned empty-handed.

On arrival home from the embarrassing U.S. visit and after hearing about Harrison's experience in Europe, Beatty decided Canada's program needed a three-star admiral. This decision, well-intentioned though it was, led to an organizational tangle which the British navy called a "dog's breakfast." Healey, fearing loss of control of the project, convinced his minister that the new admiral must report to him, and Thomas extended Beatty's directive by creating a new department as well. Rear Admiral John R. Anderson, CD, a surface sailor with little project management experience, became chief, Submarine Acquisition (CSA) in September and his new department, also known as CSA, became the repository of all SSN knowledge. Regrettably, CSA was not in the direct chain of command but sat outside the line organization, a little below ADM (Mat.) and a little above CASAP. This put Harrison, now assistant project leader, in a difficult position, but he acquiesced. The CASAP project office felt slighted, believing that their expertise had been devalued by the move and that Thomas had inserted CSA to keep an eye on the acquisition as he was no longer in Ottawa. Many thought it would have been more logical to appoint an admiral to lead an expanded CASAP without adding the extra department, and if the flag officer could have been a submariner, so much the better. In fact, there were two very able men with those credentials who could have been chosen – Jim Wood apparently refused when offered the job and Peter Cairns was not asked. CSA worked on policies, operations, infrastructure, manning, safety issues, and the impact of nuclear power on personnel and health.

Harrison quickly began to have second thoughts about having two bosses – the Treasury Board guidelines demanded that he report to ADM (Mat.), but CSA insisted that he report to him. It also became increasingly unclear who spoke for all of CASAP – was it Healey or Anderson? Was Harrison not a spokesman too? And what about Bowkett who reckoned he was responsible for the "whole" submarine? Harrison predicted this would have serious implications for the program.

The rewritten SSN Statement of Requirement (SOR), needed by CASAP to evaluate submarine designs, called for a proven design and stressed safety and reliability, modern ASW capability, and the ability to operate under the ice. It placed lesser emphasis on anti-ship capability, hydrodynamic performance and inshore operations. This translated into the need for very low noise and radiation signatures, excellent passive sonars, first-class tactical data-processing equipment, and six torpedo tubes compatible with the already-purchased Mark 48 torpedoes. Last, but definitely not least, the Canadian SSNs had to be able to surface safely through three metres of ice.[8]

When DND accepted the new SOR, it was clear that neither the British nor the French boat could meet all the Canadian requirements. For example, the French boat was not proven at sea in her Canadianized form. The Trafalgar had only five torpedo tubes and, what was worse, the Rubis's six tubes were too short for the Mark 48s. In addition, the French submarine was unable to surface through the required depth of ice. DND then softened some of the essentials, including the requirement for the need to be proven at sea and to break through three metres of ice. Alterations in SORs are not unknown in major procurements, but it was vital in the SSN project that the changes should not be allowed to jeopardize the safety of Canadian submariners.

With two such vastly dissimilar submarines, CASAP's evaluation was difficult, and comparisons almost impossible to make (see Table 3). The Trafalgar, a proven fourth-generation boat, was nearly twice as big as the unproven, second-generation Rubis/Amethyste. The major advantage of her size, determined by the large American reactor, was that it provided the necessary displacement to break through three metres of ice. Furthermore, her bigger reactor produced the power to maintain a heav-

Table 3
A Comparison of the Trafalgar and Amethyste
Nuclear-Powered Submarines

	FRANCE	BRITAIN
CLASS	RUBIS/AMETHYSTE	TRAFALGAR
PRICE	$350 million	$450 million
LOA	79.6 m (250 ft)	85.4 m (280 ft)
BEAM	7.6 m (25 ft)	9.83 m (32 ft)
MEAN DRAFT	6.4 m	8.2 m
SUB. SPEED	MORE THAN 25 knots	MORE THAN 32 knots
MAX. DEPTH	MORE THAT 300 m	MORE THAN 300 m
RANGE	UNLIMITED	UNLIMITED
DISPLACEMENT	2400 tons	4730 tons
CREW	66 (8 officers/58 men)	97-102 (12 officers/85 men)
WEAPONS (Non-nuclear)	6 21" tubes for 22 torpedoes, SM-39 missiles or mines	5 21" tubes for 25 torpedoes, Sub-Harpoon missiles or mines
PROPULSION	CIRCULATION NUCLEAR REACTOR GENERATING STEAM FOR 2 TURBINES AND 1 ELECTRIC MOTOR	PRESSURIZED WATER NUCLEAR REACTOR GENERATING STEAM FOR 2 TURBINES AND TWO AUXILIARY DIESELS.
ENDURANCE	70 DAYS' PROVISIONS	70 DAYS' PROVISIONS

ier "hotel" load (for equipment and other systems) and higher speeds. The Amethyste's compact and revolutionary nuclear reactor had enabled the French to design the world's smallest and most manoeuvrable SSN, but its lower power meant a top speed 10 knots slower than that of the Trafalgar and the Soviet boats. The Trafalgar was a deep-sea boat designed for ASW in the North Atlantic and Arctic oceans, and was quieter even than the Oberons. In contrast, the Rubis, designed for anti-shipping use in warm waters, was known to submariners as the "Mack truck" underwater. This noise came not from the reactor but from her bow configuration. Modifications were under way to improve her sound signature and accommodate Canada's longer torpedoes, but were yet to be proved quiet.

The French planned to overcome the problem of surfacing through three metres of ice by adding a retractable "icepick" to the pressure hull. After model trials France assured CASAP that it would work, but CASAP was not convinced. They maintained that the small displacement and buoyancy ratios of the Amethyste would not allow her to surface through that much ice. DND then changed their ice-depth requirement to one metre, so that the French could continue to compete for the contract, despite British and American warnings that ice of one metre did not occur frequently enough in the Arctic for safety.

Although the technical risk inherent in the French submarine was enormous and likely to increase its price significantly, the Trafalgar's U.S. reactor was its greatest drawback, because the Americans had to approve and legislate the technology transfer before the British could release their design to Canada. That the U.S. would do so was by no means a foregone conclusion.

CSA's price comparisons at the end of 1987 were based on the first hull being built in the parent yard offshore, and the rest in Canada. The Brits' unsubstantiated quote was $450 million for each Trafalgar and the French offered the Amethyste at $333 million a copy. France gave the impression that they were quoting a fixed price for the contract, which if true was hardly credible, but was certainly irresistible considering the Amethyste's inherent technical risk.

Neither submarine design was an outright winner with Canadian submariners, though the operators fiercely defended their favourites over the wardroom bars in Ottawa and Halifax. In the final analysis, they did not really care which design was chosen as long as they got new submarines, and they all despaired of having any real influence over the final choice.

CHAPTER TWENTY-EIGHT

THE NUCLEAR-POWERED SUBMARINE ACQUISITION, 1987–1989

... and the envelope, please

CASAP moved into overdrive in mid-1987, but its increased momentum did not indicate smooth sailing. On the surface the SSN project resembled most major procurements, with its tensions and glitches, but underneath the strife between the Department of Defence and other ministries became significant. One issue emerged to seriously impede the program's head-long rush.

The acquisition strategy for the nuclear-powered submarines differed from that of the diesel/electric program. The evaluation of the designs included an appraisal from the Department of External Affairs of the political implications and benefits of acquiring either the Trafalgar or the Amethyste; the Department of National Defence, not Industry, selected the boat, and the lucky winner was to be announced by country (the country of origin decision or COO), not by design. Other than special mechanisms for handling the sensitive material, the rest of the procurement was to follow the usual route, with request for proposals and project definition.

Conflicts between the ministries and departments involved developed almost immediately. Some of them originated from the acquisition process: for example, the decision to study the political ramifications of the acquisition ensured that the SSN project became highly politicized, and when External Affairs' findings began to take precedence over the boats' suitability, CASAP strenuously objected. Later, Healey's controversial decision to give an agency (probably Atomic Energy of Canada, Ltd.)

the authority not only to acquire but also to install and maintain the entire nuclear propulsion plant, for the life of the submarines, caused an uproar. Harrison, the Department of Supply and Services, Britain, France, and Canadian industry all publicly criticized the project's direction.

CASAP's rising tide of resentment towards CSA reached its height by the end of 1987. Harrison's staff had repeatedly expressed anxiety over the method of reporting, the costing, the assessment of the technical risk, the proposed locations of the SSN bases and refuelling facilities (in existing naval bases), and, most important, the inability of the French and British boats to meet the Canadian requirements. When CASAP finally confronted CSA, CSA failed to respond to its concerns and instead questioned the personnel's loyalty to the project. They left feeling marginalized and resentful. Healey acknowledged that he had trouble reconciling these differences, but felt that after he intervened the antagonism between CSA and CASAP settled down. CASAP never thought so.

By now, Harrison was seriously alarmed; he tried hard to solve the management difficulties, but soon concluded, in frustration, that if matters continued unchanged the SSNs might founder before they were built. By Christmas the situation was so grave that Harrison resigned. He cited to CSA the method of the nuclear reactor acquisition, the contravention of Treasury Board guidelines, and the unreliability of the cost estimates. Although many thought Harrison had been fired for his lack of confidence in nuclear submarines, this was definitely not the case – he simply objected to the way in which the SSN acquisition was being run. Onshore and offshore industry, all of whom respected Harrison, begged him to reconsider his decision.

Captain(N) Bruce Baxter, CD, a marine engineer with good project management experience, agreed with some reluctance to replace Harrison. When CSA refused to change its reporting procedures, Baxter persuaded the other departments to accept a paper solution to the dilemma. However, everyone knew that the rules were still being violated, and Treasury Board began to keep a very close eye on the project.

Beatty wanted the SSN design selected by December 1987 (only six months after the White Paper) but, when the acquisition teams could not manage it, he postponed it to May 1988. Beatty said that the delay was because the study on the environmental aspects of the SSN project was incomplete. However, sources indicate that as the study was not done by May either, the delay was caused by the internecine squabbles.

In the fall of 1987 Britain and France demonstrated their submarines to DND. They were unaware of the project's problems, and any they did perceive they attributed to Canada's naïveté in running a project of this magnitude at high speed. When HMS/M *Torbay* and the *Saphir* visited Halifax, DND strictly controlled their time to ensure fairness – even serving identical menus to the two groups. Perrin Beatty spent six hours on each submarine, and refrained from making comments about either. Up till now the French had believed press reports[1] that Canada favoured the Trafalgar, and that they had been included merely to give an appearance of a competition for the politicians. *Saphir's* visit made them realize they were in the running – possibly even ahead.

The response to the SSN procurement from potential prime contractors in Canada was muted in comparison with their excitement over the diesel program. Eight of the sixteen previously involved companies decided to wait for Cabinet's approval of the program before committing any more money. The rest, who expressed interest, were as follows:

- Marine Industries Ltd. (MIL), of Quebec;
- St. John Shipbuilding Ltd., of New Brunswick;
- Paramax Electronic Systems Inc., of Quebec;
- the team of Canadian Shipbuilding and Engineering Ltd., Submarine Group (CSE), and Rockwell International, of St. Catherines, Ontario; and
- the consortium of Lavalin/Halifax Dartmouth Industries/Litton Systems.

By early 1988 there were indications that the Canadian companies would form one super-consortium, as none of the five groups had the depth to manage the SSN project on its own. The British and French were delighted with the prospect of a sole-source contract that would permit the DND-funded project-definition phase to start in the fall of 1988, but CSA, needing a competition to please the politicians, encouraged the firms to form two consortia. By May a "super-group," the Canadian Submarine Consortium (CSC), led by Robert Tessier, emerged. The alignment of MIL, SNC, Lavalin, Litton Systems, and Halifax/Dartmouth Industries looked nearly invincible and deterred the remaining firms from regrouping to compete in the $37.5 million project-definition phase. However, CSC did not fare well despite its strong position and the navy's desire for speed. Documentation was not forthcoming and CSC considered CSA's lack of cooperation bizarre.

Meanwhile, at Healey's behest, staffers were again trying to pin down the cost of the SSNs. He wanted to finally quiet CASAP, Treasury Board, and DSS who stubbornly disagreed with CSA's position that twelve SSNs for $8 billion was still possible. Both DSS and CASAP had estimated $10.7 billion. Two months later Healey admitted that about $10 billion would be needed to build twelve boats at home, so he reduced the fleet to ten boats to retain the "by-now-required" figure and jobs for Canadians. Baxter has since confirmed that CASAP later found that $10 billion was not enough even for ten.

Several factors were conspiring to make the costing a nightmare. The original quotes were now out of date and were hard to translate into "Canadian-built" figures without more data, especially from the British. In their parent yards, the Trafalgar's price had risen $80 million to $530 million and the Amethyste was running 22 percent over budget ($420 million) and still rising. The cost of warship construction was known to be substantially higher in Canadian yards – up to three times as much. More worrisome was the fact that, historically, major Canadian defence procurements have come in at between 30 and 100 percent more than estimated. With the overrun averaged at 65 percent and inflation indexed over the length of the SSN acquisition, the $10 billion price tag turned into one of over $33 billion. Clearly, DND was not telling the whole story.

Throughout the SSN acquisition, CSA also wrestled with the contentious issue of the transfer to Canada of the U.S. nuclear technology in the British boat. Initial lack of an agreement with the U.S.A. reduced the amount of information on which DND could evaluate the contenders, influenced their design choice, and irritated international relations. In April the U.S. president, probably encouraged by his friend Margaret Thatcher, finally notified the Canadian prime minister that he would support the transfer of U.S. submarine technology to Canada despite the fierce objections of his defence department. Although the U.S. Congress had still to approve the technology transfer, the Canadian project began to solidify.

Just before Reagan's decision, CSA and External Affairs completed their appraisals of the contenders, duplicating much of the work done in 1986–87 by NSOS and CASAP. Although Anderson insisted that he and Healey did not know which submarine had secured the competition, many believed otherwise. Several confidential sources indicated Beatty unofficially learned of the design choice from Anderson in March or

April 1988. Naturally, the country-of-origin decision was classified, but ask anyone in Ottawa and you'll be told that it was France. The only publication that believed the British submarine had won was the French-Canadian daily, *Le Devoir.*[2]

The Cabinet was scheduled to meet on 11 May 1988 to discuss the SSN program. Only after they agreed on the concept could Cabinet approve DND's design selection and the funds for the project definition. The latter represented the key to success, because once in place the project would be difficult to stop due to the international implications of backing out. Excitement rather than anxiety was the order of the day in naval circles, and the champagne was already on ice.

When nothing happened after 11 May 1988, DND began to worry, and by the end of June even outsiders wondered what was going on. The minister of finance gave what amounted to the only explanation of the delay – Wilson said that Cabinet had postponed the sensitive SSN decision until after Britain and France attended the G7 meeting in Toronto, but mentioned using diesel/electric boats in the Atlantic and Pacific Oceans.

In fact, the Cabinet had never met, had never discussed Canadian SSNs, and had never approved the program. The May 1988 meeting was cancelled at the eleventh hour, and was never rescheduled. This non-event effectively marked the end of the Canadian nuclear-powered submarine program, though it was never public knowledge.

Why did the Canadian Cabinet *not* meet on Wednesday, 11 May 1988, to discuss the nuclear-powered submarine program? Why was the cancellation so abrupt? Who cancelled it? And why was it never rescheduled? These questions have never been fully answered because of the confidentiality of Cabinet proceedings, and because DND closed ranks. All but one official said, in answer to a direct question, that no Cabinet meeting had been arranged. After much investigation some details emerged, but few could be substantiated.

It all began when Treasury Board prepared its usual briefing note for the Cabinet on the topic to be discussed. When the Privy Council read it on Sunday, 8 May 1988, they alerted Joe Clark, the acting prime minister. Clark reacted to the brief by calling an immediate meeting with the ministers of finance and national defence. He proposed cancelling the Cabinet meeting, and Wilson supported him – it was two against one. Perrin Beatty, who declined to be interviewed, seemed quite unprepared for the contents of the brief. When he read it in the company of the two ministers, who had never liked the SSN program in the first place, his feelings must have ranged through shock and anger to embarrassment.

For starters, Treasury Board had concluded that the SSN project was improperly constituted, that the costing was flawed, that no independent program analysis had been done, even though it was a requirement, that some of the procurement decisions were questionable, and that the program directors seemed to be assuming that they were above criticism, with internal challenges stifled and external questions swept away. They objected to CSA's restricted access to the program, which meant ministers would have to vote on the SSNs without even knowing their operational requirements. But most damning of all was TB's vigorous opposition to CSA's final design choice – France's Amethyste. They believed that CSA had selected the French design with inadequate data, and that the choice carried much too much technical risk. They gave their opinion that the infrastructure and a few SSNs, probably five, could be had for $8 billion.

The Treasury Board brief appears to have been sufficiently plausible and alarming to overcome any arguments that Beatty may have made to keep the SSN program on the Cabinet's agenda. So Canada's SSN program was wrecked without the benefit of any Cabinet discussion at all. It is unlikely that Clark and Wilson deliberately attempted to sink the project, but ensuing world events, the government's reduced confidence in DND, and their cancellation of the meeting certainly worked together to hasten the SSNs' demise.

Very few people outside DND and government realized that the design choice for the new Canadian submarines had not been approved. Those in the know accused Treasury Board, and one analyst in particular, of sabotage; Treasury Board responded by saying they had simply presented the facts as they saw them. The extent to which DND tried to limit the impact of the brief is unknown, but there is evidence to suggest that the navy never recouped its position on SSNs. Mulroney allegedly ordered an independent review by Mazankowski, Clark, and de Cotret, but their findings, if indeed they exist, are unavailable.

Press reports in June first indicated that Cabinet would meet sometime in July to consider the SSN project, then that the program was under review. Later the emphasis changed again – speculation had the Tories having second thoughts about the new submarines despite Beatty's comments to the contrary. After July the media stopped commenting on the delay, and as the summer lengthened into fall Canadians began to forget about the SSN program.

The key players in the Canadian SSN program all dissembled mightily when asked to explain the delayed decision, probably to prevent more harm being done to the submarine replacement program. Healey refused to comment on it or on the elusive Cabinet meeting. "I'm *never* going to open that file again!" was his rueful comment.[3] However, once he was safely retired he did admit that the SSN choice had been made. By contrast, Anderson maintained that he never knew the successful submarine's identity and that he was unaware that a Cabinet meeting had been scheduled for 11 May 1988. Baxter knew "nothing" of the alleged Cabinet meeting but did know which design had won. Bowkett confirmed the Cabinet meeting, but stated the priorities and planning committee had advised Beatty not to present the project to his colleagues. Later, when Vice-Admiral Thomas was VCDS, he refused to comment at all, which – considering the wide disparity in explanations – was probably the most prudent course.

Treasury Board's timing of their exposé was brutal and left no time for the navy to recover. It was this, perhaps more than the contents of the brief, that gave rise to the bitter accusations of sabotage. The Canadian navy was now in a serious predicament, partly of its own making. In the rush to get nuclear-powered submarines DND had made some fundamental procurement errors. The lack of communication with the politicians, the lack of an independent analysis, and the failure to address the rising concerns of the Treasury Board were some of the major mistakes that ultimately deep-sixed the program. Informed authorities believe that the alterations made to the SOR to accommodate France's contender were almost as serious. The flawed cost estimates and the reactor acquisition policy were lesser blunders, but when added to the others they generated a festering distrust of DND in the government. It is ironic that the nuclear-power issue ended up having nothing to do with the submarines' fall from grace.

Nothing further was done in the political arena to get the SSN project back on track during the summer and fall of 1988 – the Tories were focused on another election. The acquisition staff laboured on, believing the project would eventually succeed as long as the boats were not French.

During the November 1988 federal election campaign, the remaining media support for the SSN project eroded, and with DND abdicating the field there were few to rebut the opposing arguments. By now the country was firmly against SSNs – a CBC television poll reported that 71 percent of Canadians opposed the purchase – and Prime Minister Mulroney was listening.

After the Conservatives were re-elected, Anderson expected the politicians to address the SSN program quickly. When nothing happened, and the government started to report financial shortfalls, he became mildly concerned. The traditional post-election Cabinet shuffle also worried CSA – Beatty might be moved. But worse was to come. Mulroney stated publicly that child care and free trade now had a higher priority than submarines, and DND's associate minister delayed the SSN country-of-origin announcement further. In early January, DND informed Britain and France that the submarine selection was under review but did not elaborate. Observers took this to mean one or all of three possibilities: that the SSN program was back in business, that DND was re-doing the evaluation so that the British submarine was favoured, or that less money was available.

The event the navy had been dreading came at the end of January 1989 – Beatty went to the Department of Health and Welfare. Sources indicate that it was not a moment too soon for the disenchanted defence minister, who had asked to be moved immediately after the cancellation of the May Cabinet meeting. The navy put a brave face on losing their advocate, but it concealed a desperate anxiety. Beatty was replaced by a relatively unknown MP called Bill McKnight. He was a pig farmer from Saskatchewan with a reputation for being hard-working and hard-nosed. The media interpreted Beatty's departure as the death knell of the SSN program, and a month after the new Cabinet was sworn in a well-informed source alleged that Mulroney told McKnight that the future of the SSN acquisition was dim.

By March, Britain and France were almost beside themselves with impatience and worry, and CSA was unable to calm their fears. The two countries, together with the potential prime contractors, warned DND they would soon stop sinking money into an increasingly uncertain contract unless they got some credible reassurance. CSA held them off believing all would be well.

At the same time, the departments of External Affairs and National Defence were reviewing their policies to fit the democratization of Eastern Europe and Canada's debt position. The navy managed to maintain ten SSNs in the retrenchment but the upheavals continued in the Communist-bloc countries.

Admirals Thomas and Anderson awaited the Conservative government's 27 April 1989 budget with some apprehension, as did the British and French submarine teams, who were in Canada to meet with the admirals. The night before the budget speech, Anderson had dinner with the French ambassador, the head of French military procurement, Bob Fowler (ADM [Policy]) and Ed Healey (ADM [Mat.]). Across town Thomas entertained the British high commissioner, the First Sea Lord, and the head of Vickers in Canada. At 2000, they all heard there had been a budget leak, but none of them knew how severe it was.

Anderson recalled the evening with amusement and despair. "Great dinner, shitty entertainment!" were his words. Just before 2200, Fowler took Healey aside and told him that Wilson was about to read the budget on national television because the leak had been serious. The two deputy ministers, knowing the budget's contents, immediately told the dinner party that the Canadian nuclear-powered submarine project had been cancelled. Anderson somehow maintained his outward composure, and the French were gracious and understanding in their bitter disappointment. A similar scene was played out with the British contingent. The representatives of Vickers were also stunned, though perhaps less disappointed than the French as they had the Upholder to fall back on if another diesel/electric program materialized.

The cancellation of the biggest project in Canadian defence history took only one sentence. Wilson simply announced that the SSN program would not continue further as government policy had determined against it. He gave no official reason for the decision and the government allowed the nation's growing deficit to become the excuse.

But this excuse was invalid. Wilson did not axe the SSNs for lack of immediate money (they did not need much) or for their long-term expense. Averaged over twenty-seven years, the submarines' $300 million annual cost was less than 3 percent of the defence budget, and it paled in comparison to the $53 billion per year for social services. When the author asked Anderson why the deficit was used as the reason, he shrugged and said, "You tell me. I can't explain it and no one has explained it satisfactorily to me." He declined to speculate further.

If cost was only a convenient excuse for the SSNs' cancellation in 1989, what was the real reason? Probably there was not just one, but a combination of factors: for political reasons, Mulroney dared not cancel the federal child-care program while retaining the SSNs; Beatty's departure from the defence ministry had a bearing too, but not much; and it was harder to justify SSNs in the newly emerging world order. However, the major factor, and the one never mentioned, was undoubtedly Treasury Board's exposé of the SSN project.

The cancellation of the SSN project was a last-minute budget decision – Fowler and Healey had lobbied successfully as far as they could reach. It was the committee that developed the budget "sales strategy" that advised against the SSNs, citing the increasing negativity of the electorate towards them. Wilson, never a strong proponent of the SSNs, did not argue the point, and Mulroney, ever mindful of the polls, concurred.

Reactions to the budget varied widely. Thomas was more upset over the treatment he had received from DND than over the cancellation itself. He had not been warned of the decision, nor had he been given satisfactory reasons for it. By contrast Anderson was shocked – in 1990 he looked back and spoke quietly of the traumatic time: "It was like a death in my family." The silence from Britain and France was deafening, though diplomatic channels were reporting a serious loss of face for Canada – her credibility as a maritime nation had sunk along with the 1987 White Paper. Domestic and overseas industry felt betrayed, and Canadian shipbuilders were especially concerned as the cut meant layoffs at best, and yard closures at worst. For the submariners themselves the outlook was very bleak as Beatty's abandonment of the diesel/electric program provided them with no fall-back position. They were not really demoralized, but they knew that all procurement would be politically driven from now on – their day in the sun was over.

Others cheered when the Tories axed the SSNs. The United States submarine service celebrated very privately but very thoroughly. Diesel/electric designers and builders saw a renewed opportunity for sales. The two Canadian firms that were developing air-independent propulsion systems hoped they might now get a chance. And the vociferous peace organizations took the credit for the SSNs' funeral, as if they had achieved it.

It was fortunate that the Canadian Submarine Service celebrated its 75th anniversary three weeks before the 1989 budget. If it had come later, the great party would have turned into a wake.

CHAPTER TWENTY-NINE

THE FUTURE OF THE CANADIAN SUBMARINE SERVICE

Losing the bubble

The high profile of the Canadian Submarine Service faded rapidly after the SSN cancellation. The submariners' pride in the service, their humour and their hard work were unchanged, but they were worried about the future. The Department of National Defence lay low, and CASAP was reduced to a small staff, back in the mainstream of headquarters. Their requests for a speedy renewal of a diesel/electric submarine program fell on deaf Conservative ears. The fall of the Berlin Wall at the end of 1989, which presaged the startling events in eastern Europe and the U.S.S.R., had a direct impact on the submarine acquisition and many concluded the navy had missed their boat.

After the fateful budget, CSA and the Department of Submarine Engineering and Maintenance closed, but DND retained the Directorate of Nuclear Safety (DNS). This encouraged the press to suggest that the navy were continuing to work clandestinely on the SSN option,[1] but it was not true. They simply wished to keep tabs on marine nuclear technology and to investigate the Slowpoke reactor as an air-independent propulsion (AIP) system for use in diesel submarines under the ice. CASAP stayed on for a while, expecting to restart a diesel/electric program, and rewrote the statement of requirement for SSKs with an AIP option. Thomas became the vice-chief of Defence Staff after his time as Maritime Commander and Healey soon resigned. Anderson returned to Maritime Doctrine and Operations (CMDO),[2] insisting he would continue the fight for new submarines.

But by 1990 the likelihood of replacing, let alone augmenting, the old Oberons was fast diminishing, as the Berlin Wall fell and Communism in Eastern Europe collapsed. These events brought massive defence cuts in all NATO countries, and the submarines' bargaining chip, the third batch of frigates, soon disappeared. Later the Gulf War, in which Canadian forces participated, did nothing to stiffen governmental resolve.

It was in this rapidly changing world that the navy fought, and is still fighting, to preserve the Canadian Submarine Service. When the SSN cancellation demolished the three-ocean cornerstone of the 1987 White Paper, the Tories ordered a new defence policy, hoping to rely on others for Arctic protection. But the new policy turned out to be difficult to pull together. The unification of the two Germanys, Iraq's invasion of Kuwait, the lack of defence dollars, and the inability of the three services to agree on a future force structure led to revision after revision of policy. The first draft included eight diesel boats, but in the next they were down to six, and not even certain of these.

CASAP's office closed in July 1990, and the emasculated acquisition program was renamed – CPSP (the Canadian Patrol Submarine Program). Thomas, VCDS, and the new Maritime Commander, Rear Admiral Robert George, CD, both privately predicted that if the government failed to make a decision on the submarines soon, it would be the end of the Canadian Submarine Service.

The Cabinet did not consider DND's new policy until the summer of 1991, probably because they were too preoccupied with national unity, a developing recession, and their own declining popularity to tackle another controversial subject. Thomas had already quit over the new defence policy in April, going public with his disgust at its contents. The submarine squadron assumed that Thomas's action meant that their boats had lost out in the competition for funds. Their pessimism was not improved shortly after by a visit from the new minister, Marcel Masse, who told them to expect more cuts.

Nearly two and a half years after the SSNs sank and over eighteen months after it was promised, Masse announced the new Tory defence policy. It contained virtually no emphasis on the north. The package was a trade-off between a large force with old equipment and a leaner force with high-tech equipment. Capital spending for this approach was to come mostly from money saved by closing the bases in Europe. The naval share included the second batch of frigates, six diesel/electric submarines in two batches (perhaps with AIP), twelve coastal defence vessels, and twelve fast patrol boats. The Arctic underwater fixed surveillance system received 30 percent more funds, to offset the lack of under-ice-capable submarines, and the aging Oberons were given a life extension program. The submariners breathed again.

However, the submarine acquisition was not as straightforward as it appeared. The *Globe and Mail* reported it as vague: "Sometime in the future – budgets permitting – the Canadian navy may acquire three new conventionally powered subs that may be able to operate under the ice."[3] A lot of *mays!* The *Financial Post* made it clearer – over the next fifteen years Canada would acquire "up to three of an eventual six submarines."[4] In other words, the second batch of three was illusory. Remember what happened to the fourth, fifth, and sixth Oberons? There was little public reaction to the announcement.

By November 1991 CPSP was out of the doldrums, hoping to go to Cabinet early in 1992 to seek preliminary project approval and to open a new office in the summer. Cdr. Lloyd Barnes, the project director of CPSP, reported that they were considering proven designs for 2000-tonne conventional boats, which averaged $300 million a copy, and which would be probably built offshore. They included the Upholder-class from Britain, the Walrus-class from Holland, the TR 1700 from Germany, Type 471 from Sweden (same as RAN's new Collins-class), and Amethyste (a diesel version) from France.

CPSP anticipated calling for requests for proposals immediately after Cabinet approval, and beginning construction in 1995/96 with the first submarine entering service around 2000.

In April 1992 all CPSP's revived hopes were dashed. Masse announced in DND's short-term capital acquisition program that the submarine program had been deferred for two years. He gave no reasons publicly, and none to the project manager, other than the general one of "profound geostrategic changes and the imperatives of fiscal restraint."[5] Although DND had made the decision and not the government, the Tories' deep defence cuts in the February 1992 budget were surely to blame. National Defence had insufficient money for all their planned capital projects and had to prioritize them. They chose to cancel some programs, defer some, and go ahead with others. The deferral of CPSP was based on expediency. With another general election looming, DND clearly believed that Cabinet approval would only be secured for procurements that would create jobs for Canadians. The submarine acquisition lost out as it was increasingly likely to be an offshore purchase.

The two-year delay expired in 1994 after Canada elected a new Liberal government. The Grits immediately targeted defence for sweeping cuts. Maritime Command has endeavored to reinstate CPSP within the framework of another new policy, but despite their efforts they may well not succeed.

In November the Special Joint (Senate-House) Committee issued a report that stated, among other things, that the cost of replacing the submarine fleet was prohibitive at $4 billion. In the same breath they recommended that the navy should consider new boats if they discovered a good deal and there was enough money within existing funds. However, the bargain had already been found. The 1994 White Paper, unveiled shortly afterwards, disclosed that the government intended to explore the option of acquiring four recently constructed Upholder-class submarines.

The Brits have four nearly new surplus Upholders sitting in the parking lot, which they are aching to sell. The Canadian navy is mad for them, whether or not they are suitable, and who can blame them? Although some Canadian ministers were cool to the scheme, even with sweeteners, Cabinet allowed DND to continue with negotiations. However, the discount price of about $1 billion spread over fifteen years (or thereabouts) was hard for ministers to swallow in the midst of their cost-cutting frenzy. Justification for the electorate did not come either – the new defence policy de-emphasized the ASW role of the Canadian navy for which submarines are essential – and having offensive weapons platforms to keep greedy European fishing fleets off the Grand Banks is a hard sell.

In July 1995 Chrétien and his Liberal Cabinet dropped the replacement submarines to the bottom of the defence department's shopping list. Britain, incensed for the umpteenth time by Canada's procrastination, reacted by offering the Upholders to Portugal and Chile. The navy and the squadron retain some optimism that this latest government action will not spell the end of the Canadian Submarine Service but are realistic enough to know that it might. They will continue to strive mightily towards the acquisition of new submarines while squeezing out the few remaining years left to the aging Oberons. If the politicians persist in delaying the submarine decision, there is a real possibility that the Canadian Submarine Service will die a slow and painful death in the closing years of the twentieth century.

Throughout the Canadian Submarine Service's eighty years of stops and starts, impaired governmental vision, surface-dominated procurement policies, depression, euphoria, and making-do, the Canadian submariners have endured. Not only have they endured, they have come shining

through it all with their competence and spirit intact. This proud fraternity, whose members constantly put themselves at risk for their country,
is still needed, and it deserves the best equipment Canada can provide
until there is a genuine, world-encompassing peace.

It is easy to defend the Canadian Submarine Service on sentimental
grounds, but there are also important practical reasons for promoting it.
While the nations of the world perhaps face better prospects for peaceful
co-existence than at any time in their experience, recent history indicates
that Canada cannot become complacent or isolationist in her defence and
foreign policies. Without global disarmament, she urgently needs to
modernize her three services to protect Canada and to promote peace
with freedom for herself and her allies. Part of this must include a
Canadian navy that can effectively patrol her three oceans with sufficient
numbers of Canadian-owned-and-operated submarines. The essential
components for a balanced fleet are submarines, aircraft, and surface
ships. If Canada cannot stretch to all of them, the next best solution is
submarines and aircraft; and, if only one is affordable, the choice is submarines. A navy of ships without submarines makes no sense at all today.

If Canada fails to act, Canadians will have to contract out their
defence, and thus sacrifice more of the self-reliance previous generations
worked to gain. It is not too late for the government to decide on the
submarine program, and for the citizens of Canada to be willing to accept
the obligations that go hand in hand with the benefits of independent
and collective security and peacekeeping.

Canada's submariners have served in every theatre of the world, in war
and peace, in Canadian, British, American, Australian, and a few Dutch
boats. Some have seen action and some have died in the service of their
country. A few have become heroes. The submariners of the present day
proudly uphold the tradition of excellence laid down by their predecessors, and this now has a distinctly Canadian flavour. One thread has held
the Canadian Submarine Service together throughout its eighty years of
hard-won existence. It unites the untrained boys of *CC1* and *CC2* in
1914 and the highly trained specialists who serve in HMCS/M *Ojibwa,
Onondaga,* and *Okanagan* today. That thread is dedicated professionalism; for it is the men, not the boats, who are the true essence of the
Canadian Submarine Service.

Dolphin 72a.[6]

APPENDICES

APPENDIX 1

COMMANDERS OF THE CANADIAN SUBMARINE FLOTILLAS
AND SQUADRONS

HMCS *Shearwater* (depot ship) and the CC flotilla

Lt. A.St.V. Keyes, RCN	August 1914 - January 1915
Lt. B.E. Jones, RCN	January 1915 - December 1918

Submarine depot, HMC Dockyard Halifax, and HMCS *CH14* and *CH15*

Lt. G.H.S. Edwardes, RCNVR   June 1919 - May 1920
(Only for Bermuda/Halifax passage and while laid up.)

Lt. R.C. Watson, RCN   May 1920 - June 1922
N.B. LCdr. B.L. Johnson, RNR, commanded the flotilla and *H15* before they
were given to Canada by the Royal Navy (June 1918 - December 1918).

The First Canadian Submarine Squadron

Cdr. E.G. Gigg	July 1966 - July 1969
Cdr. M. Tate	July 1969 - July 1972
Cdr. J.C. Wood	August 1972 - July 1974
Cdr. P.W. Cairns	July 1974 - July 1975
Cdr. J.E.D. Bell	July 1975 - January 1978
Cdr. R.C. Hunt	January 1978 - August 1981
Cdr. R.C. Perks	August 1981 - July 1983
Cdr. K.G. Nesbit	July 1983 - December 1984
Cdr. W.J. Sloan	December 1984 - August 1987
Cdr. K.F. McMillan	August 1987 - July 1989
Capt(N) A.B. Dunlop	July 1989 - December 1990
Capt(N) J.A.Y. Plante	December 1990 - April 1992
Cdr. F. Scherber	April 1992 - April 1994

APPENDIX 2

COMMANDING OFFICERS OF CANADIAN SUBMARINES

HMCS *CC1*

Keyes, A. St.V.	August 1914 - October 1914
Hanson, F.B.	January 1915 - December 1918

HMCS *CC2*

Jones, B.E.	August 1914 - April 1916
Lake, G.	April 1916 - November 1917
Hanson, F.B.	November 1917 - September 1918
(in charge of both during refit)	
Pitts, A.C.S.	September 1918 - December 1918

HMCS *CH14*

Wood, R.W.	April 1921 - June 1922

HMCS *CH15*

Watson, R.C.	May 1920 - June 1922

HMCS *U-190*

Wood, M. (RNVR)	May 1945 - October 1945
Holmes, E.A.D.	October 1945 - January 1946
Johnston, J.R.	January 1946 - July 1947

HMCS *U-889*

Holmes, E.A.D.	July 1945 - October 1945
Cross, J.A.	October 1945
Johnston, J.R.	October 1945 - January 1946

HMCS *Grilse*

Gigg, E.G.	May 1961 - August 1963
McMorris, G.C.	August 1963 - August 1964
Rodocanachi, J.	August 1964 - September 1966
Tate, M.	September 1966 - July 1968
Falstrem, C.E.	July 1968 - December 1968

HMCS *Rainbow*

Falstrem, C.E.	December 1968 - April 1970
Hunt, R.C.	April 1970 - July 1972
Crow, C.J.	July 1972 - August 1973
Barnes, L.W.	August 1973 - December 1974

HMCS *Ojibwa*

Tomlinson, S.G.	September 1965 - November 1966
Rodacanachi, J.	November 1966 - August 1967
Wood, J.C.	August 1967 - August 1969
Bell, J.E.D.	August 1969 - July 1971
Falstrem, C.E.	July 1971 - May 1972
Perks, R.C.	June 1972 - July 1974
Bell, J.E.D.	September 1974 - January 1975
Barnes, L.W.	January 1975 - March 1976
Sloan, W.J.	March 1976 - August 1977
Jones, J.T.O.	August 1977 - July 1979
McMillan, K.F.	July 1979 - December 1979
Ewan, J.M.	December 1979 - June 1980
Nicolson, N.P.	June 1980 - January 1984
Webster, E.P.	January 1984 - April 1985
Irvine, W.C.	April 1985 - September 1986
Plante, J.A.Y.	September 1986 - August 1987
Macdonald, A.L.	April 1988 - February 1989
Bush, R.E.	February 1989 - August 1989
Davidson, R.A.	August 1989 - December 1990
Marsaw, D.C.	December 1990 - October 1993
Kavanagh, P.T.	November 1993 -

HMCS *Okanagan*

Frawley, N.H.H.	June 1968 - August 1969
Meek, G.R.	August 1969 - November 1969
Temple, L.G.	November 1969 - December 1969
Crow, C.J.	December 1969 - December 1970
Waddell, H.R.	December 1970 - October 1971
Falstrem, C.E.	October 1971 - May 1973
Bell, J.E.D.	May 1973 - August 1974
Hunt, R.C.	August 1974 - October 1975
Nesbit, K.G.	October 1975 - June 1977
Ewan, J.M.	June 1977 - July 1978
Ferguson, J.S.	July 1978 - July 1980
Scherber, F.	July 1980 - January 1982
Dunlop, A.B.	January 1982 - May 1982
MacLean, M.B.*	May 1982 - August 1983
Webster, E.P.	August 1983 - January 1984
Plante, J.A.Y.	January 1984 - March 1984
Webb, D.F. (RAN)	March 1984 - April 1985
Webster, E.P.	April 1985 - August 1985
MacDonald, A.L.	August 1985 - March 1985
Nicholson, N.P.	March 1988 - August 1989
Irvine, W.C.	August 1989 - August 1990

Mosher, L.B.	August 1990 - May 1991
Bush, R.E.	June 1991 - June 1992
Hickey, L.M.	June 1992 -

HMCS *Onondaga*

Meek, G.R.	June 1967 - August 1968
Temple, L.G.	August 1968 - January 1970
Waddell, A.R.	October 1971 - June 1972
Cairns, P.W.	June 1972 - July 1974
Perks, R.C.	July 1974 - July 1975
Lund, W.G.	January 1977 - July 1978
Ewan, J.M.	August 1978 - November 1979
McMillan, K.F.	December 1979 - March 1981
Dunlop, A.B.	March 1981 - January 1982
Plante, J.A.Y.	December 1983 - July 1986
Hickey, L.M.	July 1986 - May 1987
Carter, R.D. (RAN)	May 1987 - December 1987
Diercks, J. (RAN)	December 1987 - July 1988
Bush, R.E.	July 1988 - January 1989
Truscott, R.M.	January 1990 - July 1992
Woodburn, W.A.	July 1992 -

APPENDIX 3

CANADIAN SUBMARINERS WHO PASSED PERISHER AND
COMMANDED ROYAL NAVY SUBMARINES IN WWI AND WWII

Cross, Lt. J.A., RCNVR

| HMS/M *Unseen* | February 1945 - August 1945 |
| *U-889* | October 1945 |

Edwards, Lt. J.G., RCN

| HMS/M *C18* | November 1918 - December 1918 |
| HMS/M *R1* | June 1919 - November 1919 |

Johnson, Capt. B.L., CBE, DSO, RD, RCNR

HMS/M *H8*	May 1915 - March 1916
HMS/M *D3*	April 1916 - November 1917
HMS/M *E54*	December 1917 - May 1918
HMS/M *H15*	June 1918 - November 1918

Maitland-Dougall, Lt. W.McK., RCN
HMS/M *D1*   September 1917 - November 1917
HMS/M *D3*   November 1917 - March 1918
(possibly took Perisher – cannot be confirmed.)

Sherwood, LCdr. F.H., DSO and bar, RCNVR.
HMS/M *P556*   March 1943 - June 1943
HMS/M *Spiteful*   July 1943 - November 1945

Watson, Lt. R.C., RCN
HMS/M *V3*   September 1918 - December 1918
HMS/M *R8*   December 1918 - May 1919
HMS/M *R2*   June 1919 - November 1919
HMS/M *H44*   February 1920 - May 1920

APPENDIX 4

CANADIAN SUBMARINERS WHO HAVE BEEN DECORATED

Forbes, SLt. E.K., RCNVR
DSC for "Distinguished services in successful patrols in HM Submarines" while first lieutenant in HMS/M *P34*. December 1942.

Johnson, LCdr. B.L., RNR
DSO for "Gallantry aboard *H8* and for continued service in submarines" while CO of *H8*. November 1917.

Sherwood, Lt. F.H., RCNVR
DSC for "Bravery in successful submarine patrols" while first lieutenant in HMCS/M *Safari*. March 1943.
Bar to DSC for "Gallant services in Far East war patrols" while CO of HMS/M *Spiteful*. July 1945.

APPENDIX 5

CANADIAN SUBMARINERS WHO LOST THEIR LIVES ON ACTIVE SERVICE

Bonnell, Lt. C.E., RCNVR. January 3rd, 1943, when HMS/M *P311* was lost off Sardinia en route to his first chariot operation.

Maitland-Dougall, Lt. W. McK., RCN. March 12th, 1918, while CO of HMS/M *D3* when the submarine was sunk in error by an Allied airship off the coast of northern France.

McCloud, PO2. L. RCN. June 16, 1953, when an experimental torpedo exploded in HMS/M *Sidon* in Portland harbour, England.

Russel, Lt. H.D.S., RCNVR. December 12th, 1942, when HMS *Traveller* was lost in the Gulf of Taranto, Italy.

Notes

Chapter 1
The Birth of the Canadian Submarine Service, 1914

1   Interview with M. Kirkpatrick-Crockett, officer in charge of Black Rock Battery, 18 May 1962, PABC, Oral History Tape No. 1306, tape 1.

2   *Vancouver Daily Province,* "Esquimalt excited when subs hove into sight," 8 February 1936.

3   Canadian Broadcasting Corporation interview with Frederick W. Crickard, broadcast on 13 December 1959; transcript, DHIST, Biography, C.

4   B.L. Johnson, *Naval Incidents 1914 to 1919,* undated, VACA, ADD MSS 581.

5   Victoria *Daily Colonist,* 5 August 1914.

6   Primary sources for this section included Edwards to PABC, 24 April 1956, PABC, O/A/Ed 9; *John Grant "Jock" Edwards. 1893-1964. Biographical Notes,* undated, Lansdell Papers (private); and Keyes's Royal Navy Record of Service, PRO, ADM 196/47, 280.

7   Primary sources for this section include the sworn evidence given at the Royal Commission on War Supplies, Arms and Munitions and Concerning the Purchase of Submarines (known as the Davidson Commission), DHIST, 80/522; NAC, RG 24, 3966/4018/11902; and the McBride papers, PABC, ADD MSS 347, vol. 1, file 7; and the Mcintosh papers (private).

8   Interview with M. Kirkpatrick-Crockett, 18 May 1962, PABC, Oral History Tape No. 1306, tape 1.

9   *Victoria Daily Times,* 5 August 1914.

10 Primary sources for this section include the Borden papers, NAC, MG 26, H-1; and G.N. Tucker, "The Naval Policy of Sir Robert Borden, 1912-14," *Canadian Historical Review,* March 1947, 3.

11 Admiralty report, 1912 (originally SECRET, now declassified by the PRO), DHIST, 81/744.

12 The Naval Aid Bill, the Borden papers, NAC, MG 26, H-1, vol. 6, reel C-4199.

13 Churchill to McBride, 9 December 1912, Mcintosh Papers (private).

14 Churchill to McBride, 7 December 1913, ibid.

Chapter 2
HMCS *CC1* and *CC2* Go into Service

1   B.L. Johnson, *Naval Incidents 1914 to 1919,* undated, VACA, ADD MSS 581.

2   Adrian St. Vincent Keyes, Record of Service, PRO, ADM 196/47, 280.

3   The primary source for this section is Johnson, *Naval Incidents 1914 to 1919.*

4   Canadian Broadcasting Corporation interview with AB F.W. Crickard, 13 December 1959; transcript, DHIST, Biography, C.

5   Johnson, *Naval Incidents 1914 to 1919.*

6   Primary sources for this section include the McBride papers, PABC, ADD MSS 347, vol. 1, file 7; and Johnson, *Naval Incidents 1914 to 1919.*

7 For a more detailed description, see J.H. Ferguson, "Maitland-Dougall," *Resolution,* Summer 1991, 11-15.

8 Norman Hacking, *The Two Barneys,* Vancouver: Gordon Soules Book Publishing Company, 1984.

9 Johnson, *Naval Incidents 1914 to 1919.*

10 Primary sources for this section include Dave Perkins, *Canada's Submariners: 1914-1923,* Erin, Ontario: Boston Mills Press, 1989; "*CC1* and *CC2*: The First Canadian Submarines," *Maritime Engineering Journal,* April 1986, 5-13; and the author's interview with Mrs. "Peggy" Mcintosh, 20 November 1985.

11 Primary sources for this section include PRO, ADM 116/1057; NAC, RG 24, 5636 and 7152; Johnson, *Naval Incidents 1914 to 1919;* DHIST, Biography, C. 38-22-1 (vol. 1); and *Crowsnest,* "Pioneer Submariner Leaves the Service," September 1956.

12 Sessional Paper No. 158, 1915, Ottawa: King's Printer, 1917, PABC, UC/265/C2A27.

13 Canadian Broadcasting Corporation interview with F.W. Crickard, 13 December 1959, DHIST, Biography, C.

14 Primary sources for this section include NAC, RG25, 578,P1/89; and the Borden papers, NAC, MG 26, H1(A), vol. 46, reel C-4235.

15 DNS to deputy minister of the Naval Service, 23 September 1914, MMBC, Sessional Paper No. 158, 1958.

Chapter 3
Questioning the Purchase and Performance of
CC1 and *CC2,* 1915

1 A.J. Marder, *From the Dreadnought to Scapa Flow,* vol. 1, *The Road to War,* Oxford: Oxford University Press, 1961.

2 Primary sources for this section include the Borden papers, NAC, MG 26, H1(A); PABC, GR 441, vol. 165; and Sessional Paper No. 158, UC/265/C2A27.

3 McBride's speech, 24 February 1915, PABC, GR 441, vol. 165, 2.

4 Primary sources for this section include NAC, RG24, 7152, 7153, 3593, and 4027.

5 Cdr. P.C.W. Howe to minister of naval service, c. July 1915, NAC, RG 24, 3593, 45-2-3.

6 Capt. Hardy, RN, CO of HMS *Avoca,* to Esquimalt Dockyard, 27 March 1917, NAC, RG24, 4027, 1062-6-10.

7 The transcript of the Davidson Commission, DHIST, 80/522.

8 Probably, Victoria *Daily Colonist,* c. 6 October 1915, editorial.

9 *Victoria Daily Times,* c. 6 October 1915, editorial.

Chapter 4
The "Canadian" H Boats, 1915–1916

1 Primary sources include the Borden papers, NAC, MG 26, H1(A); and Gaddis Smith, *The Clandestine Submarines of 1914-1915: An Essay in the History of the North Atlantic Triangle,* report of the Canadian Historical Society Annual Meeting, June 1963.

2 Fisher to Admiral Sir John Jellicoe, C-in-C Home Fleet, 3 November 1914, quoted in A.J. Marder's *Fear God and Dreadnought,* vol. 3, London: Cape 1959.

3 Smith, *The Clandestine Submarines of 1914-1915.*

4 The primary sources for this section include B.L. Johnson, *Naval Incidents 1914 to 1919,* undated, VACA, ADD MSS 581; PRO, ADM 173/2627; and PRO, ADM 137/383 and 2069, ADM 186/684.

5 Author's interview with J.H. Stevenson, April 1987. Mr. Stevenson served with Johnson in World War Two and remembers him recalling the incident.

6 Primary sources for this section include Johnson, *Naval Incidents 1914 to 1919;* PRO, ADM 137/2069 and ADM 186/684; and RNSMM, Notes on Officers.

7 *Daily Mail,* "Submarine Drama: how a mined boat returned home," 21 May 1916.

8 Ibid.

9 Report of Proceedings of HMS/M *H8,* 16-23 March 1916, PRO, ADM 137/2069.

10 Captain(S), HMS *Maidstone,* to the Admiralty, Incident Report, 24 March 1916, PRO, ADM 137/381, p. 54.

11 John G. Bower ("Klaxon"), *On Patrol,* Edinburgh and London: William Blackwood and Sons, 1919.

12 *Daily Mail*, "Submarine drama: How a mined boat returned home," 21 May 1916.

13 Notes on Officers, RNSMM.

Chapter 5
Canadian Submariners in Europe, 1915–1917

1 Primary sources for this chapter include B.L. Johnson, *Naval Incidents 1914 to 1919*, VACA, ADD MSS 581; PRO, ADM 137/383, 1363, 2077, ADM 171/78-88; and ADM 173/1032, 1033.

2 Notes on Officers, RNSMM.

Chapter 6
HMCS *CC1* and *CC2*, 1917

1 J.H. Hamilton, *Western Shores*, PABC, NW/387/H218.

2 DNS to RAdm Sir Dudley de Chair, chief of staff to the Governor General of Canada, 28 May 1917, NAC, RG 24, 4027, 1062-18-2.

3 Primary sources for this section include NAC, RG 24, 3595, 3969, 4027.

4 J.H. Hamilton, *Western Shores*.

5 The primary source for this section includes the Report of the Davidson Commission, Ottawa: King's Printer, 1917, PABC, UC/265/C2A27.

6 *Victoria Times*, undated, "Thought Aeroplanes were making Raid." An interview with the cox'n of *CC2*.

Chapter 7
Canadian Submariners in Europe, 1917–1918

1 Primary sources for this chapter include PRO, ADM 137/1551, 2076, 3598, and ADM 173/1209, 1210, 1211; B.L. Johnson, *Naval Incidents 1914 to 1919* and his personal notebooks, VACA, ADD MSS 581; the Williams papers (private); and RNSMM, Notes on Officers.

2 Dave Perkins, *Canada's Submariners: 1914-1923*, Erin, Ontario: Boston Mills Press, 1989.

3 Admiralty, No. 722/008/5, 17 March 1918, PRO, ADM 137/3598.

4 Cdr. A. Quicke, RN, to Commodore(S), 15 March 1918, ibid.

5 Admiralty, No. 722/008/5, 17 April 1918, ibid.

Chapter 8
HMCS *CC1* and *CC2*, 1918

1 The primary sources for this section include NAC, RG 24, 3593 and 3969, and NSS 1047-19-4; *Notes from the log of HMCS* Shearwater *on activities connected with hydrophone experiments and training on the Bras d'Or Lakes*, RCN History, general, 1920-30, DHIST, 81/520/1440-5, vol. VIII; and Alexander Graham Bell National Historic Park, Home Notes, vol. 112.

2 *Notes from the log of HMCS* Shearwater.

3 Ibid.

4 The primary sources for this section include B.L. Johnson, *Naval Incidents 1914 to 1919*, VACA, ADD MSS 581; NAC, RG 24, 7840; Notes on Officers, RNSMM; and correspondence with Cmdre. B. Oland, RCNR (Ret).

Chapter 9
HMCS *CH14* and *CH15*, 1919–1922

1 Primary sources for this chapter include NAC, RG 24, 4028, 3595, 5607, 5694, 7182; and DHIST, H-Class and *CH14* and *CH15*.

2 DNS to the deputy minister of the Naval Service, NAC, RG 24, 4028, 1062-22-2, vol. 1.

3 Victoria *Daily Colonist*, 15 July 1924, "Sailboat sinks and five drown," and the *Victoria Daily Times*, 14 July 1924, "Five Lost Offshore."

Chapter 10
Canadians Volunteer for Submarines in World War II, 1940–1941

1 Report of Admiral of the Fleet, Viscount Jellicoe of Scapa, GCB, OM, GCVO, on the Naval Mission to the Dominion of Canada (November-December 1919), NAC, RG 24, 5669, 78-1-14.

2 Commodore Walter Hose, RCN, to the naval historian, 23 January 1962, DHIST, RCN 1920-39, folder A, file 8.

3 The primary sources for this section include Bryant, RAdm. B. RN, DSO, DSC and Bar, *One Man Band*, London: William Kimber and Company, 1958; and PRO, ADM 199/1835.

4 Used with Mr. F. H. Sherwood's permission.

Chapter 11
Canadians in the Mediterranean, 1941–1943

1 Primary sources for this account include RNSMM, *OPR* class; and PRO, ADM 199/1888.

2 Primary sources for this section include RNSMM, the transcript of a taped account by Mr. E.K. Forbes, 28 January 1987; PRO, ADM199/1920/1825; and correspondence from Forbes to the author.

3 Primary sources for this chapter include PRO, ADM 199/1839,1921,1925, 1983; ADM 234/381; and ADM236/39.

4 The primary sources for this section are PRO, ADM 199/1921, ADM 234/381 and ADM 236/39.

Chapter 12
The Charioteers, 1942–1943

1 Captain W.R. Fell, CMG, CBE, DSC, RN, *The Sea Our Shield,* London: Cassell and Company Ltd., 1966.

2 The primary sources for this chapter include PRO, ADM 199/1833,1922 and ADM 234/381; RNSMM, A1984/60; and interviews, taped accounts, and correspondence with A.W. Moreton.

3 Captain Bill Shelford, RN (Ret), "Chariots of Fire," *Diver,* January 1979, 16–18.

4 Fell, *The Sea Our Shield.*

5 RAdm. G.W.G. "Shrimp," Simpson, CB, CBE, RN, *Periscope View,* London: MacMillan, 1972.

6 RCN Press Release, 9 March 1945, NAC, RG 24, 11754, Submarines Allied; *Toronto Evening Telegram,* "Toronto Man, One of the 'Great Heroes' of War Gave Life in Strike at Foe in 2-Man Submarine," 9 March 1945; and another Toronto newspaper, possibly the *Globe and Mail,* undated, "Toronto Officer Called 'Great Hero' of this War."

Chapter 13
The RCN Begs for Submarines, 1940–1945

1 Primary sources for this chapter include NAC, RG 24, 11019, 11100, 11101, 11128, 11543, 11574, 11575, 11580, 11647, 11652; RG 24, 83-84/167, 3514, 3613, 3924; PRO, ADM1/13037, 18651 and ADM234/381; DHIST, Admiralty Ship Movement books and Submarines 8000, general; RNSMM, COQC Attack Records; and correspondence with Cdr. L. Hill, RNR (Ret), Kapitein H. Van

Oostrom Soede, RNN (Ret), Mrs. J.A. Cross, G. McPhee, E.A.D. Holmes, and C.W. Perry.

2 Commodore Commanding Halifax Force to NSHQ, 7 January 1941, NAC, RG 24, 83-84/167, 3613, S8020-476.

3 Director of Anti-Submarine to the Naval Staff, 7 August 1942, NAC, RG 24, 83-84/167, 3613, S8020-476.

4 Minutes of a meeting of the Joint (RCN/RCAF) ASW Committee, 26 June 1943, NAC, RG 24, 11575, 01-18-3.

5 Minutes of the Naval Staff Meeting, 9 November 1943, NAC, RG 24, 83-84/167, 3613, S8020-476.

6 David Zimmerman, *The Great Naval Battle of Ottawa,* Toronto: University of Toronto Press, 1989.

7 Captain(D), Halifax, to C-in-C CNA, 25 March 1945, NAC, RG 24, 11575, D 1-18-1.

8 Original sources for this section include PRO, ADM 234/381; NAC, RG 24, 11652; RNSMM, COQC Attack Records; and correspondence with Mrs. J.A. Cross, Cdr. L.F.L. Hill, RNR (Ret), CO of *P553,* E.A.D. Holmes, W.W. Holmes and C.W. Perry.

9 George McPhee to author, 16 March 1990.

Chapter 14
Canadians in European Waters, 1943

1 *Salty Dips,* vol. 1, privately printed, NOAC, Ottawa Branch, 1983.

2 Primary sources for this section are correspondence and interviews with F.H. Sherwood.

3 *Salty Dips,* vol. 1.

4 Primary sources for this section include PRO, ADM 199/1840, 1921; RNSMM, A1944/19; and correspondence from E.K. Forbes to his mother and to the author.

5 RCN press release, 4 May 1943, NAC, RG 24, 11754, Submarines, Allied.

Chapter 15
Canadians in European Waters, 1943–1944

1 Primary sources for this chapter include PRO, ADM 199/1822, 1841, 1868; RNSMM, A1944/28; wartime correspondence from F.K. Fowler (to his mother); correspondence with R.P. Blake, F. Bunbury, F.K. Fowler, J. Gardner, and G. McPhee.

2 Third Submarine Flotilla, Recommendation for Decoration or Mention in Dispatches, 5 November 1944, RNSMM, A1944/28.

3 George McPhee to author, 16 March 1990.

Chapter 16
A Canadian Commands an X-craft, 1944

1 Composed by Lt. I. Jarvis, RN, commanding officer of the first passage crew of *XE8*, and quoted by LCdr. J.C. Ruse, RCN (Ret), in an interview with the author, 12 January 1990.

2 The primary sources for this chapter include PRO, ADM 1/18651 and 18654; and correspondence with LCdr. J.C. Ruse, RCN (Ret).

Chapter 17
Canadians in Far Eastern Waters, 1944

1 Primary sources for this chapter include PRO, ADM 199/1816, 1863, 1870, 1882, 1884, 1924, ADM 234/382; RNSMM, A1980/104 and the *Tantalus* file; correspondence from G. Carr (Cox'n HMS/M *Spiteful*), Cdr. E. Gigg, RCN (Ret), W.A. Gilmour, R. Harrison (AB in HMS/M *Spiteful*), A.W. Jorgenson, and G. McPhee.

2 *Salty Dips,* vol.1, privately printed by the NOAC, Ottawa Branch, 1985.

3 Ibid.

4 Ibid.

5 Commander (Submarines), 7th Fleet, to C-in-C, U.S. Fleet, 18 April 1945, PRO, ADM 199/1870.

6 Author's interview with R. Harrison, 25 February 1989.

7 Admiralty press release, undated, NAC, RG 24, 11754, Submarines, Allied.

8 *Tantalus* – Depth Charge Attack – September 1944, *Tantalus* file, RNSMM.

9 While attacking a 700-ton vessel with her gun, *Shakespeare* sustained severe damage and was unable to dive. Subsequent air attacks caused fifteen casualties. The submarine was towed into Trincomalee five days after the incident and was declared a total loss after arriving in England.

10 Previously called *Untamed* (*P58*), she had failed to surface following an exercise in Holy Loch on 30 May 1943. She was located and salvaged, with the loss of her entire crew.

11 Cliff Bastin, a survivor, to the Royal Navy Submarine Museum, 23 July 1980, RNSMM, A1980-104. Bastin was rescued many hours later by the Japanese and suffered at their hands for the rest of the war.

Chapter 18
The "Canadian" U-Boats, 1945

1 Primary sources for this chapter include NAC, RG 24, 11116, 11117, 11121, 11601, 11752, 11935; RG 24, 83-84/167, 3514, 3741; and correspondence with E.A.D. Holmes.

2 Admiralty to all U-boats, 1 May 1945, NAC, RG 24, 11752, C.S.-638-2, Surrender of U-boats.

3 Base Health Officer, Newfoundland, to Senior Submarine Officer, 18 May 1945, NAC, RG 24, 11935, 8000-U190.

4 NAC, RG 24, 11117, 66-1-4.

5 Senior Officer, Ship Reserve, to COAC, 17 October 1947, NAC, RG 24, 11601, SCH 8000-476/2.

Chapter 19
Canada Rents Submarines, 1946–1959

1 The Hon. Ralph Campney, PC, QC, the minister of national defence, 16 June 1955, HCD, p. 4914.

2 Primary sources for this section include NAC, RG 24, 11522 and 11580; NAC, RG 24, 83-84/167, 3923, 3924; and DHIST, *Ambrose,* 8000.

3 The Hon. B. Claxton, minister of national defence, 15 April 1953, HCD, p. 3920.

4 Minister of national defence to CNS, 22 February 1954, NAC, RG 24, 83-84/167, 3924, S8375-500SS, vol. 3.

5 Directorate of Public Relations (National Defence), press release, 12 November 1954, DHIST, *Ambrose,* 8000.

6 Primary sources for this section include RNSMM, A1956/1; and correspondence with J. Berchem and J.C. Gourdeau.

7 Author's interview with J.C. Gourdeau, 5 February 1990.

8 Ibid.

9 Primary sources for this section include House of Commons Debates; NAC, RG 24, 83-84/167, 142, 3923, 3924, and 3925.

10 FOAC to NSHQ, 12 November 1956, NAC, RG 24, 83-84/167, 3923, S8375/SS, vol. 3.

11 In declining, CNS noted that perhaps
Canada should consider paying the premi-
um to develop the necessary expertise for
her proposed submarine service.

Chapter 20
The Nuclear-Powered Submarine Acquisition, 1960–1962

1 Primary sources for this chapter include
NAC, RG 24, 83-84/167, 142, 500,
3514, and 3782; DHIST, 73/814, 75/149,
88/51, 88/64, Nuclear Propulsion, 6901-
50, and the Report of the Nuclear
Submarine Survey Team, 124.013 (D2).

2 For example, *Victoria Colonist*, "Canada-
Made, A-Powered Submarines to Form
RCN's Major Fighting Force," 10 May
1958, 1.

3 DHIST, Nuclear Propulsion, 6901-50.

4 For example, *Ottawa Citizen*, "Role of
Navy Only Sure Thing as Experts Wrestle
Estimates," 11 December 1958.

5 For example, *Saint John Telegraph Journal,*
"Six Subs to Cost $100,000,000," 18 May
1961.

Chapter 21
The Rebirth of the Canadian Submarine Service, 1961

1 Capt. B.L. Johnson, RCNR (Ret), to
RAdm. Finch-Noyes, RCN, 21 July 1961,
the Gigg papers (private).

2 The primary sources for this section
include NAC, RG 24, 8504, 20024;
NAC, RG 24, 83-84/167, 709, 3925;
DHIST 88/64, HMS/M *Grilse*, MMBC,
scrapbook of HMS/M *Grilse*, and correspondence with G. Sandecock.

3 *New London Evening Day,* 12 May 1961,
"*Burrfish* becomes Canadians' *Grilse*," and
Crowsnest, May 1961, pp. 5-7.

4 Reports of Proceedings, HMCS/M *Grilse,*
1961-66, NAC, RG 24, 83-84/167, 709,
1926-SS71.

5 Ibid.

6 Reports of Proceedings, HMCS/M *Grilse,*
11 May 1962, 1961-62, ibid.

7 Gary Sandecock to the author, 7 April
1989.

8 The diary is still in Gary Sandecock's pos-
session. Sandecock did not allow the
author to see it, but sent quotations in his
correspondence.

9 Primary sources for this section include
NAC, RG 24, 5545; NAC, RG 24, 83-
84/167 3515 and 3925; and DHIST,
88/64 and Submarines, General, 8000.

10 A minute to NSS 8000-SS (DG Ships), 28
June 1963, Gigg papers, DHIST, 88/64-6.

11 The minister of national defence, the
Hon. P. Hellyer, to the Special Committee
on Defence, 5 November 1963, Gigg
Papers. DHIST, 88/64-6.

12 *Ottawa Citizen,* "Shipbuilders protest 'sub'
plan," 8 November 1963.

Chapter 22
The Canadian O Boats

1 Author's interview with G.A. Kastner, 1
December 1988.

2 Primary sources for this section include
NAC, RG 24, 83-84/167, 3515, 3603,
3925; DHIST, 88/64, and HMS *Ambrose,*
8000; files of the Procurement Executive,
Ministry of Defence, Bath, England; cor-
respondence with N. Frawley, first CO of
HMCS/M *Okanagan,* Cdr. E. Gigg, RCN
(Ret), Lady Patricia Miers, and T. Sawyer.

3 Author's interview with S.G. Tomlinson, 5
June 1989.

4 *Replacement for HMCS* Grilse, DHIST,
Gigg papers, 88/64-2.

Chapter 23
Selection and Training of Canadian Submariners

1 Canada's area in the Atlantic stretches
from Labrador to Greenland, south to the
mid-Atlantic and from there, west to Nova
Scotia.

2 Author's interview with Capt(N). A.
Dunlop, 3 October 1990.

3 Compton-Hall, Richard. *Submarine versus
Submarine,* Newton Abbot, Devon,
England: David and Charles Publishers,
1988.

4 Primary sources for this section include
many interviews listed elsewhere; and
Rosada, P. (Capt(N). Nesbit, CD.) *Those
!@?#! Submariners,* Canadian Maritime
Warfare Technical Bulletin, vol. 6, no. 2,
Fall 1984.

5 *The All Round Look (*HMCS/M
Onondaga's unofficial newspaper), 1st ed.,
18 July 1978.

Chapter 25
Rejuvenating the O Boats, 1980–1986

1 The author is very grateful for the assistance of Robert Spittal, P.Eng, NDC, of
the Directorate of Underwater Combat
Systems of the Department of National
Defence, for his patient explanations concerning SOUP.

Chapter 26
Replacing the O Boats, 1983–1987

1 *Canada's Maritime Defence*, The Report of
the Sub-committee on National Defence
of the Standing Senate Committee on
Foreign Affairs, May 1983.

2 Cdr. E.J.M. Young (former project director of CASAP), "Submarines for the
Canadian Maritime Forces," *Canadian
Defence Quarterly*, Summer 1986, vol. 16,
no. 1.

3 Toronto *Globe and Mail*, "Builders bet on
nuclear subs," 6 April 1987.

Chapter 27
The Nuclear-Powered Submarine Acquisition,
1985–1987

1 A Department of National Defence poll in
March 1987 showed 59 percent of
Canadians supported the plan to use
SSNs. By May 1987, just before the White
Paper was made public, the support had
dropped to 45 percent but by then Beatty
had the Cabinet on board.

2 *Globe and Mail*, "Nuclear subs reported to
have Cabinet support," 2 May 1987.

3 Author's interview with Captain(N) A.
Dunlop, CD, 1 October 1990.

4 "Admiral hails 'flexibility' of nuclear subs,"
Toronto Star, 13 June 1987, B5.

5 Quoted in *Wings Magazine*, CASAP,
"Superabundance of Self-Confidence,"
1988, 60.

6 Ibid.

7 "Submarine plan sends Russians 'wrong
signals' opposition says," *Toronto Star*, 6
June 1987, A10.

8 Canada, Parliament, Minutes of
Proceedings and Evidence, Standing
Committee on National Defence, 2
February 1988.

Chapter 28
The Nuclear-Powered Submarine Acquisition,
1987–1989

1 For example, the *Financial Post*, "Frigate
contract political dilemma for Mulroney,"
30 November 1987.

2 The *Vancouver Sun*, "It's U.K. sub, paper
predicts," 29 March 1989, A7.

3 Mr. E. Healey, former assistant deputy
minister (matériel). Personal interview, 26
April 1990.

Chapter 29
The Future of the Canadian Submarine Service

1 For example, *Maclean's*, "Keeping the
dream alive," by Marc Clark, 1 January
1990, 48-50.

2 In July 1991, RAdm. J.R. Anderson, CD,
was promoted and appointed as commander, Maritime Command. He held this
position for a year before returning to
Ottawa as vice-chief of the Defence Staff
in July 1992. Anderson became chief of
Defence Staff in 1993, a position he held
for a few months.

3 "Canada to close bases in Germany," and
"True North needs less guarding, Ottawa
decides," Toronto *Globe and Mail*, 18
September 1991, pp. A1 and A6.

4 "Defence: Special Report," Toronto
Financial Post, 21 October 1991, 40-43.

5 "Defence Capital Acquisition Program
announced," National Defence News
Release, 20/92, 7 April 1992.

6 "Very well done."

INTERVIEWS

During the preparation of *Through a Canadian Periscope* the author interviewed many people, some several times. The majority of interviews were conducted in person.

PART ONE

Beaty, Mrs. B.W., (Lt. R.C. Watson's daughter).
Brown, Mr. Herbert, (Lt. T. Brown's son).
Cyr, Mr. Robert, (Abe Cyr's son – *CC1* and *CC2*).
Johnson, Mrs. J., (Lt.-Cdr. "Barney" Johnson's daughter-in-law).
Lansdell, Mrs. P. (Lt. Jock Edwards' daughter).
MacDonald, Mrs. Ine, (Lt. Jock Edwards' sister).
Mcintosh, Mr. Gregor, (Premier McBride's grandson).
Mcintosh, Mrs. Peggy, (Premier McBride's daughter).
May, Mrs. Marjorie, (Lt. Beech's daughter).
Pengelly, Mr. G.
Pitts, Mrs. Alice, (A.C.S. Pitts's wife).
Pitts, Mr. John, (A.C.S. Pitts's nephew).
Ridley, Mrs. M.
Stevenson, Mr. J.H.
Wills, Mr. A.
Wurtele, Mr. A.C.
Young, Mr. A.B.

PART TWO

Barzilay, Mr. P., (chief telegraphist in *O15*).
Bunbury, Mr. F.
Fennell, Mr. S. (Lt. R. Fennell's brother).
Gigg, Cdr. E.G.
Gilmour, Mr. W.A.
Hacking, Mr. N.
Halladay, Mrs. J.M., (Saunders' widow).
Harrison, Mr. R. (sailor in HMS/M *Spiteful*).
Holmes, Mr. Wayne W.
Johnston, Mr. J.R.
Moreton, Mr. A.W. (plus three hours of tapes).
Redmond, Mr. P., (cox'n of HMS/M *Visigoth*).
Roosjen, Mr. P. (sailor in *O15*).
Ruse, Mr. J.C. (X-craft).
Sherwood, Mr. F.H.
Thompson, Mr. G.

Welland, RAdm. R.P.
Williams, Mr. D.
Woods, Mr. J.D.

PART THREE

Anderson, VAdm. J.R., (former Chief, Submarine Acquisition)
Ashling, LCdr. D.
Barnes, Cdr. L., (project director of CPSP).
Baxter, Capt(N) B. (former project leader of CASAP)
Boivin, Mr. N.R.
Bowkett, Cmdre. E.G.A.
Bowness, Mr. G. (Staff Officer, *Oberon* construction).
Brower-Berkhoven, Mr. I.
Brown, Mr. J., (SRU(P)).
Cairns, VAdm. P.W., (former Commander, Maritime Command).
Cameron, LCdr. D., (planning officer CASAP).
Capern, Mr. R.G.
Christie, RAdm. W.B., (leader of *Oberon* construction team).
Crow, Capt(N) C.
Davies, Mr. P., (constructor, Canadian *Oberons*).
De Wolfe, VAdm. H.G.
Dobson, BGen. R.
Dunlop, Capt(N) A., (former commander of First Canadian Submarine Squadron).
Ewan, Cdr. J.M.
George, VAdm. R., (former Commander, Maritime Command).
Gigg, Cdr. E.G., (first Commander of First Canadian Submarine Squadron).
Gourdeau, Mr. J.C. (HMS/M *Sidon*).
Harrison, Capt(N) D., (former project leader of CASAP).
Healey, Mr. E.J., (former ADM (Matériel)).
Henderson, Mr. R., (VSEL UK).
Hunt, Capt(N) R.C.
Kastner, Mr. G.A.
Kirkpatrick, Mr. Justice J.R.H.
Lund, Capt(N) W.G.D.
MacLean, Capt(N) B.
McFarlane, Dr. J.R.
McKerracher, LCdr. D.
Murray, Cmdre. E.R.A.
Nesbit, Capt(N) K.G.
Newbery, Capt(N) J.E.
Nichol, Mr. R.
Nicholson, Cdr. N.
Peck, LCdr. R. (RN Submarine School).

Perks, Mr. R.C.

Rodocanachi, Mr. J.

Sargent, Mr. W., (industrial engineer, SRU(P)).

Sorrell, Mr. C.

Spittal, Mr. R.A., DND, (Underwater Combat Systems).

Temple, Cdr. J.

Thomas, VAdm. C.M., (former VCDS and Commander, Maritime Command).

Thurman, Mr. G., (constructor, Canadian *Oberons*).

Tomlinson, Mr. S.G., (first CO of *Ojibwa*).

Welland, RAdm R.P.

Wiseman, Mr. G.

Wood, VAdm. J.C., (former Commander, Maritime Command).

Young, Cdr. E.J.M., (former project director of CASAP).

And the members of the First Canadian Submarine Squadron.

BIBLIOGRAPHY

Alden, Cdr. J.D., USN (Ret.). *The fleet submarine in the U.S. Navy.* Annapolis, Maryland: Naval Institute Press, 1979.

Allard, Jean. *The Memoirs of General Jean V. Allard.* Vancouver: University of British Columbia Press, 1988.

Anderson, Frank J. *Submarines, Submariners and Submarining.* Hamden, Connecticut: The Shoestring Press Inc., c. 1963.

Anonymous. *Submarines.* London: Jade Books, 1983.

Anscomb, Charles. *Submariner.* London: William Kimber and Co., 1957.

Aster, S, ed. *The Second World War as a National Experience.* Ottawa: Canadian Committee for the History of the Second World War, 1981.

Bacon, Sir Reginald. *The Life of Lord Fisher.* Volumes 1 and 2. London: publisher unknown, c. 1929.

Bagnasco, Ermino. *Submarines of World War II.* Annapolis, Maryland: Naval Institute Press, 1977.

Baxter, Richard. *Stand by to Surface.* Toronto: Cassell and Co., 1944.

Beach. E. *Cold Is the Sea.* New York: Holt, Reinhart and Winston, 1978.

Beesly, Patrick. *Room 40 - British Naval Intelligence, 1914-18.* London: Hamish Hamilton, 1982.

Bennett, Mark. *Under the Periscope.* London: W. Collins Sons and Co., 1919.

Benson, J. and C.E.T. Warren. *Above Us the Waves: The story of midget submarines and human torpedoes.* London: Harrap, 1953.

Blair, Clay. *The Atomic Submarine and Admiral Rickover.* New York: H. Holt, 1954.

Bland, Douglas. *The Administration of Defence Policy in Canada 1947-1985.* Kingston, Ontario: Ronald P. Frye and Company, 1987.

Borden, Henry. *Memoirs of Sir Robert L. Borden.* Toronto: Macmillan Co. of Canada, 1938.

Boutilier, James A., ed. *RCN in Retrospect, 1910-1968.* Vancouver: University of British Columbia Press, 1982.

Bower, John, G. ("Klaxon"). *On Patrol.* Edinburgh and London: William Blackwood and Sons, 1919.

———. *The Story of Our Submarines.* Edinburgh and London: William Blackwood and Sons, c.1919.

Brewin, Andrew. *Stand on Guard: the Search for a Canadian Defence Policy.* Toronto: McClelland and Stewart, 1965.

Brock, Jeffry V. *With Many Voices: Memoirs of a Sailor.* In 2 volumes. Toronto: McClelland and Stewart Ltd., 1981.

Brown, D.K. *A Century of Naval Construction*. England: Conway Maritime Press, 1983.

Bryant, RAdm Ben. *One Man Band*. London: William Kimber and Company Ltd., 1958. Also as *Submarine Commander*. Bantam Books Inc., 1980.

Cameron, Stevie. *Ottawa Inside Out*. Toronto: HarperCollins Publishers Ltd., 1989.

Carr, William Guy. *By Guess and By God*. London: Hutchinson & Co. (Publishers) Ltd., undated.

Chalmers, RAdm. W.S., RN. *The Life and Letters of David, Earl Beatty, Admiral of the Fleet*. London: Hodder and Stoughton, 1951.

Chatterton, E.K. *Danger Zone: The Story of the Queenstown Command*. Unknown publisher, 1934.

Cohen, Paul. *The Realm of the Submarine*. Toronto: Macmillan and Company, 1969.

Compton-Hall, Cdr. R. *Submarine versus Submarine*. Newton Abbot, England: David-Charles Publishers, 1988. And, New York: Orion Books, 1988.

Crane, Jonathan. *Submarine*. British Broadcasting Corporation: London, 1984.

Creed, David. *Operations of the Fremantle Submarine Base 1942-45*. Sydney, Australia: Naval Historical Society of Australia, undated.

Dewitz, Baron Hrolf Von. *War's New Weapons*. New York: Dodd, Mead and Company, 1915.

Domville-Fife, Charles. *Submarines and Sea Power*. London: G. Bell and Sons Ltd., 1919.

Douglas, Dr. W.A.B. "Conflict and Innovation in the Royal Canadian Navy, 1939-45" in *Naval Strategy in the Twentieth Century*. Edited by G. Jordan. New York: Crane Russack, 1977, 210-32.

Douglas, W.A.B, ed. *The RCN in Transition 1910-1985*. Vancouver: University of British Columbia Press, 1988.

Douglas, W.A.B, and Brereton Greenhous. *Out of the Shadows: Canada in the Second World War*. Toronto: Dundurn Press Ltd., 1993.

Eayrs, James. *In Defence of Canada*. In five volumes. Toronto: University of Toronto Press, 1965.

Essex, James W. *Victory in the St. Lawrence: Canada's Unknown War*. Erin, Ontario: The Boston Mills Press, 1984.

Everitt, Don. *The K-Boats*. London: Harrap and Co. Ltd., 1963.

Fell, Captain W.R., CMG, CBE, DSC, RN. *The Sea Our Shield*. London: Cassell and Company Ltd., 1966.

Foster, J.A. *Heart of Oak*. Toronto: Methuen, 1985.

Friedman, Norman. *Submarine Design and Development*. Annapolis, Maryland: Naval Institute Press, 1984.

German, Tony. *The Sea Is at Our Gates: The History of the Canadian Navy.* Toronto: McClelland and Stewart Inc., 1990.

Gibbons, Tony. *Modern Military Techniques: Submarines.* London: Collins Publishing Group, 1986.

Gough, Barry M. *Distant Dominion: Britain and the Northwest Coast of North America, 1579-1809.* Vancouver: University of British Columbia Press, 1980.

Granatstein, J.L. *Canadian Foreign Policy Since 1945: Middle Power or Satellite?* Toronto: The Copp Clark Publishing Company, 1970.

———. *MacKenzie King: His Life and World.* Toronto: McGraw-Hill Ryerson Ltd., 1977.

———. *Twentieth Century Canada.* Toronto: McGraw-Hill Ryerson, 1983.

———. *Canada 1957-1967: The Years of Uncertainty and Innovation.* Toronto: McCelland and Stewart Ltd., 1986.

Granatstein, J.L., and D. Morton. *Marching to Armageddon: Canada and the Great War.* Lester and Orpen Dennys, 1989.

Gray, Colin S. *Canadian Defence Priorities: a question of relevance.* Toronto: Clarke, Irwin and Company, 1972.

Gray, E. *A Damned Un-English Weapon.* London: Seeley Service and Co. Ltd., 1971.

Hacking, Norman. *The Two Barneys.* Vancouver: Gordon Soules Book Publishing Co., 1984.

Hackman, Willen. *Seek and Strike: A History of ASDIC.* London: Her Majesty's Stationery Office, 1984.

Hadley, Michael L. *U-Boats against Canada: German Submarines in Canadian Waters.* Montreal: McGill-Queen's University Press, 1985.

Hamilton, J.H. *Western Shores.* Vancouver: Progress Publishing Company Ltd., 1933.

Hart, B.H. Liddle. *Defence of the West.* Westport, Connecticut: Greenwood Press, 1970.

Hart, Sydney. *Discharged Dead.* London: White Lion Publishers Ltd., 1976.

Hellyer, Paul. *Damn the Torpedoes: My Fight to Unify Canada's Armed Forces.* Toronto: McClelland and Stewart Inc., 1990.

Henry, D. "British submarine policy 1918-1939." In *British Naval Policy 1860-1939.* Edited by B. Ranft. London: Hodder and Stoughton, 1977.

Hough, Richard. *Former Naval Person.* London: Weidenfeld and Nicolson Ltd., 1985.

———. *The Pursuit of Admiral Von Spee.* London: publisher unknown, 1969.

———. *The Great War at Sea 1914-18.* Oxford and New York: Oxford University Press, 1983.

Howarth, David. *The Shetland Bus.* Morley, England: The Elmsfield Press, 1976.

Humble, Richard. *Submarines: The Illustrated History.* London: Basinghall Books Ltd., 1981.

Hunter, Anthony, and Peter Shankland. *Dardanelles Patrol.* London: Mayflower Books, 1971.

Jameson, RAdm Sir William S. *The Most Formidable Thing.* London: R. Hart-Davis, 1965.

———. *Submariners V.C.* London: Davies, 1962.

Jellicoe, Admiral of the Fleet, The Rt. Hon., The Earl. *The Submarine Peril: Admiralty Policy in 1917.* London: Cassell and Co. Ltd., 1917.

Keegan, John. *The Price of Admiralty: The Evolution of Naval Warfare.* Markham, Ontario: Penguin Books Canada Ltd., 1988.

Kemp, P.K. *The British Sailor: A Social History of the Lower Deck.* London: J.M. Dent and Sons Ltd., 1970.

———. *H.M. Submarines.* London: Herbert Jenkins, 1952.

Kennedy, Paul M. *The Rise and Fall of British Naval Mastery.* New York: Scribner, 1976.

Keyes, Admiral of the Fleet, Sir Roger J.B. *Naval Memoirs of Admiral of the Fleet, Sir Roger Keyes.* In 2 vols. London: Thornton Butterworth Ltd., 1934-35.

Kipling, Rudyard. *Sea Warfare.* London: Macmillan and Co., 1916.

Lamb, James B. *The Corvette Navy: True stories from Canada's Atlantic War.* Toronto: Macmillan of Canada, 1977.

Lanctot, Gustave. *A History of Canada.* In 3 vols. Toronto: Clarke, Irwin, 1963-1964.

Lawrence, Hal. *A Bloody War: One man's memories of the Canadian Navy 1939-1945.* Scarborough, Ontario: Macmillan-NAL Publishers, 1980.

Lay, H.N. *Memoirs of a Mariner.* Ottawa: Lowe-Martin Company, 1982.

Liddle, Peter H. *The Sailors' War 1914-1918.* Poole, Dorset: Blandford Press Ltd., 1985.

Link, Arthur S. *The Struggle for Neutrality.* New York: Princeton, 1962.

Lipscombe, Cdr F.W. *The British Submarine.* Second edition, London: Conway Maritime Press, 1975.

Macintyre, Captain Donald, DSO and 2 bars, DSC, RN. *Fighting under the Sea.* London: Evans Brothers Ltd., 1965.

Macpherson K., and J. Burgess. *The Ships of Canada's Naval Forces, 1910-1981.* Toronto: Collins, 1981.

McInnis, Edgar. *Canada: A Political and Social History.* Third edition, Toronto: Holt, Rinehart and Winston, 1969.

McKee, Fraser. *Volunteers for Sea Service: A Brief History of the Royal Canadian Navy Volunteer Reserve.* Toronto: Houstons Standard, 1973.

McLin, Jon B. *Canada's Changing Defense Policy, 1957-1963: The Problems of a Middle Power in Alliance.* Baltimore: Johns Hopkins Press, 1967.

Mahan, Alfred Thayer. *The Influence of Sea Power upon History 1660-1783.* London: Methuen, 1965.

Marder, A.J. *Fear God and Dread Nought: The Correspondence of Admiral of the Fleet Lord Fisher of Kilverstone.* In 3 volumes. London: Cape. 1952-1959.

Marder, A.J. *From the Dreadnought to Scapa Flow: The Road to War 1904-14.* London and New York: Oxford University Press, 1961.

Mars, Alistair. *British Submarines at War 1939-1945.* Annapolis, Maryland: Naval Institute Press, 1971.

Metson, G., ed. *The Halifax Explosion.* Toronto: McGraw-Hill Ryerson Ltd., 1978.

Milner, Marc. *North Atlantic Run.* Toronto: University of Toronto Press, 1985.

Morton, Desmond. *Canada and War: A Military and Political History.* Toronto: Butterworths, 1971.

Mottola, Karl, ed. *The Arctic Challenge: Nordic and Canadian Approaches to Security and Cooperation in an Emerging International Region.* Boulder, Colorado: Westview Press, 1988.

Naval Officers' Associations of Canada. *Salty Dips.* In 3 volumes. Privately printed.

Neilsen, Erik. *The House Is Not a Home.* Toronto: Macmillan of Canada, 1989.

Nolan, Brian, and Brian J. Street. *Champagne Navy: Canada's Small Boat Raiders of the Second World War.* Toronto: Random House of Canada Ltd., 1991.

Paine, T.O. *Submarining: Three Thousand Books and Articles.* Santa Barbara, California: General Electric Company – TEMPO, Center for Advanced Studies, 1971.

Parkin, J.H. *Bell and Baldwin.* Toronto: University of Toronto Press, 1964.

Pearson, Lester B. *Mike.* In 3 volumes. Edited by John A. Munro and Alex I. Inglis. Toronto: University of Toronto Press, 1975.

Perkins, J. Dave. *Canada's Submariners: 1914-1923.* Erin, Ontario: The Boston Mills Press, 1989.

Polmar, Norman. *The American Submarine.* Annapolis: Nautical and Aviation Publishing Company of America, 1981.

Poolman, Kenneth. *Periscope Depth.* London: William Kimber and Co. Ltd., 1981.

Preston, Anthony. *Sea Combat off the Falklands.* London: Willow Books, 1982.

Rohmer, Richard. *Red Arctic.* Markham, Ontario: Fitzhenry and Whiteside, 1989.

Shaw, James L. *Ships of the Panama Canal.* Annapolis, Maryland: United States Naval Institute, 1985.

Simpson, RAdm. G.W.G. "Shrimp," CB, CBE, RN. *Periscope View.* London: Macmillan London Ltd., 1972.

Smith, Gaddis. *Britain's Clandestine Submarines 1914 - 1915.* Montreal: McGill Press, 1964.

Stacey, Charles P. *Arms, Men and Governments: the War Policies of Canada 1939-45.* Ottawa: Queen's Printer (with authority of the minister of national defence), 1970.

————. *A Very Double Life: The Private World of MacKenzie King.* Toronto: Macmillan, 1976.

————. *Canada and the Age of Conflict: A History of Canadian External Policies.* In 2 vols. Toronto: Macmillan of Canada, 1977 and 1981.

Sullivan, George. *Inside Nuclear Submarines.* New York: Dodd, Mead, 1982.

Taylor, Dianne J. *There's No Wife Like It.* Victoria, B.C: Braemar Books, 1985.

Thomas, David A. *Submarine Victory.* Toronto: publisher unkown, 1961.

————. *The Companion to the Royal Navy.* London: Harrap, 1988.

Thomas, Lowell. *Raiders of the Deep.* New York: Doubleday, Doran and Company Inc., 1928.

Thompson, John Herd, and Allen Seager. *Canada 1922-1939: Decades of Discord.* Toronto: McCelland and Stewart, 1973.

Tucker, Gilbert N. *The Naval Service of Canada – Its Official History.* In 2 volumes. Ottawa: King's Printer, 1952.

Tugwell, Dr. Maurice. *Peace with Freedom.* Toronto: Key Porter Books Ltd., 1988.

Turner, J.F. *Periscope Patrol: The Saga of Malta Submarines.* Toronto: Clark Irwin and Co. Ltd., 1957.

Tyler, Patrick. *Running Critical.* New York: Harper and Row, 1986.

Usborne, VAdm. C.V., CB, CMG, RN. *Smoke on the Horizon: Mediterranean Fighting 1914-1918.* London: Hodder and Stoughton Ltd., 1933.

van der Vat, Dan. *The Atlantic Campaign: World War II's Great Struggle at Sea.* New York: Harper and Row, 1988.

Walker, F., and P. Mellor. *The Mystery of X5: Lieutenant H. Henty Creer's Attack on the Tirpitz.* London: William Kimber and Co. Ltd., 1988.

Warnock, John W. *Partner to a Behemoth: A Military Policy of a Satellite Canada.* Toronto: New Press, 1970.

Wheeler, Keith. *War Under the Pacific.* New York: Time-Life Books Inc., 1980.

Whitehouse, Arch. *Subs and Submariners.* New York: Doubleday and Company Inc., 1961.

Wilmott, Ned. *Strategy and Tactics of Sea Warfare.* Secaucus, New Jersey: Chartwell Books, 1979.

Wilson, Michael. *Baltic Assignment: British submariners in Russia 1914-1919.* London: Secker and Warburg Ltd., 1985.

Wingate, John. *Go Deep.* London: George Weidenfeld and Nicolson Ltd., 1985.

Winton, John. *Ultra at Sea.* London: Leo Cooper Ltd., 1988.

————. *The Fighting Tenth: The Tenth Submarine Flotilla and the Siege of Malta.* London: Leo Cooper, 1991.

Young, Cdr E.P., DSO, DSC, RNVR. *One of Our Submarines.* London: Rupert Hart-Davies Ltd., 1952.

Zimmerman, David. *The Great Battle of Ottawa.* Toronto: University of Toronto Press, 1989.

INDEX

Note: No ranks have been used in the index, as many of the individuals were promoted several times during the period covered by this book.

All surface ships and naval bases are indexed under Ships and all submarines are indexed under Submarines.

King Alfred, HMS (shore base) 119, 143
Leipzig (German), 8, 13, 30
Lutzow (German), 185
Maidstone, HMS (submarine depot ship), 54, 62, 135, 206-7, 239
Malaspina (harbour examination vessel), 3-4
Medway, HMS (submarine depot ship), 121; sinking of, 131
Mont Blanc, MV, 82
Naden, HMCS, 107-8
Newcastle, HMS, 33
Niobe, HMCS, 16, 105
Nurnberg (German), 8, 30
Ontario, HMCS, 204
Prinz Eugen (German), 122
Q13 (British), 69
Q27 (British), 69
Queen Elizabeth, HMS, 145
Rainbow, HMCS, 16, 42
Rockcliffe, HMCS, 225
Rodney, HMS, 156
St. Boniface, HMCS, 161
Salvor (tug), 12
Saxonia (German), 43
Scharnhorst (German), 121
Shearwater, HMCS (Canadian submarine depot ship), 16, 30, 43, 82, 93-95, 99; voyage to Halifax, 75-80
Swift Current, HMCS, 167
Thames, HMS (shore base) 84
Thorlock, HMCS, 225
Tirpitz (German): chariots, target of, 144, 147, 155, 157; X-craft, target of, 184, 185, 201-2
Titania, HMS (submarine depot ship), 101, 150, 153, 154
Valiant, HMS, 145
Varbel, HMS (shore base), 199, 201, 203
Victoriaville, HMCS, 225
Vulcan, HMS (submarine depot ship), 72
Wisteria, HMS, 107

Simpson, George ("Shrimp"), CB, CBE, RN, 128, 130, 138
Sonar: acoustic properties of seawater, 163, 170, 173; equipment in Canadian O-boats, 1960s, 271; equipment in Canadian O-boats, 1980s, 298; experiments, early, 93-95; WWII, 163
SOTC. *See* Submarine Officers Training Course
SOUP. *See* Submarine Operational Update Program
Sovereignty (Canadian), 307, 310, 311-13; Arctic, 312-13
Spencer, B., RCN, 241
SSBN, nuclear-powered ballistic missile submarine. *See under* Submarines, *by name*

SSK, diesel/electric submarine. *See under* Submarines, *by name*
SSN, nuclear-powered hunter/killer submarine. *See under* Submarines, *by name*
Submarine Committee, the 1962, 250-51
Submarine flotillas: WWI, 8th, 54, 65-66; WWII, 4th (Far East), 206, 219; 6th (Home Waters), 121; 8th (Mediterranean), 135; 8th (Far East), 206, 210; 10th (Mediterranean), 128, 130-31, 138; 12th (chariots and X-craft), 146, 198-204
Submarine Officers' Continuation Training Course (Canadian), 277, 287
Submarine Officers' Training Course (SOTC), 120-21, 283-84
Submarine Operational Update Program (SOUP), 298-99
Submarine policy, Canadian: 1920-39, 117; 1939-45, 118; 1946-59, 234-37, 241; 1960s-present, 259, 261, 309, 330
Submarine squadrons: 6th (RN), 236-37, 241, 243, 249, 255, 259, 261, 265
Submarine squadrons (Canadian). *See* First Canadian Submarine Squadron
Submarine warfare: attacks, WWI, 70-72; Mediterranean, 1941-43, 135, 139; tactics, WWI, 69, 70-72; unrestricted, 68, 117, 163
Submariners (Canadian): career progression of, 280; conscription of, 277-78; description of, 275, 278-81; leisure at sea, 281-82; training of, 1966-present, 266, 282-84; training in RN (1955-60), 238-39

Submarines:
A-class, 237, 251
Alderney, HMS, 235, 237
Alliance, HMS, 234
Ambush, HMS, 237
Amethyste-class (French SSN), 318, 319, 331
Ammiraglio Millo (Italian), 129
Antofagasta (*CC2*), 8, 12-13, 15
Argonaut, USS. *See Rainbow*, HMCS
Artemis, HMS, 234
Astute, HMS, 237
Barbel-class (US), 247-49, 251, 297
Bronzo (Italian), 137
Burrfish, USS. *See Grilse*, HMCS
CC1 and *CC2* (HMCS): acquisition of, 7-13; arrival in Esquimalt, 3-5, 13; ASW training targets, 94-95; communications, 44; crews of, 20, 22, 41-43, 94; crew selection, 21; crew training, 21-22, 29, 31-32; description of, 8-9, 26-29; east coast service of, 81-82; escape from Seattle, 10-12; Halifax Explosion, effects of, 82-83; inspection of, 12-13; investigation into purchase and